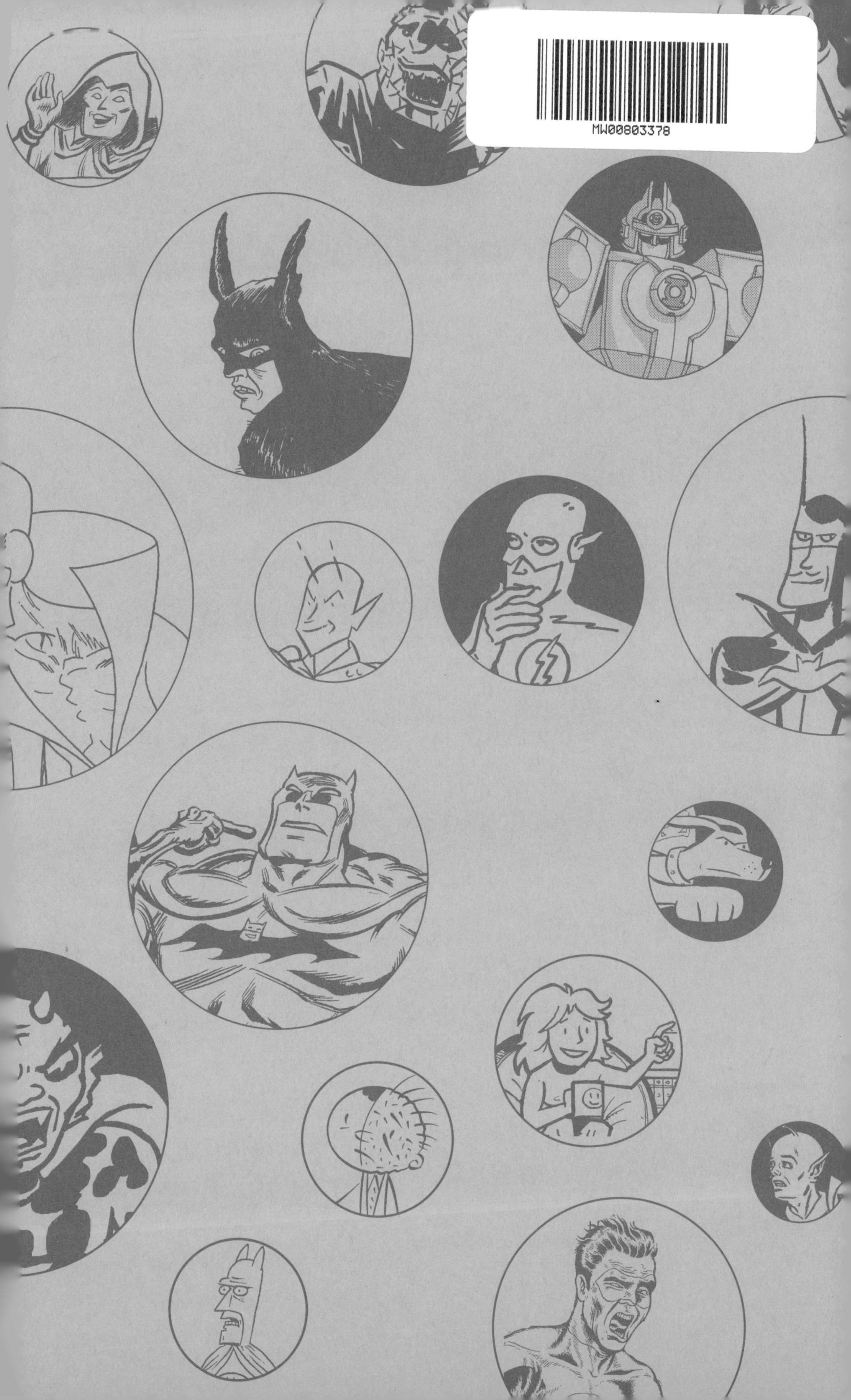

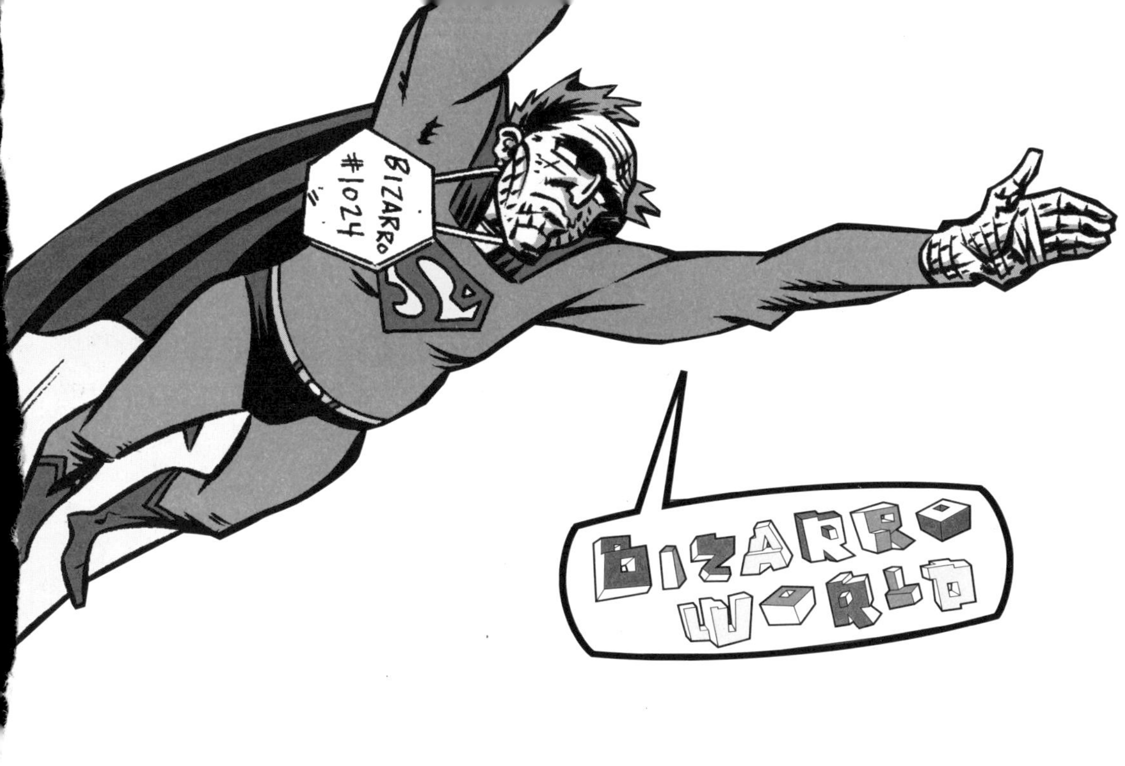
BIZARRO #1024
BIZARRO WORLD

Cover art by **Jaime Hernandez**
Cover color by **Coco Shinomiya**
Logo design by **Rian Hughes**

Special Thanks:
Kelly Sue DeConnick

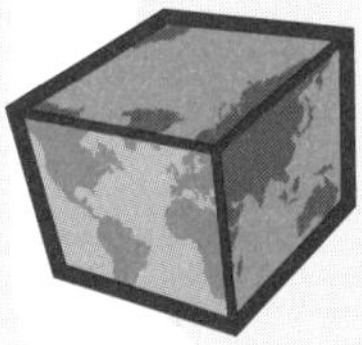

SUPERMAN created by
JERRY SIEGEL and JOE SHUSTER

BATMAN created by BOB KANE

WONDER WOMAN created by
WILLIAM MOULTON MARSTON

AQUAMAN created by
PAUL NORRIS

KAMANDI created by
JACK KIRBY

THE DEMON created by
JACK KIRBY

Original GREEN LANTERN
character created by MARTIN
NODELL and BILL FINGER

BIZARRO WORLD. Published by DC Comics,
1700 Broadway, New York, NY 10019. Cover, compilation,
and biographies copyright © 2005 DC Comics. All Rights
Reserved. All characters featured in this issue, the distinctive
likenesses thereof and related elements are trademarks of
DC Comics. The stories, characters and incidents mentioned in this magazine
are entirely fictional. DC Comics does not read or accept unsolicited
submissions of ideas, stories or artwork.
Printed in Canada. First Printing.
HC ISBN: 1-4012-0656-5 • SC ISBN: 1-4012-0657-3
DC Comics, a Warner Bros. Enertainment Company.

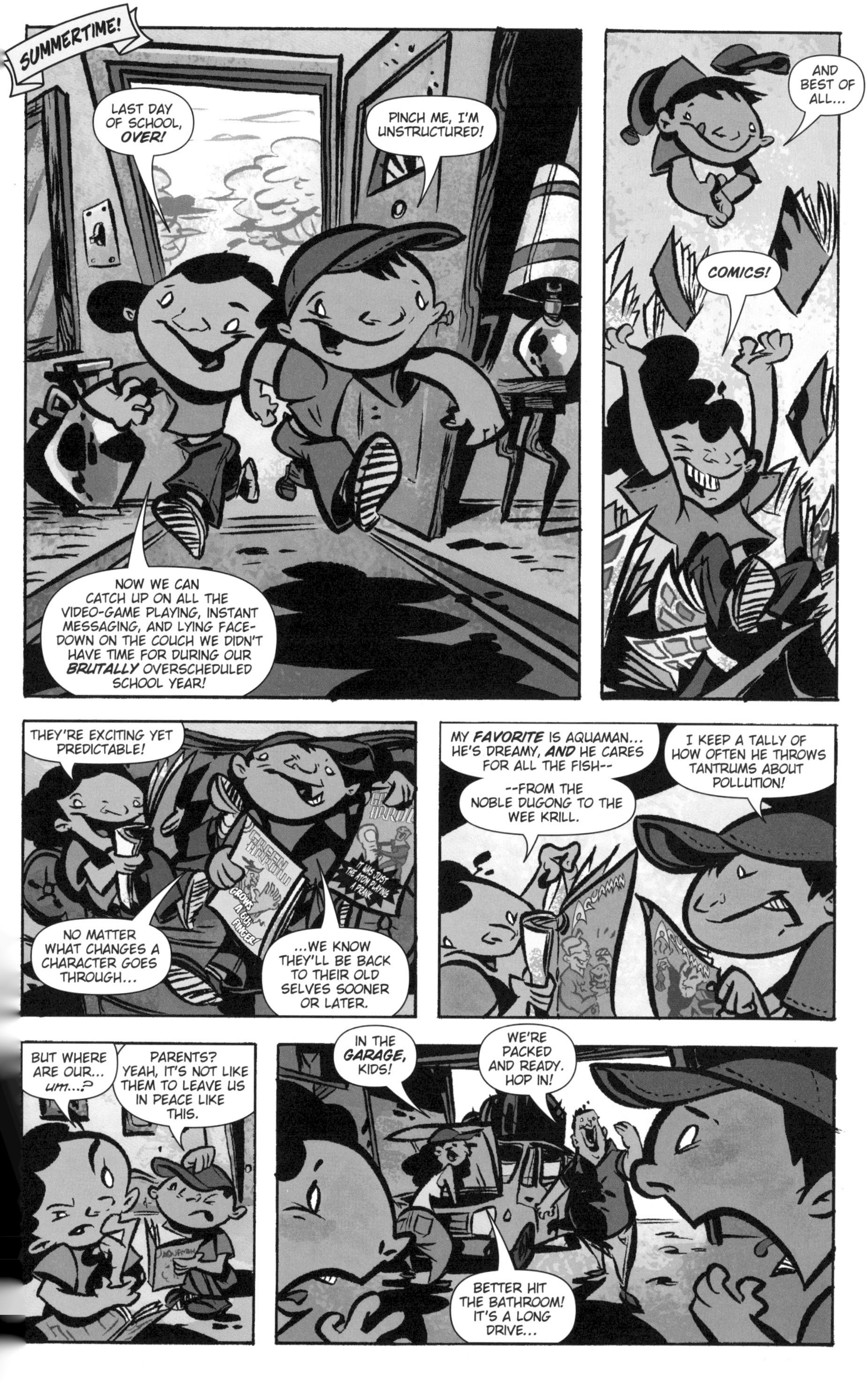
SUMMERTIME!
LAST DAY OF SCHOOL, OVER!
PINCH ME, I'M UNSTRUCTURED!
NOW WE CAN CATCH UP ON ALL THE VIDEO-GAME PLAYING, INSTANT MESSAGING, AND LYING FACE-DOWN ON THE COUCH WE DIDN'T HAVE TIME FOR DURING OUR BRUTALLY OVERSCHEDULED SCHOOL YEAR!
AND BEST OF ALL...
COMICS!
THEY'RE EXCITING YET PREDICTABLE!
GREEN ARROW
GROWS A 6th FINGER!
IT WAS JUST THE ATOM PLAYING A PRANK.
NO MATTER WHAT CHANGES A CHARACTER GOES THROUGH...
...WE KNOW THEY'LL BE BACK TO THEIR OLD SELVES SOONER OR LATER.
MY FAVORITE IS AQUAMAN... HE'S DREAMY, AND HE CARES FOR ALL THE FISH--
--FROM THE NOBLE DUGONG TO THE WEE KRILL.
I KEEP A TALLY OF HOW OFTEN HE THROWS TANTRUMS ABOUT POLLUTION!
AQUAMAN
BUT WHERE ARE OUR... um...?
PARENTS? YEAH, IT'S NOT LIKE THEM TO LEAVE US IN PEACE LIKE THIS.
IN THE GARAGE, KIDS!
WE'RE PACKED AND READY. HOP IN!
BETTER HIT THE BATHROOM! IT'S A LONG DRIVE...

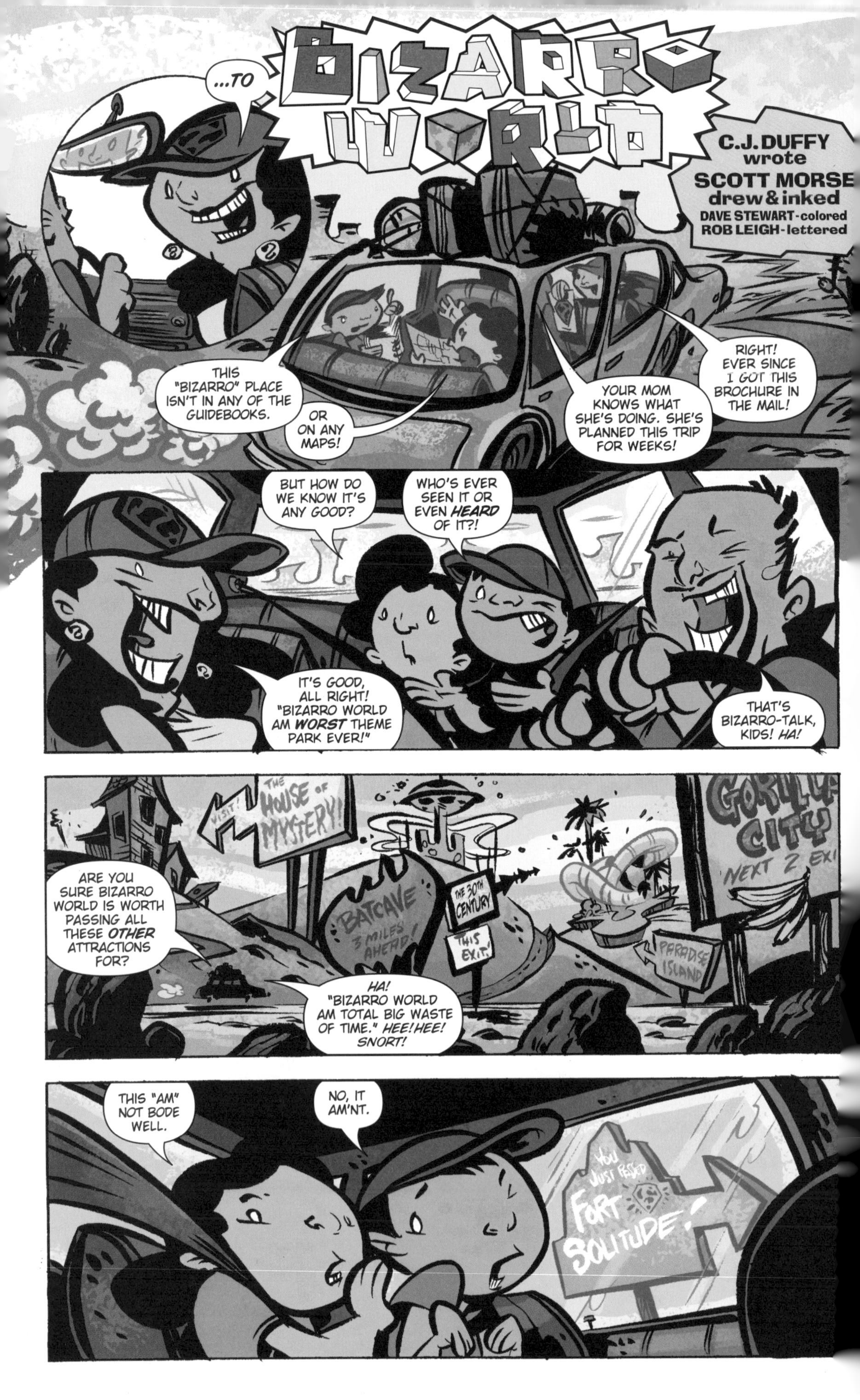
...TO
BIZARRO WORLD
C.J. DUFFY wrote
SCOTT MORSE drew & inked
DAVE STEWART-colored
ROB LEIGH-lettered
THIS "BIZARRO" PLACE ISN'T IN ANY OF THE GUIDEBOOKS.
OR ON ANY MAPS!
YOUR MOM KNOWS WHAT SHE'S DOING. SHE'S PLANNED THIS TRIP FOR WEEKS!
RIGHT! EVER SINCE I GOT THIS BROCHURE IN THE MAIL!
BUT HOW DO WE KNOW IT'S ANY GOOD?
WHO'S EVER SEEN IT OR EVEN HEARD OF IT?!
IT'S GOOD, ALL RIGHT! "BIZARRO WORLD AM WORST THEME PARK EVER!"
THAT'S BIZARRO-TALK, KIDS! HA!
VISIT! THE HOUSE OF MYSTERY!
BATCAVE 3 MILES AHEAD!
THE 30TH CENTURY
THIS EXIT!
GORILLA CITY NEXT 2 EXI
PARADISE ISLAND
ARE YOU SURE BIZARRO WORLD IS WORTH PASSING ALL THESE OTHER ATTRACTIONS FOR?
HA! "BIZARRO WORLD AM TOTAL BIG WASTE OF TIME." HEE! HEE! SNORT!
THIS "AM" NOT BODE WELL.
NO, IT AM'NT.
YOU JUST PASSED FORT SOLITUDE!

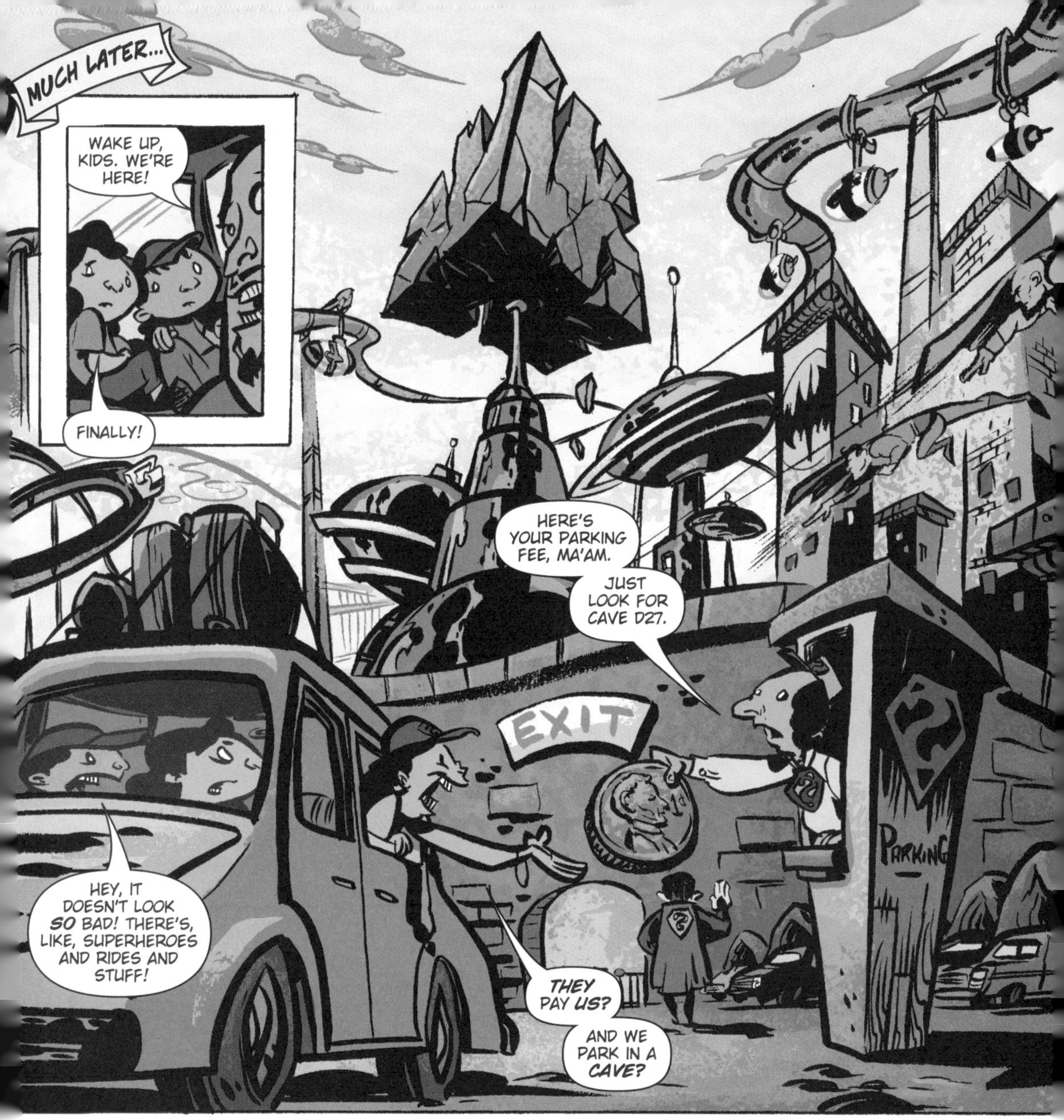
MUCH LATER...
WAKE UP, KIDS. WE'RE HERE!
FINALLY!
HERE'S YOUR PARKING FEE, MA'AM.
JUST LOOK FOR CAVE D27.
EXIT
PARKING
HEY, IT DOESN'T LOOK **SO** BAD! THERE'S, LIKE, SUPERHEROES AND RIDES AND STUFF!
THEY PAY ***US?***
AND WE PARK IN A ***CAVE?***

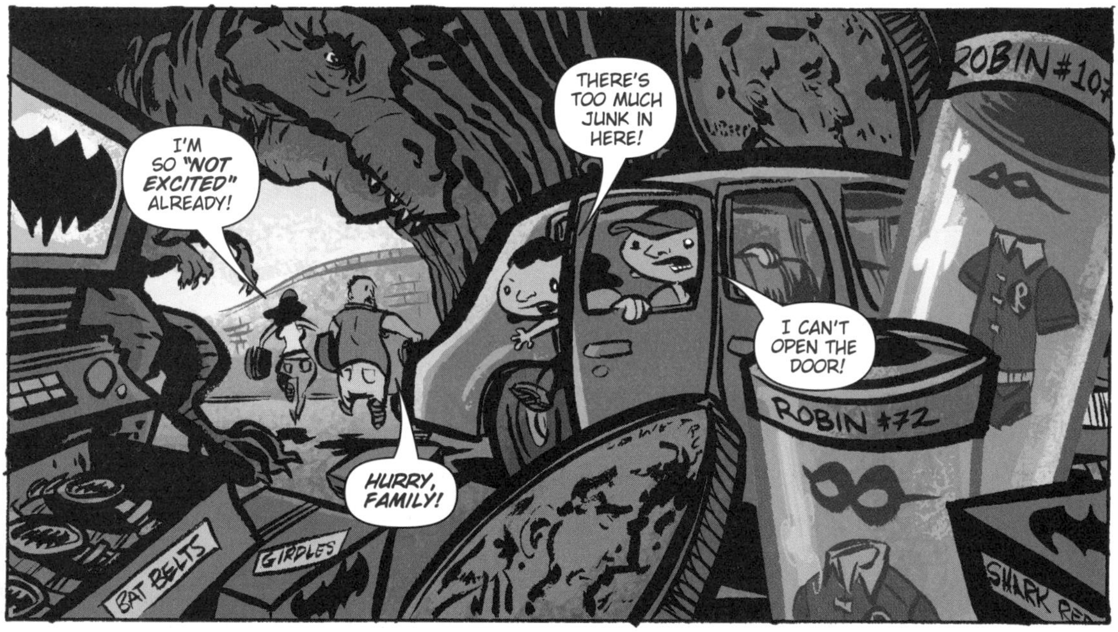
I'M SO ***"NOT EXCITED"*** ALREADY!
THERE'S TOO MUCH JUNK IN HERE!
I CAN'T OPEN THE DOOR!
HURRY, FAMILY!
ROBIN #72
BAT BELTS
GIRDLES

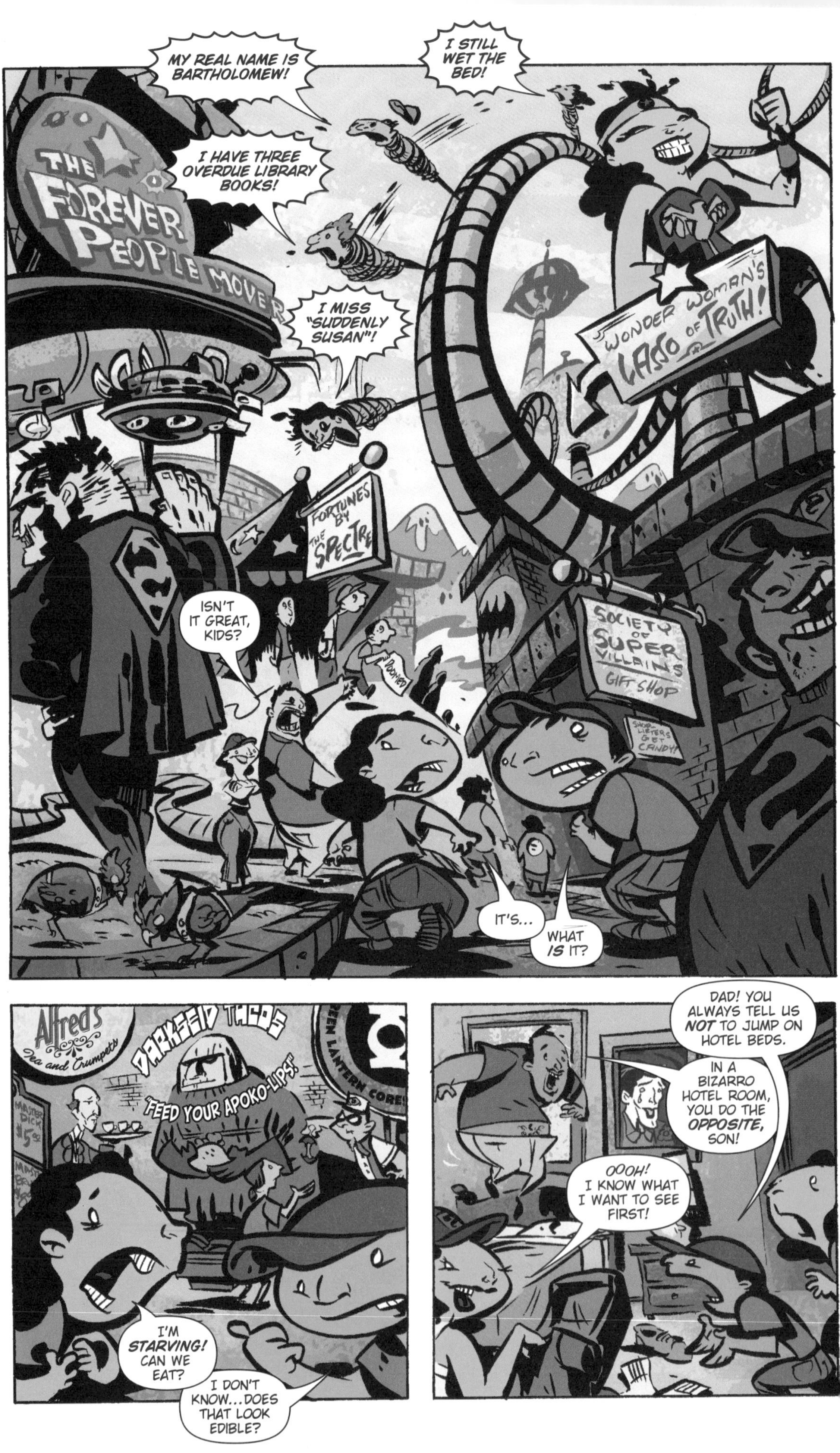
MY REAL NAME IS BARTHOLOMEW!
I STILL WET THE BED!
I HAVE THREE OVERDUE LIBRARY BOOKS!
I MISS "SUDDENLY SUSAN"!
THE FOREVER PEOPLE MOVER
WONDER WOMAN'S LASSO OF TRUTH!
FORTUNES BY THE SPECTRE
ISN'T IT GREAT, KIDS?
SOCIETY OF SUPER VILLAINS GIFT SHOP
SHOP-LIFTERS GET CANDY!
IT'S...
WHAT IS IT?
Alfred's Tea and Crumpets
DARKSEID TACOS
"FEED YOUR APOKO-LIPS!"
GREEN LANTERN CORES
I'M STARVING! CAN WE EAT?
I DON'T KNOW... DOES THAT LOOK EDIBLE?
DAD! YOU ALWAYS TELL US NOT TO JUMP ON HOTEL BEDS.
IN A BIZARRO HOTEL ROOM, YOU DO THE OPPOSITE, SON!
OOOH! I KNOW WHAT I WANT TO SEE FIRST!

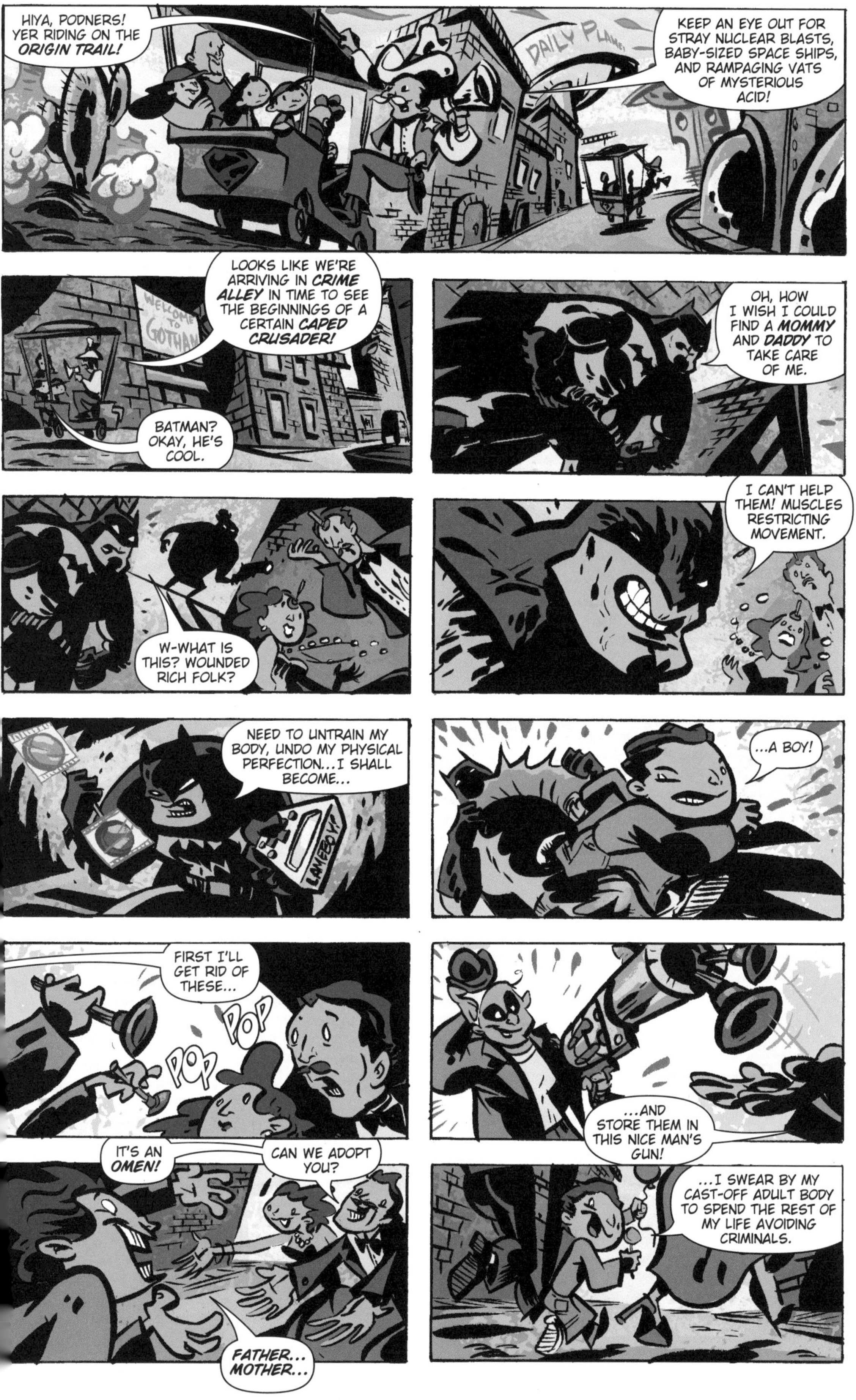
HIYA, PODNERS! YER RIDING ON THE ORIGIN TRAIL!
DAILY PLANET
KEEP AN EYE OUT FOR STRAY NUCLEAR BLASTS, BABY-SIZED SPACE SHIPS, AND RAMPAGING VATS OF MYSTERIOUS ACID!
WELCOME TO GOTHAM
LOOKS LIKE WE'RE ARRIVING IN CRIME ALLEY IN TIME TO SEE THE BEGINNINGS OF A CERTAIN CAPED CRUSADER!
BATMAN? OKAY, HE'S COOL.
OH, HOW I WISH I COULD FIND A MOMMY AND DADDY TO TAKE CARE OF ME.
W-WHAT IS THIS? WOUNDED RICH FOLK?
I CAN'T HELP THEM! MUSCLES RESTRICTING MOVEMENT.
NEED TO UNTRAIN MY BODY, UNDO MY PHYSICAL PERFECTION...I SHALL BECOME...
LAMEBOY!
...A BOY!
FIRST I'LL GET RID OF THESE...
POP
POP
...AND STORE THEM IN THIS NICE MAN'S GUN!
IT'S AN OMEN!
CAN WE ADOPT YOU?
FATHER... MOTHER...
...I SWEAR BY MY CAST-OFF ADULT BODY TO SPEND THE REST OF MY LIFE AVOIDING CRIMINALS.

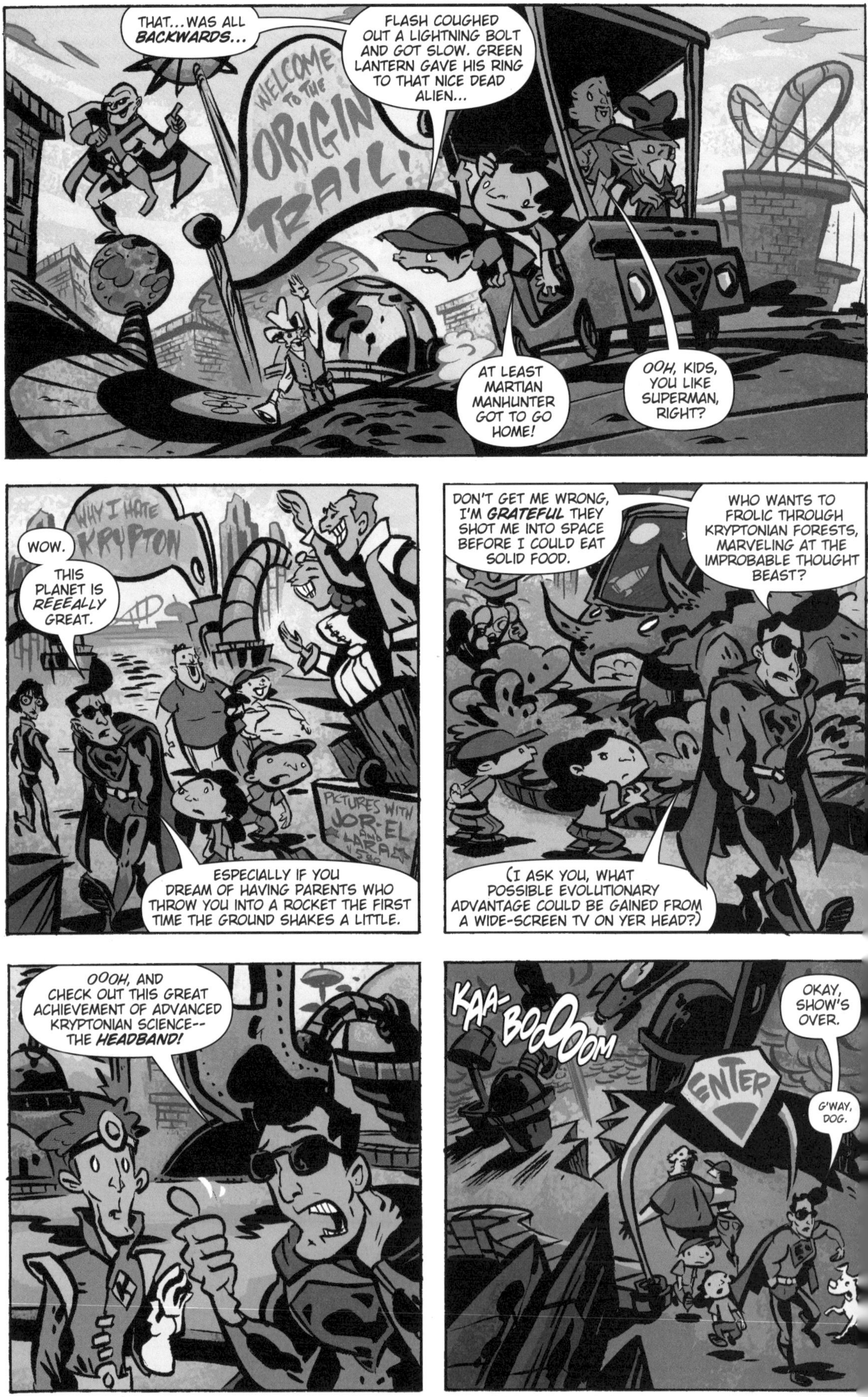
THAT...WAS ALL *BACKWARDS*...
FLASH COUGHED OUT A LIGHTNING BOLT AND GOT SLOW. GREEN LANTERN GAVE HIS RING TO THAT NICE DEAD ALIEN...
WELCOME TO THE ORIGIN TRAIL!
AT LEAST MARTIAN MANHUNTER GOT TO GO HOME!
OOH, KIDS, YOU LIKE SUPERMAN, RIGHT?
WHY I HATE KRYPTON
WOW.
THIS PLANET IS *REEEALLY* GREAT.
ESPECIALLY IF YOU DREAM OF HAVING PARENTS WHO THROW YOU INTO A ROCKET THE FIRST TIME THE GROUND SHAKES A LITTLE.
PICTURES WITH JOR-EL AND LARA
DON'T GET ME WRONG, I'M *GRATEFUL* THEY SHOT ME INTO SPACE BEFORE I COULD EAT SOLID FOOD.
WHO WANTS TO FROLIC THROUGH KRYPTONIAN FORESTS, MARVELING AT THE IMPROBABLE THOUGHT BEAST?
(I ASK YOU, WHAT POSSIBLE EVOLUTIONARY ADVANTAGE COULD BE GAINED FROM A WIDE-SCREEN TV ON YER HEAD?)
OOOH, AND CHECK OUT THIS GREAT ACHIEVEMENT OF ADVANCED KRYPTONIAN SCIENCE-- THE *HEADBAND!*
KAA-BOOOOOOM
ENTER
OKAY, SHOW'S OVER.
G'WAY, DOG.

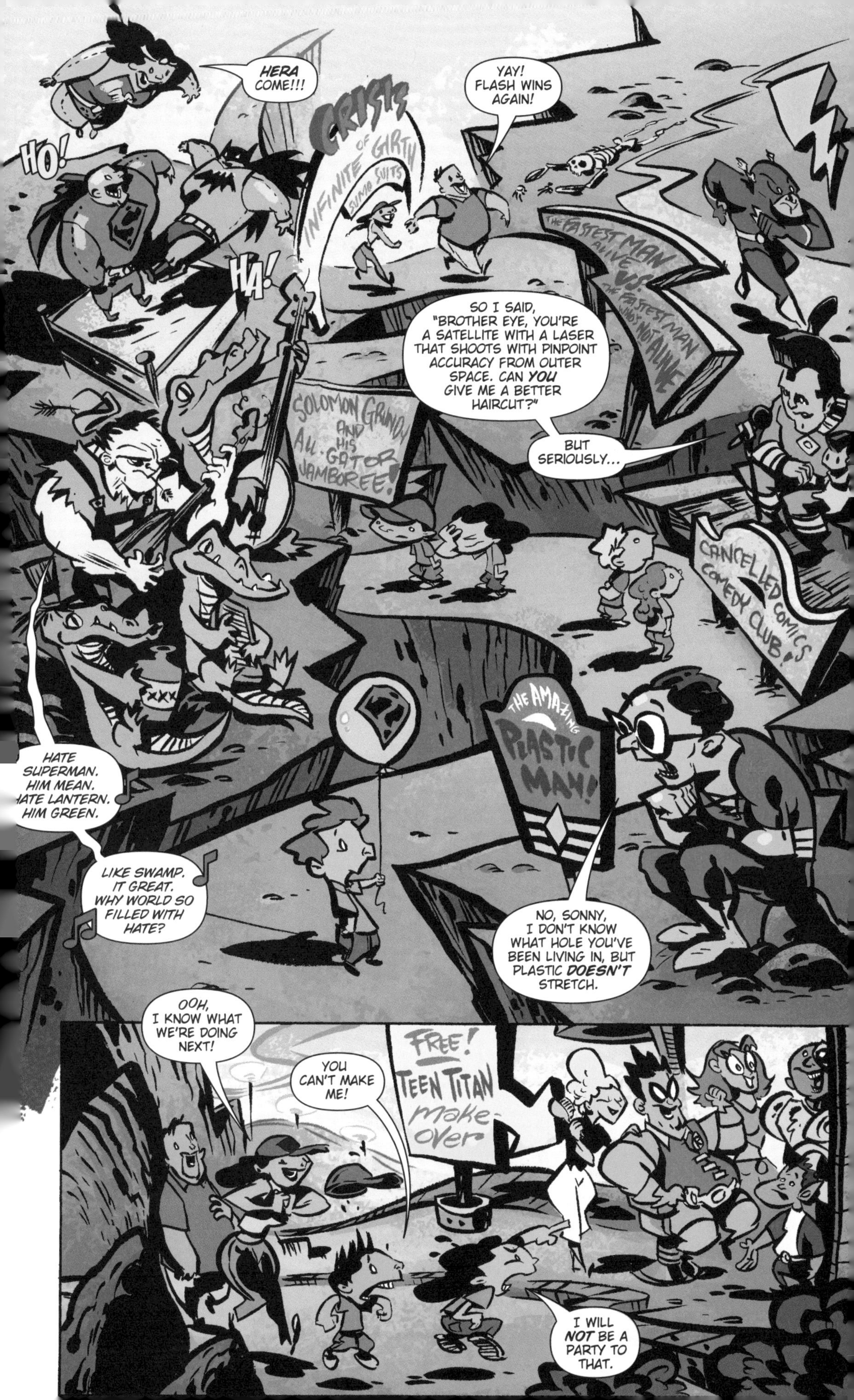
HERA COME!!!
HO!
HA!
CRISTE OF INFINITE GIRTH SUMO SUITS
YAY! FLASH WINS AGAIN!
THE FASTEST MAN ALIVE VS. THE FASTEST MAN WHO'S NOT ALIVE
SO I SAID, "BROTHER EYE, YOU'RE A SATELLITE WITH A LASER THAT SHOOTS WITH PINPOINT ACCURACY FROM OUTER SPACE. CAN YOU GIVE ME A BETTER HAIRCUT?"
BUT SERIOUSLY...
SOLOMON GRUNDY AND HIS ALL-GATOR JAMBOREE!
CANCELLED COMICS COMEDY CLUB!
HATE SUPERMAN. HIM MEAN. HATE LANTERN. HIM GREEN.
LIKE SWAMP. IT GREAT. WHY WORLD SO FILLED WITH HATE?
THE AMAZING PLASTIC MAN!
NO, SONNY, I DON'T KNOW WHAT HOLE YOU'VE BEEN LIVING IN, BUT PLASTIC DOESN'T STRETCH.
OOH, I KNOW WHAT WE'RE DOING NEXT!
YOU CAN'T MAKE ME!
FREE! TEEN TITAN make-over
I WILL NOT BE A PARTY TO THAT.

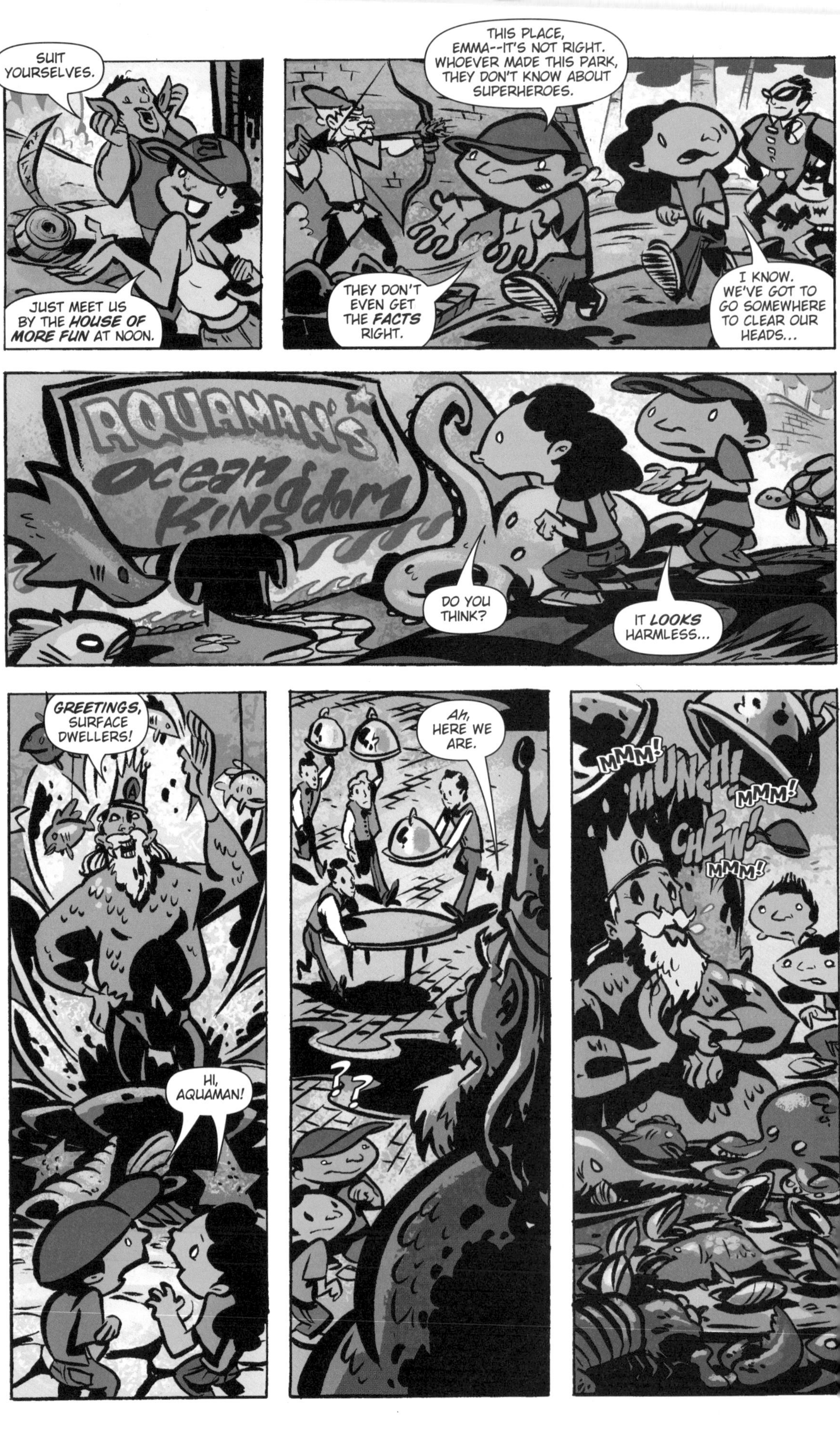
SUIT YOURSELVES.
JUST MEET US BY THE HOUSE OF MORE FUN AT NOON.
THIS PLACE, EMMA--IT'S NOT RIGHT. WHOEVER MADE THIS PARK, THEY DON'T KNOW ABOUT SUPERHEROES.
THEY DON'T EVEN GET THE FACTS RIGHT.
I KNOW. WE'VE GOT TO GO SOMEWHERE TO CLEAR OUR HEADS...
AQUAMAN'S Ocean Kingdom
DO YOU THINK?
IT LOOKS HARMLESS...
GREETINGS, SURFACE DWELLERS!
HI, AQUAMAN!
Ah, HERE WE ARE.
??
MMM!
MUNCH!
MMM!
CHEW!
MMM!

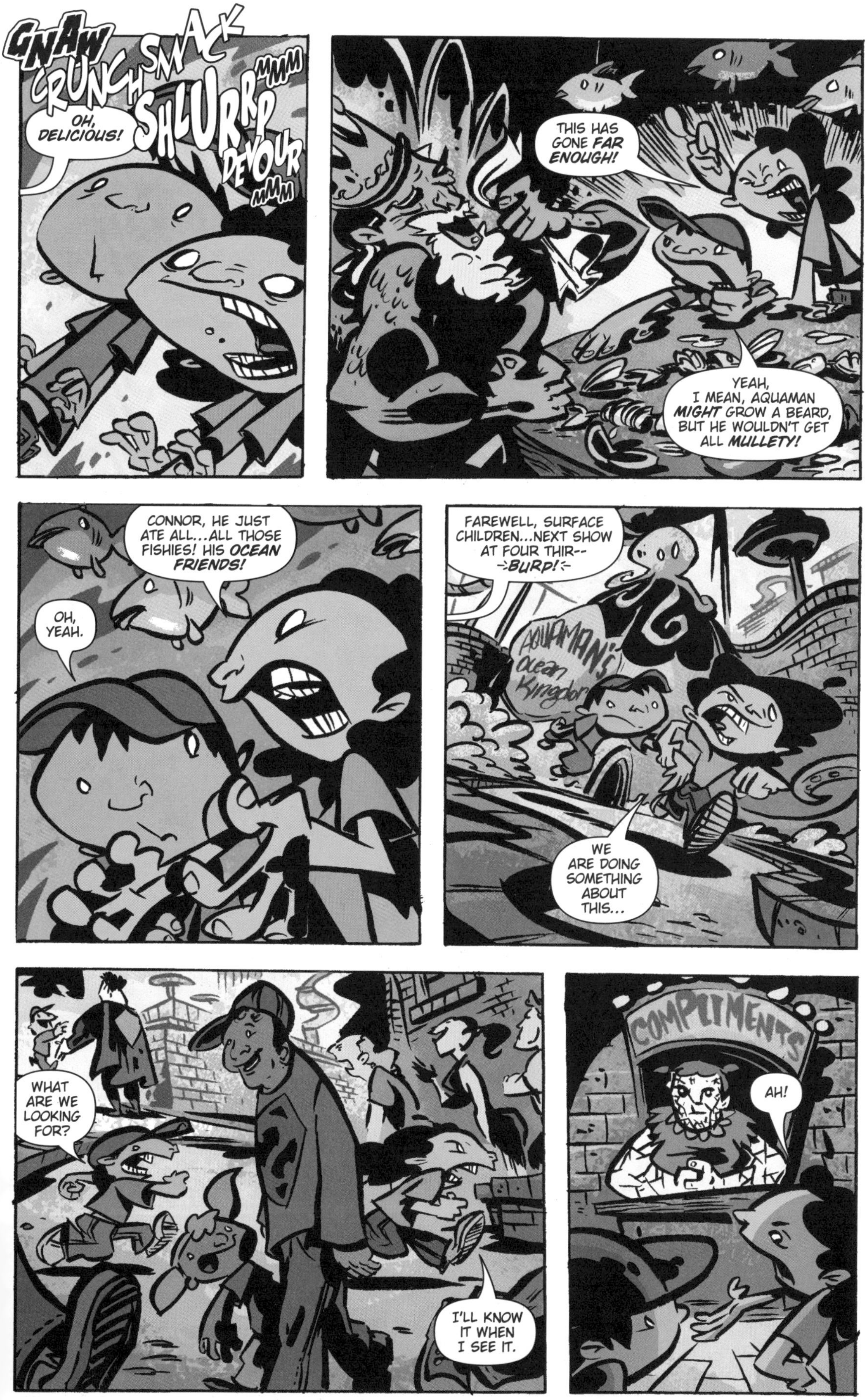
GNAW
CRUNCH
SMACK
SHLURRP
MMM
DEVOUR
MMM
OH, DELICIOUS!
THIS HAS GONE FAR ENOUGH!
YEAH, I MEAN, AQUAMAN MIGHT GROW A BEARD, BUT HE WOULDN'T GET ALL MULLETY!
CONNOR, HE JUST ATE ALL...ALL THOSE FISHIES! HIS OCEAN FRIENDS!
OH, YEAH.
FAREWELL, SURFACE CHILDREN...NEXT SHOW AT FOUR THIR-- BURP!
AQUAMAN'S Ocean Kingdom
WE ARE DOING SOMETHING ABOUT THIS...
WHAT ARE WE LOOKING FOR?
I'LL KNOW IT WHEN I SEE IT.
COMPLIMENTS
AH!

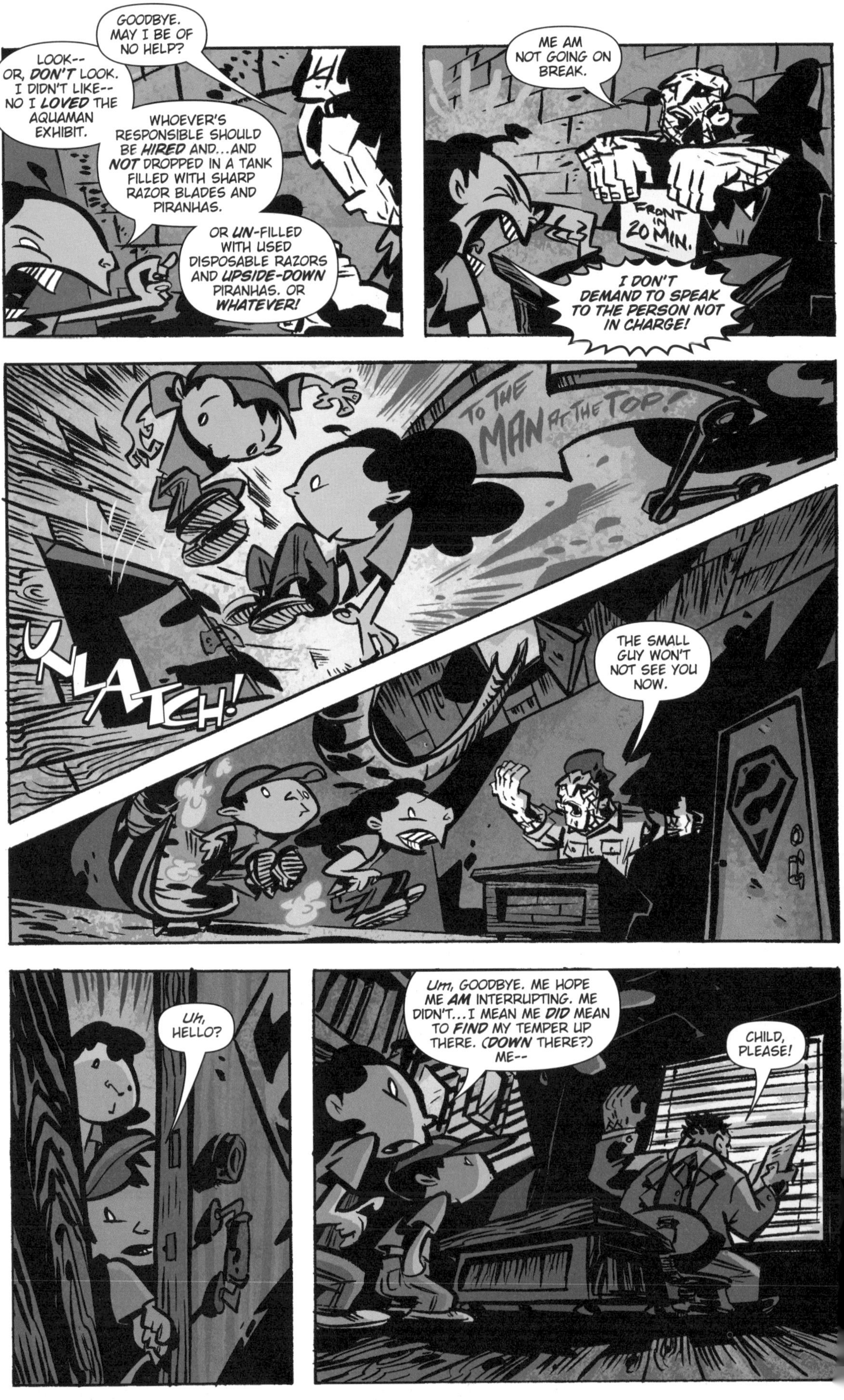
LOOK-- OR, DON'T LOOK. I DIDN'T LIKE-- NO I LOVED THE AQUAMAN EXHIBIT.
GOODBYE. MAY I BE OF NO HELP?
WHOEVER'S RESPONSIBLE SHOULD BE HIRED AND...AND NOT DROPPED IN A TANK FILLED WITH SHARP RAZOR BLADES AND PIRANHAS.
OR UN-FILLED WITH USED DISPOSABLE RAZORS AND UPSIDE-DOWN PIRANHAS. OR WHATEVER!
ME AM NOT GOING ON BREAK.
FRONT IN 20 MIN.
I DON'T DEMAND TO SPEAK TO THE PERSON NOT IN CHARGE!
TO THE MAN AT THE TOP!
UNLATCH!
THE SMALL GUY WON'T NOT SEE YOU NOW.
Uh, HELLO?
Um, GOODBYE. ME HOPE ME AM INTERRUPTING. ME DIDN'T...I MEAN ME DID MEAN TO FIND MY TEMPER UP THERE. (DOWN THERE?) ME--
CHILD, PLEASE!

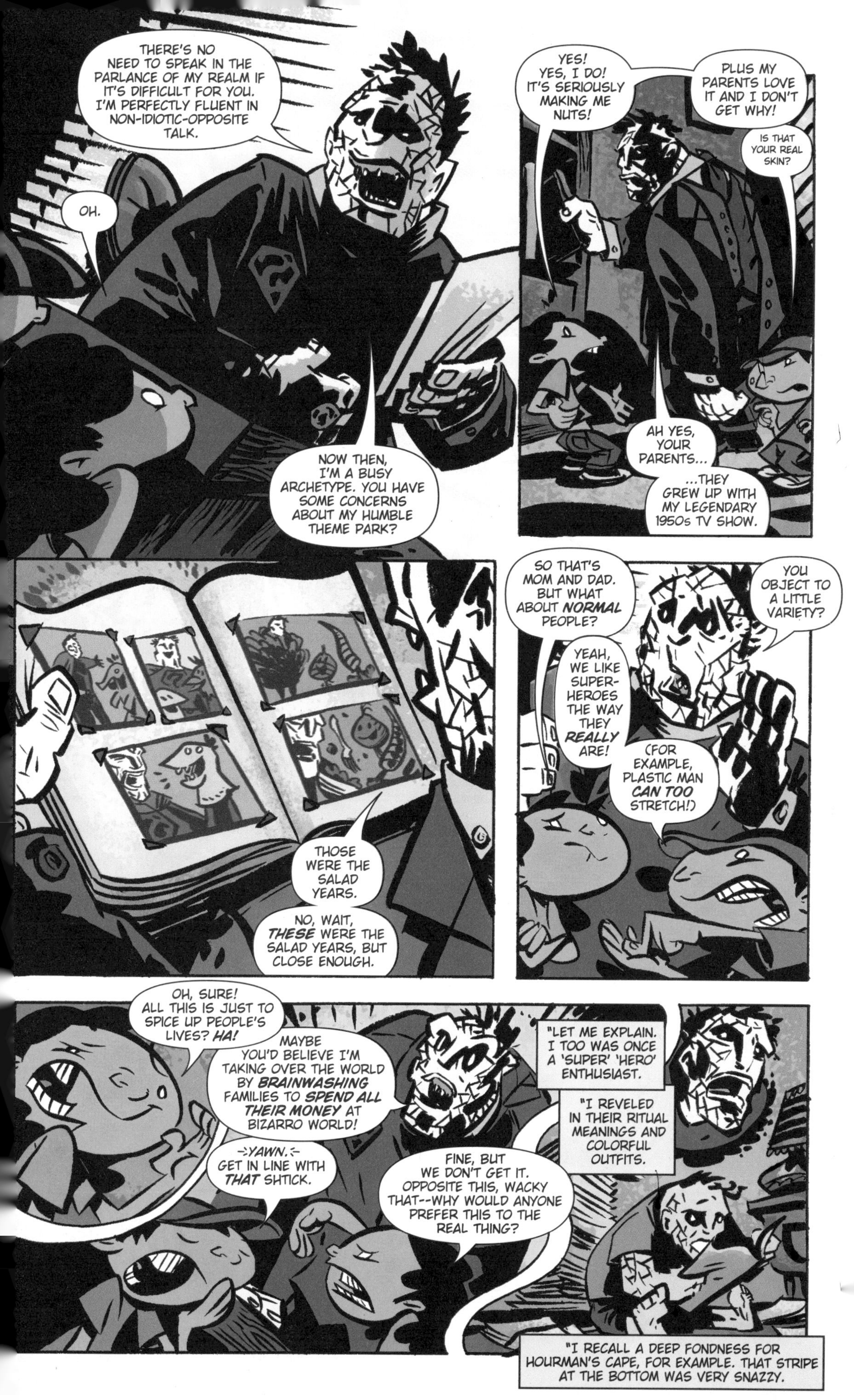
THERE'S NO NEED TO SPEAK IN THE PARLANCE OF MY REALM IF IT'S DIFFICULT FOR YOU. I'M PERFECTLY FLUENT IN NON-IDIOTIC-OPPOSITE TALK.
OH.
NOW THEN, I'M A BUSY ARCHETYPE. YOU HAVE SOME CONCERNS ABOUT MY HUMBLE THEME PARK?
YES! YES, I DO! IT'S SERIOUSLY MAKING ME NUTS!
PLUS MY PARENTS LOVE IT AND I DON'T GET WHY!
IS THAT YOUR REAL SKIN?
AH YES, YOUR PARENTS...
...THEY GREW UP WITH MY LEGENDARY 1950s TV SHOW.
THOSE WERE THE SALAD YEARS.
NO, WAIT, THESE WERE THE SALAD YEARS, BUT CLOSE ENOUGH.
SO THAT'S MOM AND DAD. BUT WHAT ABOUT NORMAL PEOPLE?
YOU OBJECT TO A LITTLE VARIETY?
YEAH, WE LIKE SUPER-HEROES THE WAY THEY REALLY ARE!
(FOR EXAMPLE, PLASTIC MAN CAN TOO STRETCH!)
OH, SURE! ALL THIS IS JUST TO SPICE UP PEOPLE'S LIVES? HA!
MAYBE YOU'D BELIEVE I'M TAKING OVER THE WORLD BY BRAINWASHING FAMILIES TO SPEND ALL THEIR MONEY AT BIZARRO WORLD!
YAWN. GET IN LINE WITH THAT SHTICK.
FINE, BUT WE DON'T GET IT. OPPOSITE THIS, WACKY THAT--WHY WOULD ANYONE PREFER THIS TO THE REAL THING?
"LET ME EXPLAIN. I TOO WAS ONCE A 'SUPER' 'HERO' ENTHUSIAST.
"I REVELED IN THEIR RITUAL MEANINGS AND COLORFUL OUTFITS.
"I RECALL A DEEP FONDNESS FOR HOURMAN'S CAPE, FOR EXAMPLE. THAT STRIPE AT THE BOTTOM WAS VERY SNAZZY.

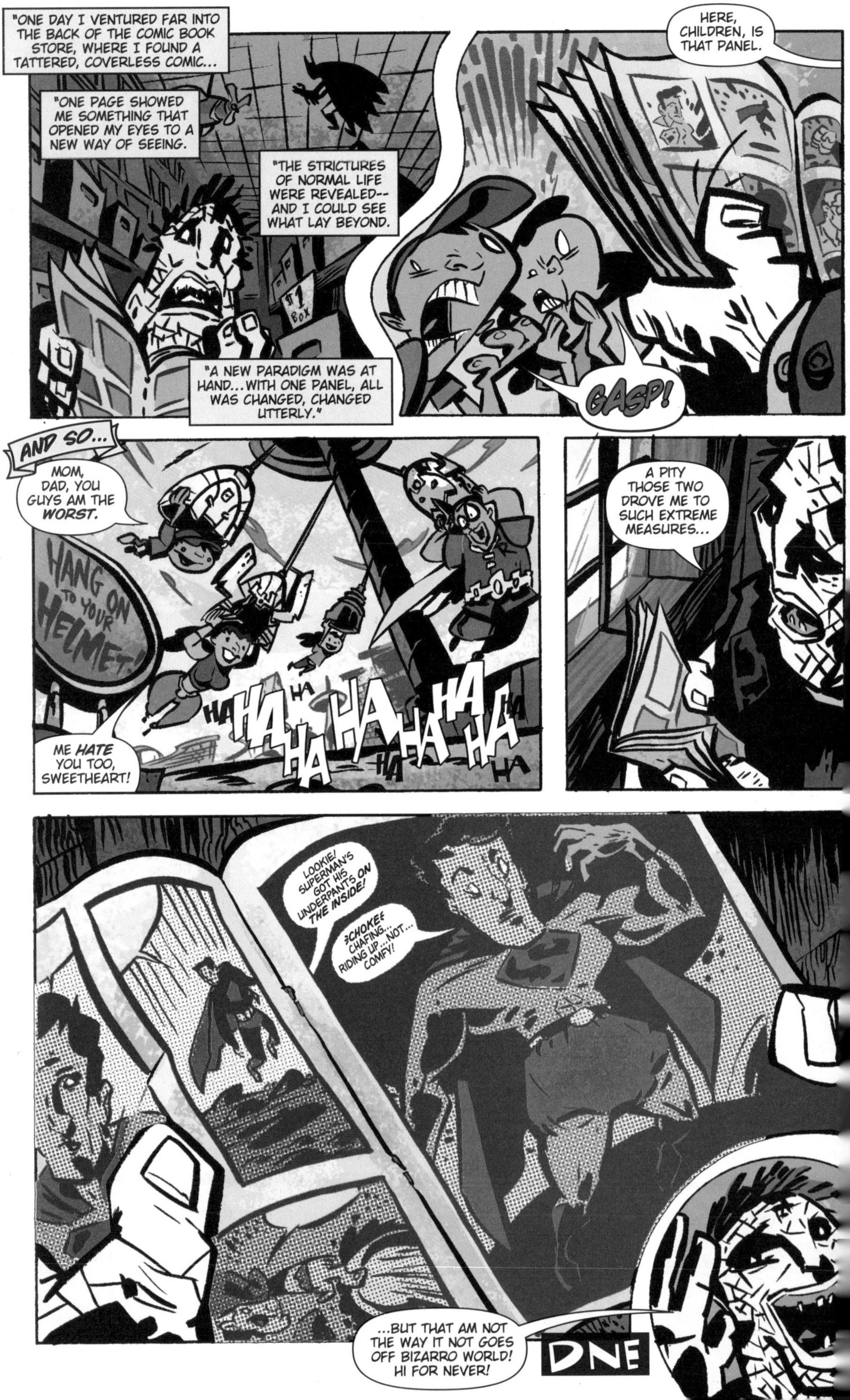
"ONE DAY I VENTURED FAR INTO THE BACK OF THE COMIC BOOK STORE, WHERE I FOUND A TATTERED, COVERLESS COMIC...
"ONE PAGE SHOWED ME SOMETHING THAT OPENED MY EYES TO A NEW WAY OF SEEING.
"THE STRICTURES OF NORMAL LIFE WERE REVEALED-- AND I COULD SEE WHAT LAY BEYOND.
$1 BOX
"A NEW PARADIGM WAS AT HAND...WITH ONE PANEL, ALL WAS CHANGED, CHANGED UTTERLY."
HERE, CHILDREN, IS THAT PANEL.
GASP!
AND SO...
MOM, DAD, YOU GUYS AM THE WORST.
HANG ON TO YOUR HELMET!
HA HA HA HA HA HA HA HA HA HA HA HA
ME HATE YOU TOO, SWEETHEART!
A PITY THOSE TWO DROVE ME TO SUCH EXTREME MEASURES...
LOOKIE! SUPERMAN'S GOT HIS UNDERPANTS ON THE INSIDE!
≠CHOKE≠ CHAFING... RIDING UP...NOT... COMFY!
...BUT THAT AM NOT THE WAY IT NOT GOES OFF BIZARRO WORLD! HI FOR NEVER!
DNE

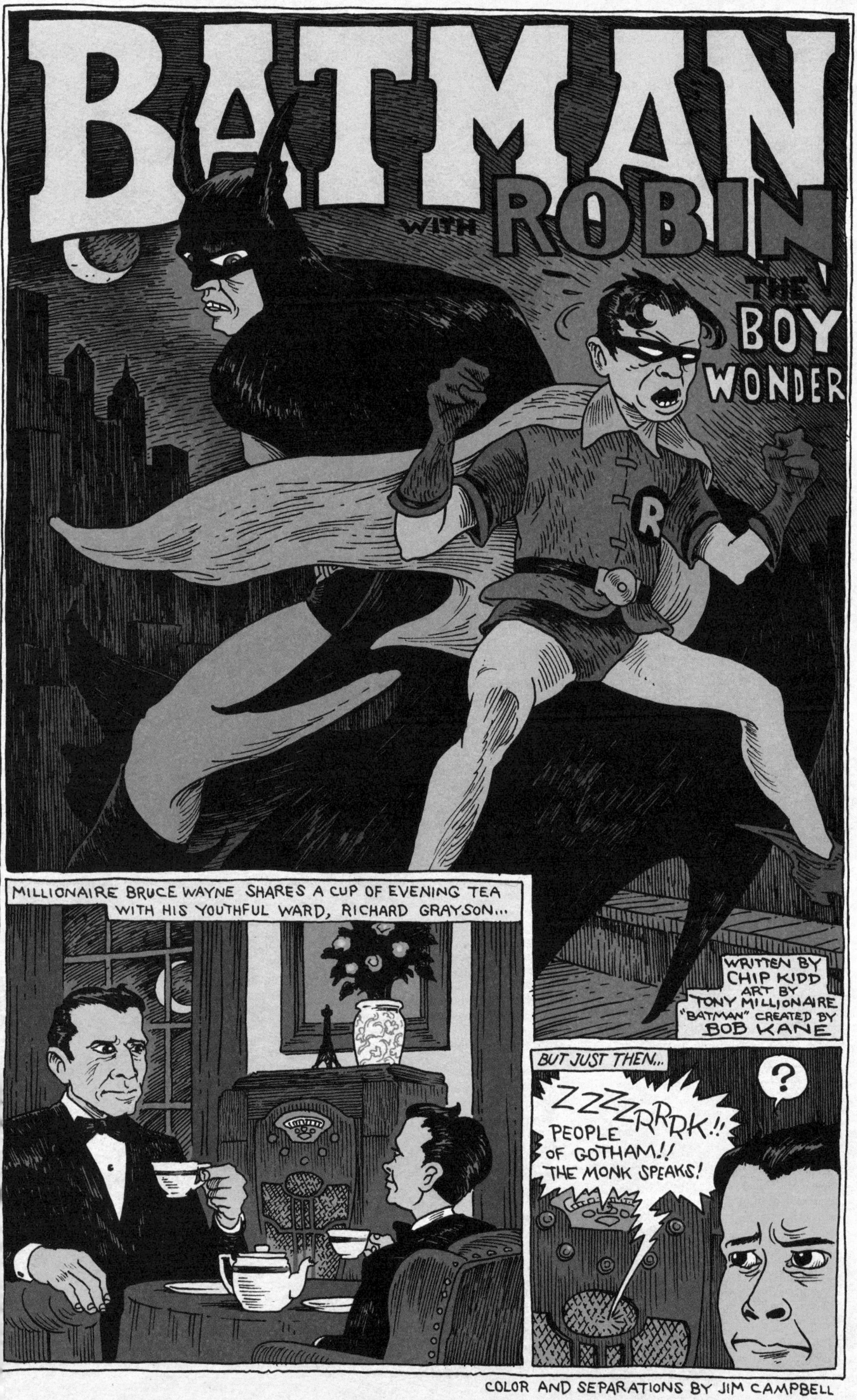
BATMAN
WITH ROBIN
THE BOY WONDER
WRITTEN BY CHIP KIDD
ART BY TONY MILLIONAIRE
"BATMAN" CREATED BY BOB KANE
MILLIONAIRE BRUCE WAYNE SHARES A CUP OF EVENING TEA WITH HIS YOUTHFUL WARD, RICHARD GRAYSON...
BUT JUST THEN...
ZZZZRRRK!! PEOPLE OF GOTHAM!! THE MONK SPEAKS!
?

COLOR AND SEPARATIONS BY JIM CAMPBELL

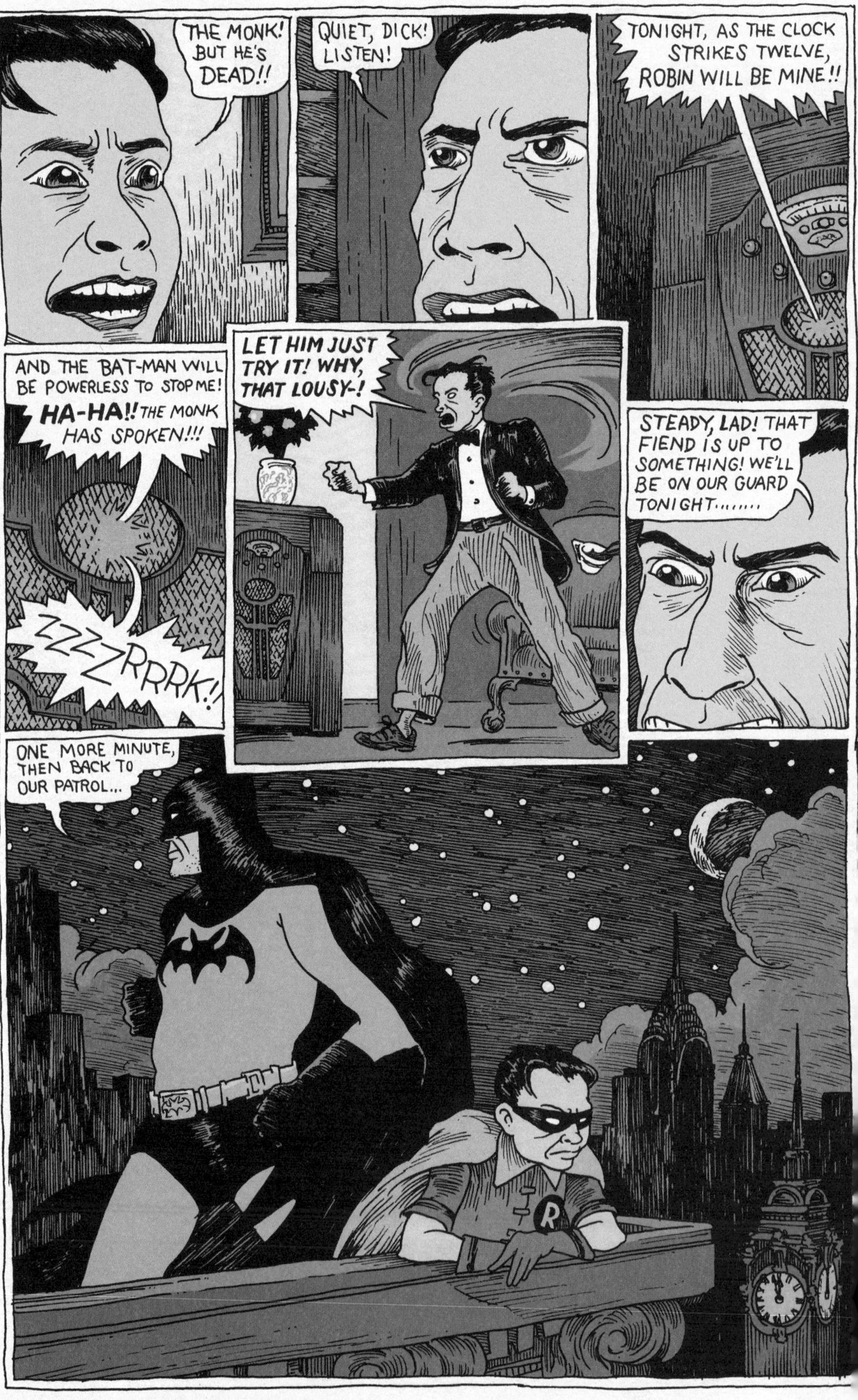
THE MONK! BUT HE'S DEAD!!
QUIET, DICK! LISTEN!
TONIGHT, AS THE CLOCK STRIKES TWELVE, ROBIN WILL BE MINE!!
AND THE BAT-MAN WILL BE POWERLESS TO STOP ME! HA-HA!! THE MONK HAS SPOKEN!!!
ZZZZZRRRRK!!
LET HIM JUST TRY IT! WHY, THAT LOUSY-!
STEADY, LAD! THAT FIEND IS UP TO SOMETHING! WE'LL BE ON OUR GUARD TONIGHT........
ONE MORE MINUTE, THEN BACK TO OUR PATROL...

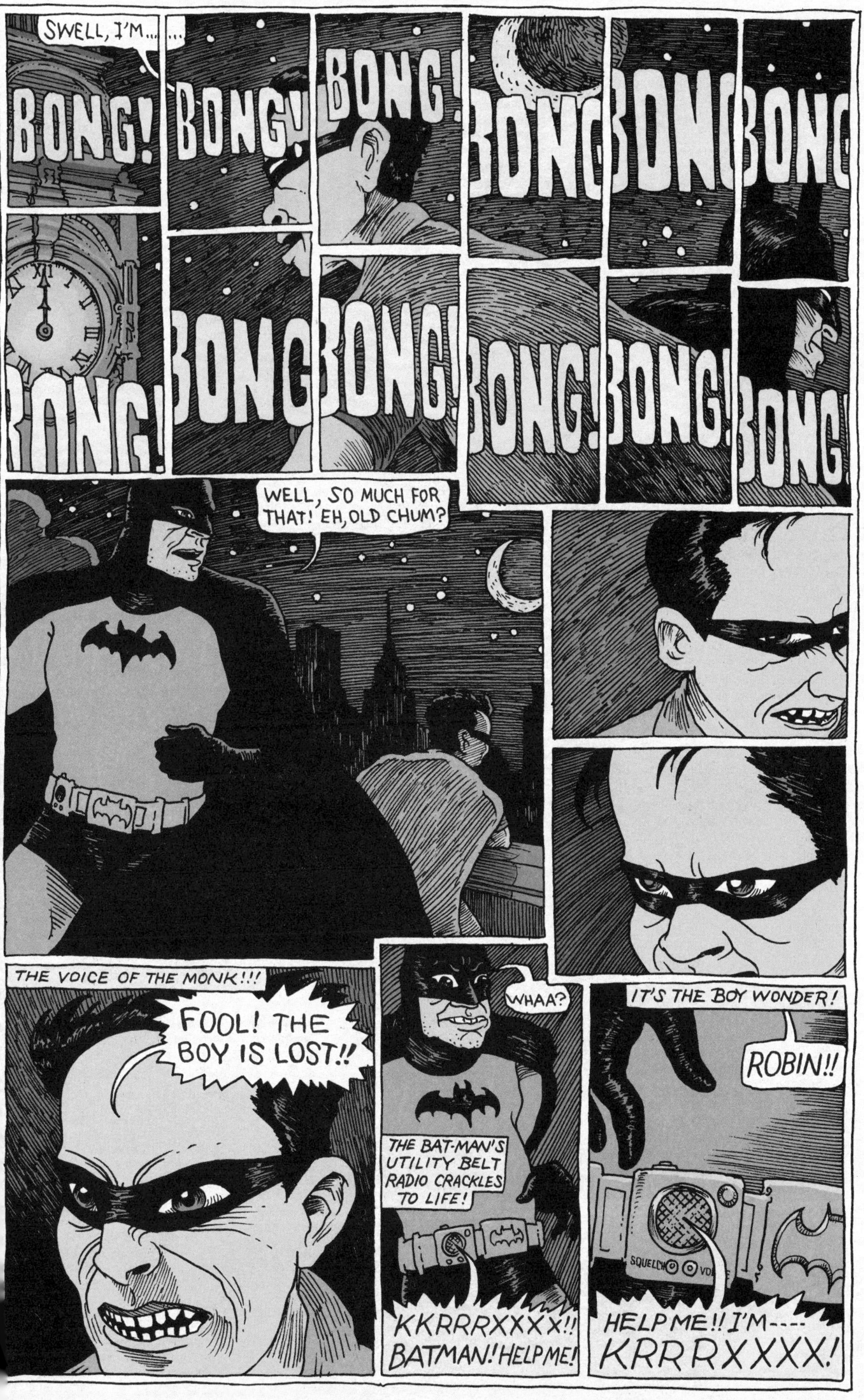

SWELL, I'M.... ....
BONG!
BONG!
BONG!
BONG
BONG
BONG
BONG!
BONG
BONG!
BONG!
BONG!
BONG!
WELL, SO MUCH FOR THAT! EH, OLD CHUM?
THE VOICE OF THE MONK!!!
FOOL! THE BOY IS LOST!!
WHAA?
THE BAT-MAN'S UTILITY BELT RADIO CRACKLES TO LIFE!
KKRRRXXXX!! BATMAN! HELP ME!
IT'S THE BOY WONDER!
ROBIN!!
SQUELCH
VOL
HELP ME!! I'M----
KRRRXXXX!

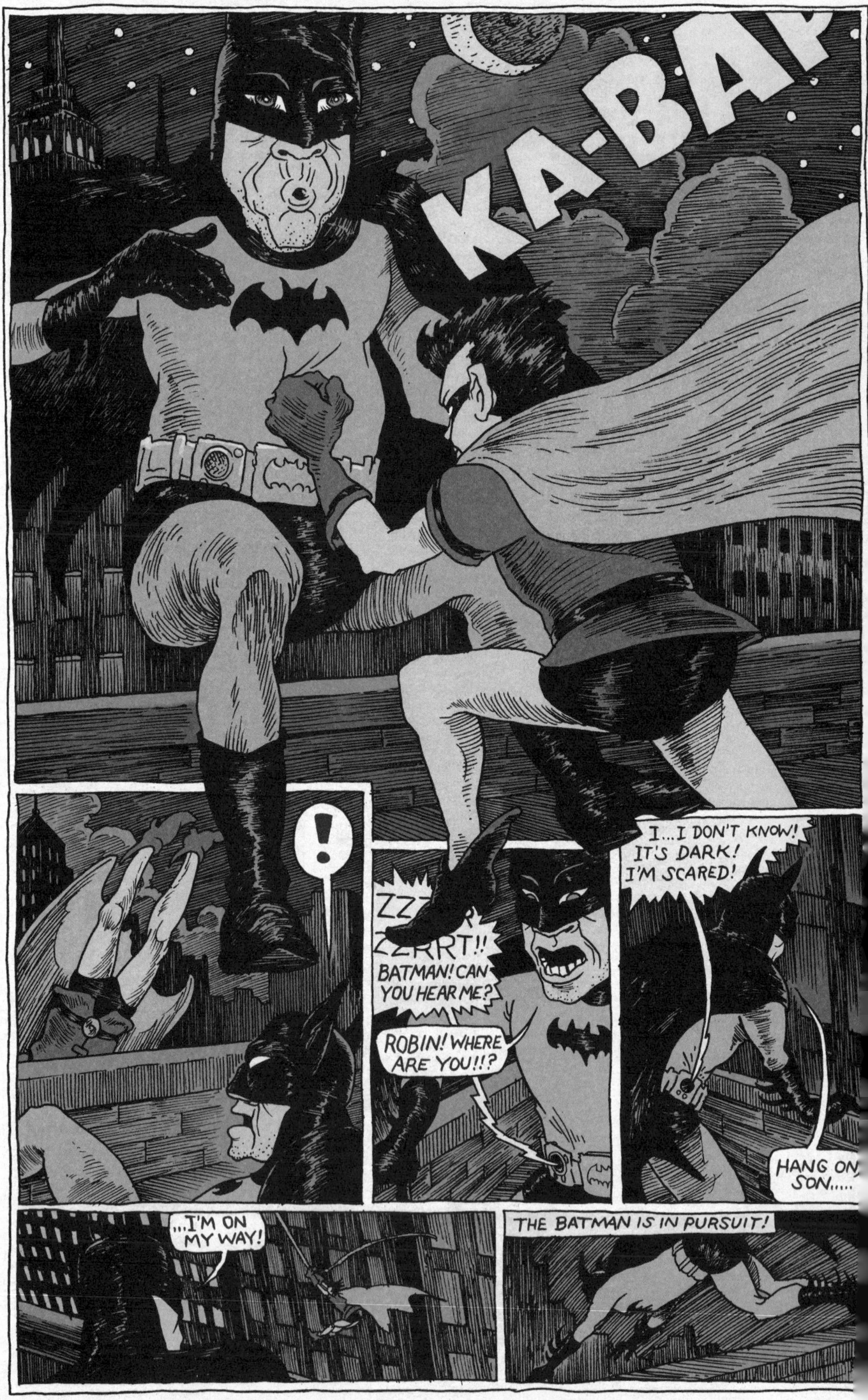
KA-BA
!
ZZRRT!!
BATMAN! CAN YOU HEAR ME?
ROBIN! WHERE ARE YOU!!?
I...I DON'T KNOW! IT'S DARK! I'M SCARED!
HANG ON, SON.....
...I'M ON MY WAY!
THE BATMAN IS IN PURSUIT!

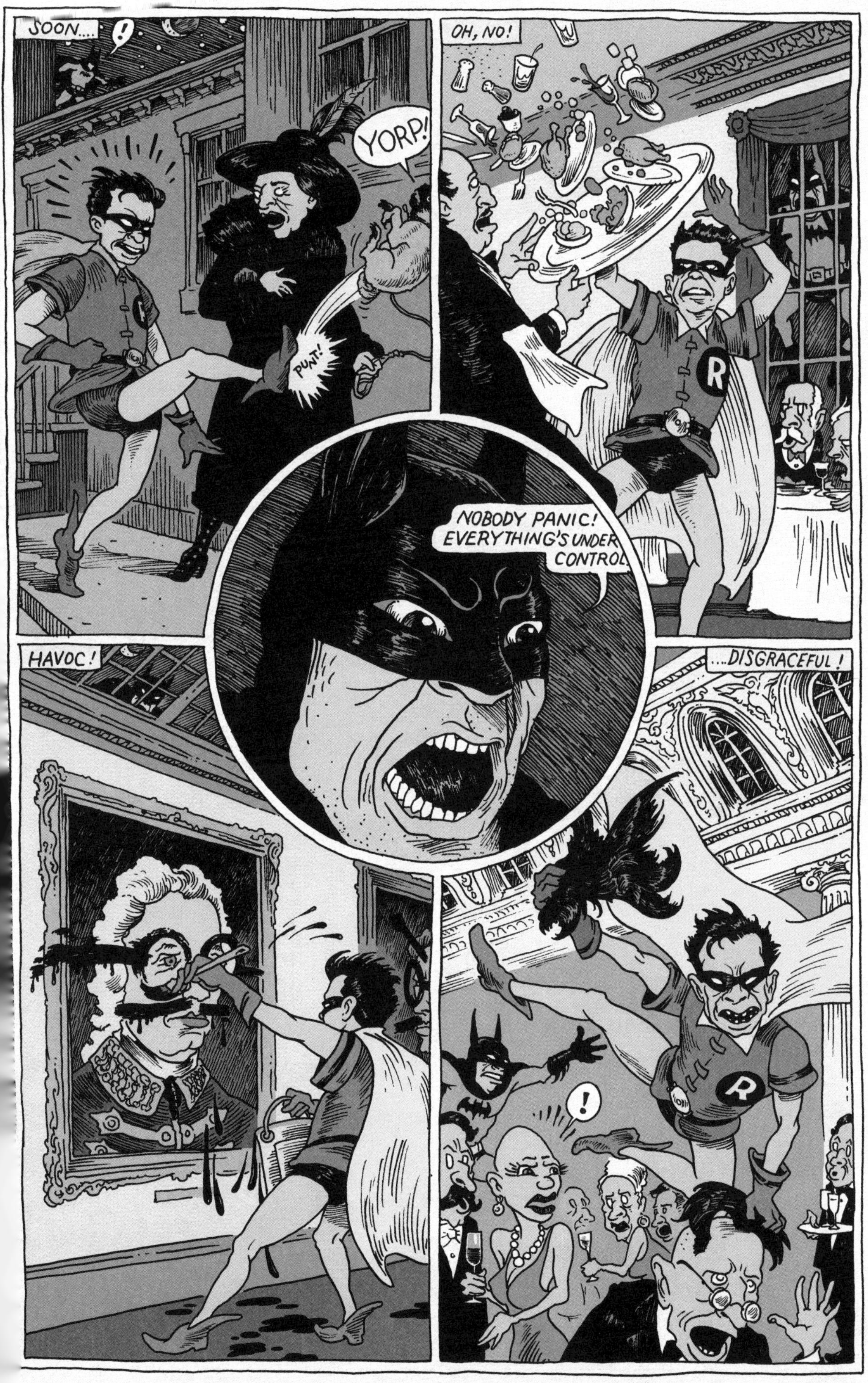
SOON....
!
YORP!
PUNT!
OH, NO!
NOBODY PANIC! EVERYTHING'S UNDER CONTROL
HAVOC!
....DISGRACEFUL!
!

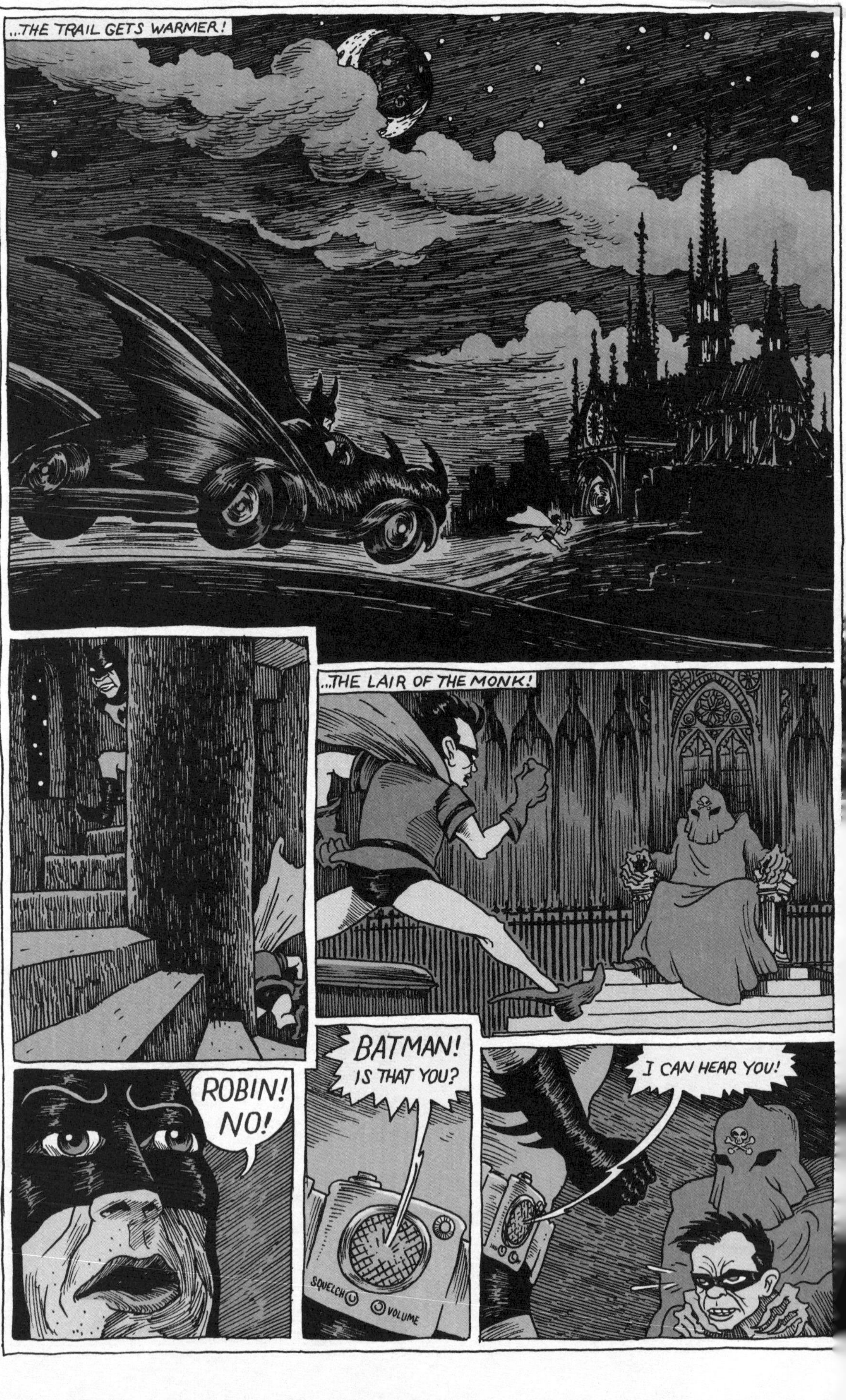
...THE TRAIL GETS WARMER!
...THE LAIR OF THE MONK!
ROBIN! NO!
BATMAN! IS THAT YOU?
SQUELCH
VOLUME
I CAN HEAR YOU!

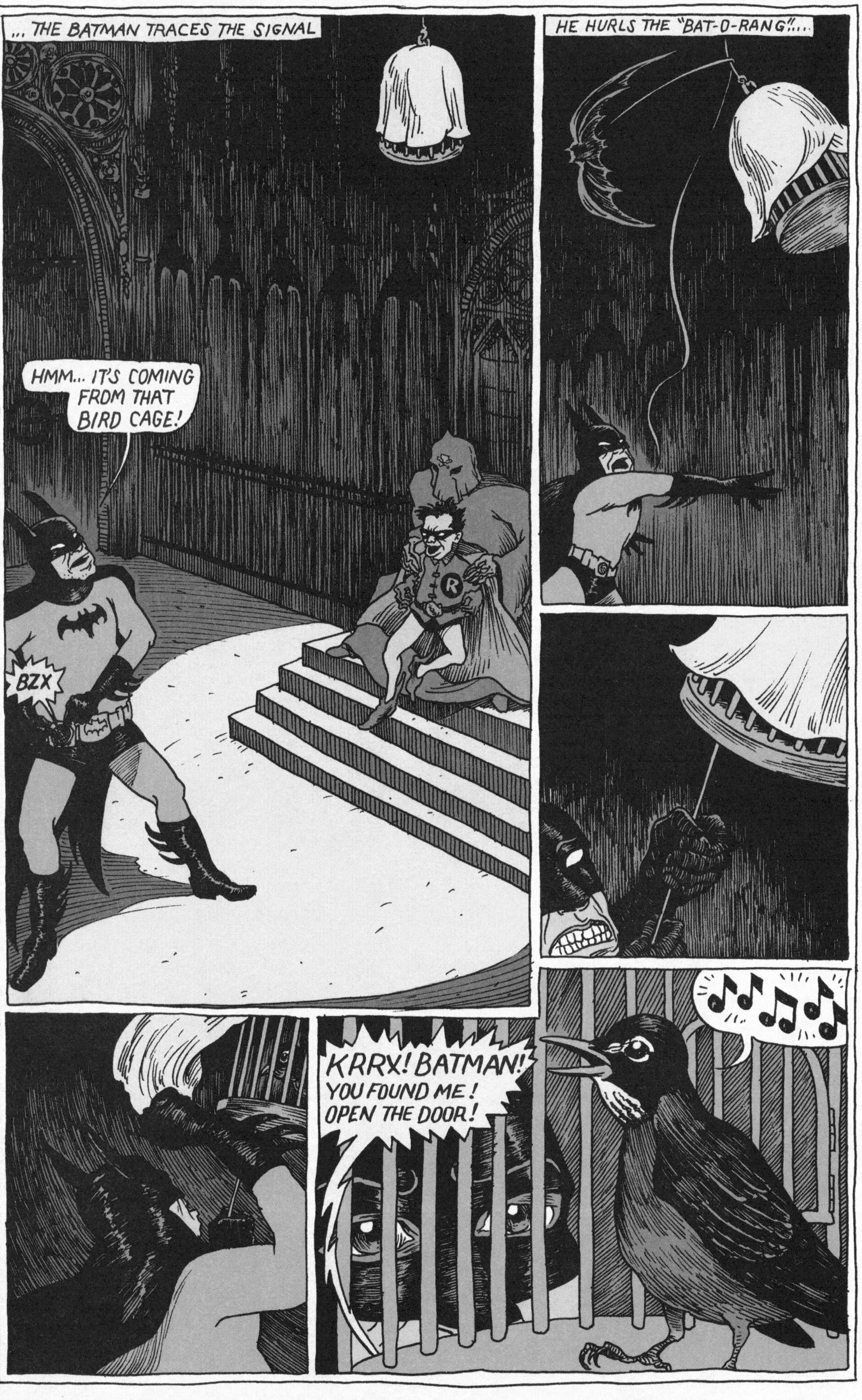
... THE BATMAN TRACES THE SIGNAL
HMM... IT'S COMING FROM THAT BIRD CAGE!
BZX
HE HURLS THE "BAT-O-RANG"!...
KRRX! BATMAN! YOU FOUND ME! OPEN THE DOOR!

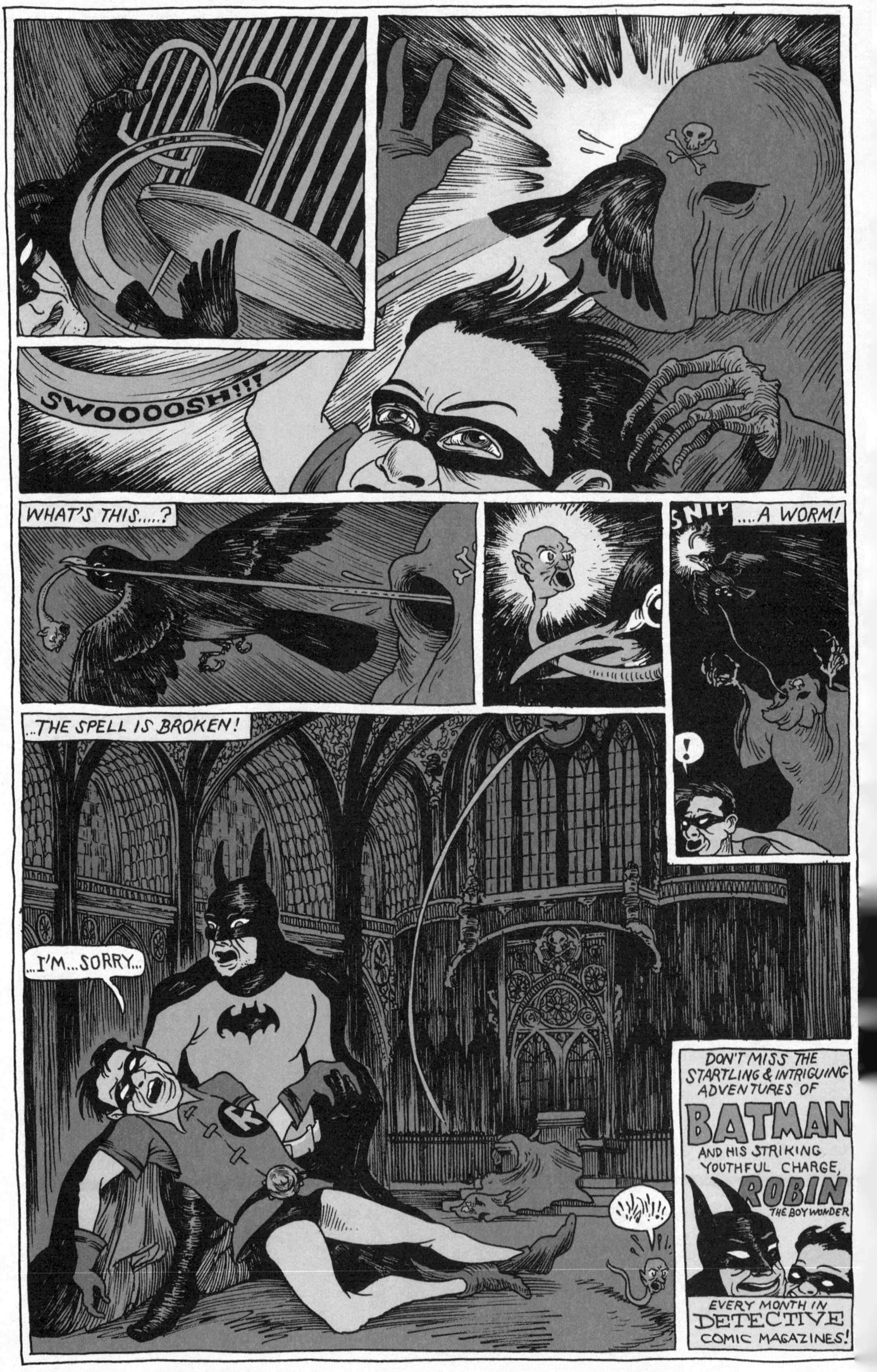
SWOOOOSH!!!
WHAT'S THIS.....?
SNIP
....A WORM!
!
...THE SPELL IS BROKEN!
...I'M...SORRY...
!!?!!!
DON'T MISS THE STARTLING & INTRIGUING ADVENTURES OF
BATMAN
AND HIS STRIKING YOUTHFUL CHARGE,
ROBIN
THE BOY WONDER
EVERY MONTH IN
DETECTIVE
COMIC MAGAZINES!

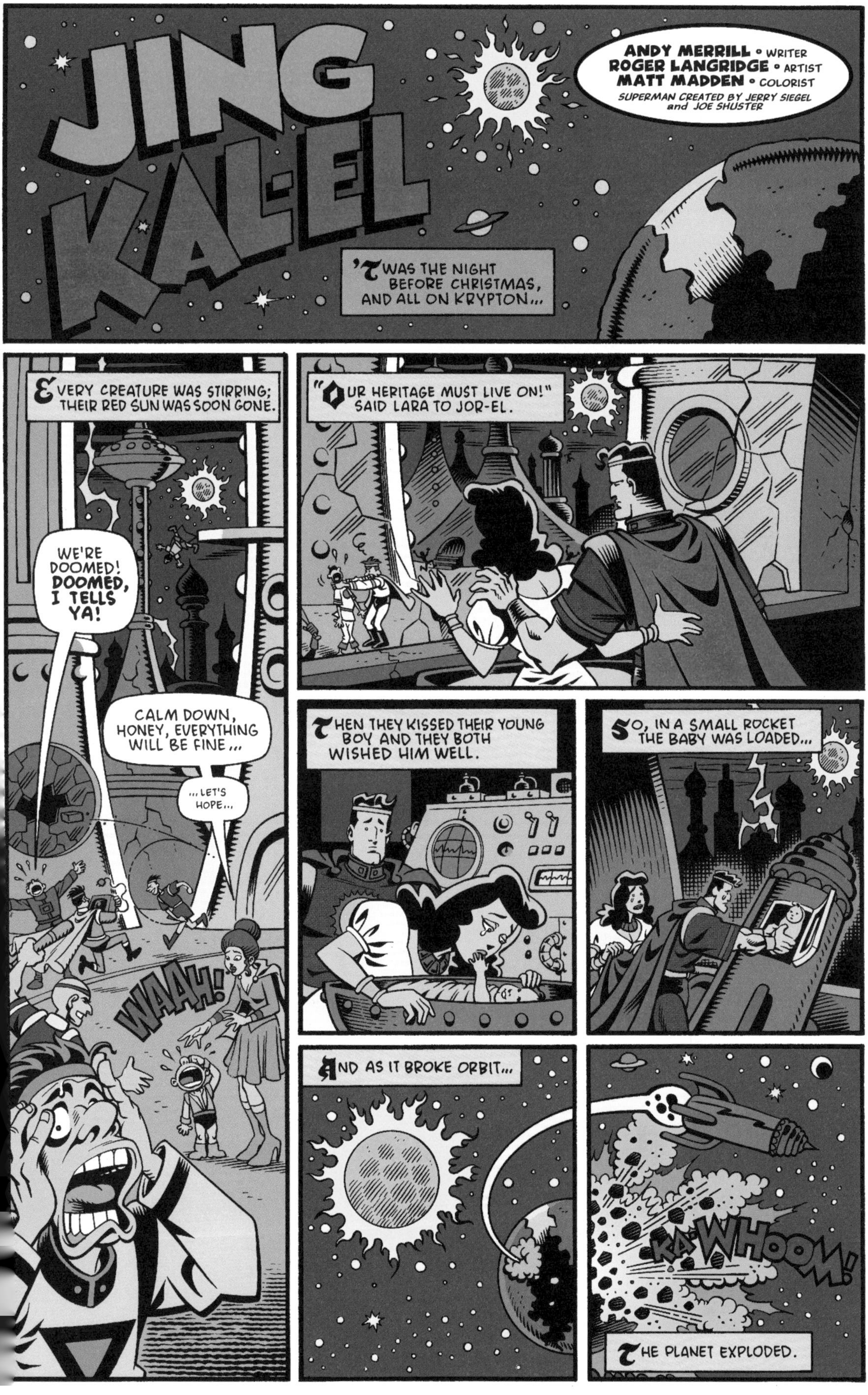
JING KAL-EL
ANDY MERRILL • WRITER
ROGER LANGRIDGE • ARTIST
MATT MADDEN • COLORIST
SUPERMAN CREATED BY JERRY SIEGEL and JOE SHUSTER
'TWAS THE NIGHT BEFORE CHRISTMAS, AND ALL ON KRYPTON...
EVERY CREATURE WAS STIRRING; THEIR RED SUN WAS SOON GONE.
WE'RE DOOMED! DOOMED, I TELLS YA!
CALM DOWN, HONEY, EVERYTHING WILL BE FINE...
...LET'S HOPE...
WAAH!
"OUR HERITAGE MUST LIVE ON!" SAID LARA TO JOR-EL.
THEN THEY KISSED THEIR YOUNG BOY AND THEY BOTH WISHED HIM WELL.
SO, IN A SMALL ROCKET THE BABY WAS LOADED...
AND AS IT BROKE ORBIT...
KA-WHOOM!
THE PLANET EXPLODED.

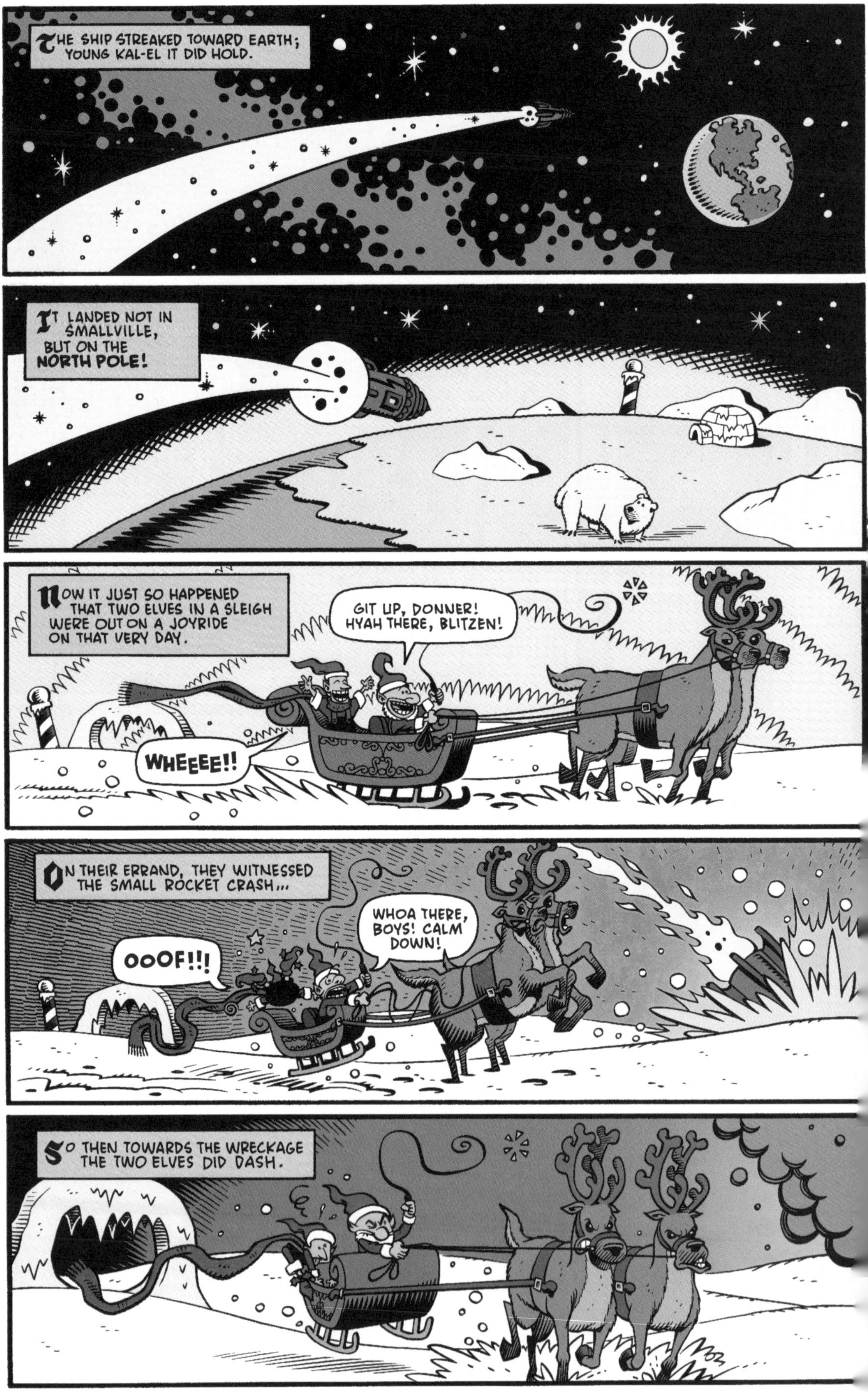
THE SHIP STREAKED TOWARD EARTH; YOUNG KAL-EL IT DID HOLD.
IT LANDED NOT IN SMALLVILLE, BUT ON THE NORTH POLE!
NOW IT JUST SO HAPPENED THAT TWO ELVES IN A SLEIGH WERE OUT ON A JOYRIDE ON THAT VERY DAY.
GIT UP, DONNER! HYAH THERE, BLITZEN!
WHEEEE!!
ON THEIR ERRAND, THEY WITNESSED THE SMALL ROCKET CRASH...
WHOA THERE, BOYS! CALM DOWN!
OOOF!!!
SO THEN TOWARDS THE WRECKAGE THE TWO ELVES DID DASH.

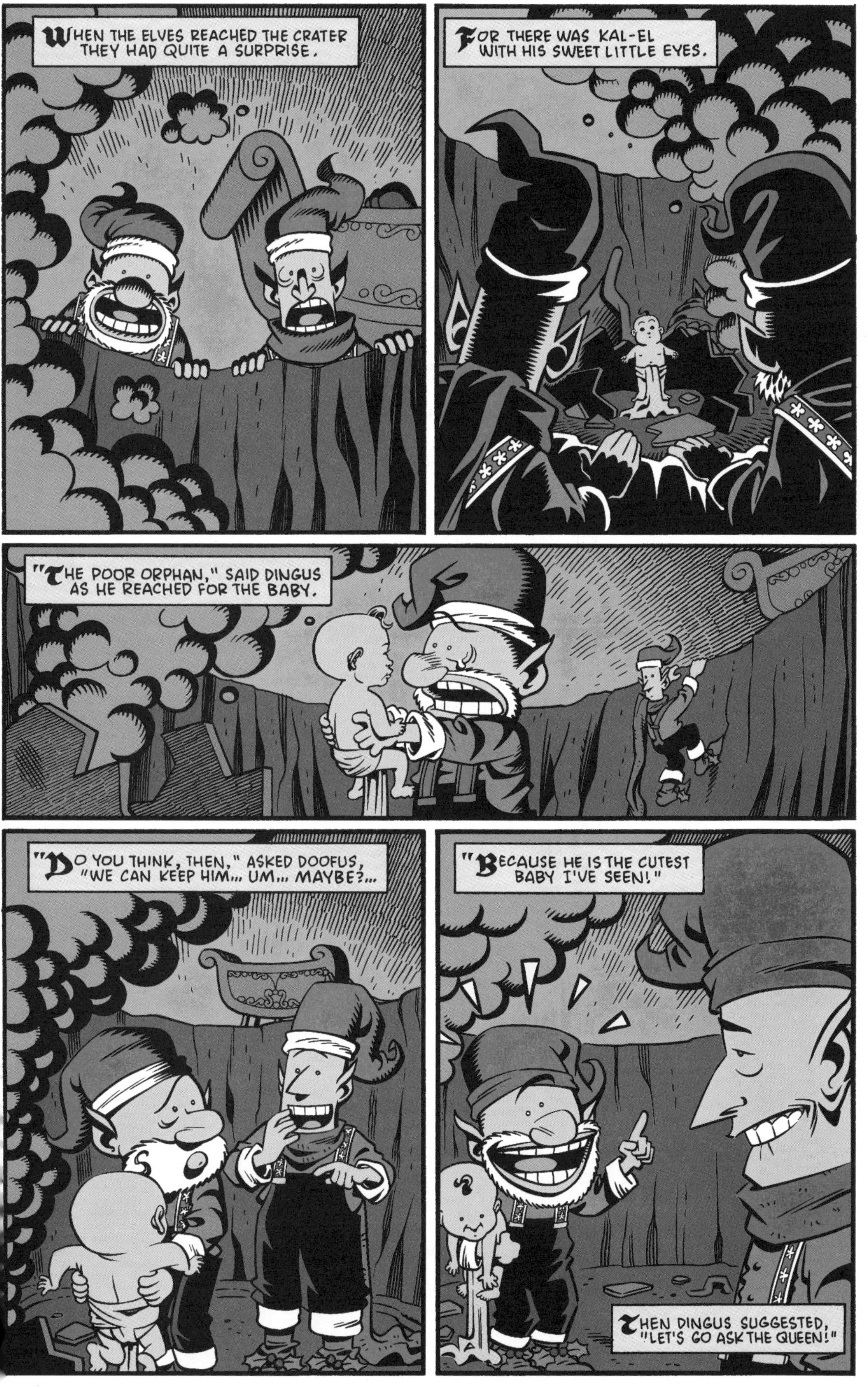
When the elves reached the crater they had quite a surprise.
For there was Kal-El with his sweet little eyes.
"The poor orphan," said Dingus as he reached for the baby.
"Do you think, then," asked Doofus, "we can keep him... um... maybe?...
"Because he is the cutest baby I've seen!"
Then Dingus suggested, "Let's go ask the queen!"

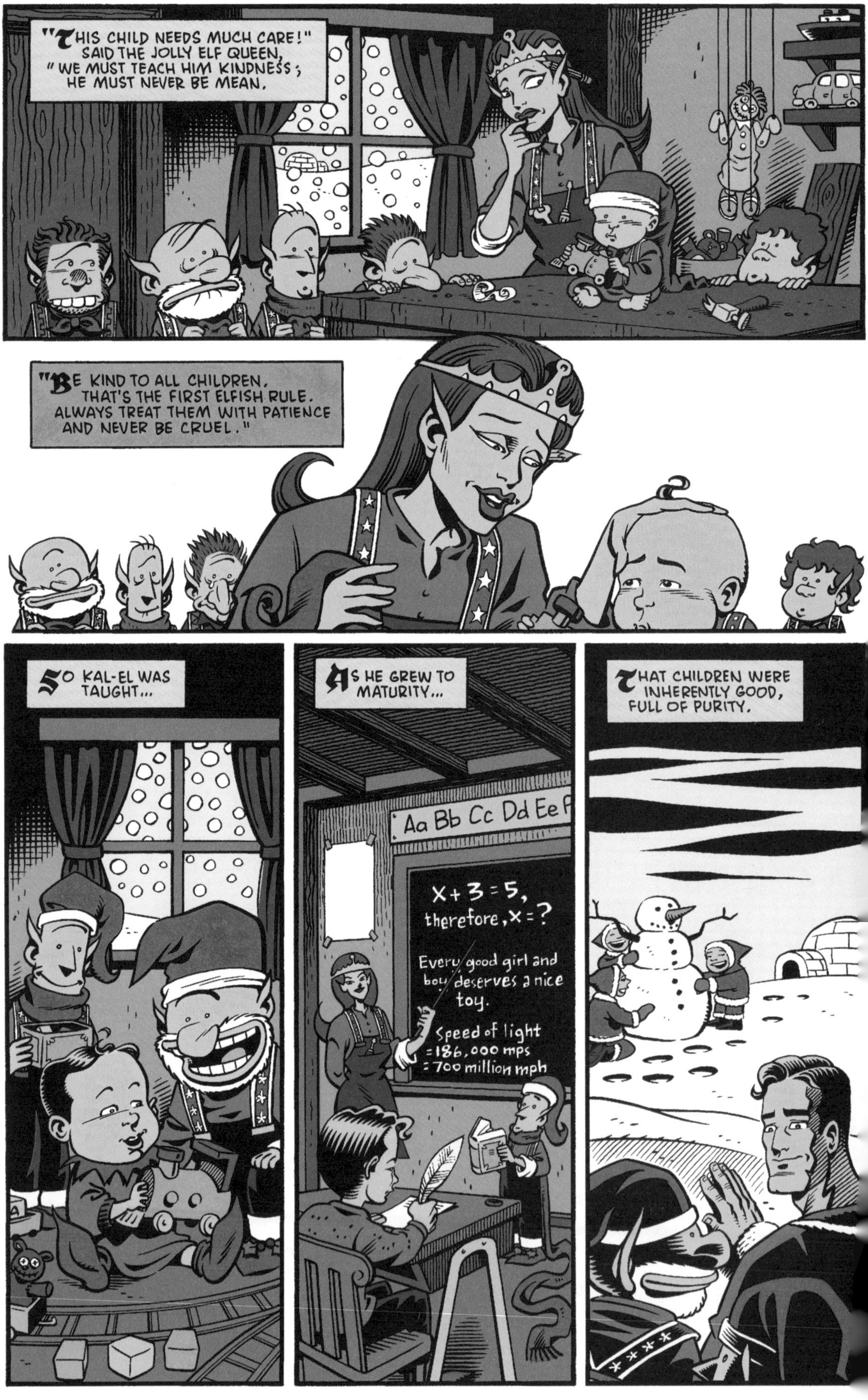
"THIS CHILD NEEDS MUCH CARE!" SAID THE JOLLY ELF QUEEN, "WE MUST TEACH HIM KINDNESS; HE MUST NEVER BE MEAN.
"BE KIND TO ALL CHILDREN. THAT'S THE FIRST ELFISH RULE. ALWAYS TREAT THEM WITH PATIENCE AND NEVER BE CRUEL."
SO KAL-EL WAS TAUGHT...
AS HE GREW TO MATURITY...
Aa Bb Cc Dd Ee F
X + 3 = 5, therefore, X = ?
Every good girl and boy deserves a nice toy.
Speed of light =186,000 mps =700 million mph
THAT CHILDREN WERE INHERENTLY GOOD, FULL OF PURITY.

AND AS HE GREW OLD, HIS LOVE FOR CHILDREN DID TOO.

HO HO!

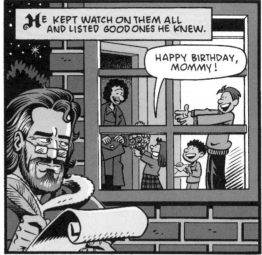

HE KEPT WATCH ON THEM ALL AND LISTED GOOD ONES HE KNEW.

HAPPY BIRTHDAY, MOMMY!

SO, WITH THE HELP OF THOSE ELVES AND REINDEER GIFTED WITH FLIGHT...

HE BRINGS GOOD CHILDREN PRESENTS EVERY CHRISTMAS EVE NIGHT.

SO WHEN YOU GO TO BED ON THAT NIGHT, STOP AND PAUSE...

AND LEAVE A COOKIE AND MILK FOR SANTA "KAL-EL" CLAUS.

HO HO HO!!!

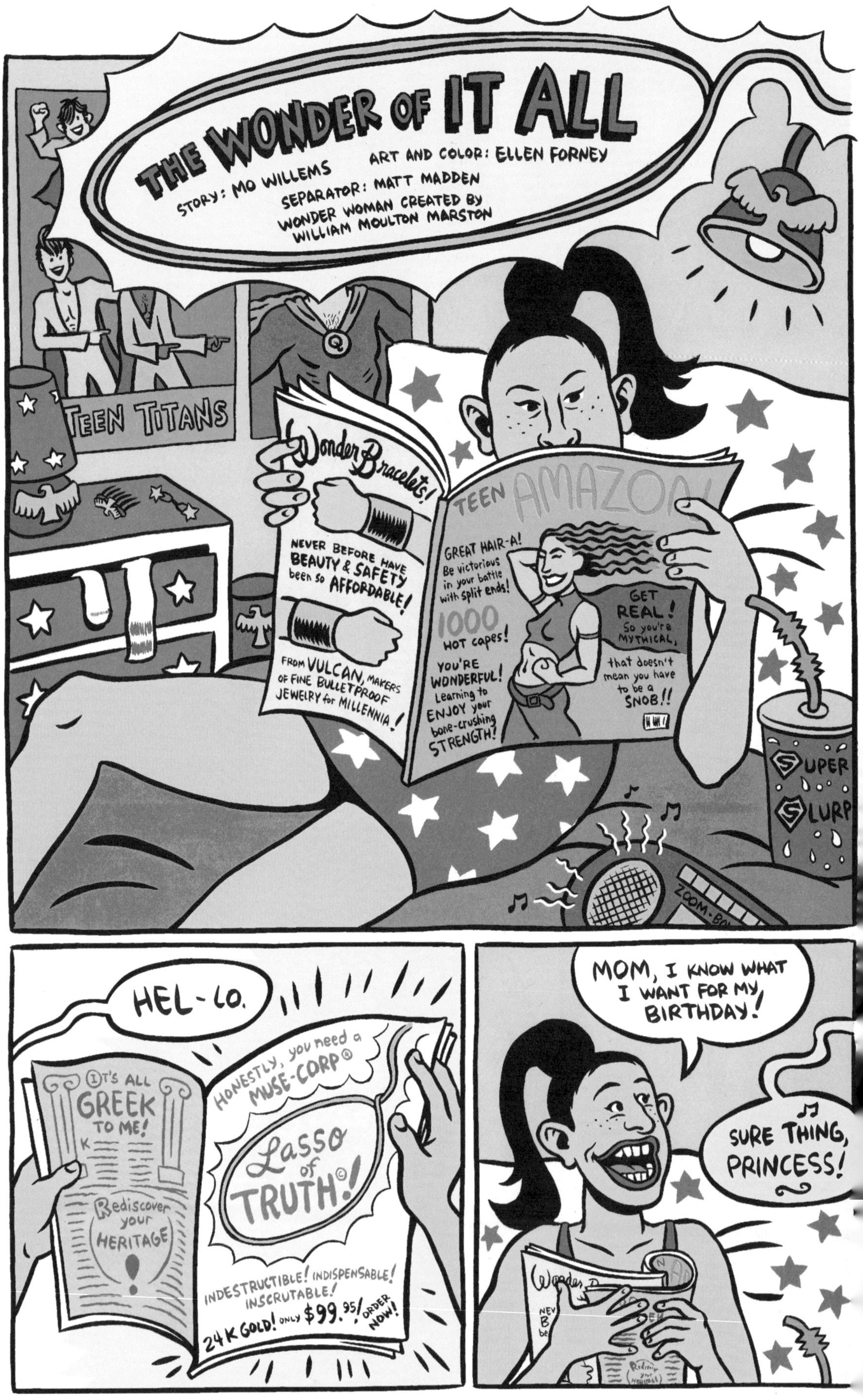
THE WONDER OF IT ALL
STORY: MO WILLEMS
ART AND COLOR: ELLEN FORNEY
SEPARATOR: MATT MADDEN
WONDER WOMAN CREATED BY WILLIAM MOULTON MARSTON
TEEN TITANS
Wonder Bracelets!
NEVER BEFORE HAVE BEAUTY & SAFETY been so AFFORDABLE!
FROM VULCAN, MAKERS OF FINE BULLETPROOF JEWELRY for MILLENNIA!
TEEN AMAZON!
GREAT HAIR-A! Be victorious in your battle with split ends!
1000 HOT capes!
YOU'RE WONDERFUL! Learning to ENJOY your bone-crushing STRENGTH!
GET REAL! So you're MYTHICAL, that doesn't mean you have to be a SNOB!!
SUPER SLURP
ZOOM-BO
HEL-LO.
IT'S ALL GREEK TO ME!
Rediscover your HERITAGE!
HONESTLY, you need a MUSE-CORP®
Lasso of TRUTH©!
INDESTRUCTIBLE! INDISPENSABLE! INSCRUTABLE!
24K GOLD! ONLY $99.95! ORDER NOW!
MOM, I KNOW WHAT I WANT FOR MY BIRTHDAY!
SURE THING, PRINCESS!

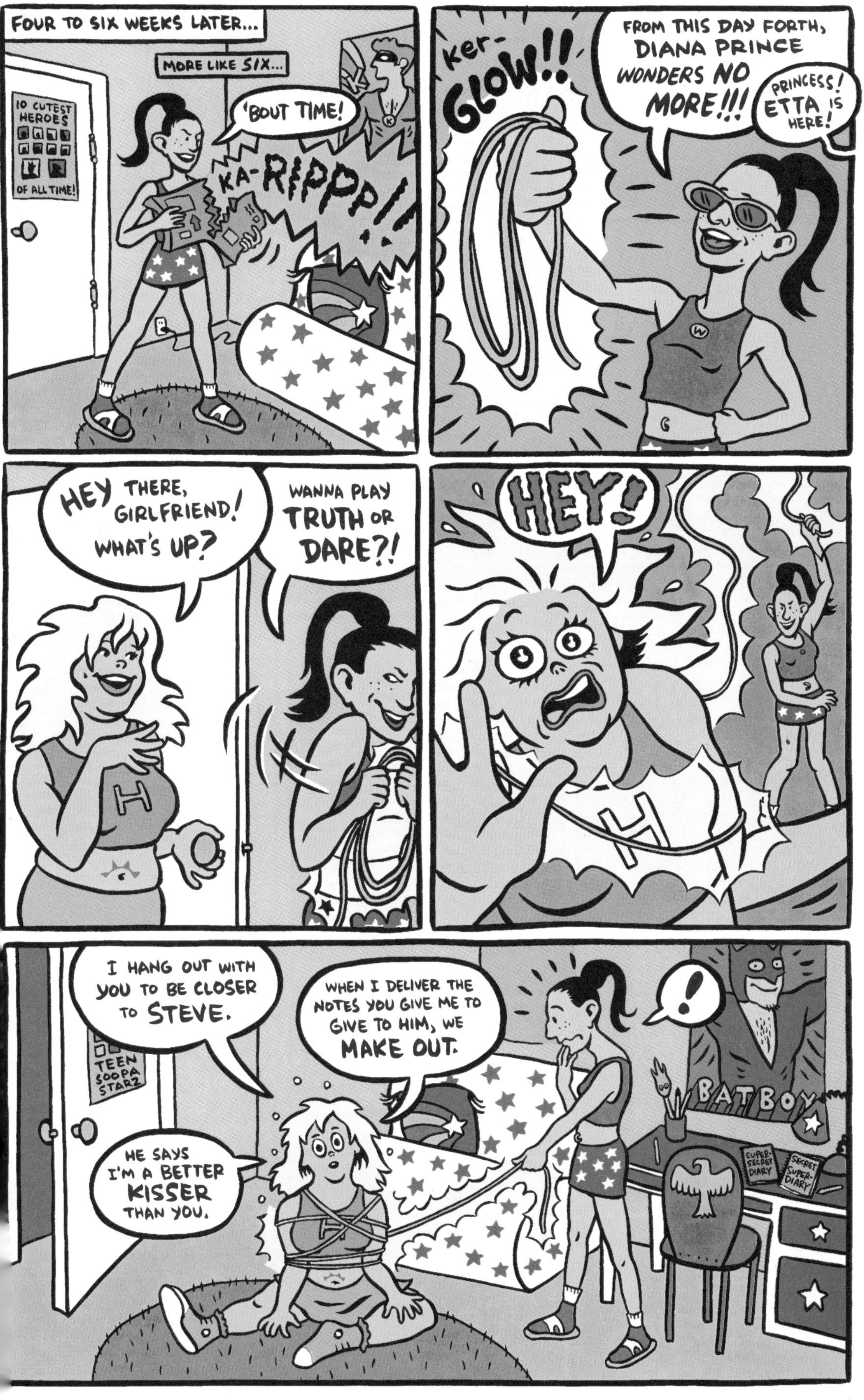
FOUR TO SIX WEEKS LATER...
MORE LIKE SIX...
10 CUTEST HEROES OF ALL TIME!
'BOUT TIME!
KA-RIPPP!!
ker-GLOW!!
FROM THIS DAY FORTH, DIANA PRINCE WONDERS NO MORE!!!
PRINCESS! ETTA IS HERE!
HEY THERE, GIRLFRIEND! WHAT'S UP?
WANNA PLAY TRUTH OR DARE?!
HEY!
I HANG OUT WITH YOU TO BE CLOSER TO STEVE.
WHEN I DELIVER THE NOTES YOU GIVE ME TO GIVE TO HIM, WE MAKE OUT.
HE SAYS I'M A BETTER KISSER THAN YOU.
TEEN SOOPA STARZ
BATBOY
SUPER-SECRET DIARY
SECRET SUPER-DIARY

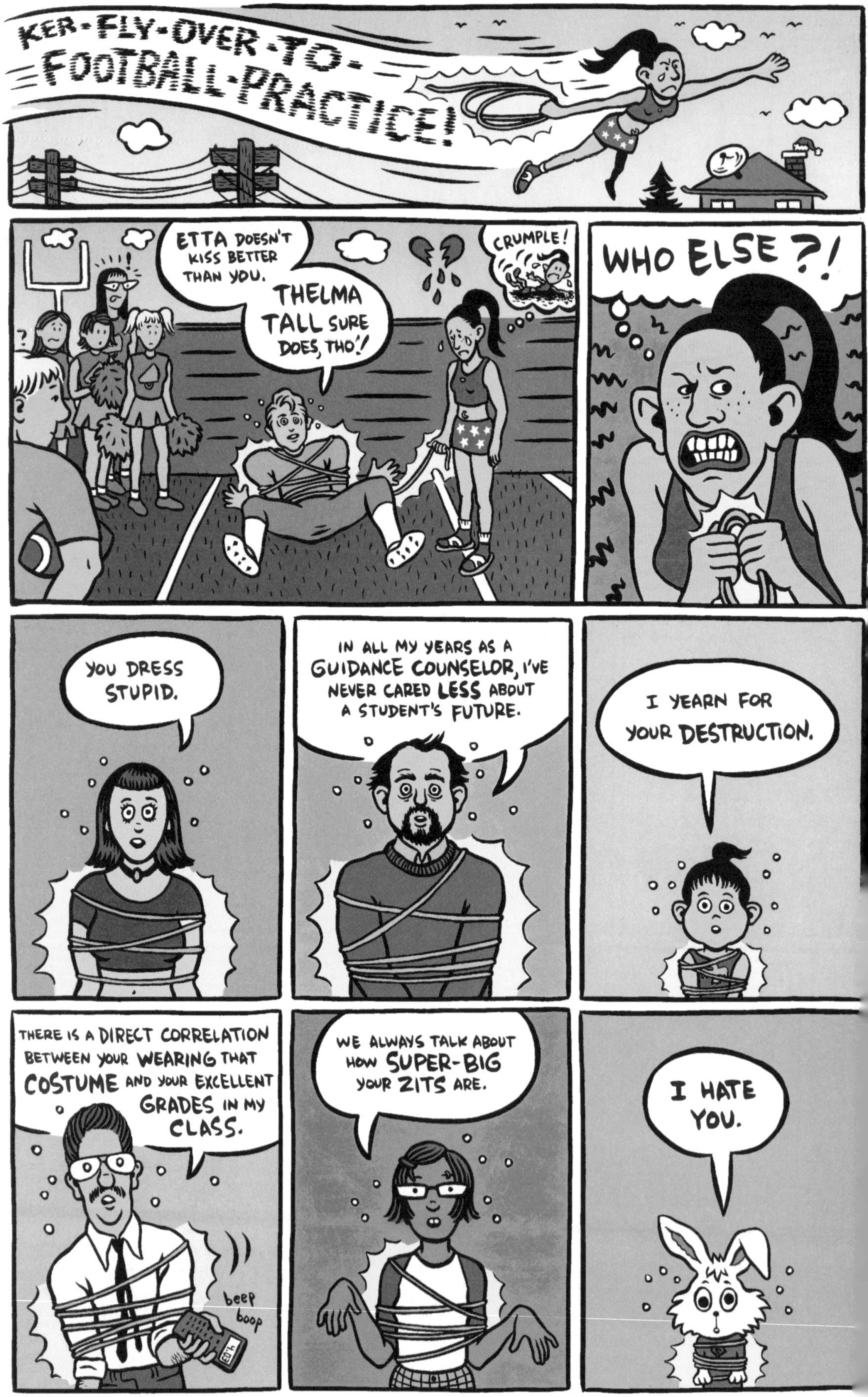
KER-FLY-OVER-TO-FOOTBALL-PRACTICE!
ETTA DOESN'T KISS BETTER THAN YOU.
THELMA TALL SURE DOES, THO'!
CRUMPLE!
WHO ELSE?!
YOU DRESS STUPID.
IN ALL MY YEARS AS A GUIDANCE COUNSELOR, I'VE NEVER CARED LESS ABOUT A STUDENT'S FUTURE.
I YEARN FOR YOUR DESTRUCTION.
THERE IS A DIRECT CORRELATION BETWEEN YOUR WEARING THAT COSTUME AND YOUR EXCELLENT GRADES IN MY CLASS.
beep boop
WE ALWAYS TALK ABOUT HOW SUPER-BIG YOUR ZITS ARE.
I HATE YOU.

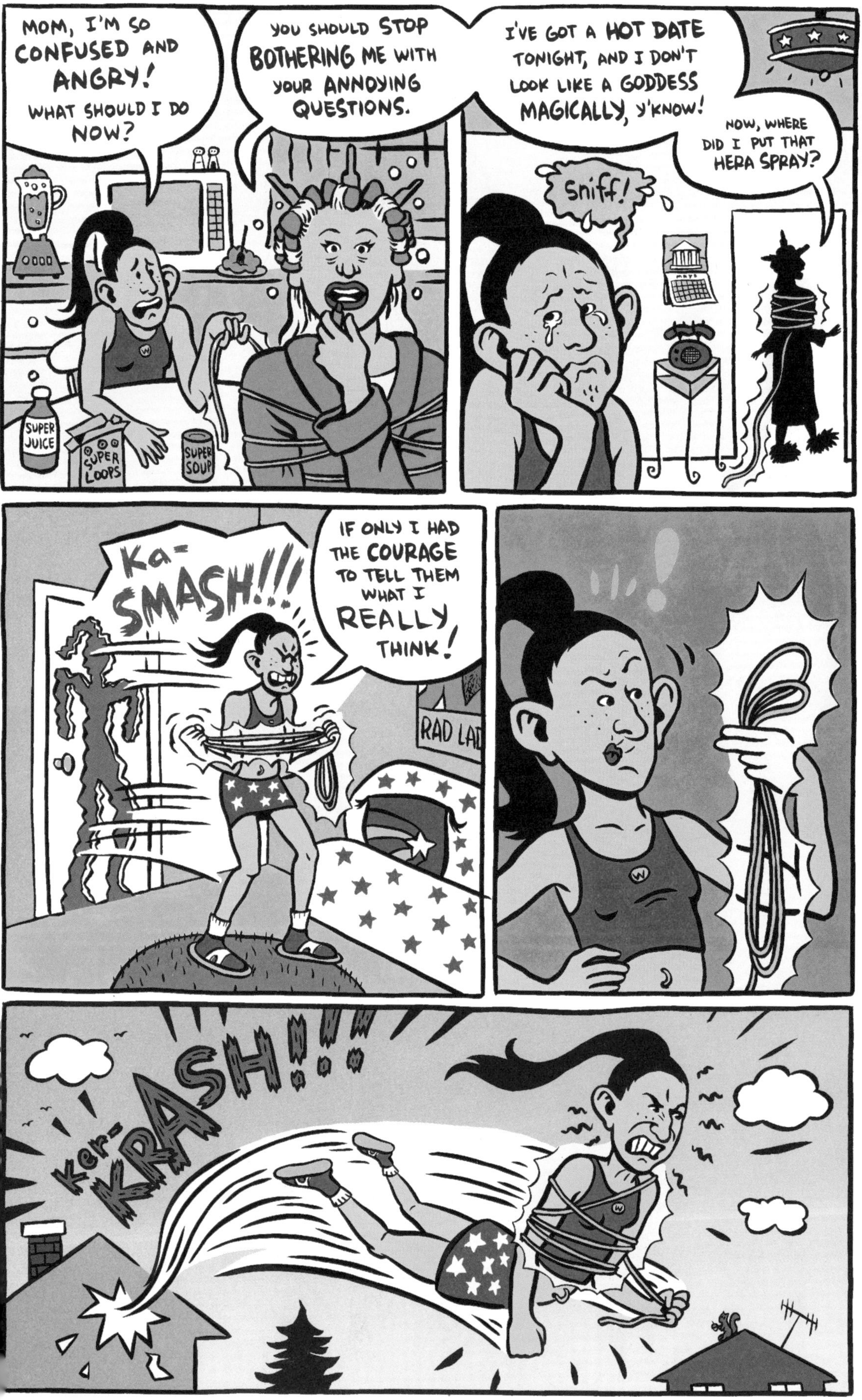
MOM, I'M SO CONFUSED AND ANGRY! WHAT SHOULD I DO NOW?
YOU SHOULD STOP BOTHERING ME WITH YOUR ANNOYING QUESTIONS.
I'VE GOT A HOT DATE TONIGHT, AND I DON'T LOOK LIKE A GODDESS MAGICALLY, Y'KNOW!
NOW, WHERE DID I PUT THAT HERA SPRAY?
SUPER JUICE
SUPER LOOPS
SUPER SOUP
Sniff!
KA-SMASH!!!
IF ONLY I HAD THE COURAGE TO TELL THEM WHAT I REALLY THINK!
RAD LAD
KER-KRASH!!!

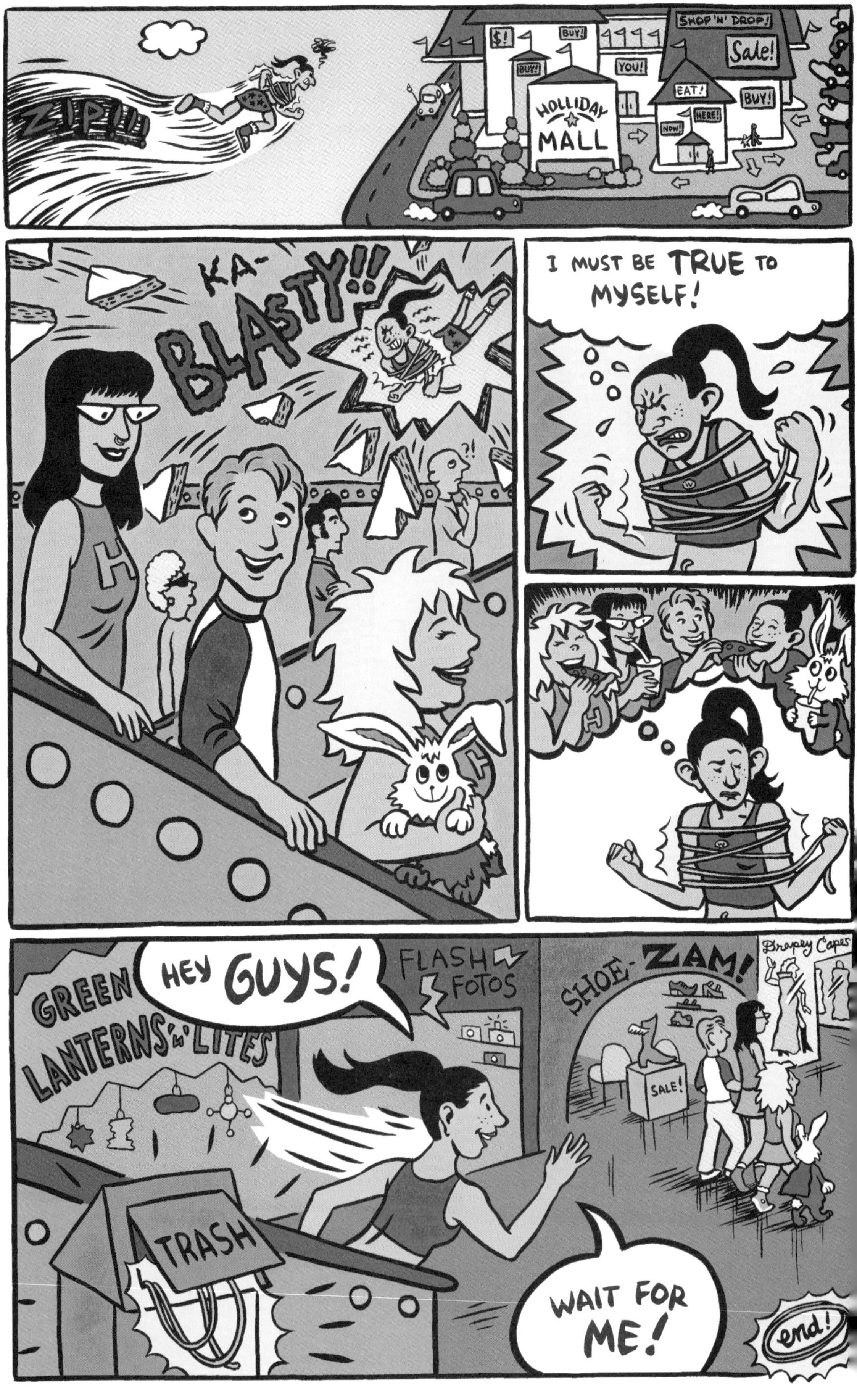
ZIP!!!
SHOP 'N' DROP!
$!
BUY!
Sale!
BUY!
YOU!
EAT!
BUY!
HOLLIDAY MALL
HERE!
NOW!
KA-BLASTY!!
?!
I MUST BE TRUE TO MYSELF!
GREEN LANTERNS 'n' LITES
HEY GUYS!
FLASH FOTOS
SHOE-ZAM!
Drapey Capes
SALE!
TRASH
WAIT FOR ME!
end!

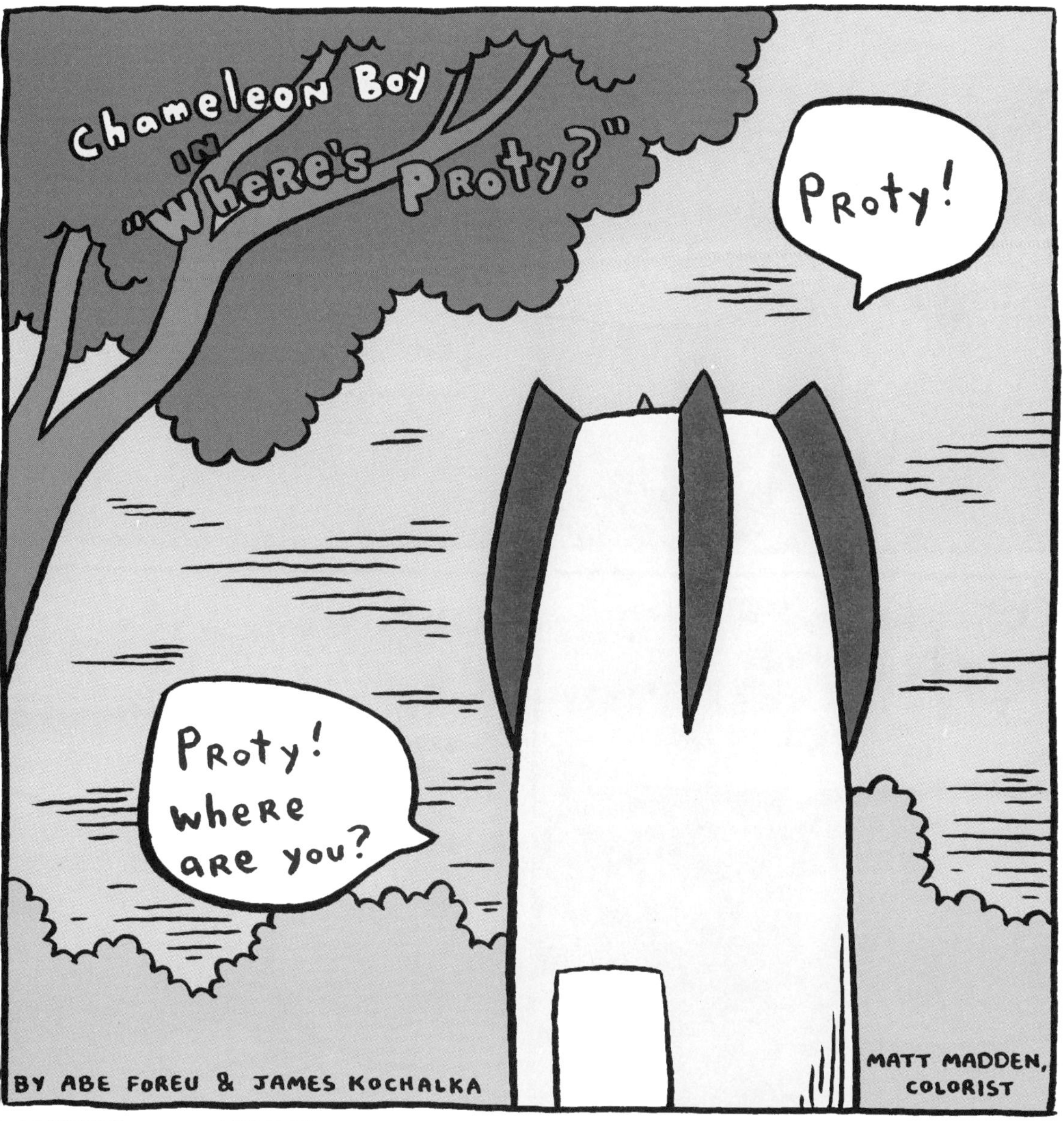
Chameleon Boy
in
"Where's Proty?"
Proty!
Proty! where are you?
BY ABE FOREU & JAMES KOCHALKA
MATT MADDEN, COLORIST

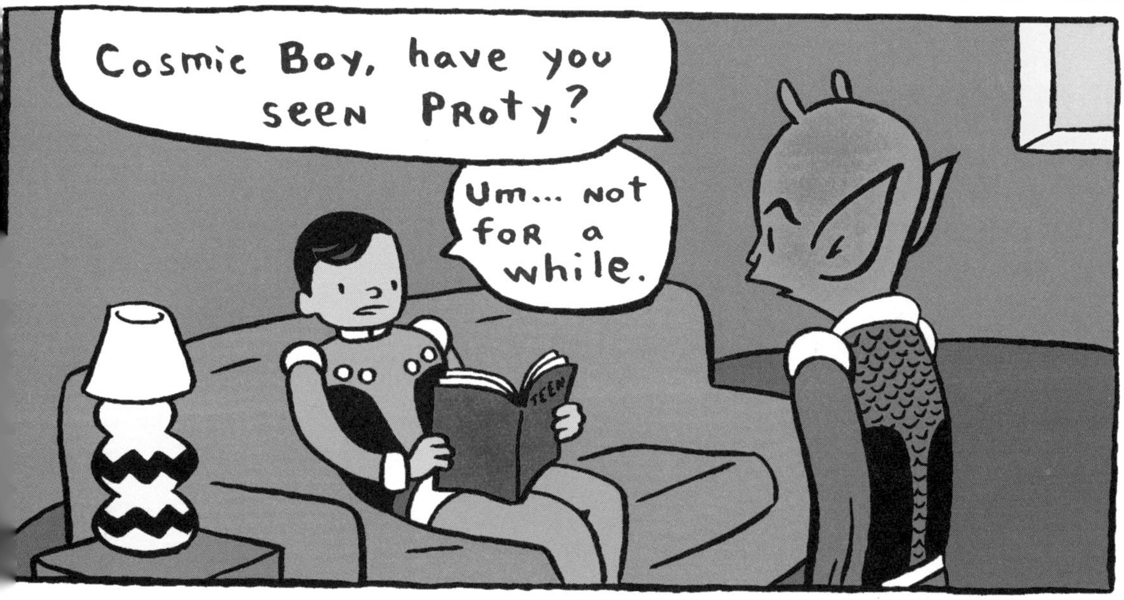
Cosmic Boy, have you seen Proty?
Um... not for a while.
TEEN

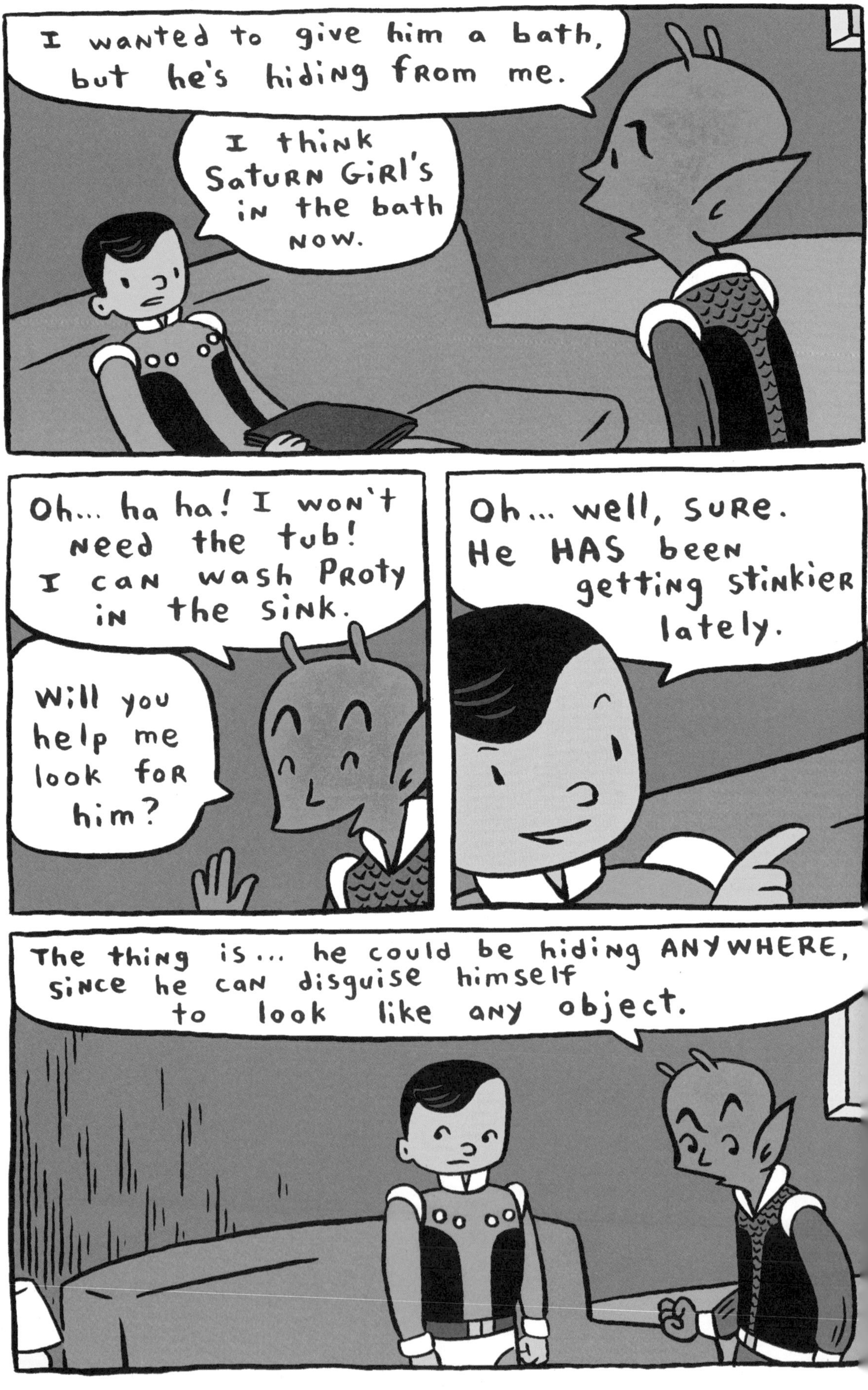
I wanted to give him a bath, but he's hiding from me.
I think Saturn Girl's in the bath now.
Oh... ha ha! I won't need the tub! I can wash Proty in the sink.
Will you help me look for him?
Oh... well, sure. He HAS been getting stinkier lately.
The thing is... he could be hiding ANYWHERE, since he can disguise himself to look like any object.

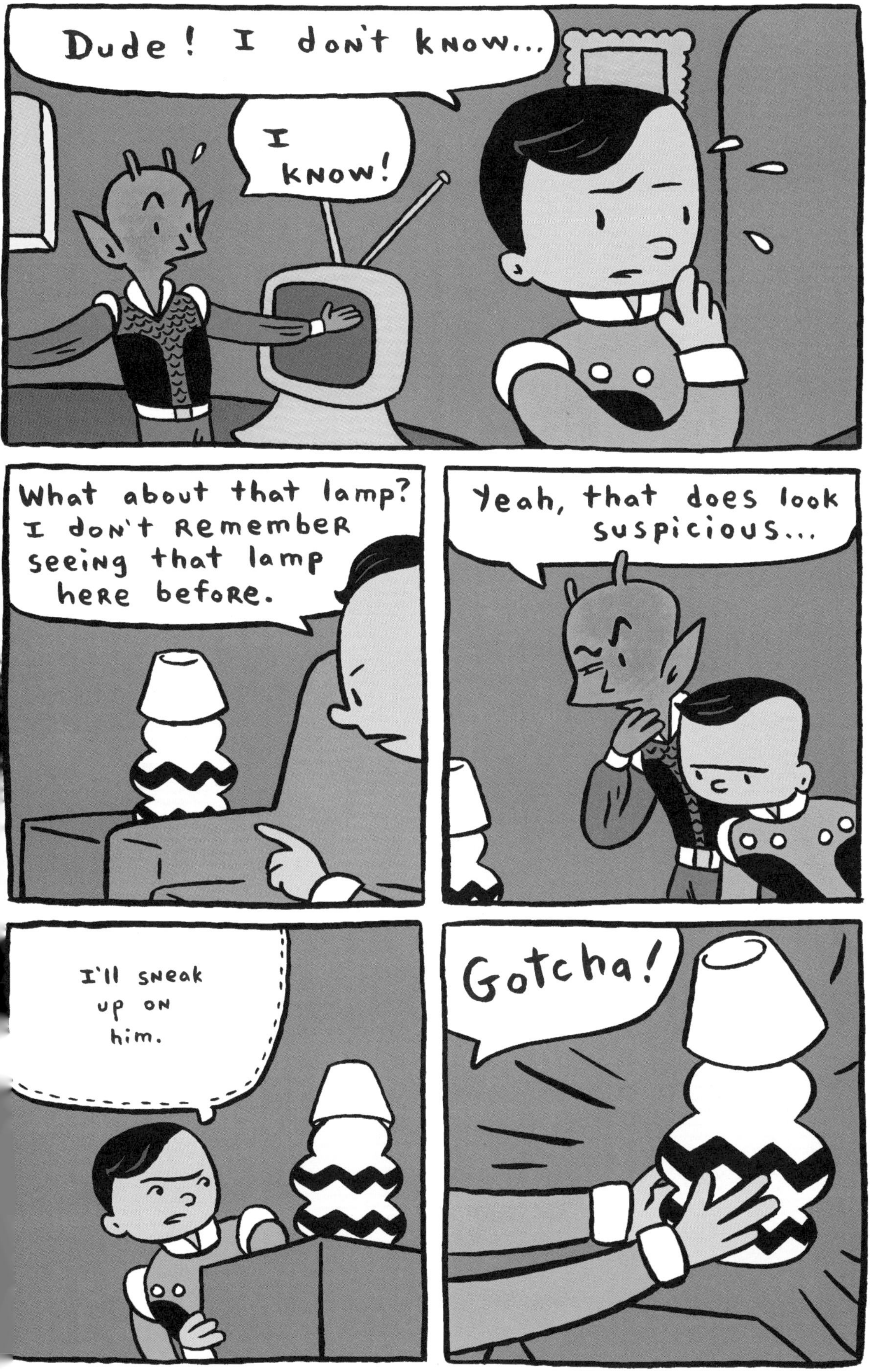
Dude! I don't know...
I know!
What about that lamp? I don't remember seeing that lamp here before.
Yeah, that does look suspicious...
I'll sneak up on him.
Gotcha!

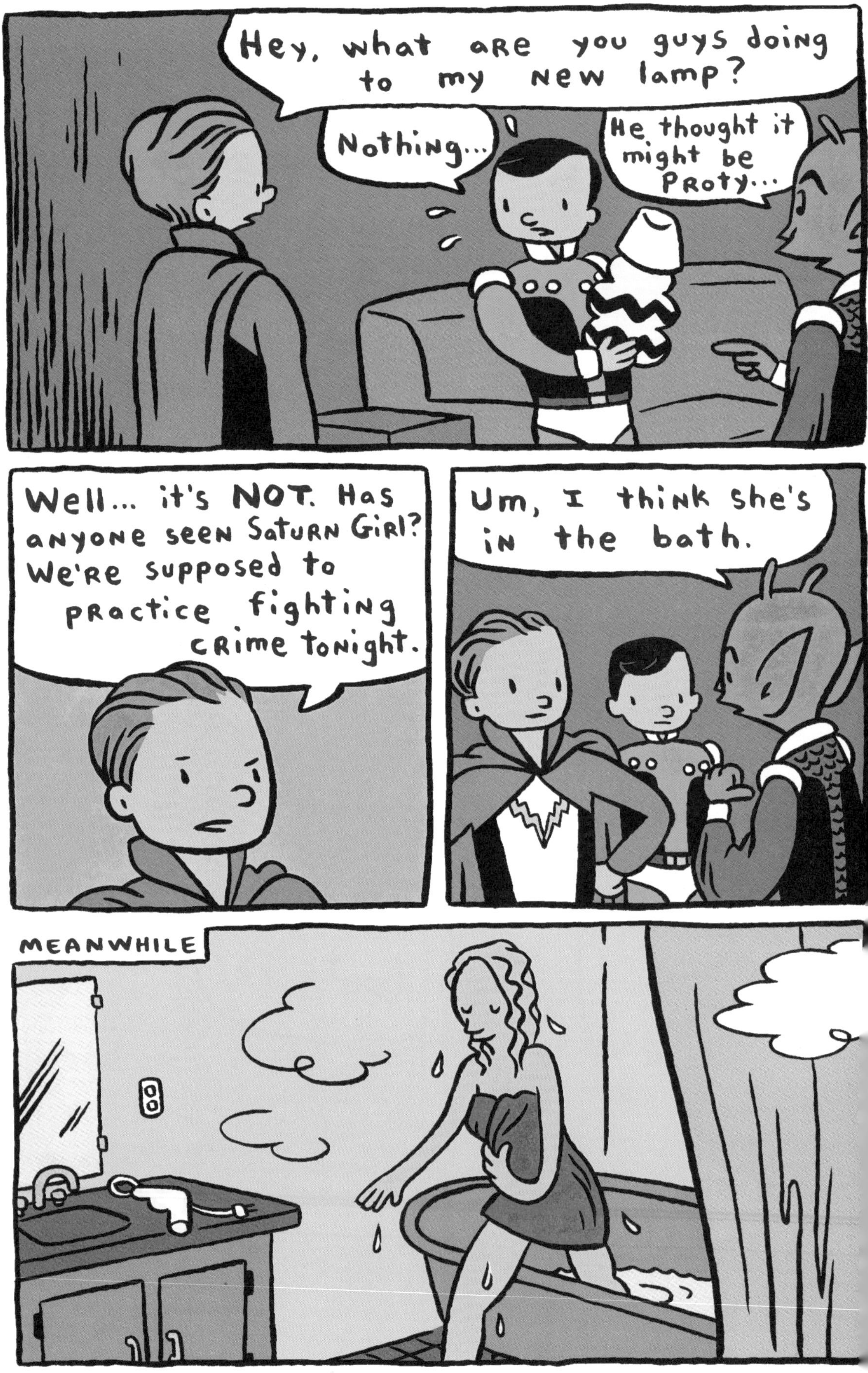

Hey, what are you guys doing to my new lamp?
Nothing...
He thought it might be Proty...
Well... it's NOT. Has anyone seen Saturn Girl? We're supposed to practice fighting crime tonight.
Um, I think she's in the bath.
MEANWHILE

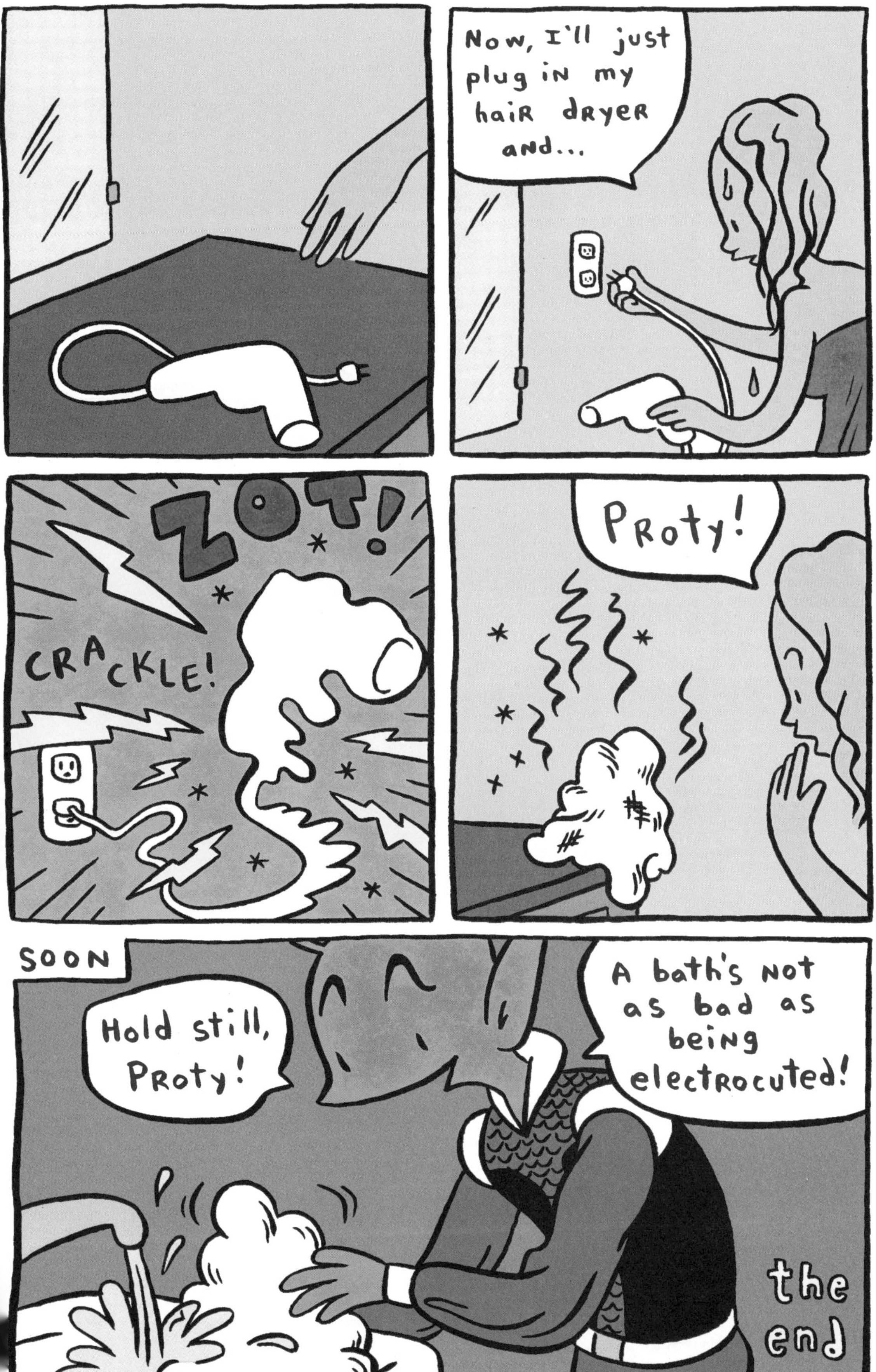
Now, I'll just plug in my hair dryer and...
ZOT!
CRACKLE!
Proty!
SOON
Hold still, Proty!
A bath's not as bad as being electrocuted!
the end

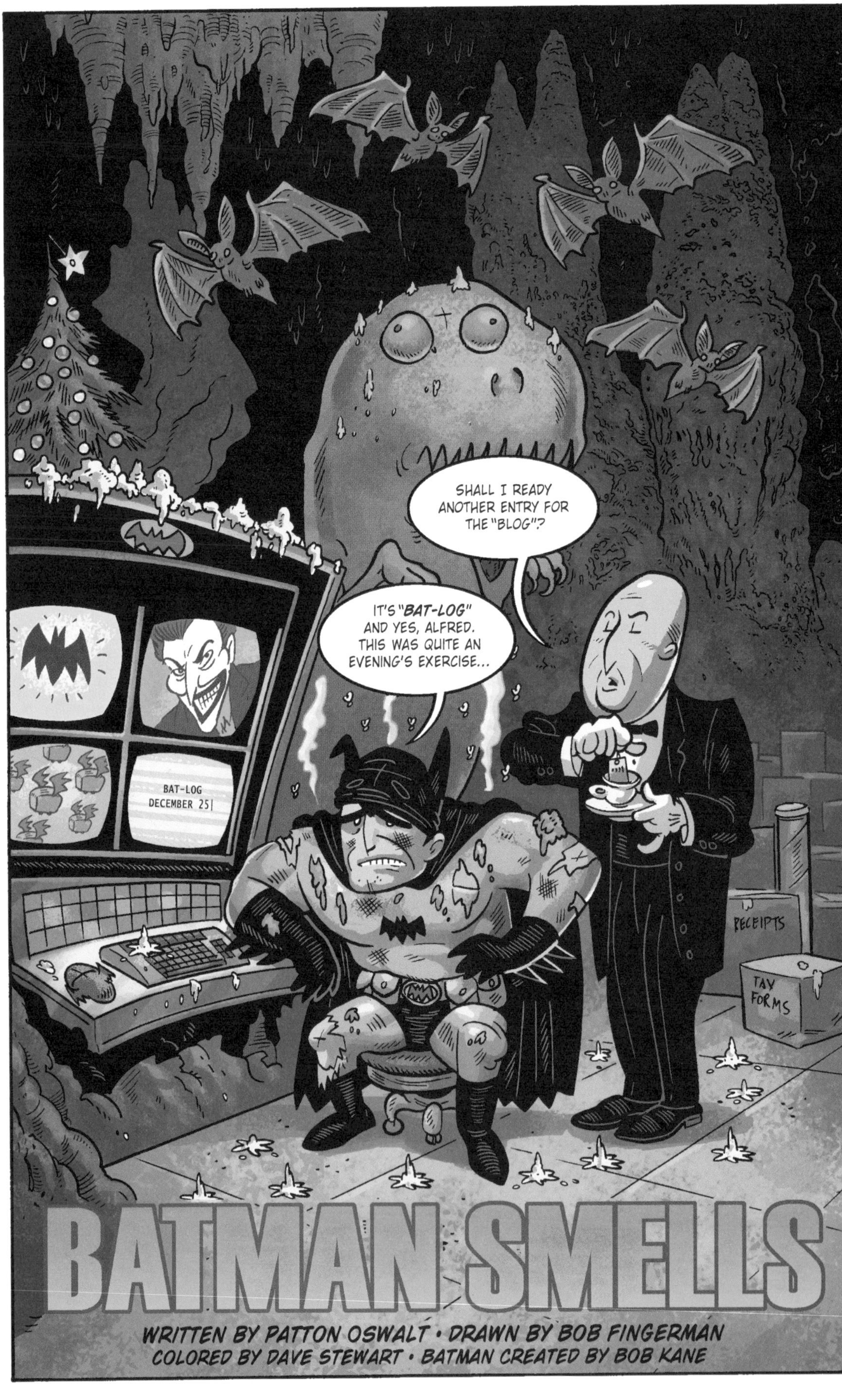

SHALL I READY ANOTHER ENTRY FOR THE "BLOG"?
IT'S "BAT-LOG" AND YES, ALFRED. THIS WAS QUITE AN EVENING'S EXERCISE...
BAT-LOG DECEMBER 25
RECEIPTS
TAX FORMS
BATMAN SMELLS
WRITTEN BY PATTON OSWALT • DRAWN BY BOB FINGERMAN
COLORED BY DAVE STEWART • BATMAN CREATED BY BOB KANE

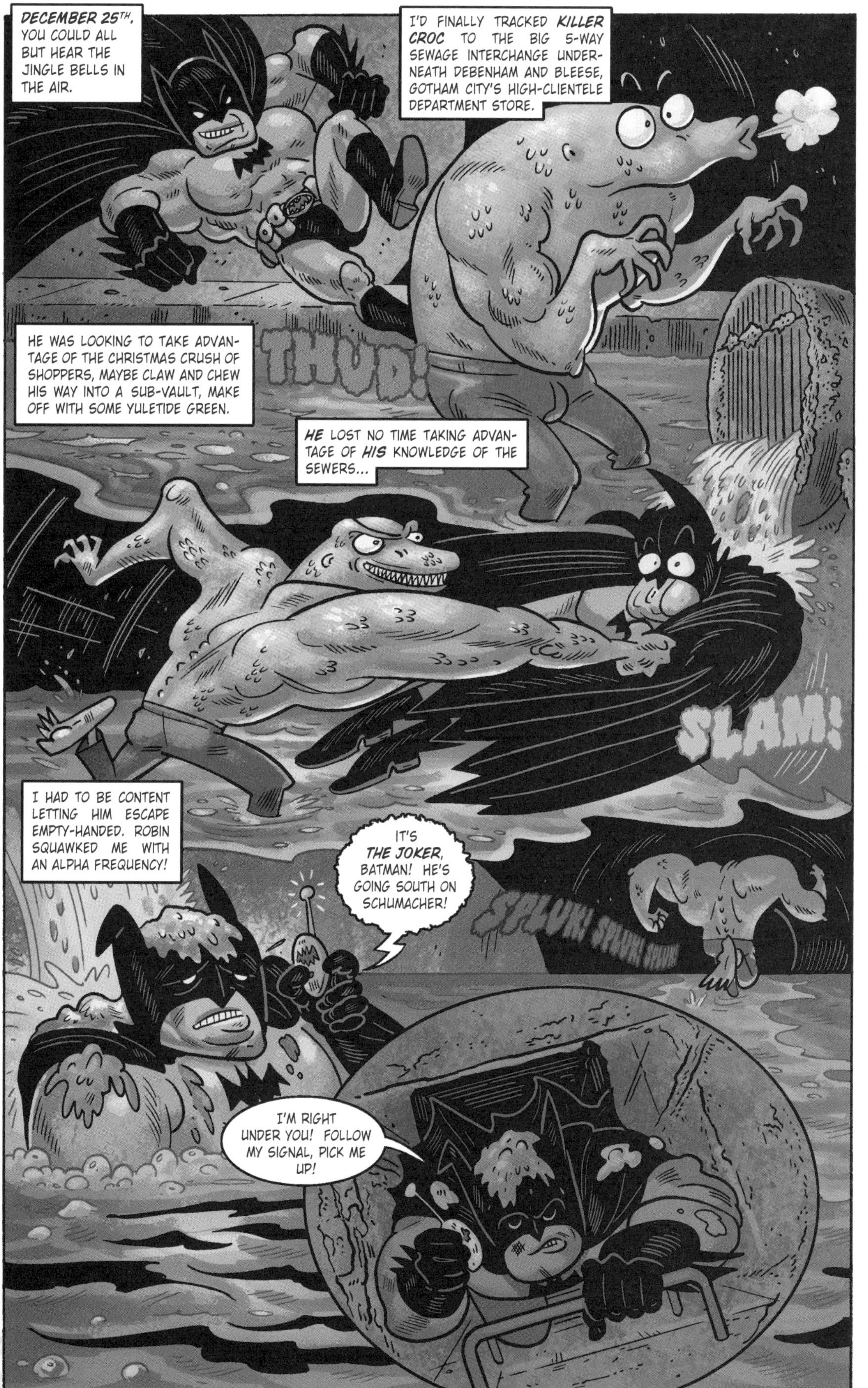
DECEMBER 25TH. YOU COULD ALL BUT HEAR THE JINGLE BELLS IN THE AIR.
I'D FINALLY TRACKED KILLER CROC TO THE BIG 5-WAY SEWAGE INTERCHANGE UNDERNEATH DEBENHAM AND BLEESE, GOTHAM CITY'S HIGH-CLIENTELE DEPARTMENT STORE.
HE WAS LOOKING TO TAKE ADVANTAGE OF THE CHRISTMAS CRUSH OF SHOPPERS, MAYBE CLAW AND CHEW HIS WAY INTO A SUB-VAULT, MAKE OFF WITH SOME YULETIDE GREEN.
THUD!
HE LOST NO TIME TAKING ADVANTAGE OF HIS KNOWLEDGE OF THE SEWERS...
SLAM!
I HAD TO BE CONTENT LETTING HIM ESCAPE EMPTY-HANDED. ROBIN SQUAWKED ME WITH AN ALPHA FREQUENCY!
IT'S THE JOKER, BATMAN! HE'S GOING SOUTH ON SCHUMACHER!
SPLUK! SPLUK! SPLUK!
I'M RIGHT UNDER YOU! FOLLOW MY SIGNAL, PICK ME UP!

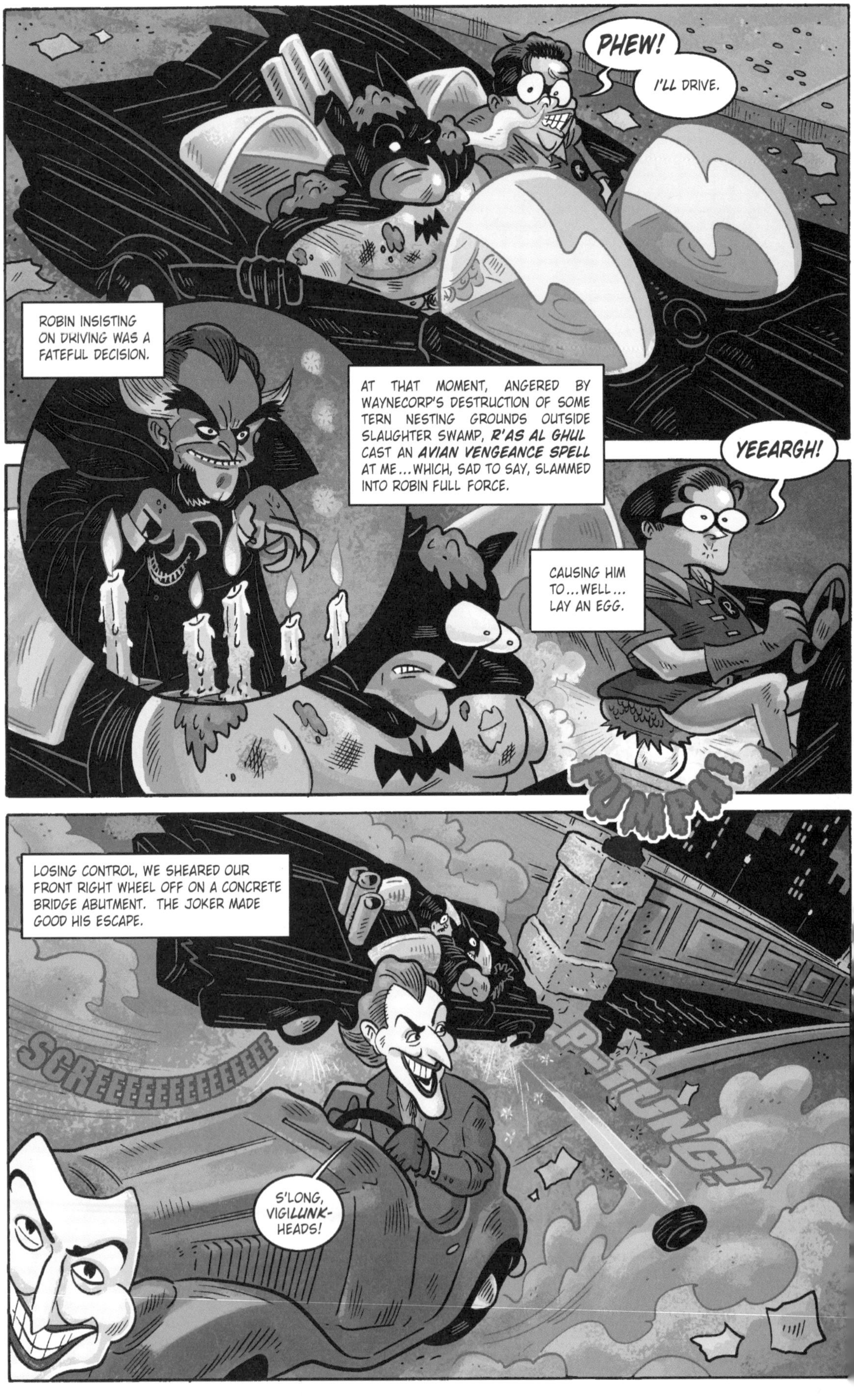
PHEW!
I'LL DRIVE.
ROBIN INSISTING ON DRIVING WAS A FATEFUL DECISION.
AT THAT MOMENT, ANGERED BY WAYNECORP'S DESTRUCTION OF SOME TERN NESTING GROUNDS OUTSIDE SLAUGHTER SWAMP, ***R'AS AL GHUL*** CAST AN ***AVIAN VENGEANCE SPELL*** AT ME... WHICH, SAD TO SAY, SLAMMED INTO ROBIN FULL FORCE.
YEEARGH!
CAUSING HIM TO... WELL... LAY AN EGG.
FUMPH
LOSING CONTROL, WE SHEARED OUR FRONT RIGHT WHEEL OFF ON A CONCRETE BRIDGE ABUTMENT. THE JOKER MADE GOOD HIS ESCAPE.
SCREEEEEEEEEEEE
P-TUNG!
S'LONG, VIGI***LUNK***-HEADS!

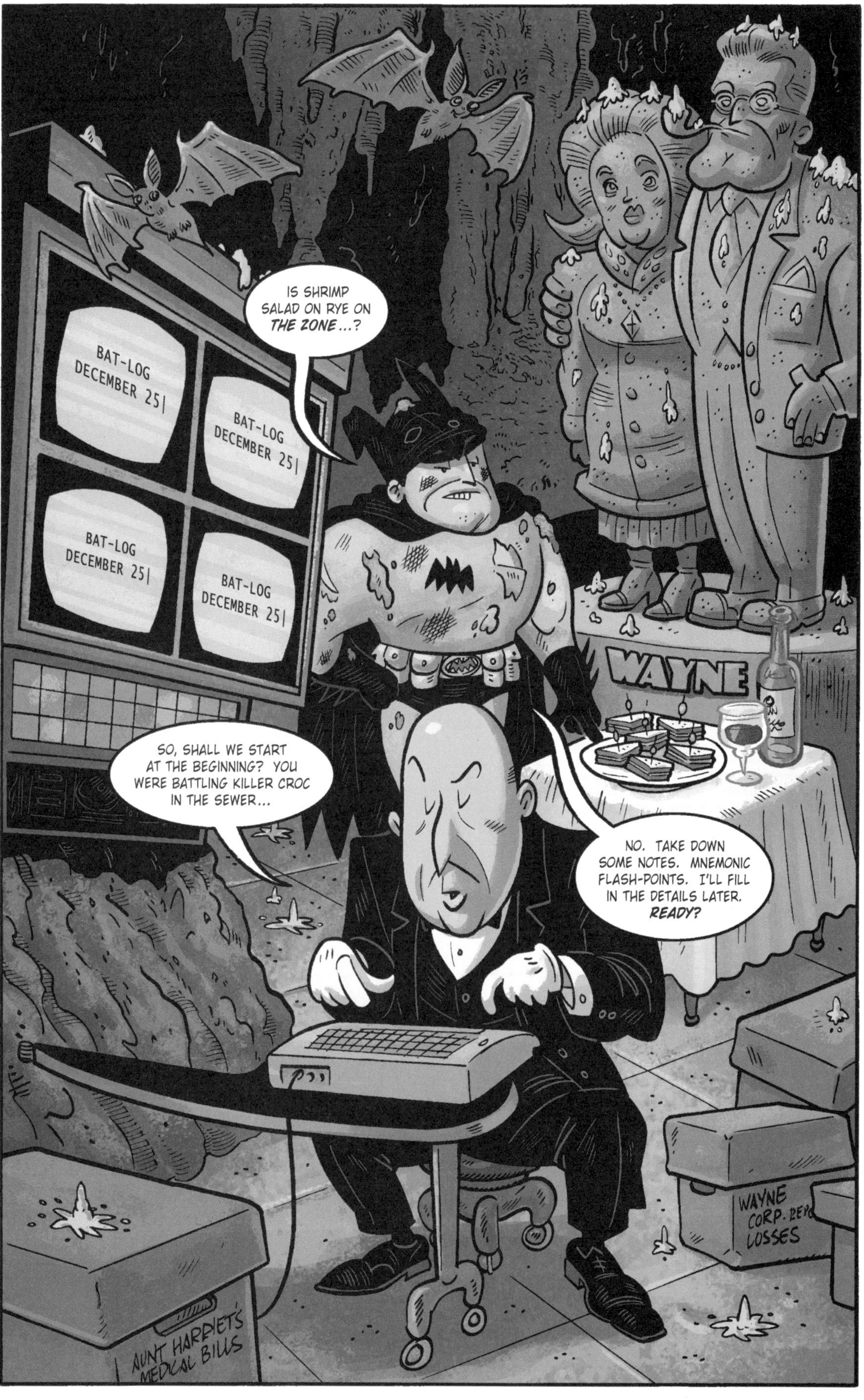
BAT-LOG DECEMBER 25
BAT-LOG DECEMBER 25
BAT-LOG DECEMBER 25
BAT-LOG DECEMBER 25
IS SHRIMP SALAD ON RYE ON ***THE ZONE...?***
WAYNE
SO, SHALL WE START AT THE BEGINNING? YOU WERE BATTLING KILLER CROC IN THE SEWER...
NO. TAKE DOWN SOME NOTES. MNEMONIC FLASH-POINTS. I'LL FILL IN THE DETAILS LATER. ***READY?***
WAYNE CORP. LOSSES
AUNT HARRIET'S MEDICAL BILLS

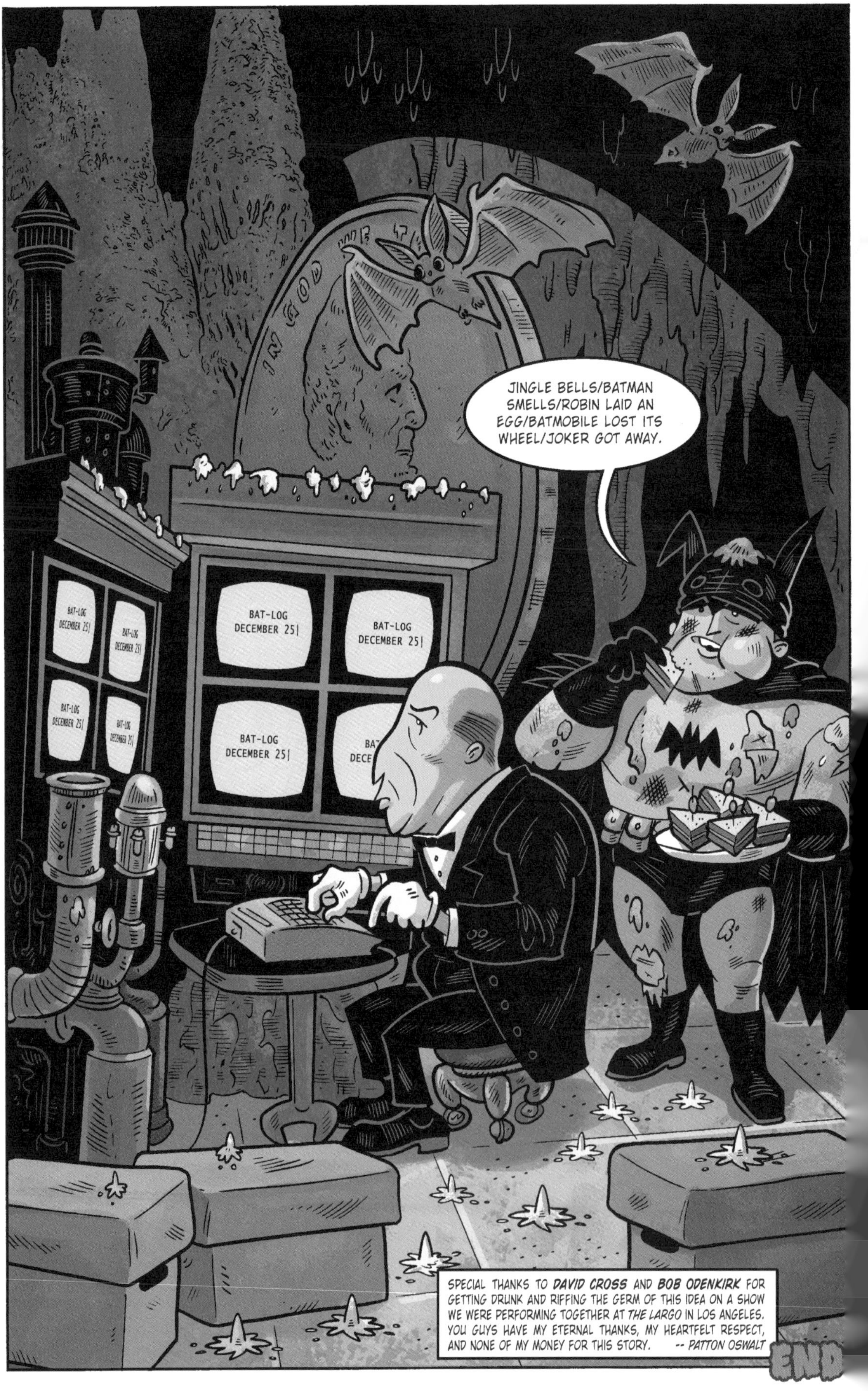

BAT-LOG DECEMBER 25
BAT-LOG DECEMBER 25
BAT-LOG DECEMBER 25
BAT-LOG DECEMBER 25
BAT-LOG DECEMBER 25
BAT-LOG DECEMBER 25
BAT-LOG DECEMBER 25
JINGLE BELLS/BATMAN SMELLS/ROBIN LAID AN EGG/BATMOBILE LOST ITS WHEEL/JOKER GOT AWAY.
SPECIAL THANKS TO *DAVID CROSS* AND *BOB ODENKIRK* FOR GETTING DRUNK AND RIFFING THE GERM OF THIS IDEA ON A SHOW WE WERE PERFORMING TOGETHER AT *THE LARGO* IN LOS ANGELES. YOU GUYS HAVE MY ETERNAL THANKS, MY HEARTFELT RESPECT, AND NONE OF MY MONEY FOR THIS STORY. -- *PATTON OSWALT*
END

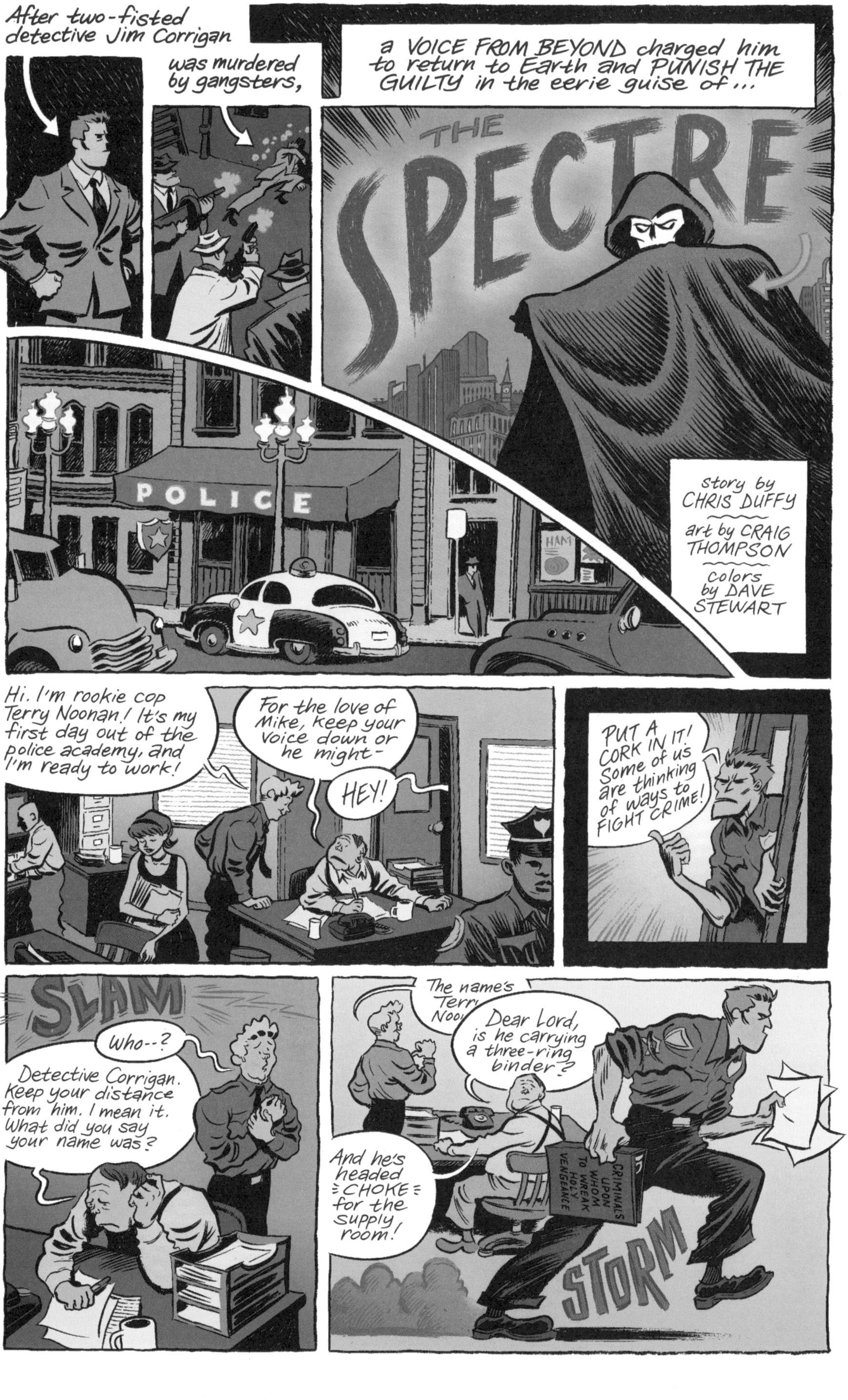
After two-fisted detective Jim Corrigan
was murdered by gangsters,
a VOICE FROM BEYOND charged him to return to Earth and PUNISH THE GUILTY in the eerie guise of...
THE SPECTRE
story by CHRIS DUFFY
art by CRAIG THOMPSON
colors by DAVE STEWART
POLICE
HAM
Hi. I'm rookie cop Terry Noonan! It's my first day out of the police academy, and I'm ready to work!
For the love of Mike, keep your voice down or he might-
HEY!
PUT A CORK IN IT! Some of us are thinking of ways to FIGHT CRIME!
SLAM
Who--?
Detective Corrigan. Keep your distance from him. I mean it. What did you say your name was?
The name's Terr Noon
Dear Lord, is he carrying a three-ring binder?
And he's headed CHOKE for the supply room!
CRIMINALS UPON TO WHOM WREAK HOLY VENGEANCE
STORM

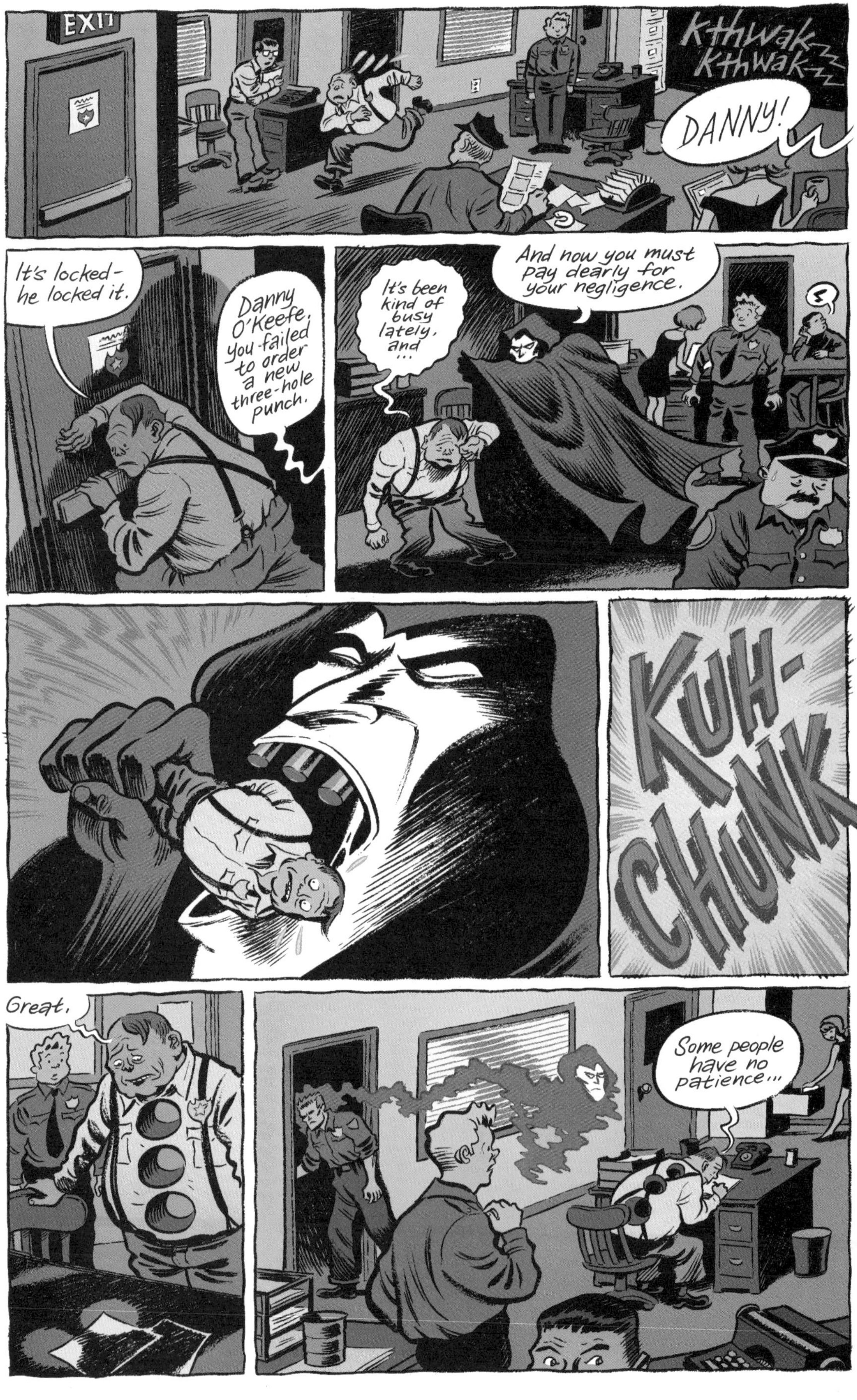

EXIT
kthwak kthwak
DANNY!
It's locked- he locked it.
Danny O'Keefe, you failed to order a new three-hole punch.
It's been kind of busy lately, and ...
And now you must pay dearly for your negligence.
KUH-CHUNK
Great.
Some people have no patience...

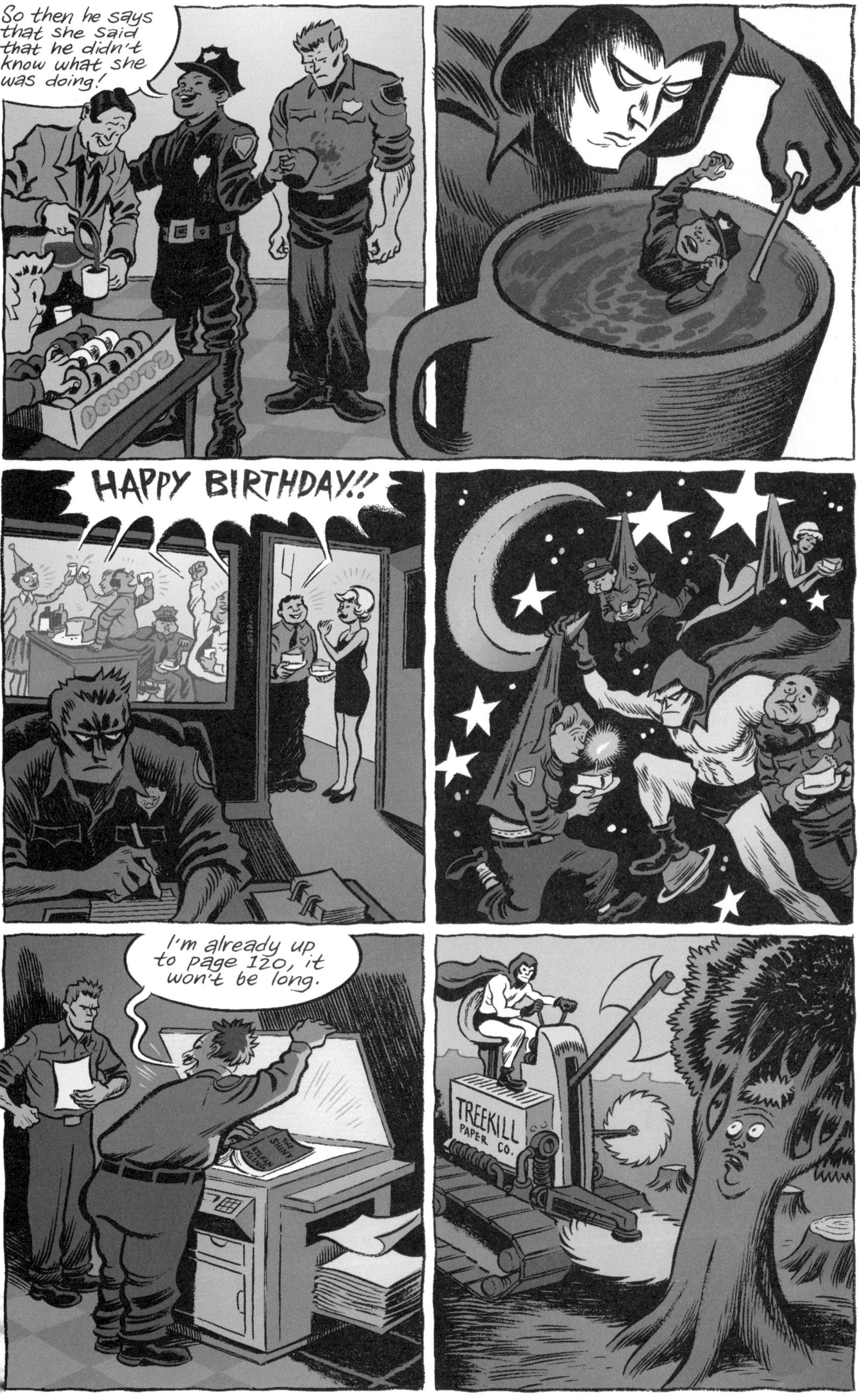

So then he says that she said that he didn't know what she was doing!
HAPPY BIRTHDAY!!
I'm already up to page 120, it won't be long.
TREEKILL PAPER CO.

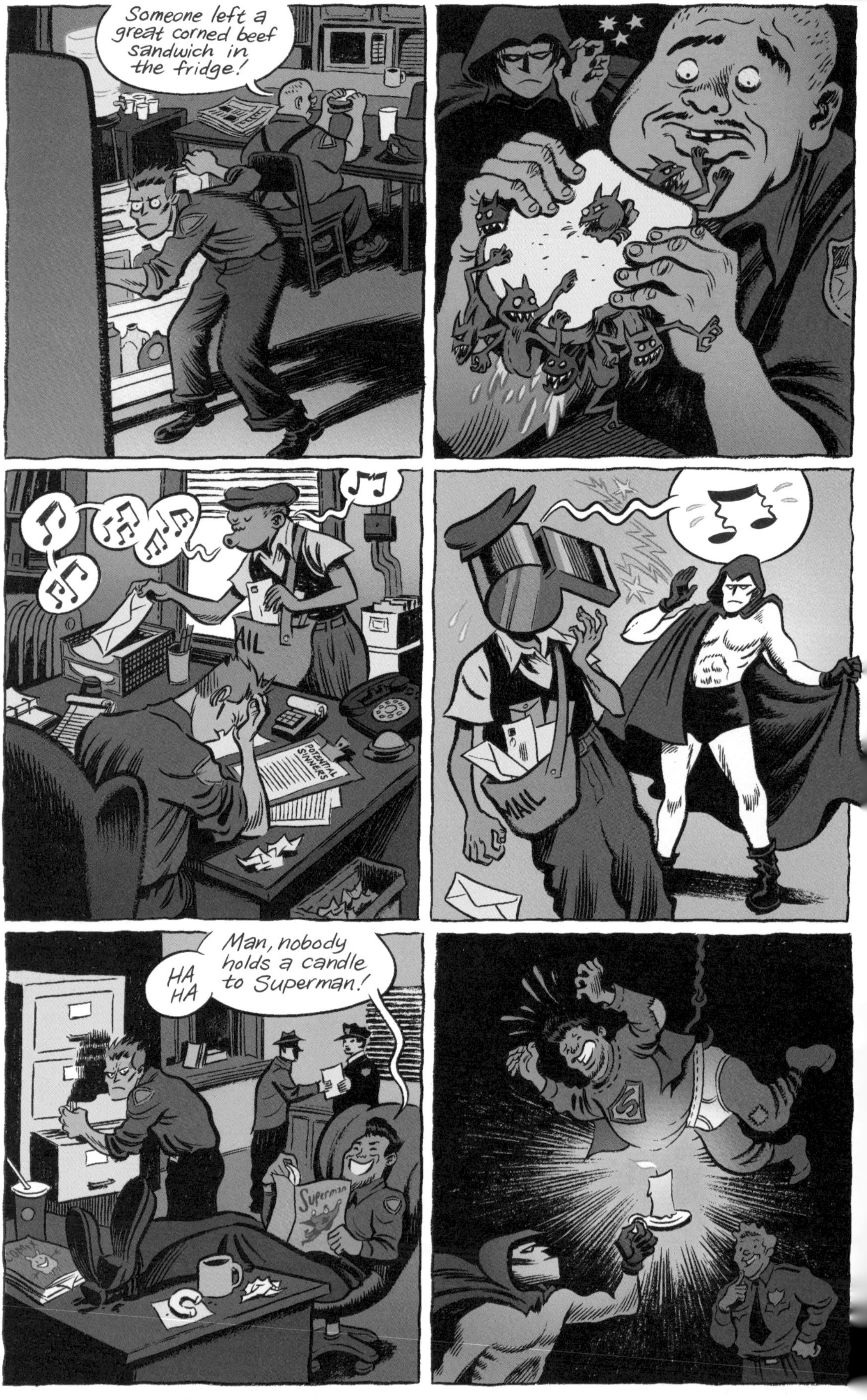
Someone left a great corned beef sandwich in the fridge!
MAIL
POTENTIAL SINNERS
MAIL
HA HA
Man, nobody holds a candle to Superman!
Superman

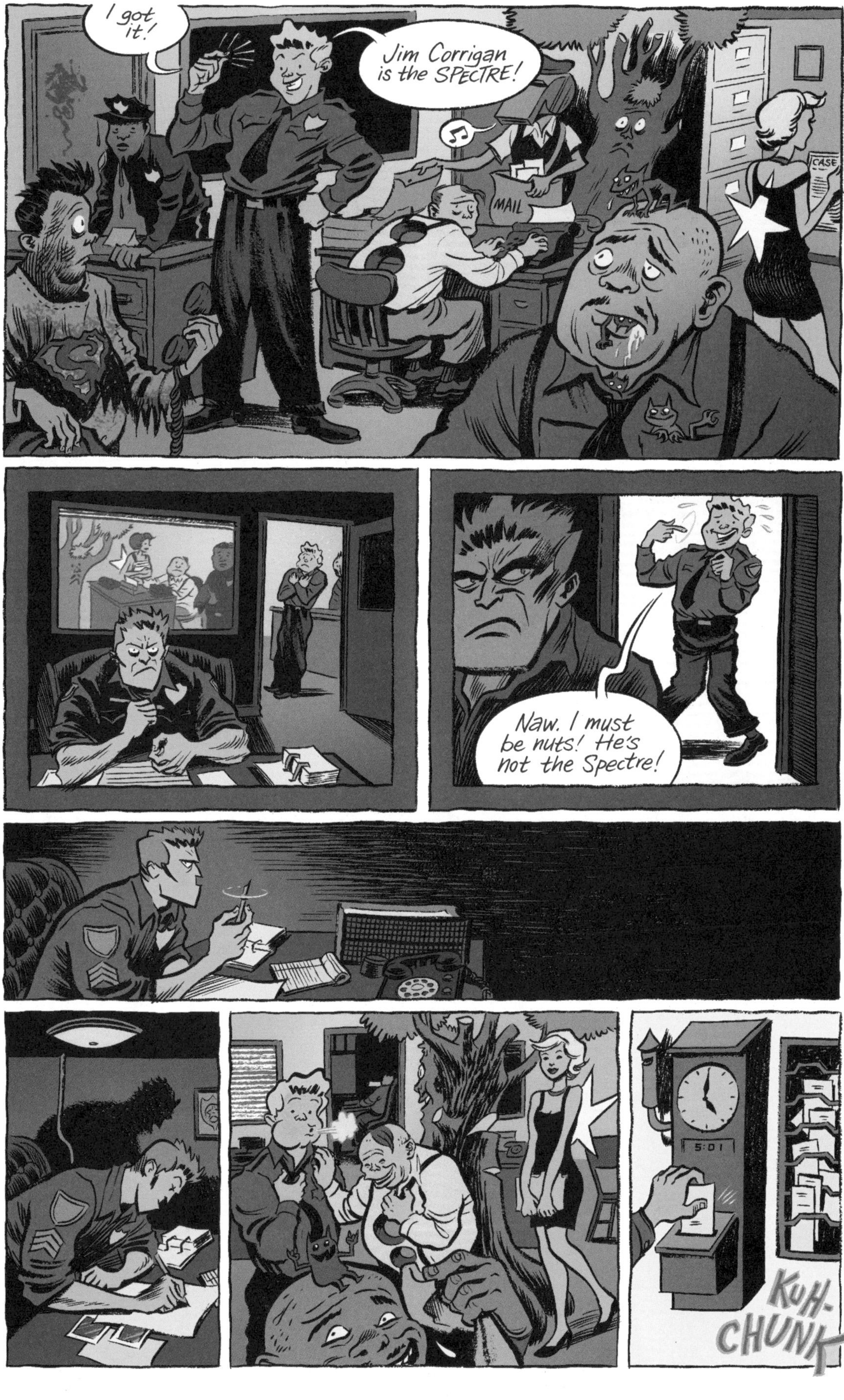
I got it!
Jim Corrigan is the SPECTRE!
MAIL
CASE
Naw. I must be nuts! He's not the Spectre!
5:01
KUH-CHUNK

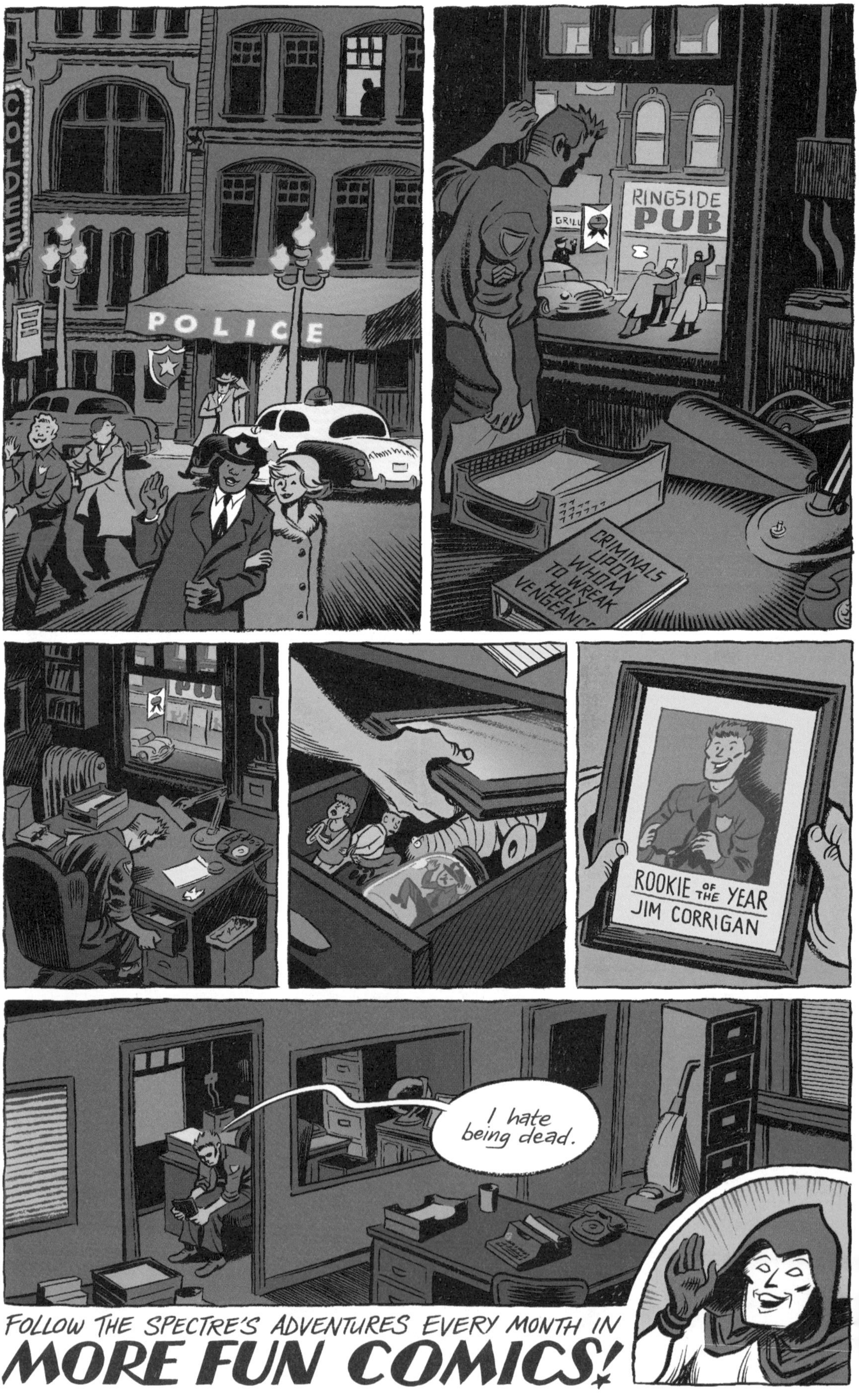
COLDEE
POLICE
RINGSIDE PUB
GRILL
CRIMINALS UPON WHOM TO WREAK HOLY VENGEANC
ROOKIE OF THE YEAR
JIM CORRIGAN
I hate being dead.
FOLLOW THE SPECTRE'S ADVENTURES EVERY MONTH IN
MORE FUN COMICS!

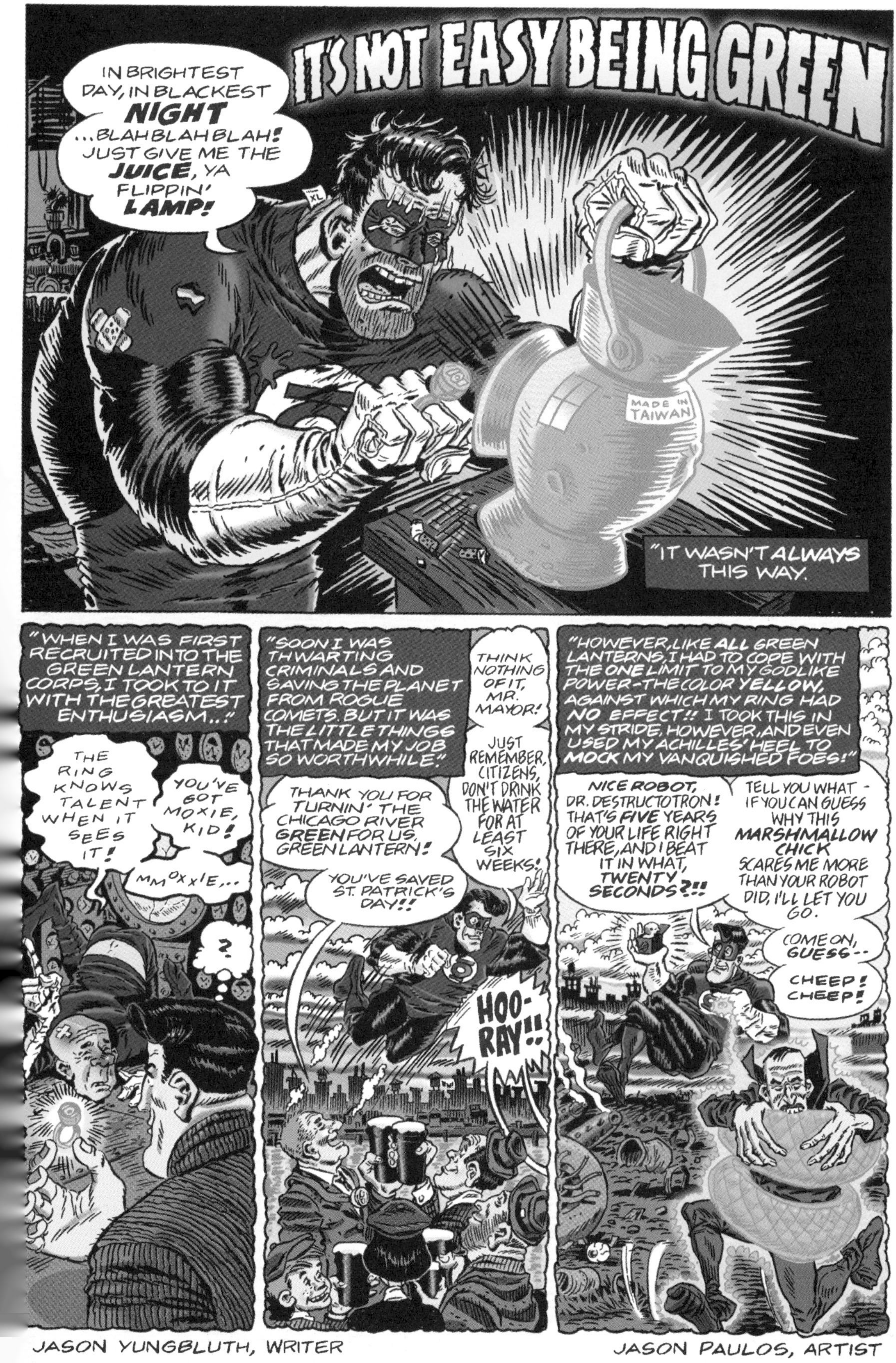

IT'S NOT EASY BEING GREEN
IN BRIGHTEST DAY, IN BLACKEST NIGHT ...BLAH BLAH BLAH! JUST GIVE ME THE JUICE, YA FLIPPIN' LAMP!
XL
MADE IN TAIWAN
"IT WASN'T ALWAYS THIS WAY.
"WHEN I WAS FIRST RECRUITED INTO THE GREEN LANTERN CORPS, I TOOK TO IT WITH THE GREATEST ENTHUSIASM..."
THE RING KNOWS TALENT WHEN IT SEES IT!
YOU'VE GOT MOXIE, KID!
MMOXXIE...
?
"SOON I WAS THWARTING CRIMINALS AND SAVING THE PLANET FROM ROGUE COMETS. BUT IT WAS THE LITTLE THINGS THAT MADE MY JOB SO WORTHWHILE."
THINK NOTHING OF IT, MR. MAYOR!
JUST REMEMBER, CITIZENS, DON'T DRINK THE WATER FOR AT LEAST SIX WEEKS!
THANK YOU FOR TURNIN' THE CHICAGO RIVER GREEN FOR US, GREEN LANTERN!
YOU'VE SAVED ST. PATRICK'S DAY!!
HOO-RAY!!
"HOWEVER, LIKE ALL GREEN LANTERNS, I HAD TO COPE WITH THE ONE LIMIT TO MY GODLIKE POWER-THE COLOR YELLOW, AGAINST WHICH MY RING HAD NO EFFECT!! I TOOK THIS IN MY STRIDE, HOWEVER, AND EVEN USED MY ACHILLES' HEEL TO MOCK MY VANQUISHED FOES!"
NICE ROBOT, DR. DESTRUCTOTRON! THAT'S FIVE YEARS OF YOUR LIFE RIGHT THERE, AND I BEAT IT IN WHAT, TWENTY SECONDS?!!
TELL YOU WHAT - IF YOU CAN GUESS WHY THIS MARSHMALLOW CHICK SCARES ME MORE THAN YOUR ROBOT DID, I'LL LET YOU GO.
COME ON, GUESS--
CHEEP! CHEEP!

JASON YUNGBLUTH, WRITER

JASON PAULOS, ARTIST

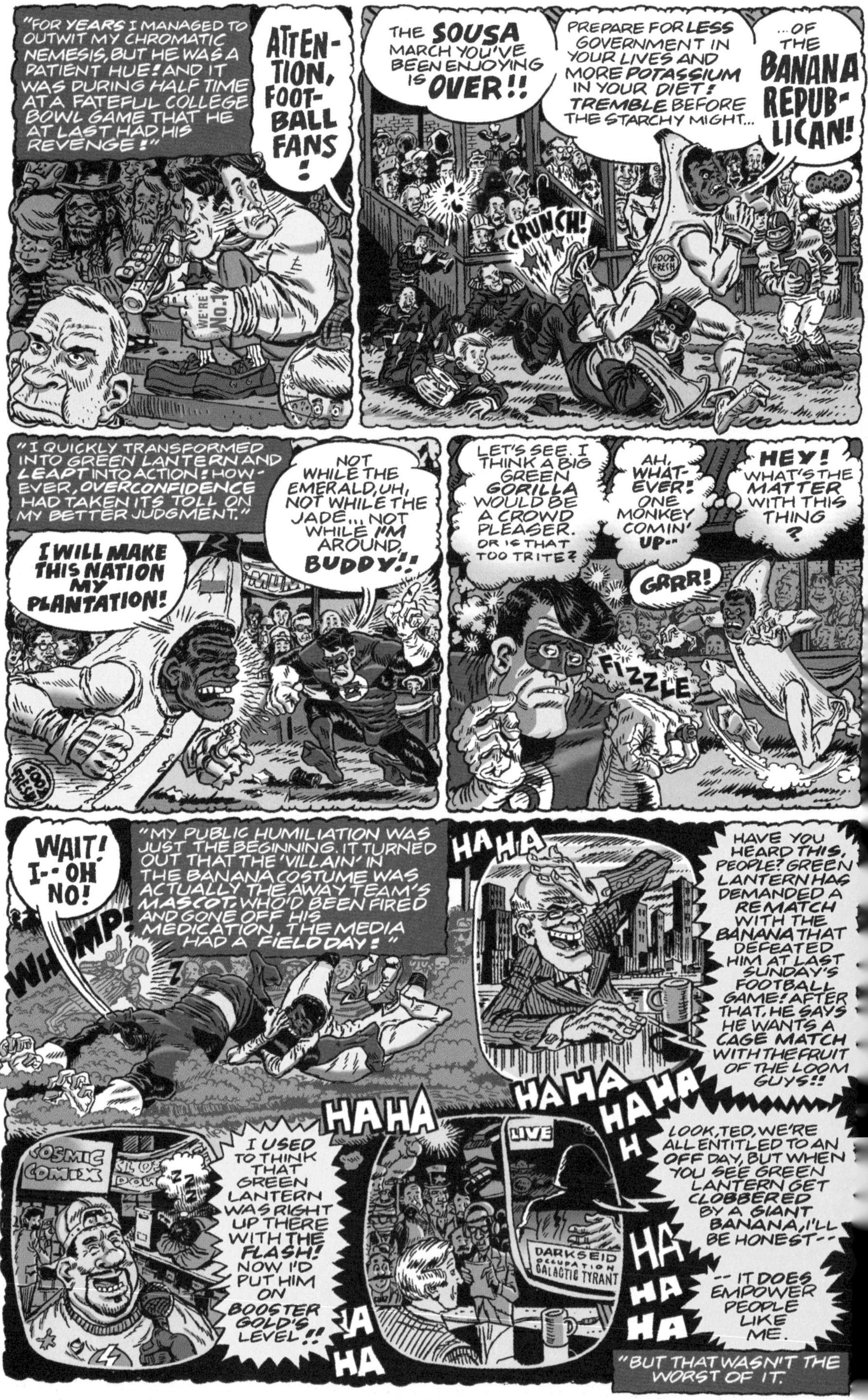
"FOR YEARS I MANAGED TO OUTWIT MY CHROMATIC NEMESIS, BUT HE WAS A PATIENT HUE! AND IT WAS DURING HALF TIME AT A FATEFUL COLLEGE BOWL GAME THAT HE AT LAST HAD HIS REVENGE!"
ATTEN-TION, FOOT-BALL FANS!
WE'RE No.1
THE SOUSA MARCH YOU'VE BEEN ENJOYING IS OVER!!
CRUNCH!
PREPARE FOR LESS GOVERNMENT IN YOUR LIVES AND MORE POTASSIUM IN YOUR DIET! TREMBLE BEFORE THE STARCHY MIGHT...
...OF THE BANANA REPUB-LICAN!
100% FRESH
"I QUICKLY TRANSFORMED INTO GREEN LANTERN AND LEAPT INTO ACTION! HOW-EVER, OVERCONFIDENCE HAD TAKEN ITS TOLL ON MY BETTER JUDGMENT."
I WILL MAKE THIS NATION MY PLANTATION!
NOT WHILE THE EMERALD, UH, NOT WHILE THE JADE... NOT WHILE I'M AROUND, BUDDY!!
LET'S SEE. I THINK A BIG GREEN GORILLA WOULD BE A CROWD PLEASER. OR IS THAT TOO TRITE?
AH, WHAT-EVER! ONE MONKEY COMIN' UP..
HEY! WHAT'S THE MATTER WITH THIS THING?
GRRR!
FIZZLE
WAIT! I-- OH NO!
"MY PUBLIC HUMILIATION WAS JUST THE BEGINNING. IT TURNED OUT THAT THE 'VILLAIN' IN THE BANANA COSTUME WAS ACTUALLY THE AWAY TEAM'S MASCOT, WHO'D BEEN FIRED AND GONE OFF HIS MEDICATION. THE MEDIA HAD A FIELD DAY!"
WHOMP!
HA HA
HAVE YOU HEARD THIS, PEOPLE? GREEN LANTERN HAS DEMANDED A REMATCH WITH THE BANANA THAT DEFEATED HIM AT LAST SUNDAY'S FOOTBALL GAME! AFTER THAT, HE SAYS HE WANTS A CAGE MATCH WITH THE FRUIT OF THE LOOM GUYS!!
HA HA HA HA HA H
COSMIC COMIX
I USED TO THINK THAT GREEN LANTERN WAS RIGHT UP THERE WITH THE FLASH! NOW I'D PUT HIM ON BOOSTER GOLD'S LEVEL!!
HAHA
LIVE
DARKSEID OCCUPATION GALACTIC TYRANT
LOOK, TED, WE'RE ALL ENTITLED TO AN OFF DAY, BUT WHEN YOU SEE GREEN LANTERN GET CLOBBERED BY A GIANT BANANA, I'LL BE HONEST--
HA HA HA HA
-- IT DOES EMPOWER PEOPLE LIKE ME.
HA HA
"BUT THAT WASN'T THE WORST OF IT.

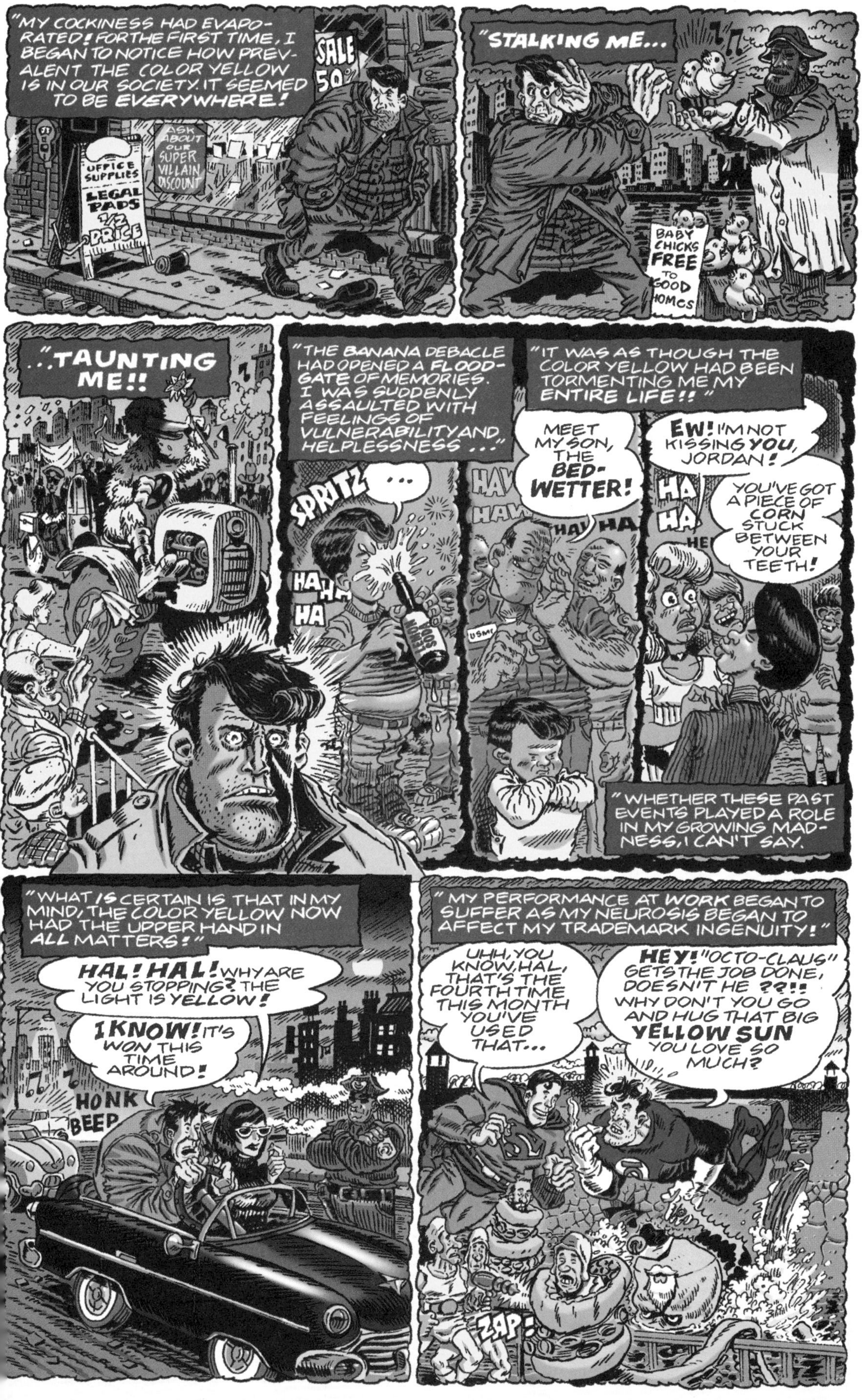
"MY COCKINESS HAD EVAPORATED! FOR THE FIRST TIME, I BEGAN TO NOTICE HOW PREVALENT THE COLOR YELLOW IS IN OUR SOCIETY. IT SEEMED TO BE EVERYWHERE!
SALE 50%
ASK ABOUT OUR SUPER VILLAIN DISCOUNT
OFFICE SUPPLIES LEGAL PADS 1/2 PRICE
"STALKING ME...
BABY CHICKS FREE TO GOOD HOMES
"...TAUNTING ME!!
"THE BANANA DEBACLE HAD OPENED A FLOODGATE OF MEMORIES. I WAS SUDDENLY ASSAULTED WITH FEELINGS OF VULNERABILITY AND HELPLESSNESS..."
"IT WAS AS THOUGH THE COLOR YELLOW HAD BEEN TORMENTING ME MY ENTIRE LIFE!!"
SPRITZ
...
HA HA HA
MEET MY SON, THE BED-WETTER!
HAW HAW HAW HA
EW! I'M NOT KISSING YOU, JORDAN!
HA HA HE
YOU'VE GOT A PIECE OF CORN STUCK BETWEEN YOUR TEETH!
"WHETHER THESE PAST EVENTS PLAYED A ROLE IN MY GROWING MADNESS, I CAN'T SAY.
"WHAT IS CERTAIN IS THAT IN MY MIND, THE COLOR YELLOW NOW HAD THE UPPER HAND IN ALL MATTERS!"
HAL! HAL! WHY ARE YOU STOPPING? THE LIGHT IS YELLOW!
I KNOW! IT'S WON THIS TIME AROUND!
HONK BEEP
"MY PERFORMANCE AT WORK BEGAN TO SUFFER AS MY NEUROSIS BEGAN TO AFFECT MY TRADEMARK INGENUITY!"
UHH, YOU KNOW, HAL, THAT'S THE FOURTH TIME THIS MONTH YOU'VE USED THAT...
HEY! "OCTO-CLAUS" GETS THE JOB DONE, DOESN'T HE ??!! WHY DON'T YOU GO AND HUG THAT BIG YELLOW SUN YOU LOVE SO MUCH?
ZAP!

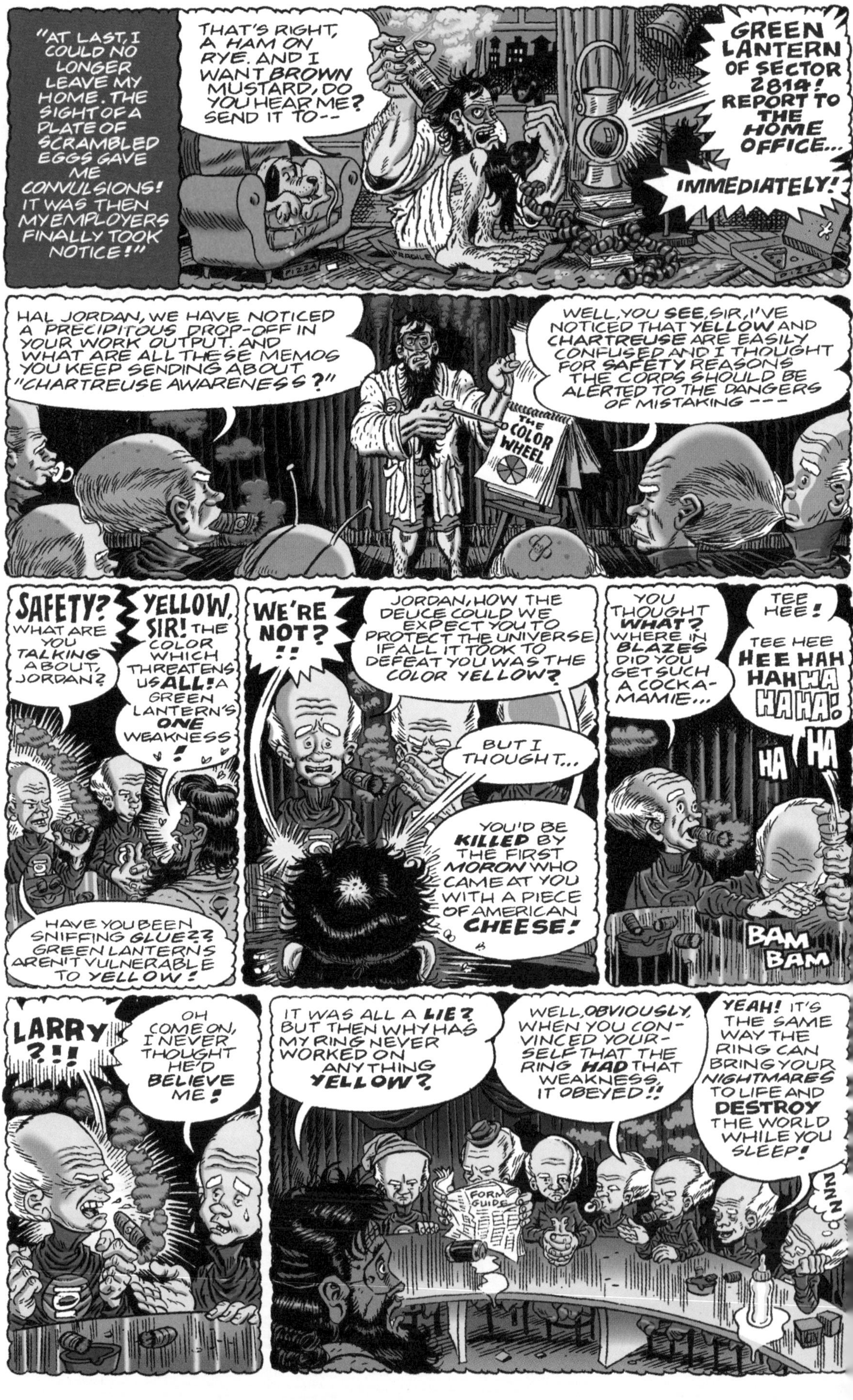
"AT LAST, I COULD NO LONGER LEAVE MY HOME. THE SIGHT OF A PLATE OF SCRAMBLED EGGS GAVE ME CONVULSIONS! IT WAS THEN MY EMPLOYERS FINALLY TOOK NOTICE!"
THAT'S RIGHT, A HAM ON RYE. AND I WANT BROWN MUSTARD, DO YOU HEAR ME? SEND IT TO--
GREEN LANTERN OF SECTOR 2814! REPORT TO THE HOME OFFICE...
IMMEDIATELY!
PIZZA
FRAGILE
PIZZA
HAL JORDAN, WE HAVE NOTICED A PRECIPITOUS DROP-OFF IN YOUR WORK OUTPUT. AND WHAT ARE ALL THESE MEMOS YOU KEEP SENDING ABOUT "CHARTREUSE AWARENESS?"
WELL, YOU SEE, SIR, I'VE NOTICED THAT YELLOW AND CHARTREUSE ARE EASILY CONFUSED AND I THOUGHT FOR SAFETY REASONS THE CORPS SHOULD BE ALERTED TO THE DANGERS OF MISTAKING ---
THE COLOR WHEEL
SAFETY? WHAT ARE YOU TALKING ABOUT, JORDAN?
YELLOW, SIR! THE COLOR WHICH THREATENS US ALL! A GREEN LANTERN'S ONE WEAKNESS!
HAVE YOU BEEN SNIFFING GLUE?? GREEN LANTERNS AREN'T VULNERABLE TO YELLOW!
WE'RE NOT?!!
JORDAN, HOW THE DEUCE COULD WE EXPECT YOU TO PROTECT THE UNIVERSE IF ALL IT TOOK TO DEFEAT YOU WAS THE COLOR YELLOW?
BUT I THOUGHT...
YOU'D BE KILLED BY THE FIRST MORON WHO CAME AT YOU WITH A PIECE OF AMERICAN CHEESE!
YOU THOUGHT WHAT? WHERE IN BLAZES DID YOU GET SUCH A COCKAMAMIE...
TEE HEE!
TEE HEE HEE HAH HAH HA HA HA!
HA HA
BAM BAM
LARRY?!!
OH COME ON, I NEVER THOUGHT HE'D BELIEVE ME!
IT WAS ALL A LIE? BUT THEN WHY HAS MY RING NEVER WORKED ON ANYTHING YELLOW?
WELL, OBVIOUSLY, WHEN YOU CONVINCED YOURSELF THAT THE RING HAD THAT WEAKNESS, IT OBEYED!!
YEAH! IT'S THE SAME WAY THE RING CAN BRING YOUR NIGHTMARES TO LIFE AND DESTROY THE WORLD WHILE YOU SLEEP!
ZZZ
FORM GUIDE

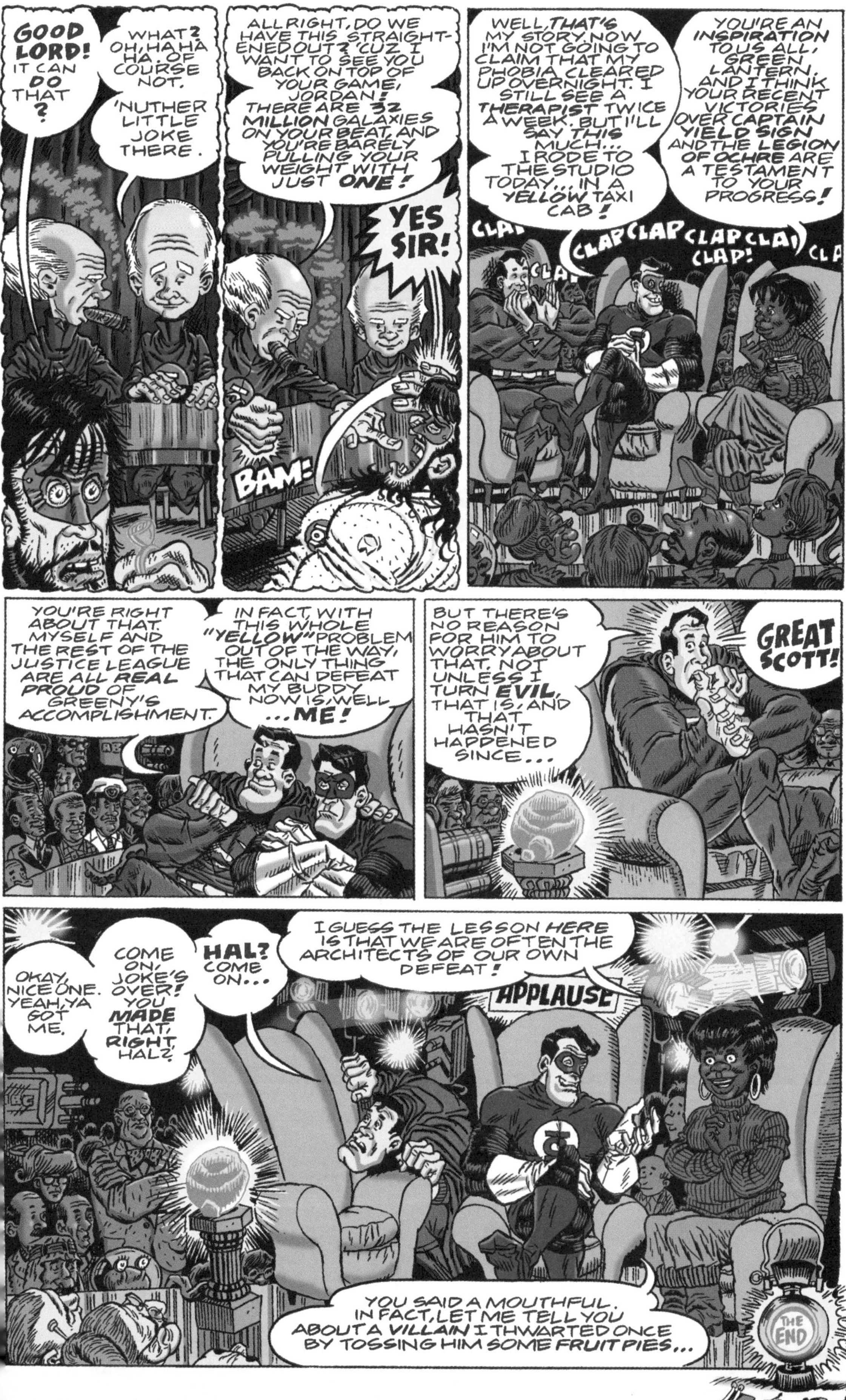
GOOD LORD! IT CAN DO THAT?
WHAT? OH, HA HA HA. OF COURSE NOT.
'NUTHER LITTLE JOKE THERE.
ALL RIGHT, DO WE HAVE THIS STRAIGHTENED OUT? 'CUZ I WANT TO SEE YOU BACK ON TOP OF YOUR GAME, JORDAN! THERE ARE 32 MILLION GALAXIES ON YOUR BEAT, AND YOU'RE BARELY PULLING YOUR WEIGHT WITH JUST ONE!
YES SIR!
BAM!
WELL, THAT'S MY STORY. NOW I'M NOT GOING TO CLAIM THAT MY PHOBIA CLEARED UP OVERNIGHT. I STILL SEE A THERAPIST TWICE A WEEK. BUT I'LL SAY THIS MUCH... I RODE TO THE STUDIO TODAY... IN A YELLOW TAXI CAB!
YOU'RE AN INSPIRATION TO US ALL, GREEN LANTERN. AND I THINK YOUR RECENT VICTORIES OVER CAPTAIN YIELD SIGN AND THE LEGION OF OCHRE ARE A TESTAMENT TO YOUR PROGRESS!
CLAP CLAP CLAP CLAP CLAP CLAP CLAP! CLAP
YOU'RE RIGHT ABOUT THAT. MYSELF AND THE REST OF THE JUSTICE LEAGUE ARE ALL REAL PROUD OF GREENY'S ACCOMPLISHMENT.
IN FACT, WITH THIS WHOLE "YELLOW" PROBLEM OUT OF THE WAY, THE ONLY THING THAT CAN DEFEAT MY BUDDY NOW IS, WELL ...ME!
BUT THERE'S NO REASON FOR HIM TO WORRY ABOUT THAT. NOT UNLESS I TURN EVIL, THAT IS, AND THAT HASN'T HAPPENED SINCE...
GREAT SCOTT!
OKAY, NICE ONE. YEAH, YA GOT ME.
COME ON, JOKE'S OVER! YOU MADE THAT, RIGHT, HAL?
HAL? COME ON...
I GUESS THE LESSON HERE IS THAT WE ARE OFTEN THE ARCHITECTS OF OUR OWN DEFEAT!
APPLAUSE
YOU SAID A MOUTHFUL. IN FACT, LET ME TELL YOU ABOUT A VILLAIN I THWARTED ONCE BY TOSSING HIM SOME FRUIT PIES...
THE END

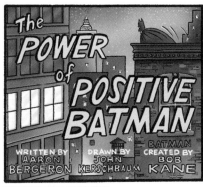

The POWER of POSITIVE BATMAN

WRITTEN BY AARON BERGERON · DRAWN BY JOHN KERSCHBAUM · BATMAN CREATED BY BOB KANE

CRASH!

DR. MILLIKEN, WE NEED TO TALK.

MY COUCH IS YOURS.

I'D RATHER STAND.

I'VE BEEN THINKING...

..., AND YOU'RE RIGHT.

MY PARENTS' DEATHS ARE NOT MY FAULT. THERE'S NOTHING I CAN DO TO BRING THEM BACK. I NEED TO STOP TORTURING MYSELF.

I NEED TO LET GO OF THE PAST.

IT'S WONDERFUL YOU'RE INTERNALIZING OUR DISCUSSIONS, BATMAN.

THEY'VE BEEN INCREDIBLY POSITIVE AND HAVE LED ME TO THIS:

I DON'T NEED OR WANT TO BE BATMAN.

I'M CURED.

WHAT?!

I'M CURED. THERE'S NO REASON FOR ME TO FIGHT CRIME AND WEAR A COWL. I MEAN, WHAT DO I HAVE TO PROVE?

zip!

BRUCE WAYNE?!

YEAH!

AND I'M GONNA SAIL A TRIMARAN TO NEW ZEALAND!

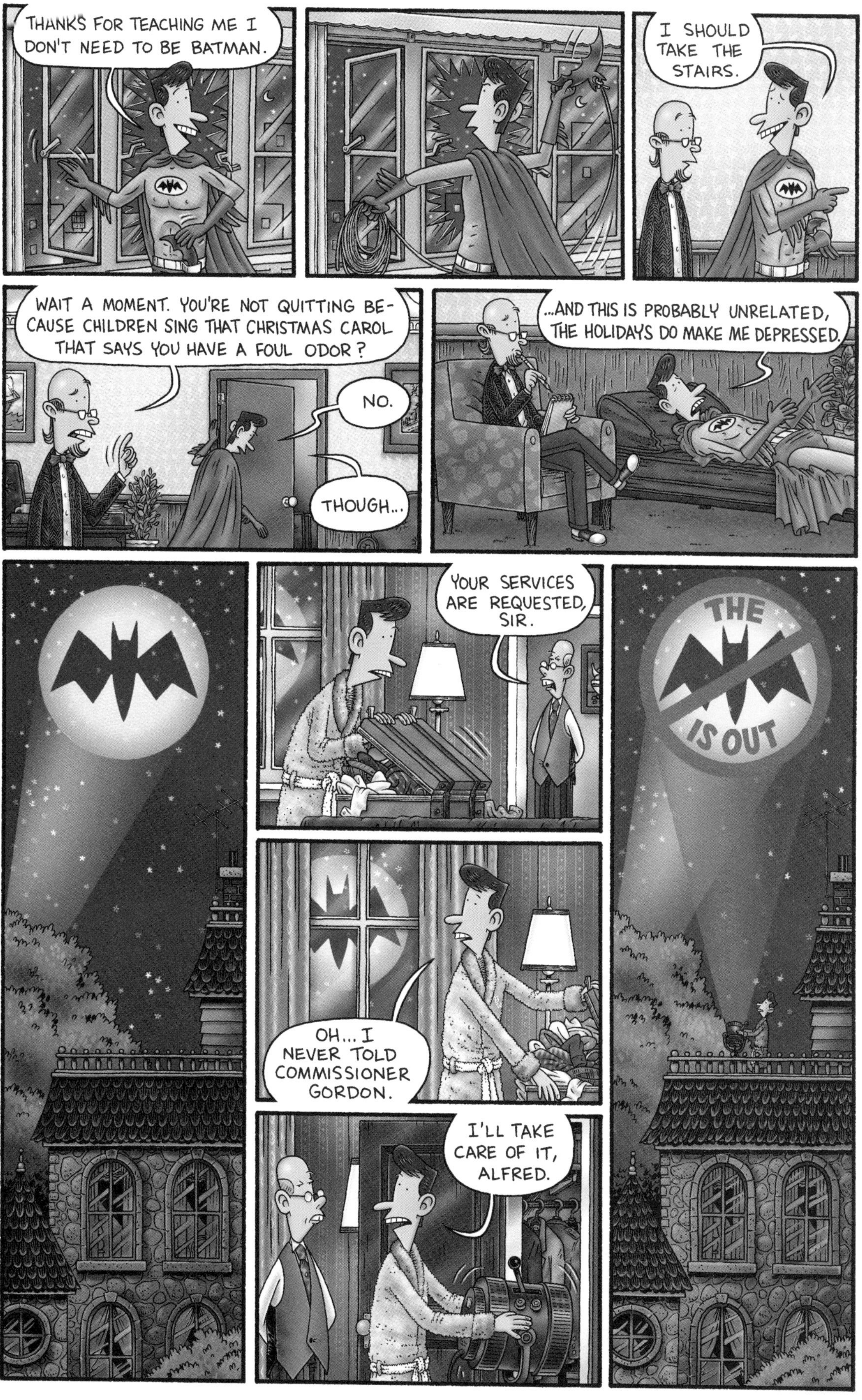
THANKS FOR TEACHING ME I DON'T NEED TO BE BATMAN.
I SHOULD TAKE THE STAIRS.
WAIT A MOMENT. YOU'RE NOT QUITTING BE-CAUSE CHILDREN SING THAT CHRISTMAS CAROL THAT SAYS YOU HAVE A FOUL ODOR?
NO.
THOUGH...
...AND THIS IS PROBABLY UNRELATED, THE HOLIDAYS DO MAKE ME DEPRESSED.
YOUR SERVICES ARE REQUESTED, SIR.
OH... I NEVER TOLD COMMISSIONER GORDON.
I'LL TAKE CARE OF IT, ALFRED.
THE IS OUT

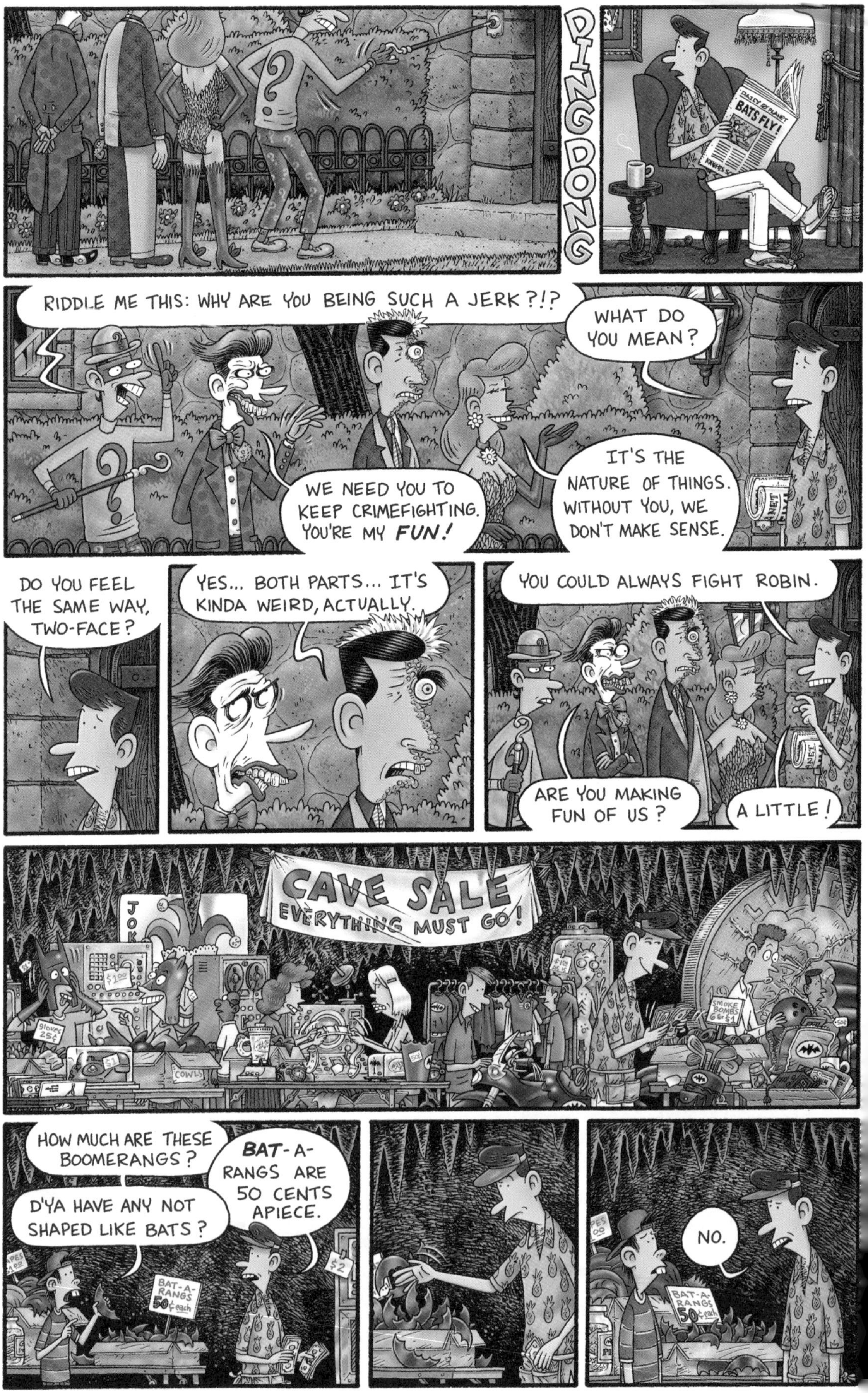
DING DONG
DAILY PLANET
BATS FLY!
RIDDLE ME THIS: WHY ARE YOU BEING SUCH A JERK?!?
WHAT DO YOU MEAN?
WE NEED YOU TO KEEP CRIMEFIGHTING. YOU'RE MY FUN!
IT'S THE NATURE OF THINGS. WITHOUT YOU, WE DON'T MAKE SENSE.
DO YOU FEEL THE SAME WAY, TWO-FACE?
YES... BOTH PARTS... IT'S KINDA WEIRD, ACTUALLY.
YOU COULD ALWAYS FIGHT ROBIN.
ARE YOU MAKING FUN OF US?
A LITTLE!
CAVE SALE
EVERYTHING MUST GO!
GLOVES 25¢
$1.00
COWLS
SMOKE BOMBS 6 for $1
HOW MUCH ARE THESE BOOMERANGS?
BAT-A-RANGS ARE 50 CENTS APIECE.
D'YA HAVE ANY NOT SHAPED LIKE BATS?
BAT-A-RANGS 50¢ each
$2
NO.
BAT-A-RANGS 50¢ each

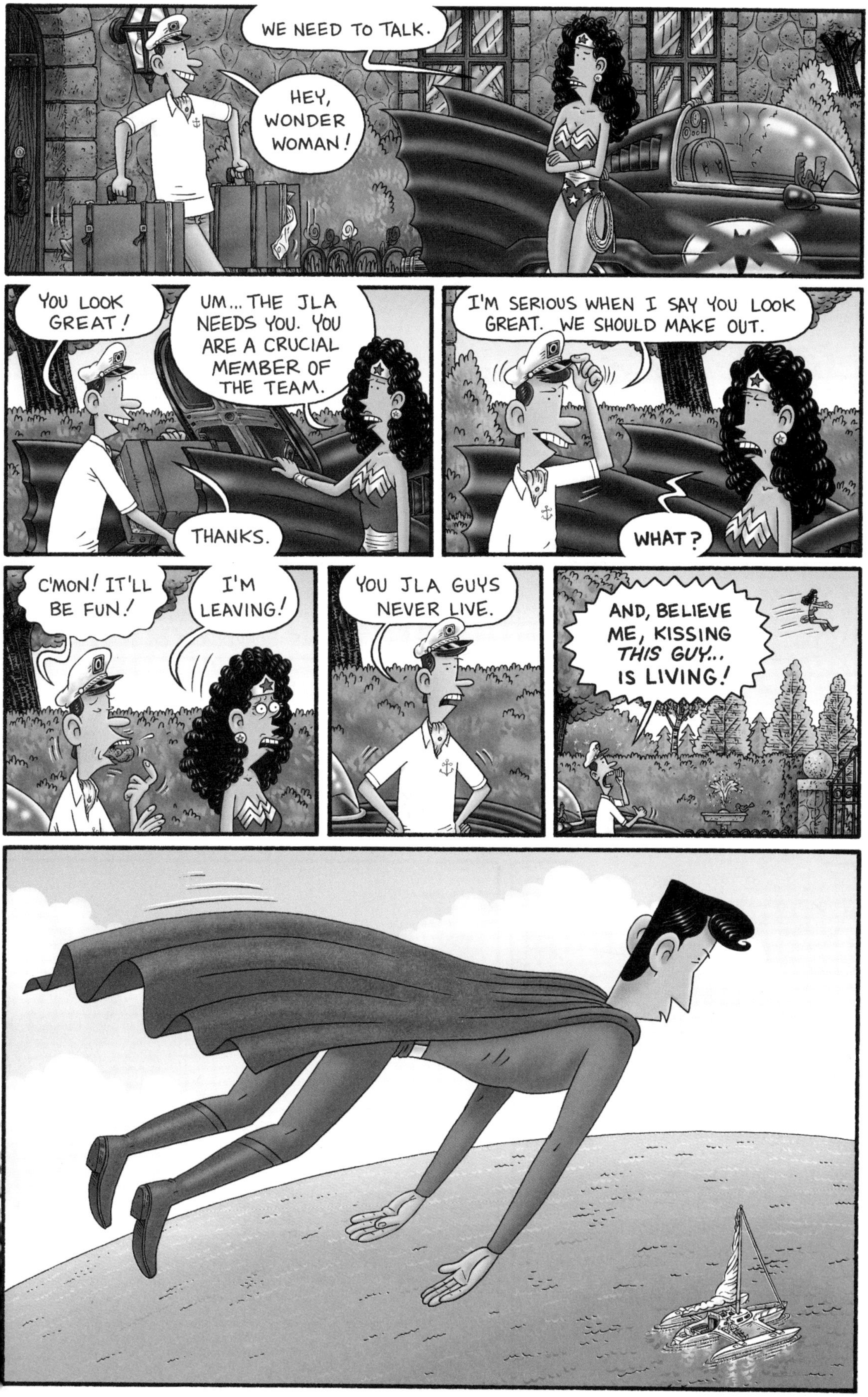
WE NEED TO TALK.
HEY, WONDER WOMAN!
YOU LOOK GREAT!
UM... THE JLA NEEDS YOU. YOU ARE A CRUCIAL MEMBER OF THE TEAM.
THANKS.
I'M SERIOUS WHEN I SAY YOU LOOK GREAT. WE SHOULD MAKE OUT.
WHAT?
C'MON! IT'LL BE FUN!
I'M LEAVING!
YOU JLA GUYS NEVER LIVE.
AND, BELIEVE ME, KISSING *THIS GUY*... IS LIVING!

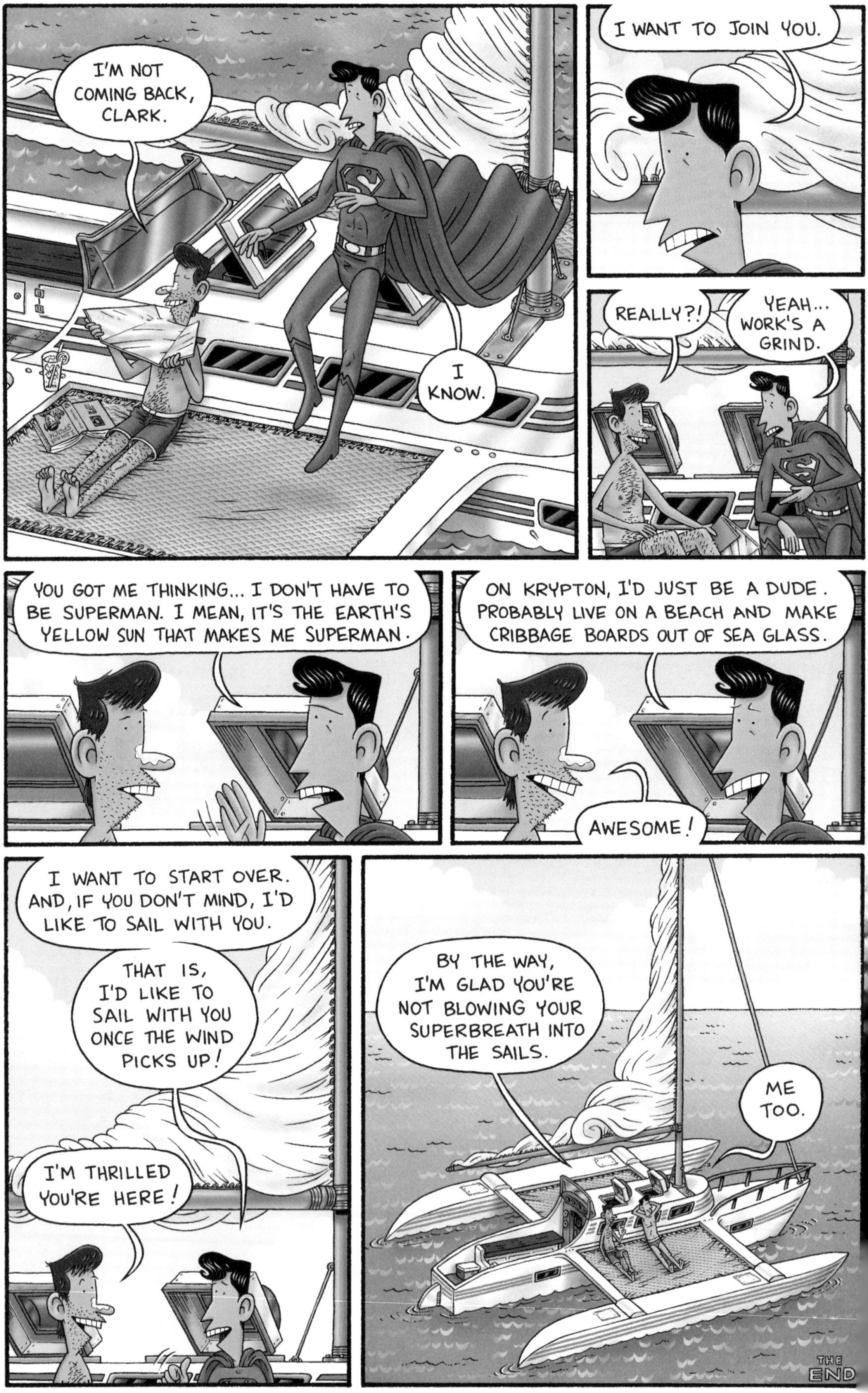

I'M NOT COMING BACK, CLARK.
I KNOW.
I WANT TO JOIN YOU.
REALLY?!
YEAH... WORK'S A GRIND.
YOU GOT ME THINKING... I DON'T HAVE TO BE SUPERMAN. I MEAN, IT'S THE EARTH'S YELLOW SUN THAT MAKES ME SUPERMAN.
ON KRYPTON, I'D JUST BE A DUDE. PROBABLY LIVE ON A BEACH AND MAKE CRIBBAGE BOARDS OUT OF SEA GLASS.
AWESOME!
I WANT TO START OVER. AND, IF YOU DON'T MIND, I'D LIKE TO SAIL WITH YOU.
THAT IS, I'D LIKE TO SAIL WITH YOU ONCE THE WIND PICKS UP!
I'M THRILLED YOU'RE HERE!
BY THE WAY, I'M GLAD YOU'RE NOT BLOWING YOUR SUPERBREATH INTO THE SAILS.
ME TOO.
THE END

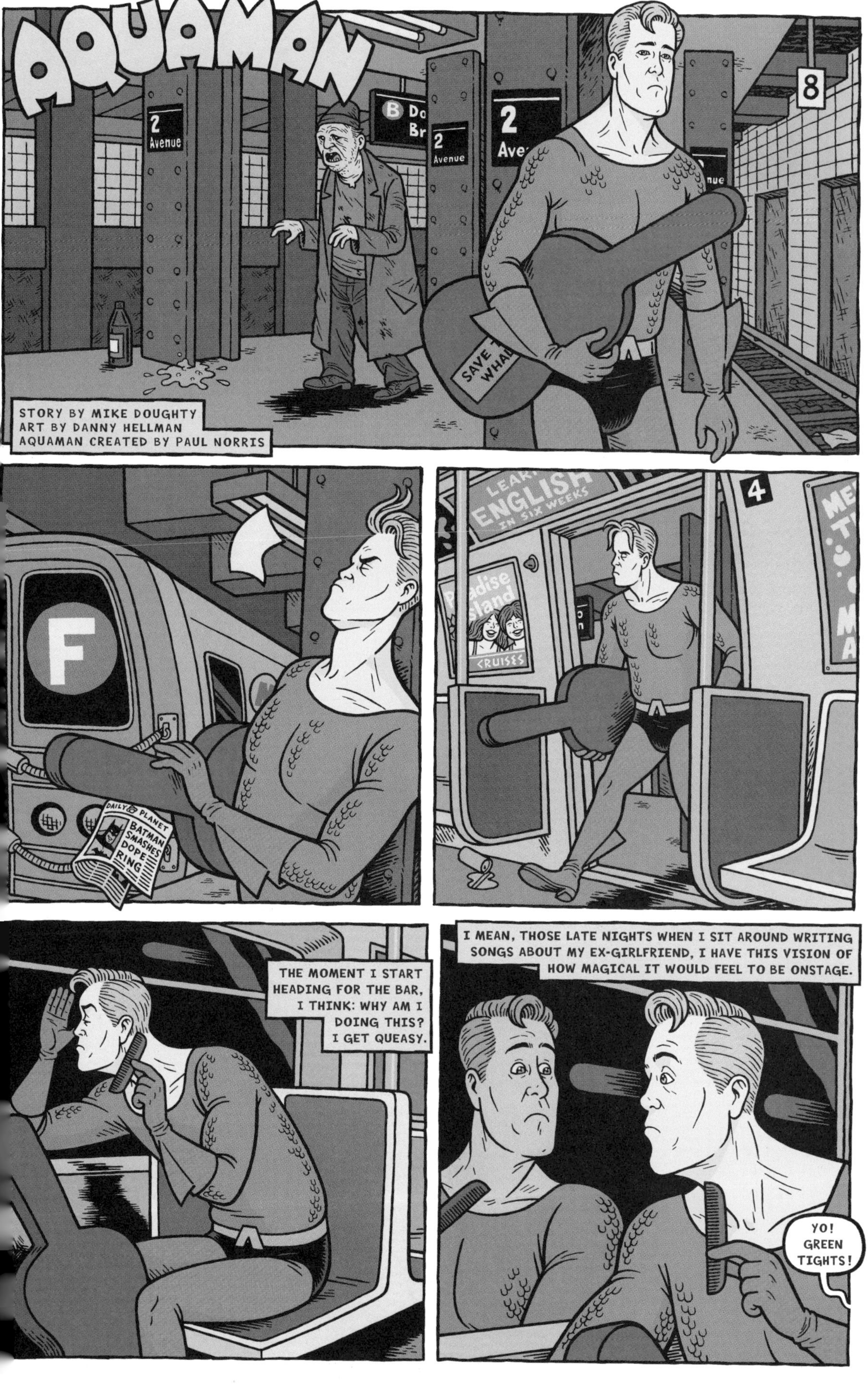
AQUAMAN
8
2 Avenue
STORY BY MIKE DOUGHTY
ART BY DANNY HELLMAN
AQUAMAN CREATED BY PAUL NORRIS
F
DAILY PLANET
BATMAN SMASHES DOPE RING
LEARN ENGLISH IN SIX WEEKS
4
CRUISES
THE MOMENT I START HEADING FOR THE BAR, I THINK: WHY AM I DOING THIS? I GET QUEASY.
I MEAN, THOSE LATE NIGHTS WHEN I SIT AROUND WRITING SONGS ABOUT MY EX-GIRLFRIEND, I HAVE THIS VISION OF HOW MAGICAL IT WOULD FEEL TO BE ONSTAGE.
YO! GREEN TIGHTS!

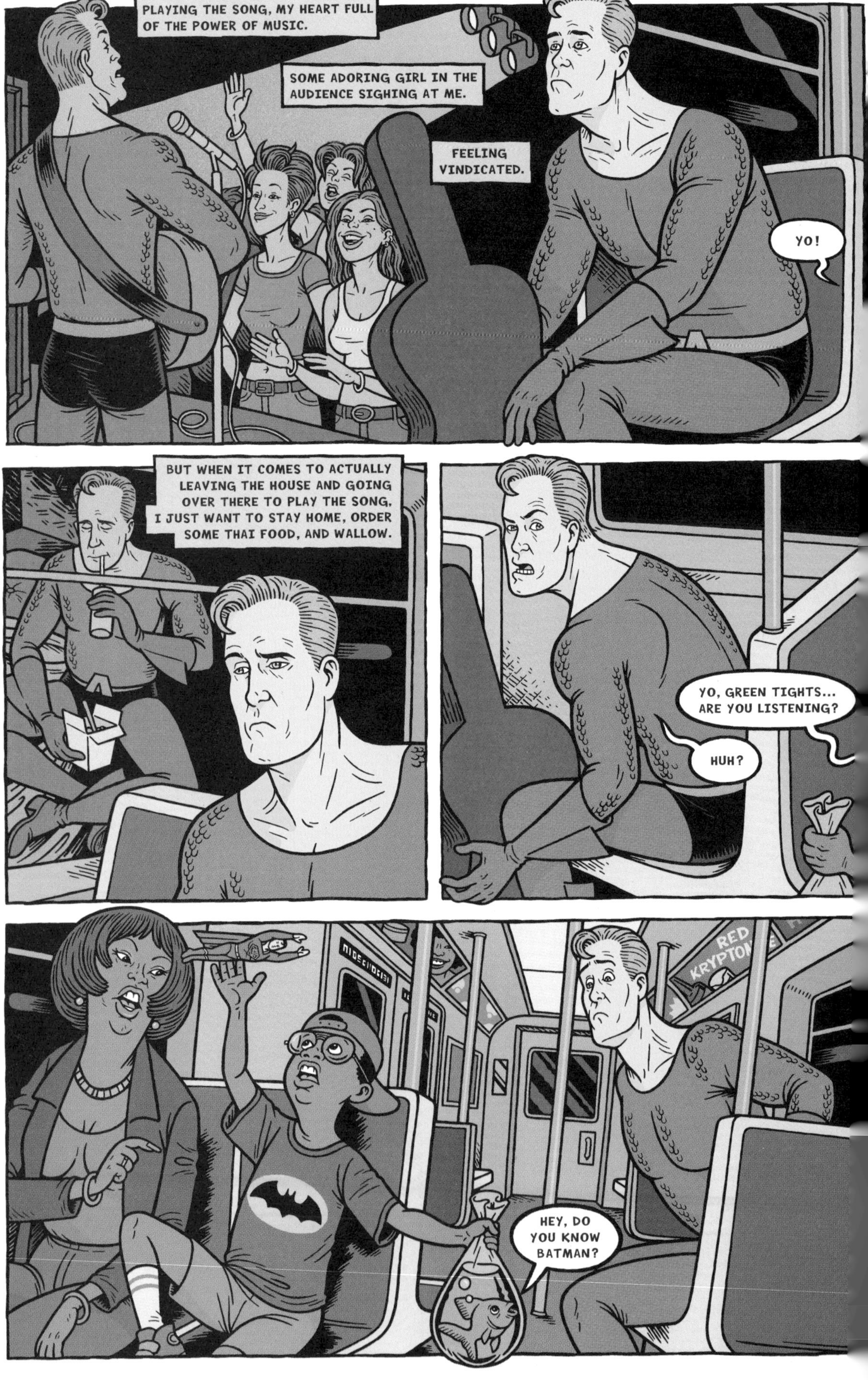
PLAYING THE SONG, MY HEART FULL OF THE POWER OF MUSIC.
SOME ADORING GIRL IN THE AUDIENCE SIGHING AT ME.
FEELING VINDICATED.
YO!
BUT WHEN IT COMES TO ACTUALLY LEAVING THE HOUSE AND GOING OVER THERE TO PLAY THE SONG, I JUST WANT TO STAY HOME, ORDER SOME THAI FOOD, AND WALLOW.
YO, GREEN TIGHTS... ARE YOU LISTENING?
HUH?
RED
HEY, DO YOU KNOW BATMAN?

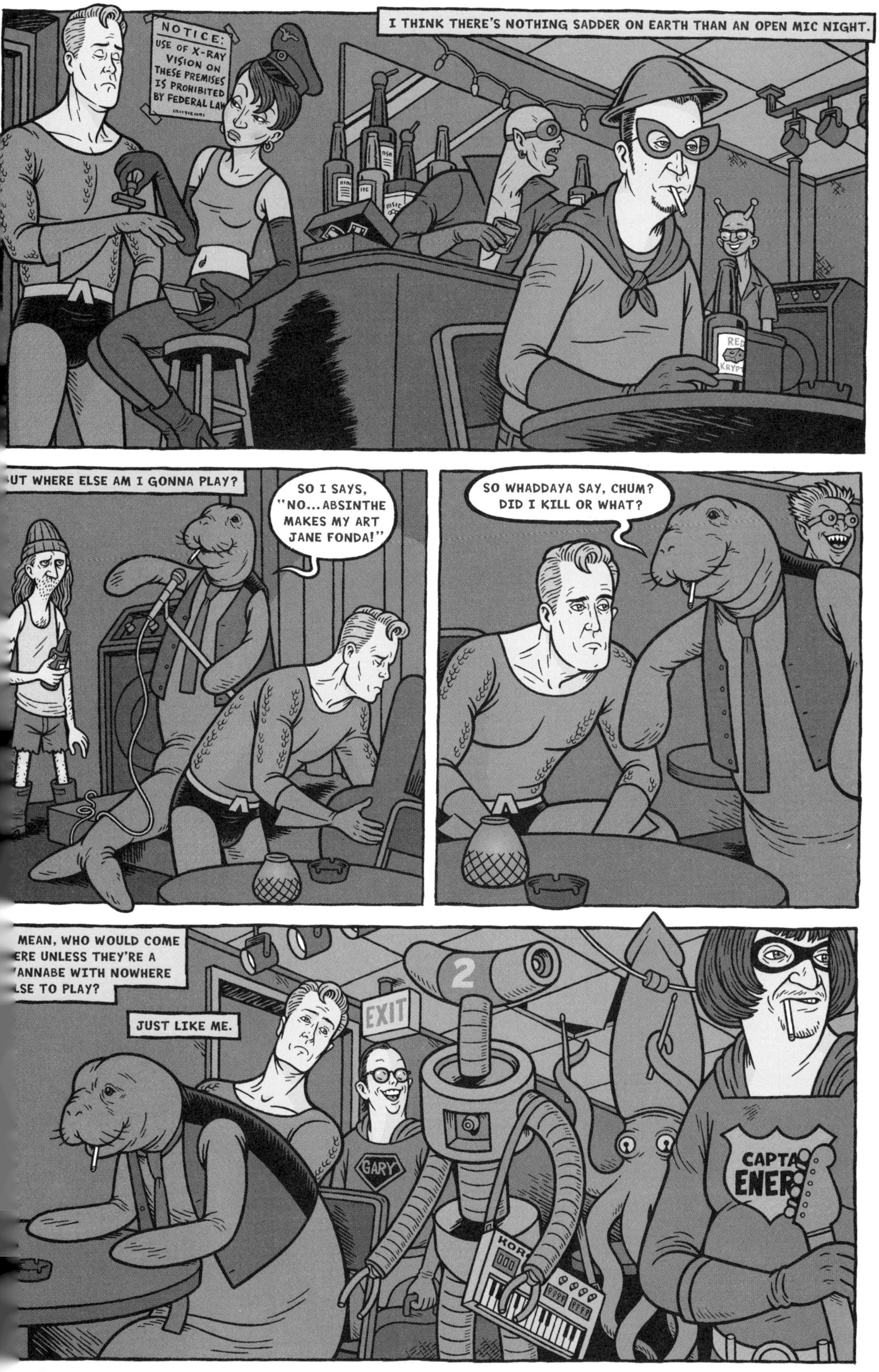
NOTICE:
USE OF X-RAY VISION ON THESE PREMISES IS PROHIBITED BY FEDERAL LAW
I THINK THERE'S NOTHING SADDER ON EARTH THAN AN OPEN MIC NIGHT.
UT WHERE ELSE AM I GONNA PLAY?
SO I SAYS, "NO...ABSINTHE MAKES MY ART JANE FONDA!"
SO WHADDAYA SAY, CHUM? DID I KILL OR WHAT?
MEAN, WHO WOULD COME
ERE UNLESS THEY'RE A
ANNABE WITH NOWHERE
LSE TO PLAY?
JUST LIKE ME.
EXIT
2
GARY
CAPTA
ENER

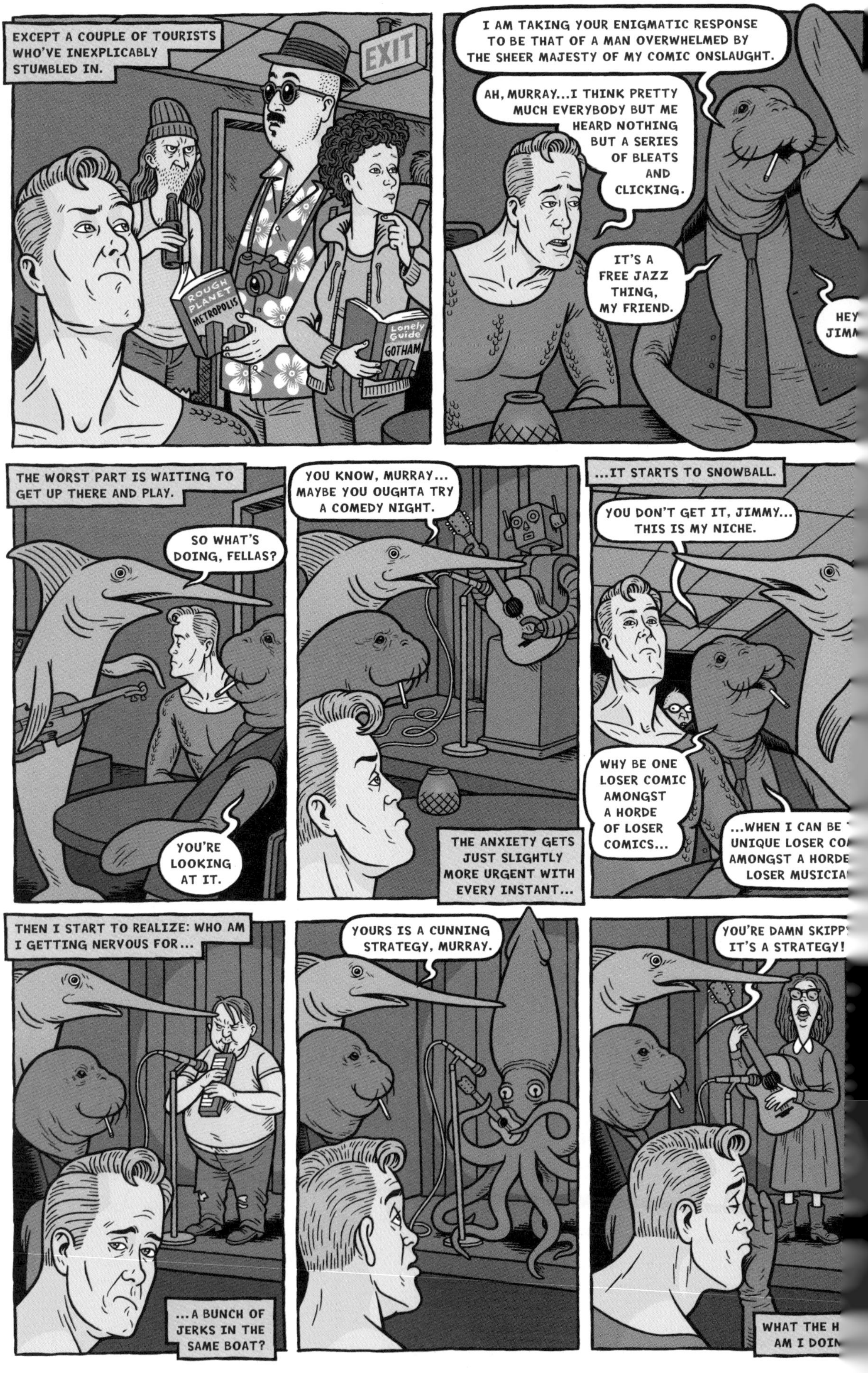

EXCEPT A COUPLE OF TOURISTS WHO'VE INEXPLICABLY STUMBLED IN.
EXIT
ROUGH PLANET METROPOLIS
Lonely Guide GOTHAM
I AM TAKING YOUR ENIGMATIC RESPONSE TO BE THAT OF A MAN OVERWHELMED BY THE SHEER MAJESTY OF MY COMIC ONSLAUGHT.
AH, MURRAY...I THINK PRETTY MUCH EVERYBODY BUT ME HEARD NOTHING BUT A SERIES OF BLEATS AND CLICKING.
IT'S A FREE JAZZ THING, MY FRIEND.
HEY JIMM
THE WORST PART IS WAITING TO GET UP THERE AND PLAY.
SO WHAT'S DOING, FELLAS?
YOU'RE LOOKING AT IT.
YOU KNOW, MURRAY... MAYBE YOU OUGHTA TRY A COMEDY NIGHT.
THE ANXIETY GETS JUST SLIGHTLY MORE URGENT WITH EVERY INSTANT...
...IT STARTS TO SNOWBALL.
YOU DON'T GET IT, JIMMY... THIS IS MY NICHE.
WHY BE ONE LOSER COMIC AMONGST A HORDE OF LOSER COMICS...
...WHEN I CAN BE UNIQUE LOSER CO AMONGST A HORDE LOSER MUSICIA
THEN I START TO REALIZE: WHO AM I GETTING NERVOUS FOR...
...A BUNCH OF JERKS IN THE SAME BOAT?
YOURS IS A CUNNING STRATEGY, MURRAY.
YOU'RE DAMN SKIPP IT'S A STRATEGY!
WHAT THE H AM I DOIN

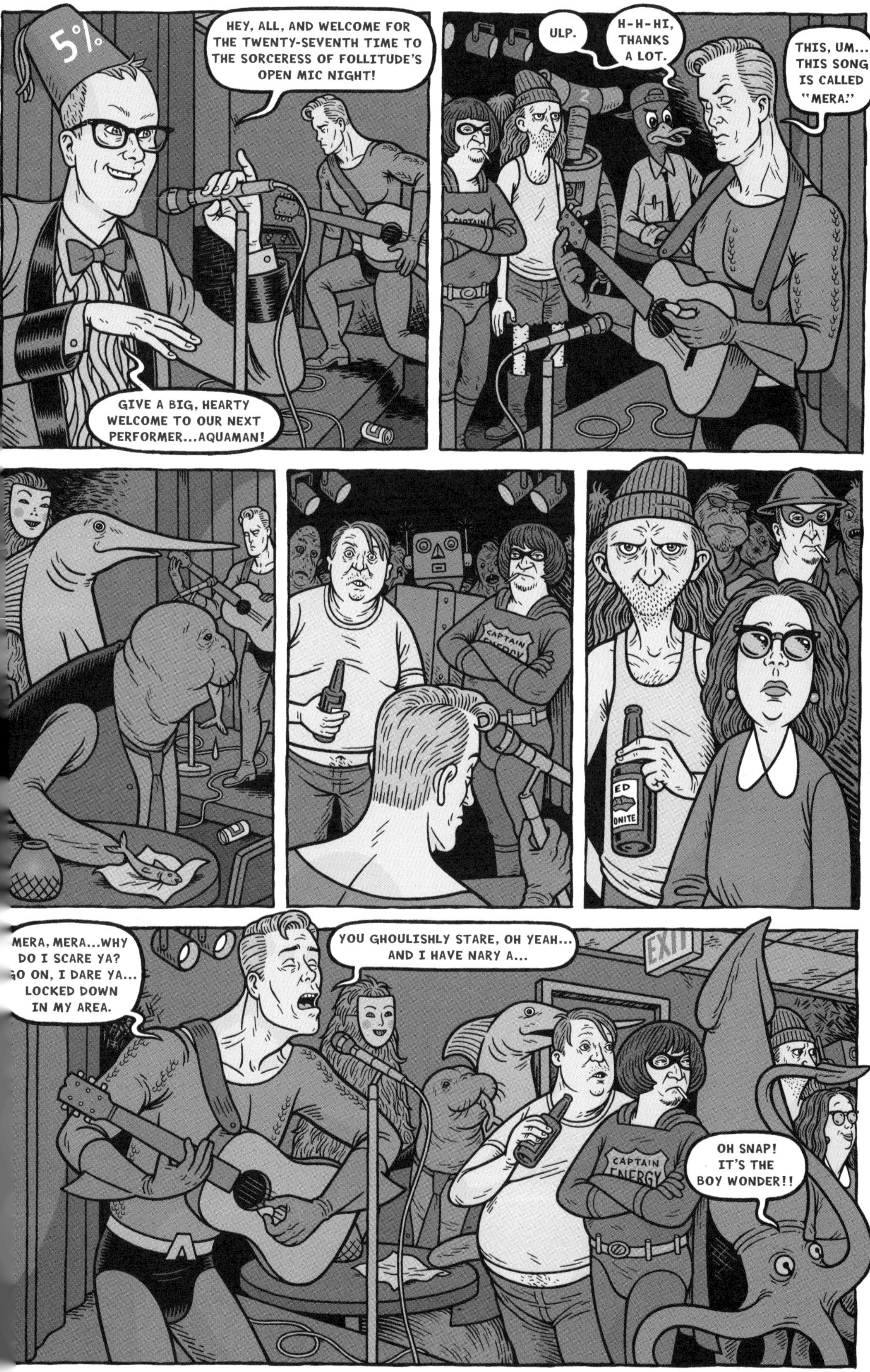
5%
HEY, ALL, AND WELCOME FOR THE TWENTY-SEVENTH TIME TO THE SORCERESS OF FOLLITUDE'S OPEN MIC NIGHT!
GIVE A BIG, HEARTY WELCOME TO OUR NEXT PERFORMER...AQUAMAN!
ULP.
H-H-HI, THANKS A LOT.
THIS, UM... THIS SONG IS CALLED "MERA."
CAPTAIN ENERGY
MERA, MERA...WHY DO I SCARE YA?
GO ON, I DARE YA... LOCKED DOWN IN MY AREA.
YOU GHOULISHLY STARE, OH YEAH... AND I HAVE NARY A...
EXIT
CAPTAIN ENERGY
OH SNAP! IT'S THE BOY WONDER!!

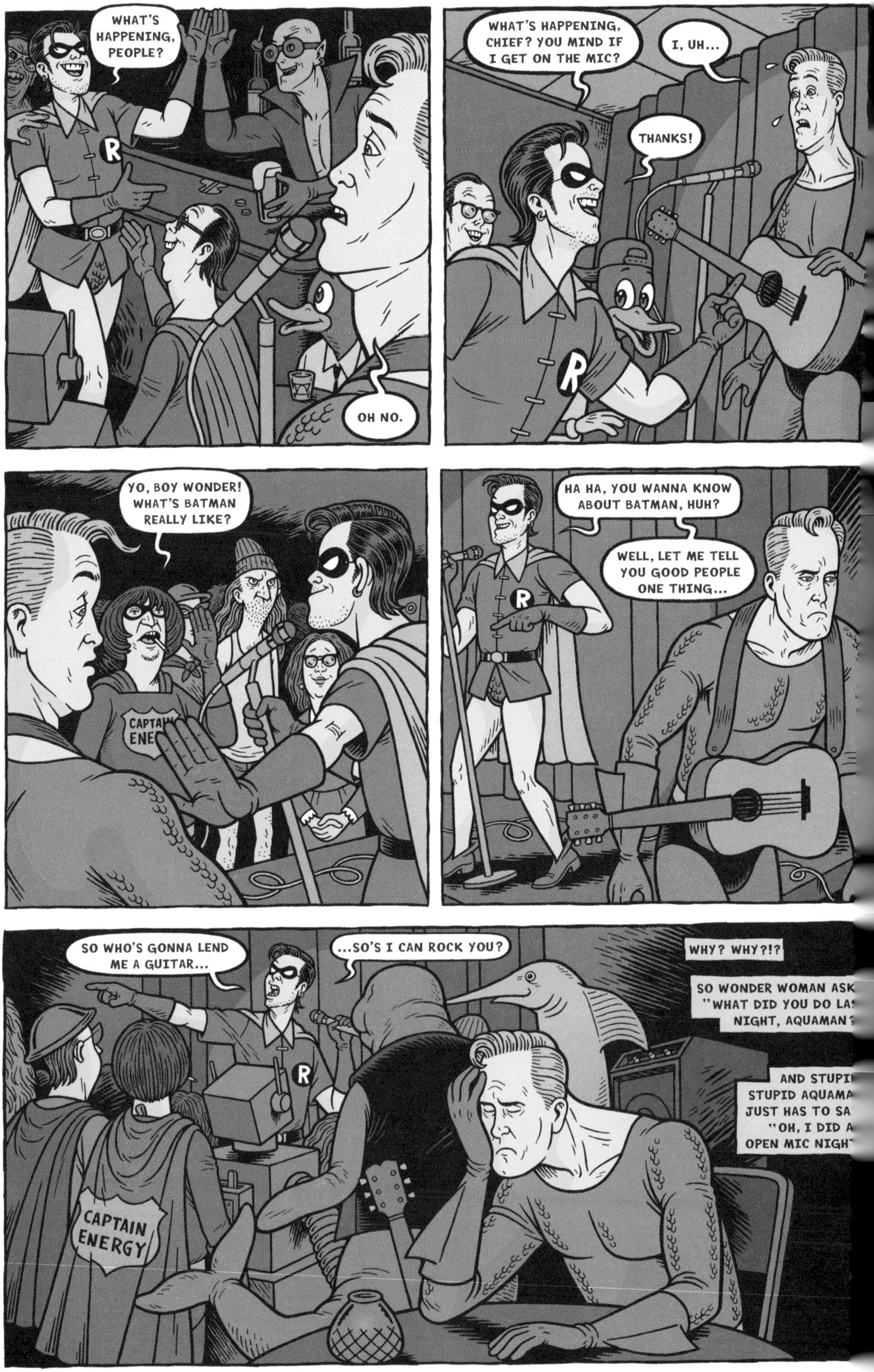
WHAT'S HAPPENING, PEOPLE?
OH NO.
WHAT'S HAPPENING, CHIEF? YOU MIND IF I GET ON THE MIC?
I, UH...
THANKS!
YO, BOY WONDER! WHAT'S BATMAN REALLY LIKE?
CAPTAIN ENE
HA HA, YOU WANNA KNOW ABOUT BATMAN, HUH?
WELL, LET ME TELL YOU GOOD PEOPLE ONE THING...
SO WHO'S GONNA LEND ME A GUITAR...
...SO'S I CAN ROCK YOU?
WHY? WHY?!?
SO WONDER WOMAN ASK
"WHAT DID YOU DO LAS
NIGHT, AQUAMAN?
AND STUPI
STUPID AQUAMA
JUST HAS TO SA
"OH, I DID A
OPEN MIC NIGH
CAPTAIN ENERGY

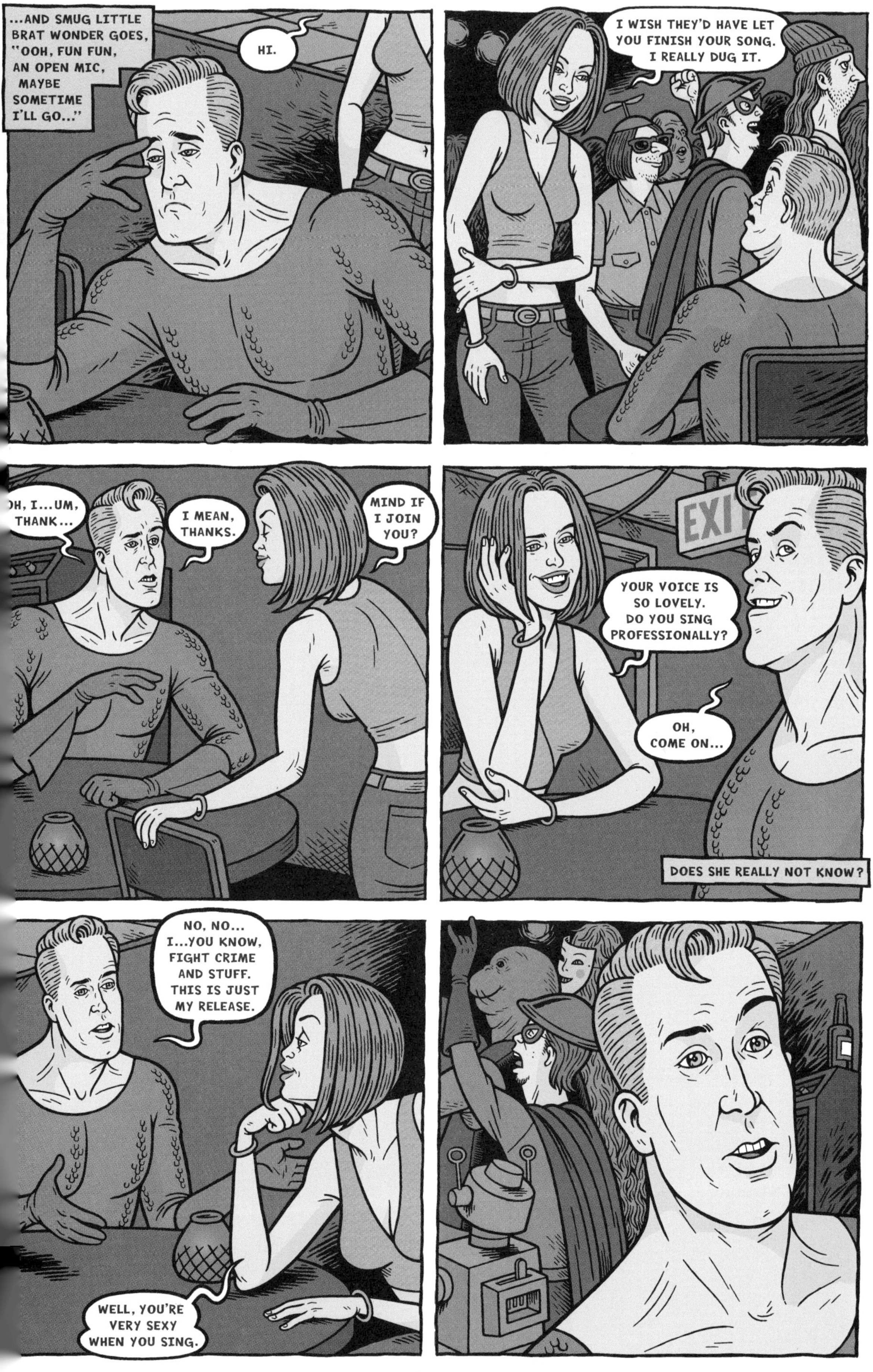
...AND SMUG LITTLE BRAT WONDER GOES, "OOH, FUN FUN, AN OPEN MIC, MAYBE SOMETIME I'LL GO..."
HI.
I WISH THEY'D HAVE LET YOU FINISH YOUR SONG. I REALLY DUG IT.
OH, I...UM, THANK...
I MEAN, THANKS.
MIND IF I JOIN YOU?
EXIT
YOUR VOICE IS SO LOVELY. DO YOU SING PROFESSIONALLY?
OH, COME ON...
DOES SHE REALLY NOT KNOW?
NO, NO... I...YOU KNOW, FIGHT CRIME AND STUFF. THIS IS JUST MY RELEASE.
WELL, YOU'RE VERY SEXY WHEN YOU SING.

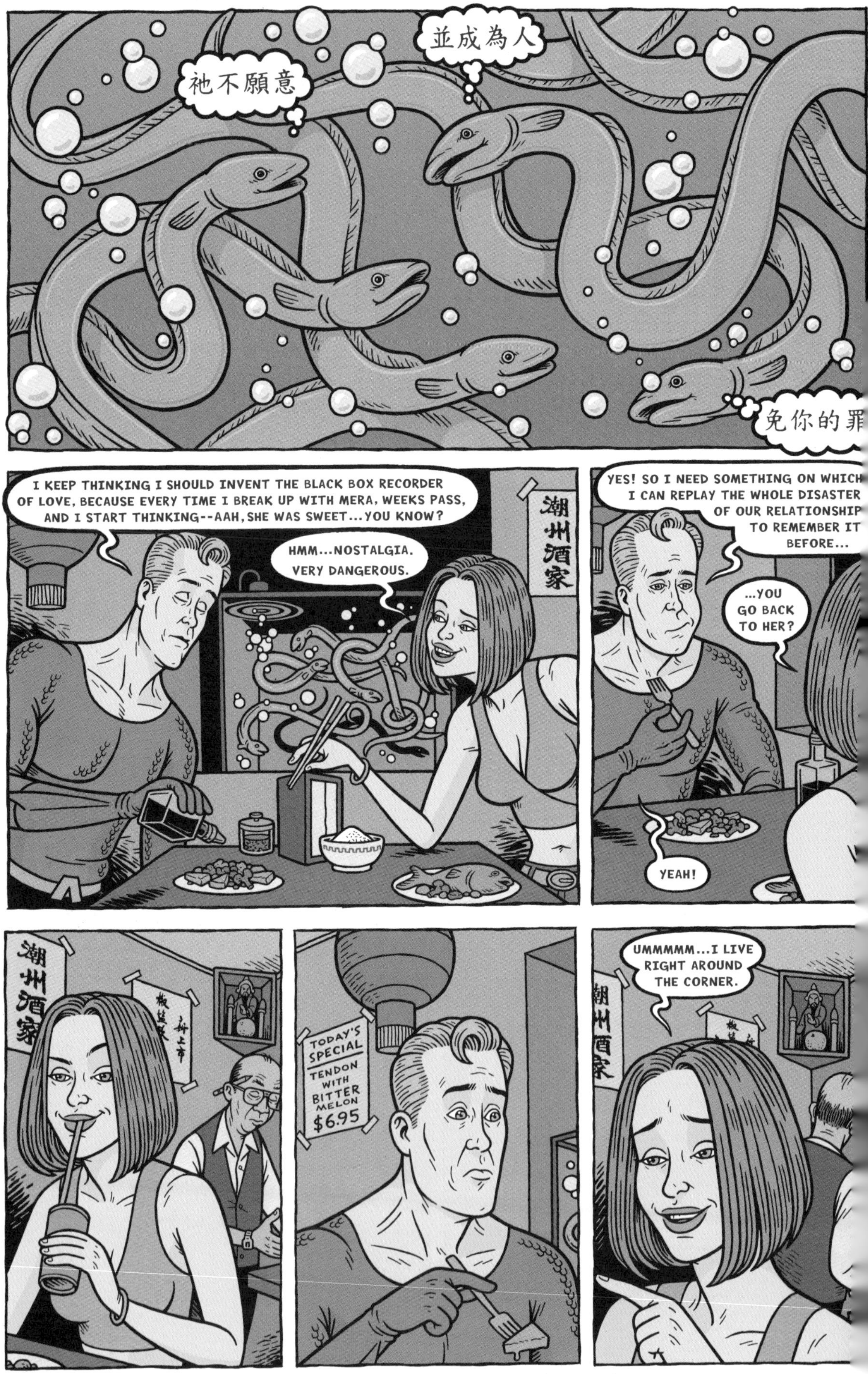
祂不願意
並成為人
免你的罪
I KEEP THINKING I SHOULD INVENT THE BLACK BOX RECORDER OF LOVE, BECAUSE EVERY TIME I BREAK UP WITH MERA, WEEKS PASS, AND I START THINKING--AAH, SHE WAS SWEET... YOU KNOW?
潮州酒家
HMM...NOSTALGIA. VERY DANGEROUS.
YES! SO I NEED SOMETHING ON WHICH I CAN REPLAY THE WHOLE DISASTER OF OUR RELATIONSHIP TO REMEMBER IT BEFORE...
...YOU GO BACK TO HER?
YEAH!
潮州酒家
TODAY'S SPECIAL
TENDON WITH BITTER MELON
$6.95
UMMMMM...I LIVE RIGHT AROUND THE CORNER.
潮州酒家

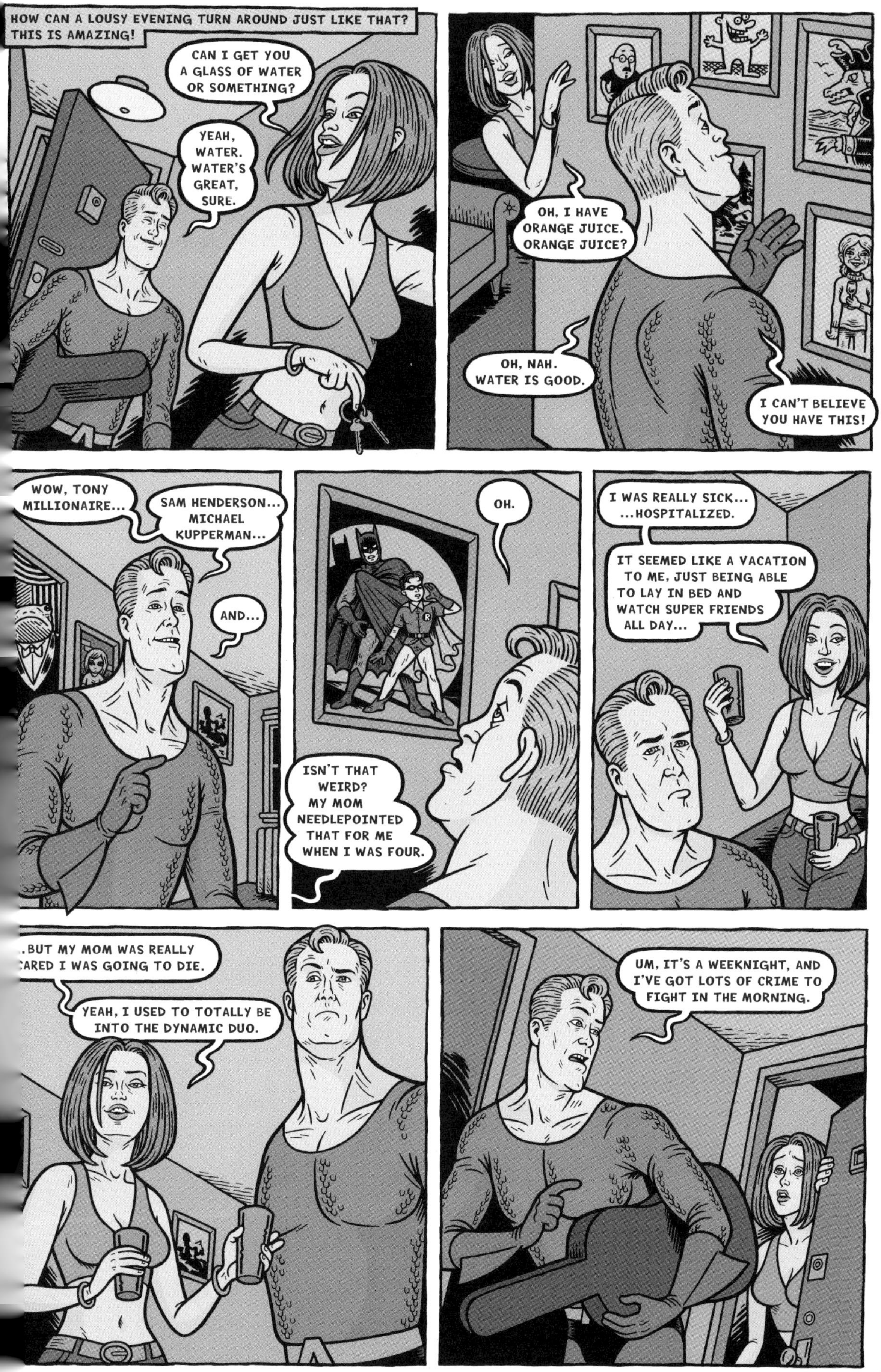
HOW CAN A LOUSY EVENING TURN AROUND JUST LIKE THAT? THIS IS AMAZING!
CAN I GET YOU A GLASS OF WATER OR SOMETHING?
YEAH, WATER. WATER'S GREAT, SURE.
OH, I HAVE ORANGE JUICE. ORANGE JUICE?
OH, NAH. WATER IS GOOD.
I CAN'T BELIEVE YOU HAVE THIS!
WOW, TONY MILLIONAIRE...
SAM HENDERSON... MICHAEL KUPPERMAN...
AND...
OH.
ISN'T THAT WEIRD? MY MOM NEEDLEPOINTED THAT FOR ME WHEN I WAS FOUR.
I WAS REALLY SICK... ...HOSPITALIZED.
IT SEEMED LIKE A VACATION TO ME, JUST BEING ABLE TO LAY IN BED AND WATCH SUPER FRIENDS ALL DAY...
.BUT MY MOM WAS REALLY CARED I WAS GOING TO DIE.
YEAH, I USED TO TOTALLY BE INTO THE DYNAMIC DUO.
UM, IT'S A WEEKNIGHT, AND I'VE GOT LOTS OF CRIME TO FIGHT IN THE MORNING.

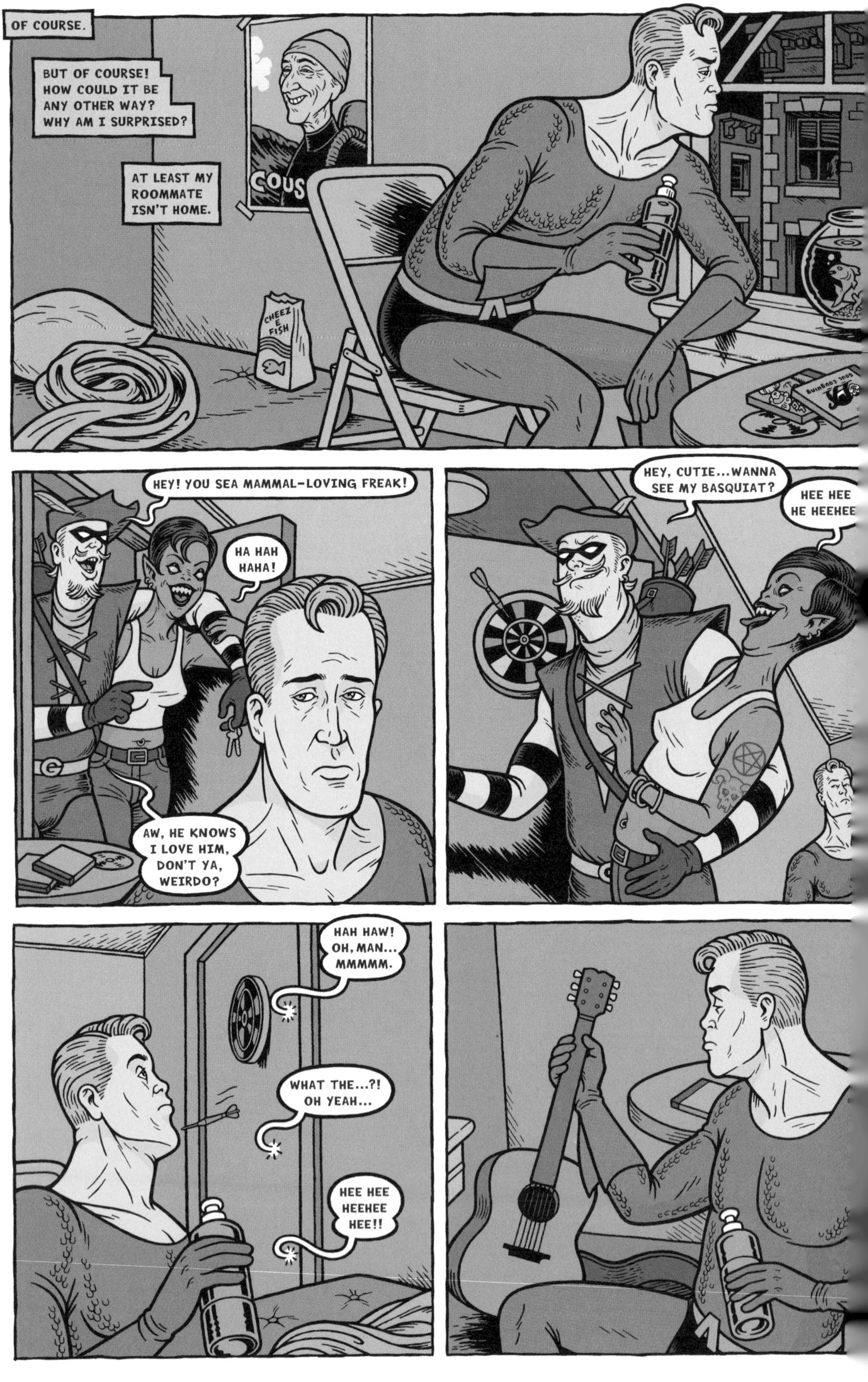
OF COURSE.
BUT OF COURSE! HOW COULD IT BE ANY OTHER WAY? WHY AM I SURPRISED?
AT LEAST MY ROOMMATE ISN'T HOME.
COUS
CHEEZ E FISH
HEY! YOU SEA MAMMAL-LOVING FREAK!
HA HAH HAHA!
AW, HE KNOWS I LOVE HIM, DON'T YA, WEIRDO?
HEY, CUTIE...WANNA SEE MY BASQUIAT?
HEE HEE HE HEEHEE
HAH HAW! OH, MAN... MMMMM.
WHAT THE...?! OH YEAH...
HEE HEE HEEHEE HEE!!

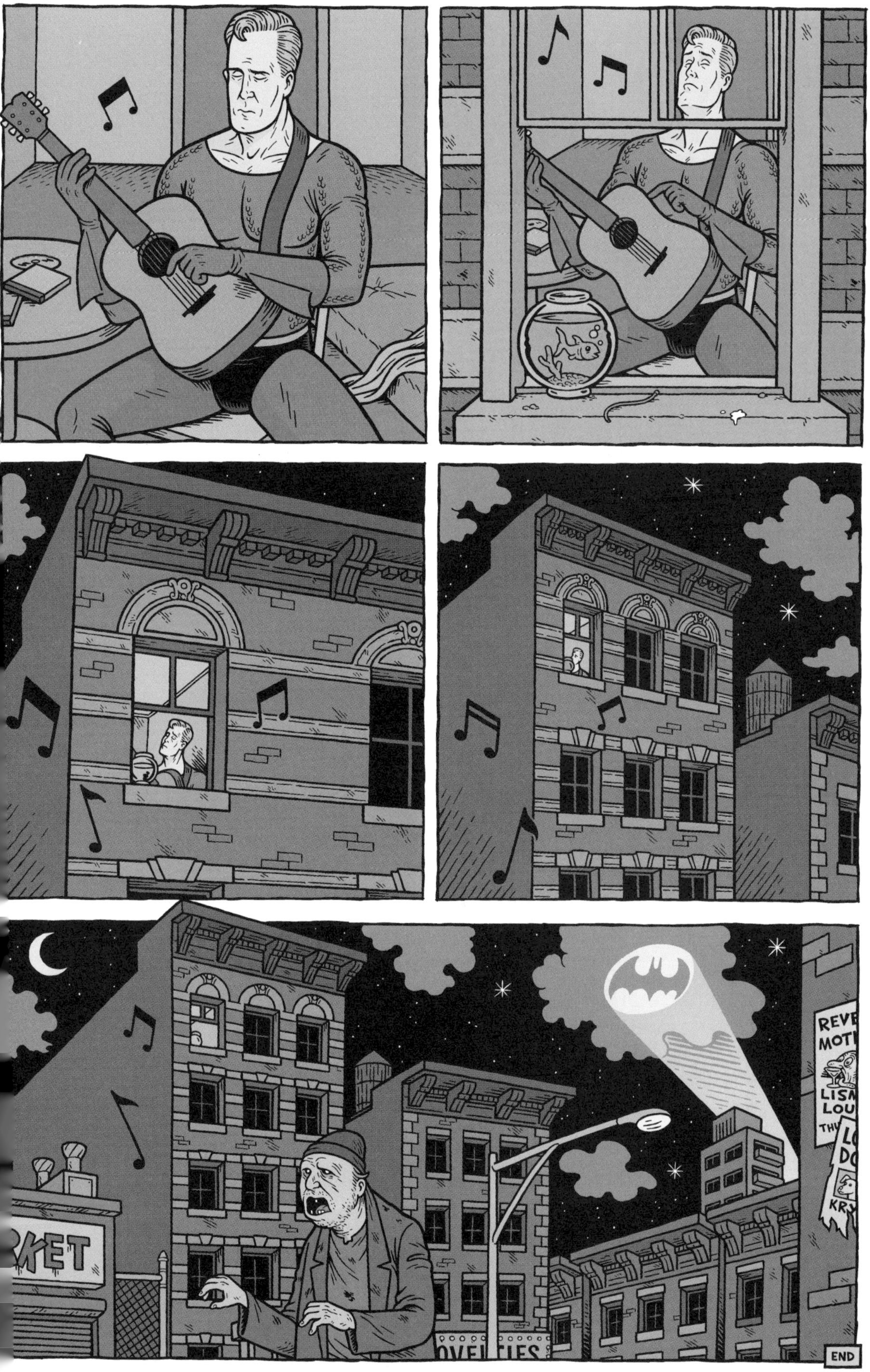
END

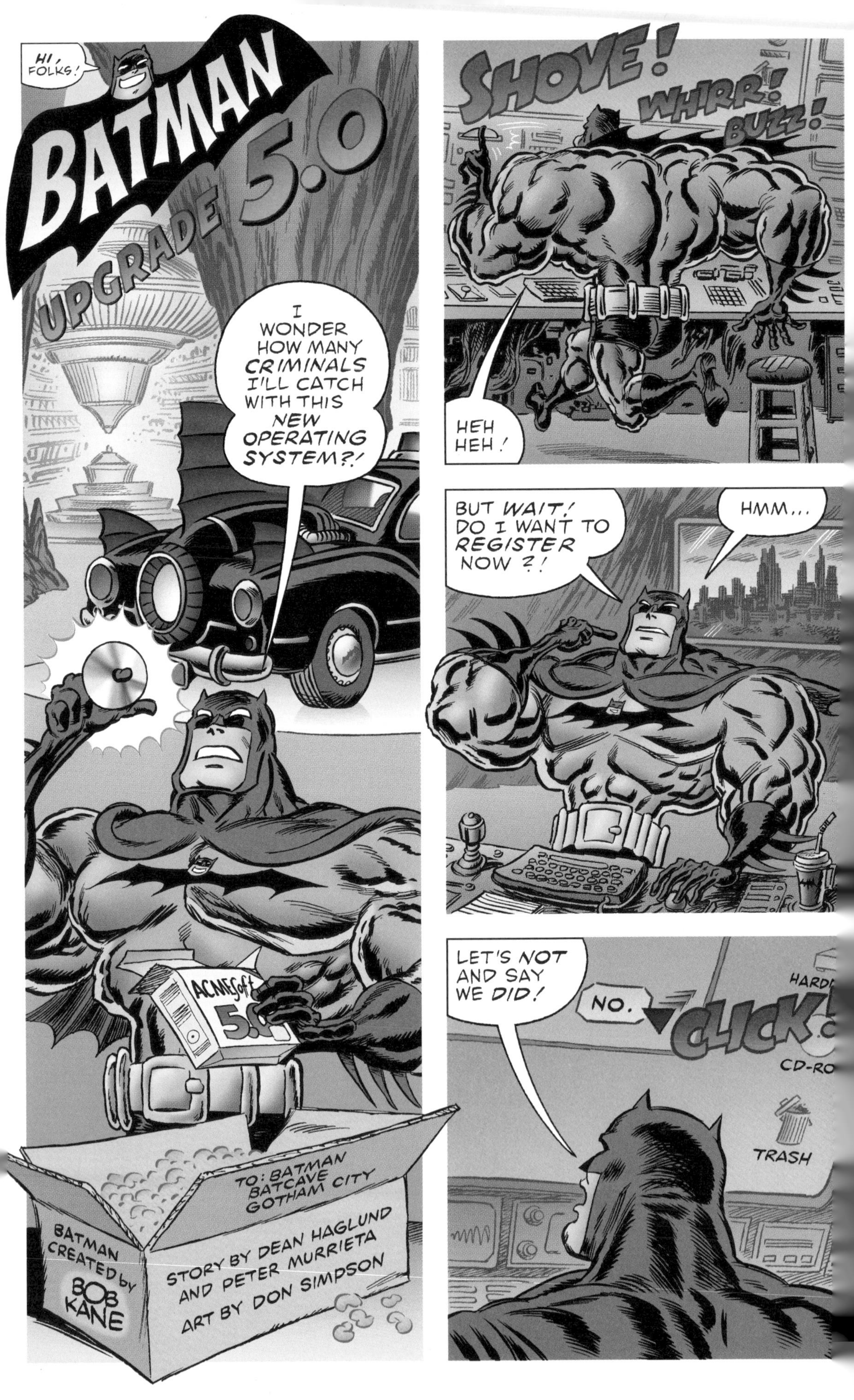
HI, FOLKS!
BATMAN
UPGRADE 5.0
I WONDER HOW MANY CRIMINALS I'LL CATCH WITH THIS NEW OPERATING SYSTEM?!
ACMESoft 5.0
TO: BATMAN BATCAVE GOTHAM CITY
BATMAN CREATED by BOB KANE
STORY BY DEAN HAGLUND AND PETER MURRIETA
ART BY DON SIMPSON
SHOVE!
WHIRR!
BUZZ!
HEH HEH!
BUT WAIT! DO I WANT TO REGISTER NOW?!
HMM...
LET'S NOT AND SAY WE DID!
NO.
CLICK!
TRASH

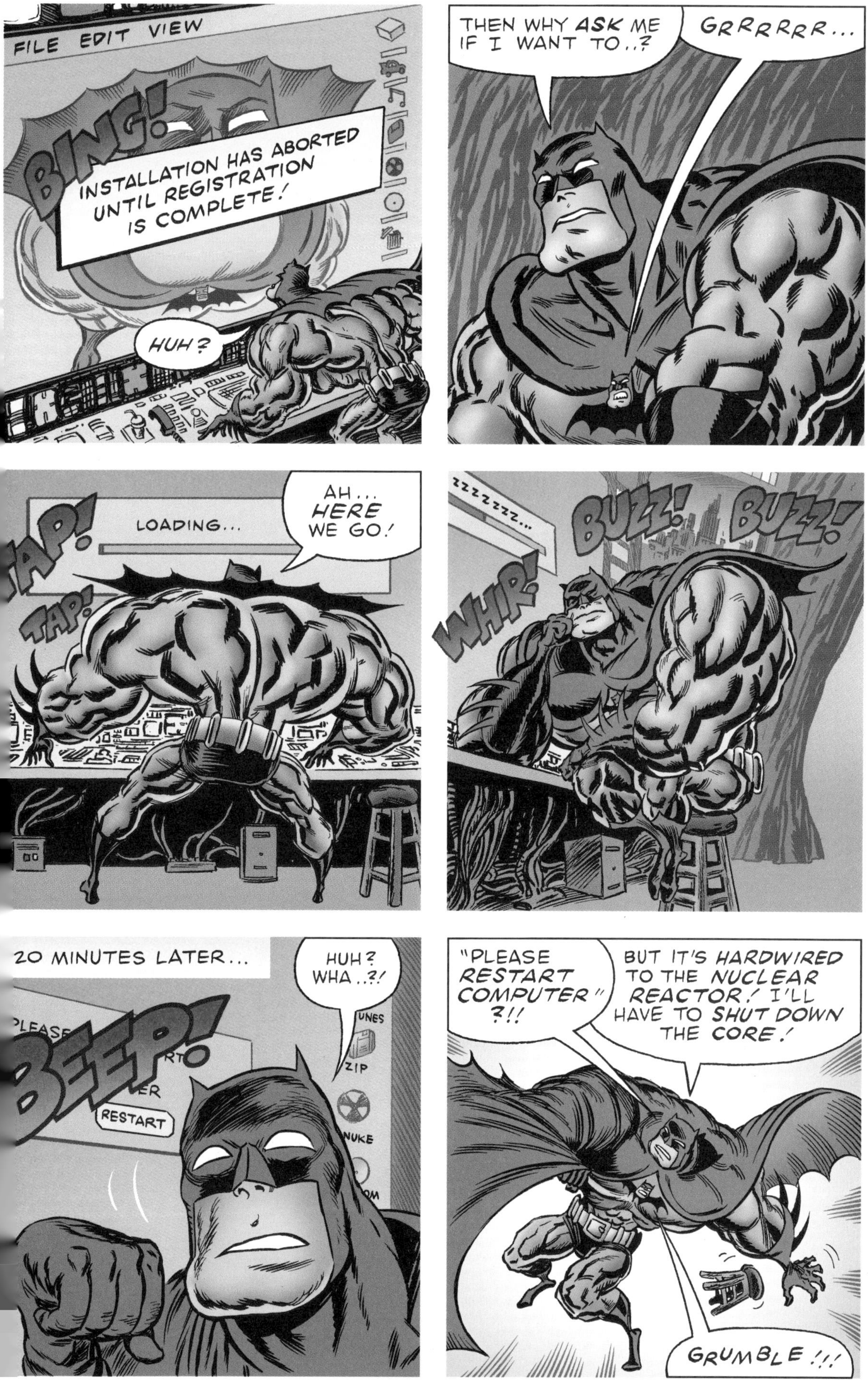

FILE EDIT VIEW
BING!
INSTALLATION HAS ABORTED UNTIL REGISTRATION IS COMPLETE!
HUH?
THEN WHY ASK ME IF I WANT TO..?
GRRRRRR...
LOADING...
AH... HERE WE GO!
TAP!
TAP!
ZZZZZZZ...
BUZZ! BUZZ!
WHIR!
20 MINUTES LATER...
HUH? WHA..?!
BEEP!
RESTART
ZIP
NUKE
"PLEASE RESTART COMPUTER" ?!!
BUT IT'S HARDWIRED TO THE NUCLEAR REACTOR! I'LL HAVE TO SHUT DOWN THE CORE!
GRUMBLE!!!

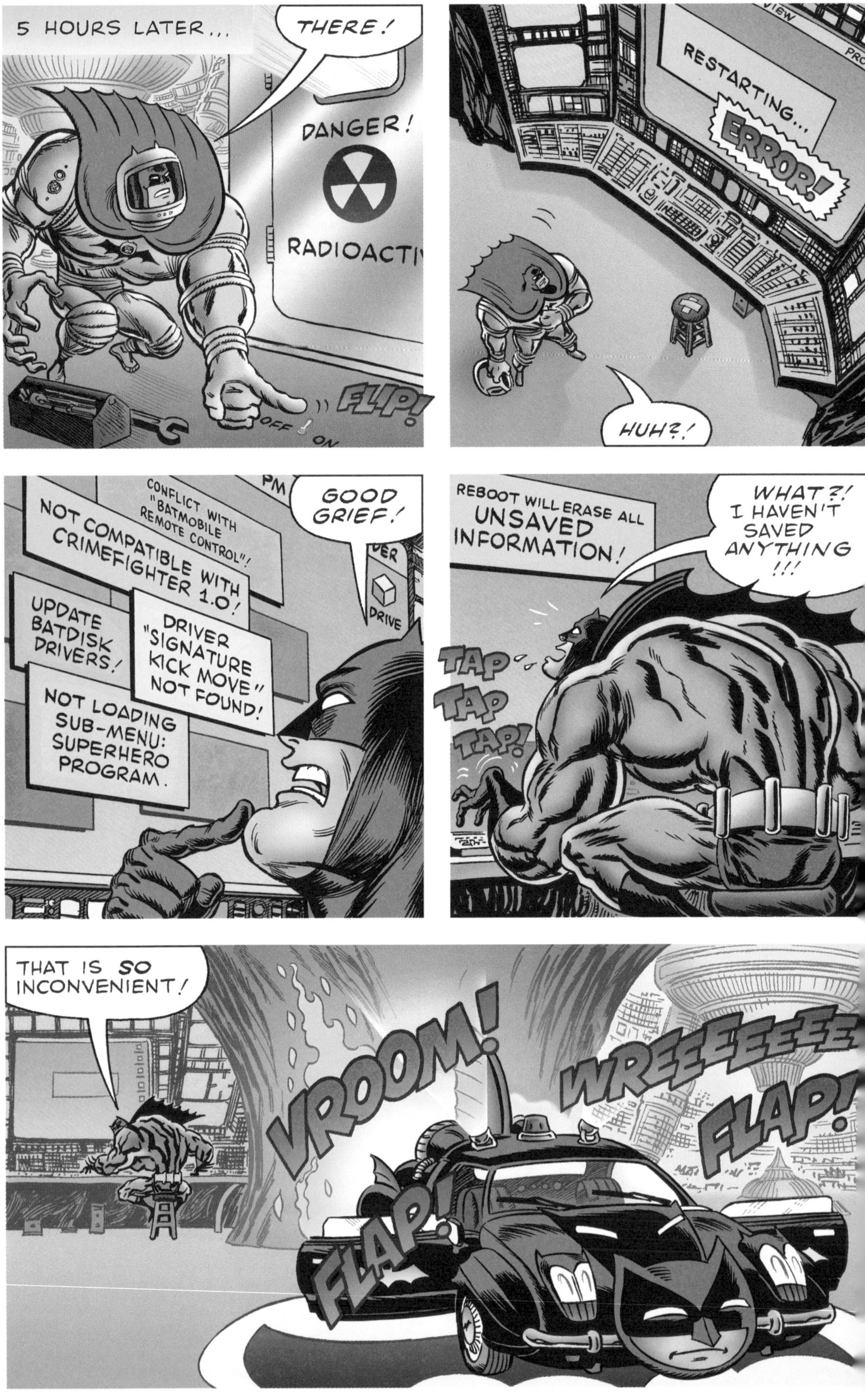
5 HOURS LATER...
THERE!
DANGER!
RADIOACTI
FLIP!
OFF
ON
RESTARTING...
ERROR!
HUH?!
CONFLICT WITH "BATMOBILE REMOTE CONTROL"!
NOT COMPATIBLE WITH CRIMEFIGHTER 1.0!
UPDATE BATDISK DRIVERS!
DRIVER "SIGNATURE KICK MOVE" NOT FOUND!
NOT LOADING SUB-MENU: SUPERHERO PROGRAM.
GOOD GRIEF!
DRIVE
REBOOT WILL ERASE ALL UNSAVED INFORMATION!
WHAT?! I HAVEN'T SAVED ANYTHING !!!
TAP TAP TAP!
THAT IS SO INCONVENIENT!
VROOM!
WREEEEEEE
FLAP!
FLAP!

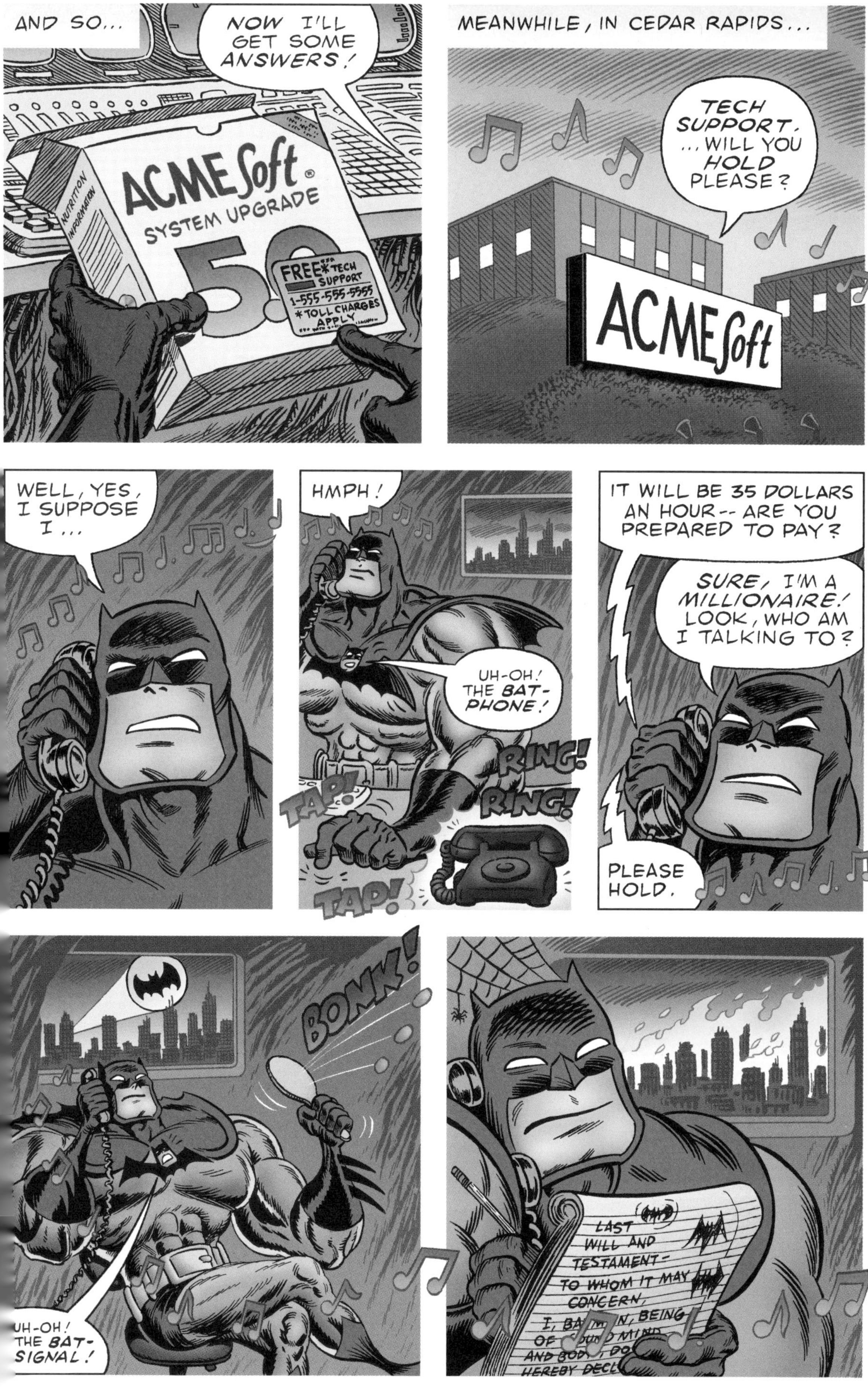
AND SO...
NOW I'LL GET SOME ANSWERS!
ACME Soft®
SYSTEM UPGRADE
5.0
NUTRITION INFORMATION
FREE* TECH SUPPORT
1-555-555-5555
*TOLL CHARGES APPLY
MEANWHILE, IN CEDAR RAPIDS...
TECH SUPPORT. ...WILL YOU HOLD PLEASE?
ACME Soft
WELL, YES, I SUPPOSE I...
HMPH!
UH-OH! THE BAT-PHONE!
TAP!
RING!
RING!
TAP!
IT WILL BE 35 DOLLARS AN HOUR-- ARE YOU PREPARED TO PAY?
SURE, I'M A MILLIONAIRE! LOOK, WHO AM I TALKING TO?
PLEASE HOLD.
BONK!
UH-OH! THE BAT-SIGNAL!
LAST WILL AND TESTAMENT—
TO WHOM IT MAY CONCERN,

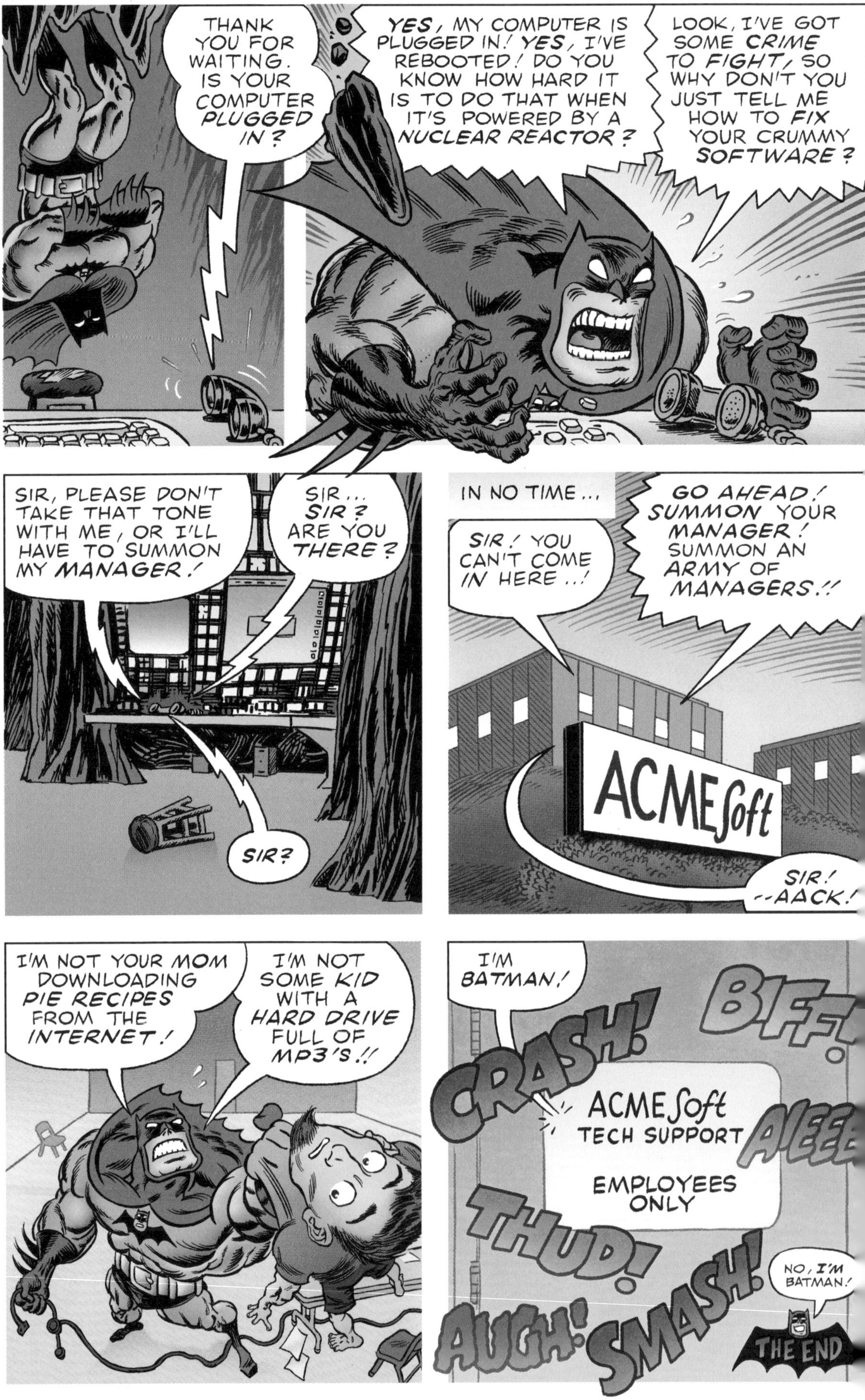
THANK YOU FOR WAITING. IS YOUR COMPUTER PLUGGED IN?
YES, MY COMPUTER IS PLUGGED IN! YES, I'VE REBOOTED! DO YOU KNOW HOW HARD IT IS TO DO THAT WHEN IT'S POWERED BY A NUCLEAR REACTOR?
LOOK, I'VE GOT SOME CRIME TO FIGHT, SO WHY DON'T YOU JUST TELL ME HOW TO FIX YOUR CRUMMY SOFTWARE?
SIR, PLEASE DON'T TAKE THAT TONE WITH ME, OR I'LL HAVE TO SUMMON MY MANAGER!
SIR... SIR? ARE YOU THERE?
SIR?
IN NO TIME...
SIR! YOU CAN'T COME IN HERE...!
GO AHEAD! SUMMON YOUR MANAGER! SUMMON AN ARMY OF MANAGERS!!
ACME Soft
SIR! --AACK!
I'M NOT YOUR MOM DOWNLOADING PIE RECIPES FROM THE INTERNET!
I'M NOT SOME KID WITH A HARD DRIVE FULL OF MP3'S!!
I'M BATMAN!
CRASH!
BIFF!
ACME Soft TECH SUPPORT
EMPLOYEES ONLY
AIEEE
THUD!
SMASH!
AUGH!
NO, I'M BATMAN!
THE END

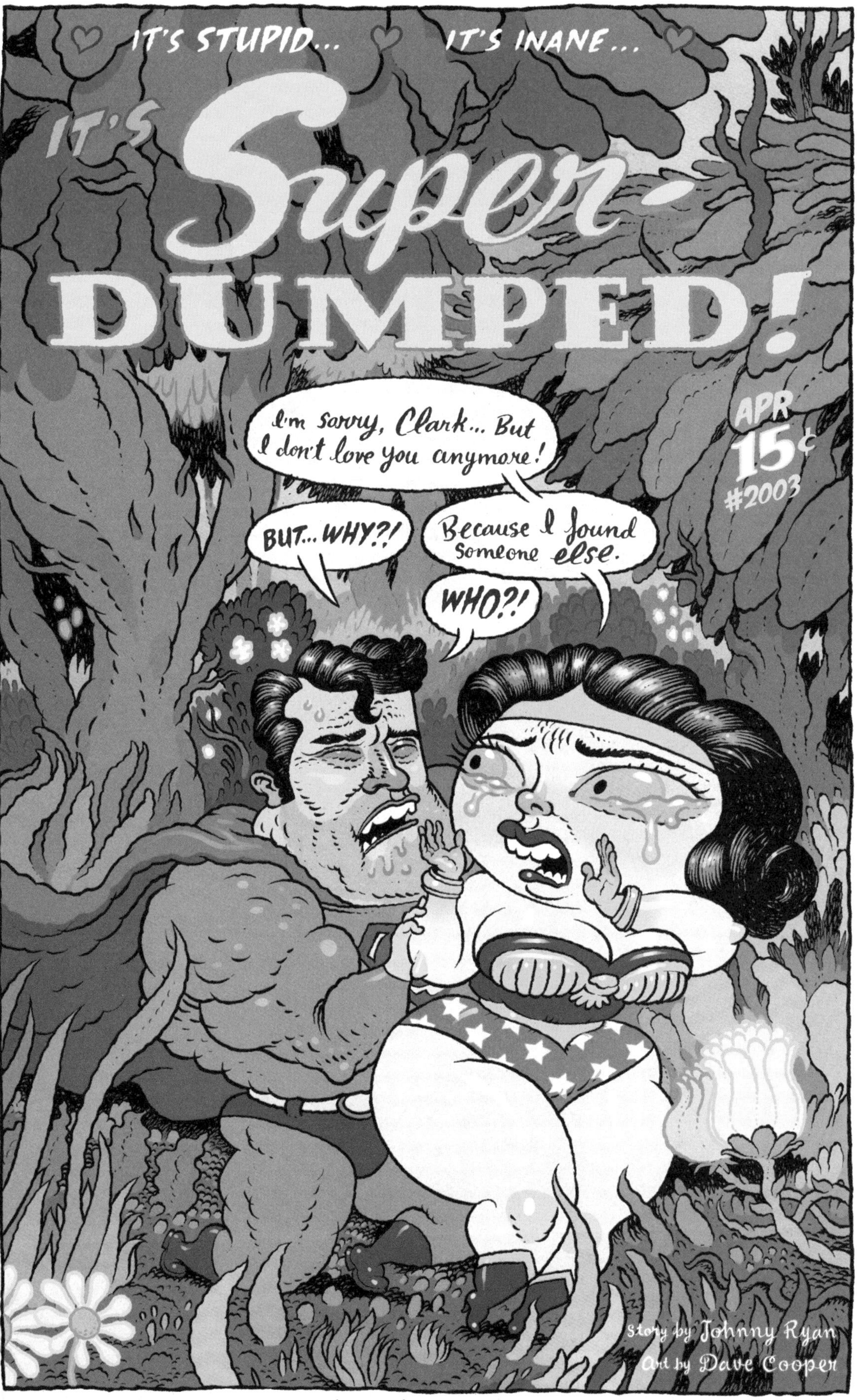
IT'S STUPID...
IT'S INANE...
IT'S Super-DUMPED!
APR
15¢
#2003
I'm sorry, Clark... But I don't love you anymore!
BUT...WHY?!
Because I found someone else.
WHO?!
Story by Johnny Ryan
Art by Dave Cooper

Superman created by Jerry Siegel & Joe Shuster. Wonder Woman created by William Moulton Marston

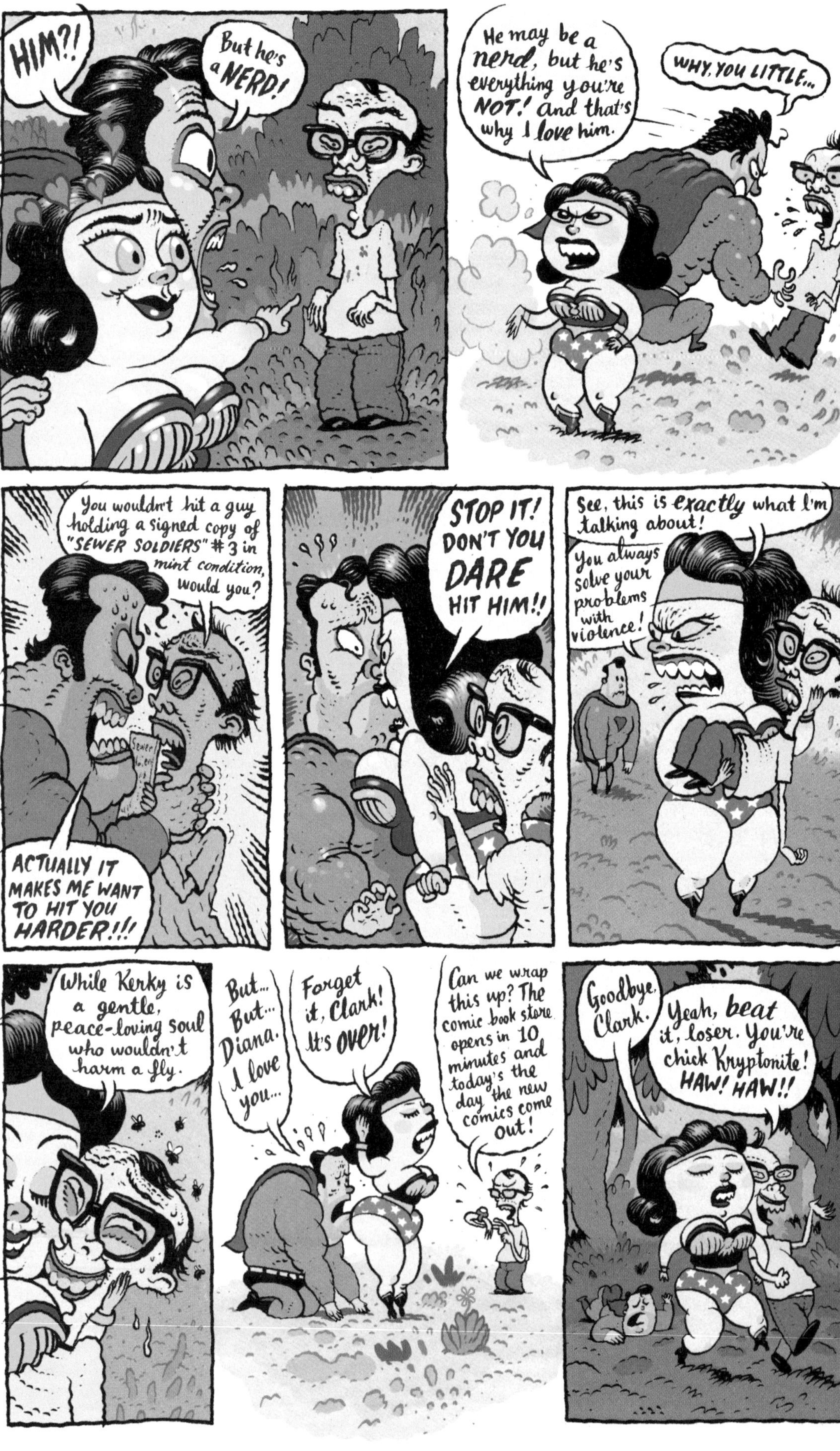
HIM?!
But he's a NERD!
He may be a nerd, but he's everything you're NOT! And that's why I love him.
WHY, YOU LITTLE...
You wouldn't hit a guy holding a signed copy of "SEWER SOLDIERS" #3 in mint condition, would you?
ACTUALLY IT MAKES ME WANT TO HIT YOU HARDER!!!
STOP IT! DON'T YOU DARE HIT HIM!!
See, this is exactly what I'm talking about!
You always solve your problems with violence!
While Kerky is a gentle, peace-loving soul who wouldn't harm a fly.
But... But... Diana. I love you...
Forget it, Clark! It's OVER!
Can we wrap this up? The comic book store opens in 10 minutes and today's the day the new comics come out!
Goodbye, Clark.
Yeah, beat it, loser. You're chick Kryptonite! HAW! HAW!!

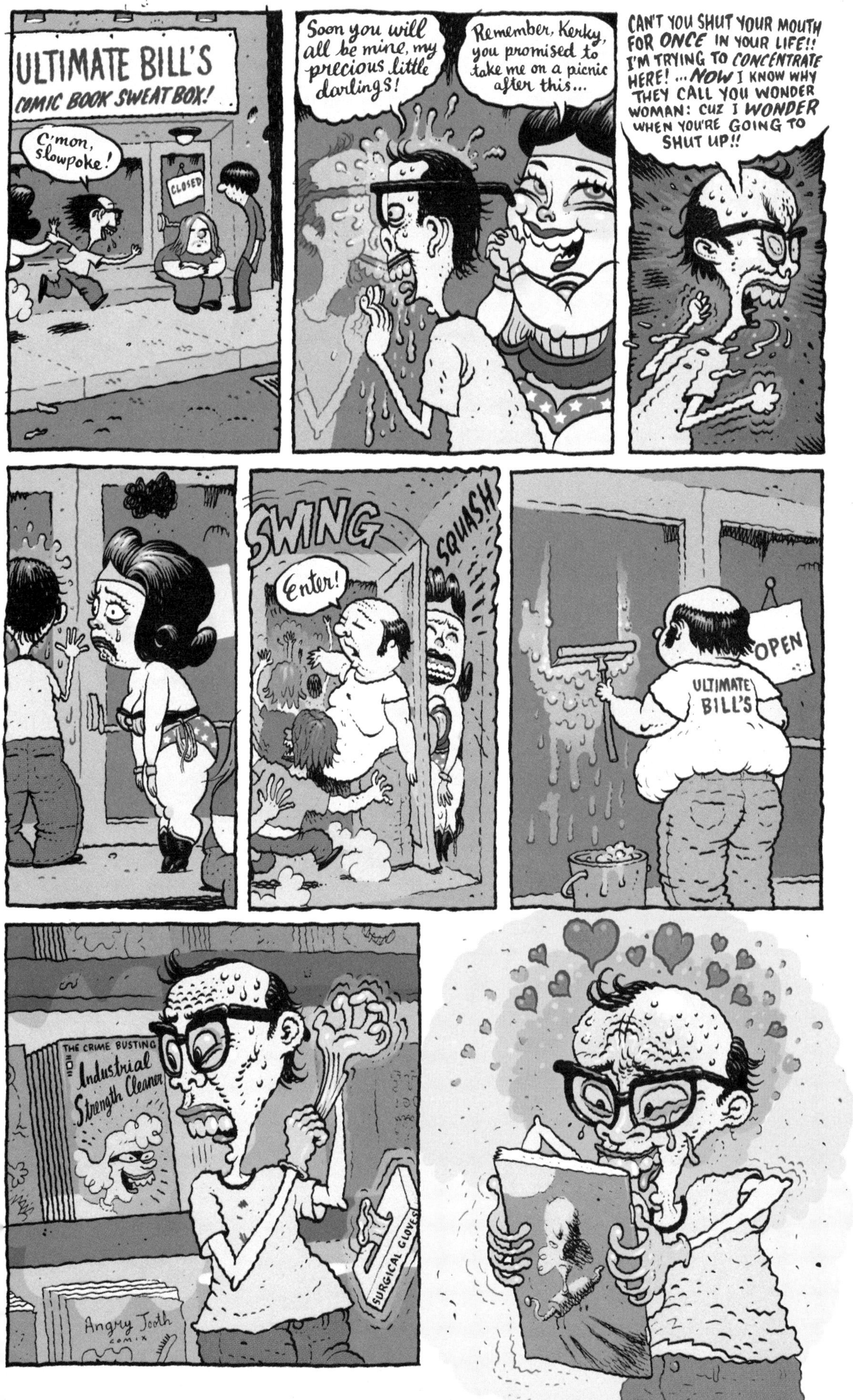
ULTIMATE BILL'S
COMIC BOOK SWEAT BOX!
C'mon, slowpoke!
CLOSED
Soon you will all be mine, my precious little darlings!
Remember, Kerky, you promised to take me on a picnic after this...
CAN'T YOU SHUT YOUR MOUTH FOR ONCE IN YOUR LIFE!! I'M TRYING TO CONCENTRATE HERE! ...NOW I KNOW WHY THEY CALL YOU WONDER WOMAN: CUZ I WONDER WHEN YOU'RE GOING TO SHUT UP!!
SWING
SQUASH
Enter!
OPEN
ULTIMATE BILL'S
THE CRIME BUSTING
Industrial Strength Cleaner
SURGICAL GLOVES
Angry Tooth comix

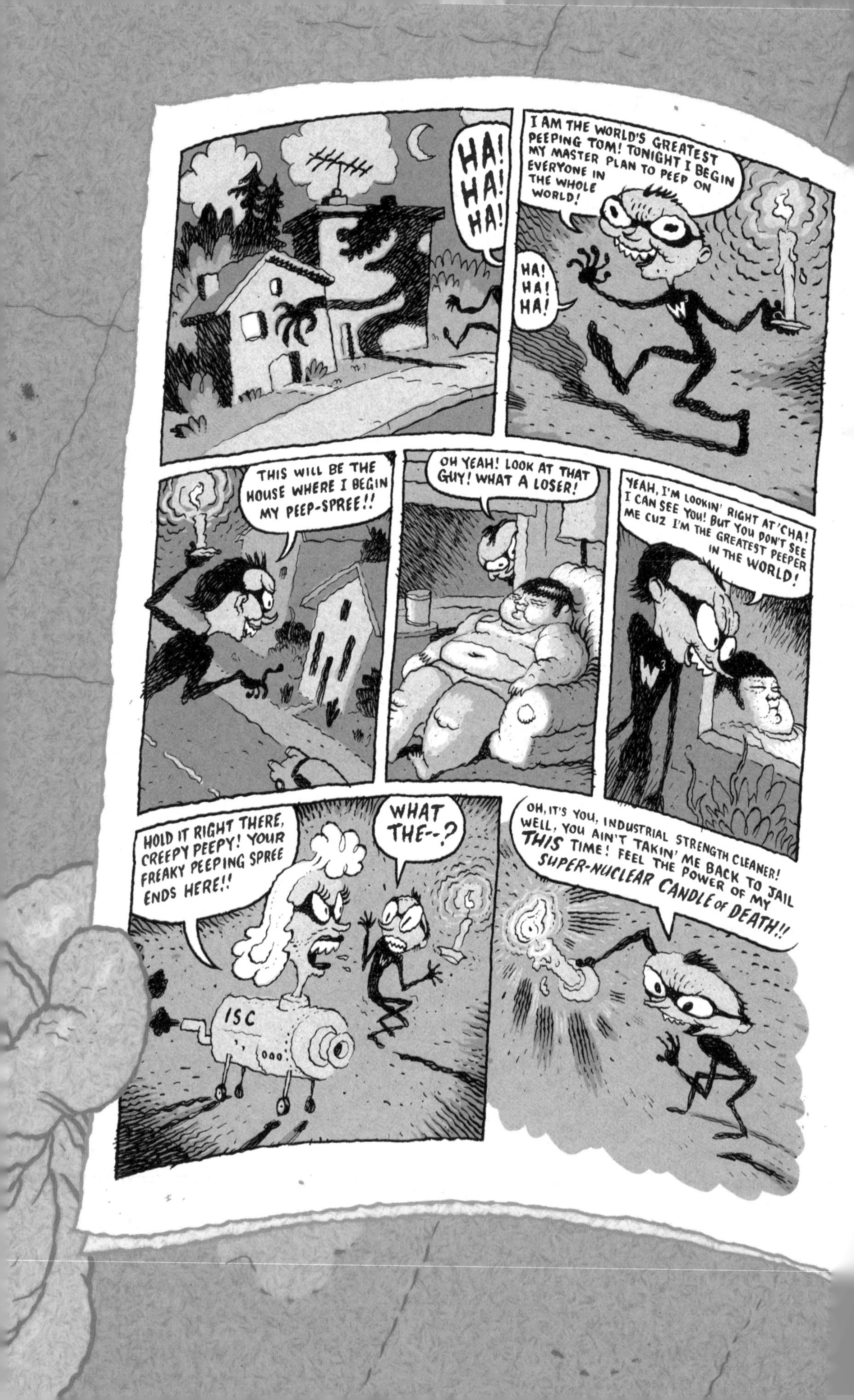
HA! HA! HA!
I AM THE WORLD'S GREATEST PEEPING TOM! TONIGHT I BEGIN MY MASTER PLAN TO PEEP ON EVERYONE IN THE WHOLE WORLD!
HA! HA! HA!
THIS WILL BE THE HOUSE WHERE I BEGIN MY PEEP-SPREE!!
OH YEAH! LOOK AT THAT GUY! WHAT A LOSER!
YEAH, I'M LOOKIN' RIGHT AT 'CHA! I CAN SEE YOU! BUT YOU DON'T SEE ME CUZ I'M THE GREATEST PEEPER IN THE WORLD!
HOLD IT RIGHT THERE, CREEPY PEEPY! YOUR FREAKY PEEPING SPREE ENDS HERE!!
WHAT THE--?
ISC
OH, IT'S YOU, INDUSTRIAL STRENGTH CLEANER! WELL, YOU AIN'T TAKIN' ME BACK TO JAIL THIS TIME! FEEL THE POWER OF MY SUPER-NUCLEAR CANDLE OF DEATH!!

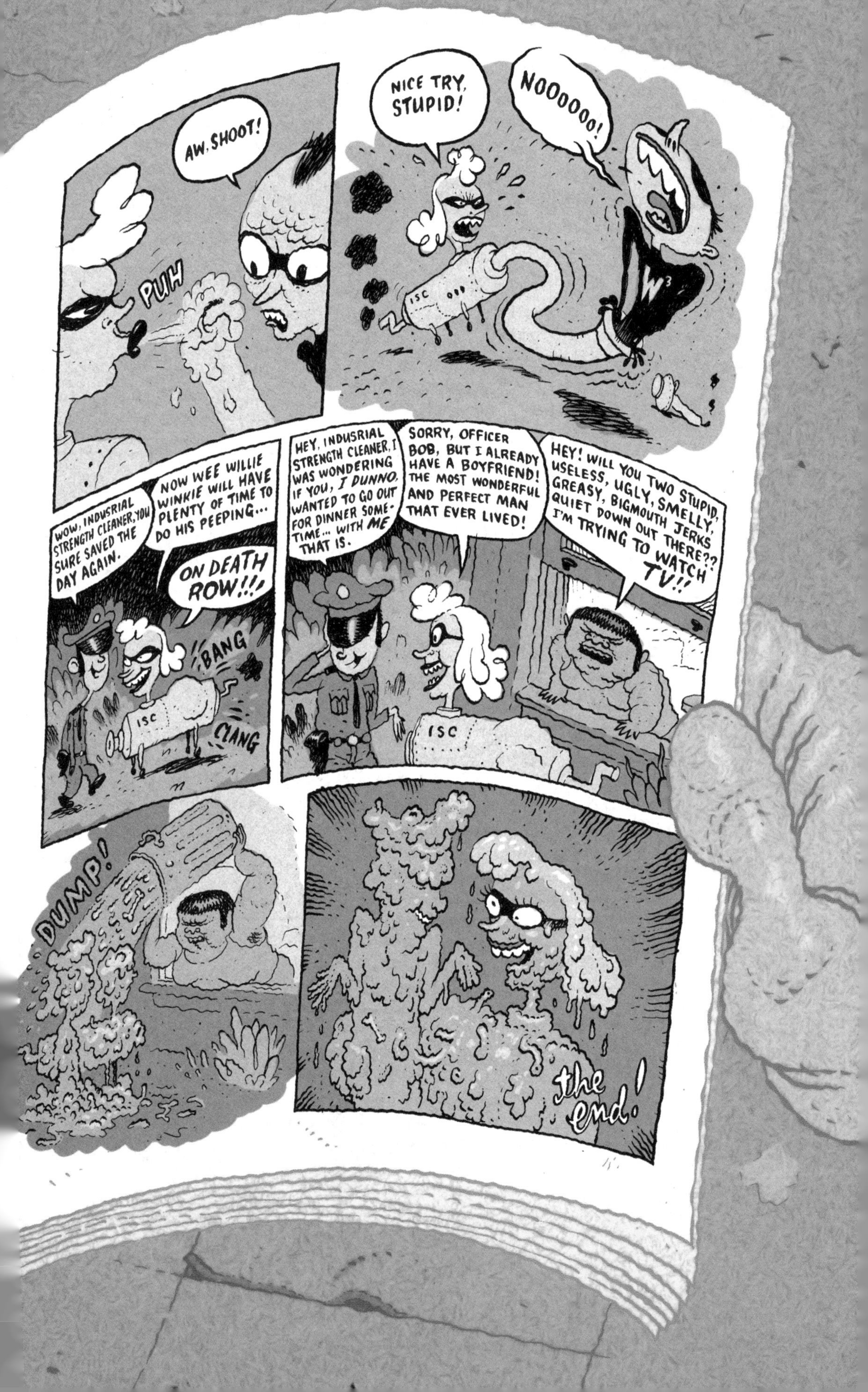
AW, SHOOT!
PUH
NICE TRY, STUPID!
NOOOOOO!
ISC
WOW, INDUSRIAL STRENGTH CLEANER, YOU SURE SAVED THE DAY AGAIN.
NOW WEE WILLIE WINKIE WILL HAVE PLENTY OF TIME TO DO HIS PEEPING...
ON DEATH ROW!!!
BANG
CLANG
HEY, INDUSRIAL STRENGTH CLEANER, I WAS WONDERING IF YOU, I DUNNO, WANTED TO GO OUT FOR DINNER SOME-TIME... WITH ME THAT IS.
SORRY, OFFICER BOB, BUT I ALREADY HAVE A BOYFRIEND! THE MOST WONDERFUL AND PERFECT MAN THAT EVER LIVED!
HEY! WILL YOU TWO STUPID, USELESS, UGLY, SMELLY, GREASY, BIGMOUTH JERKS QUIET DOWN OUT THERE?? I'M TRYING TO WATCH TV!!
DUMP!
the end!

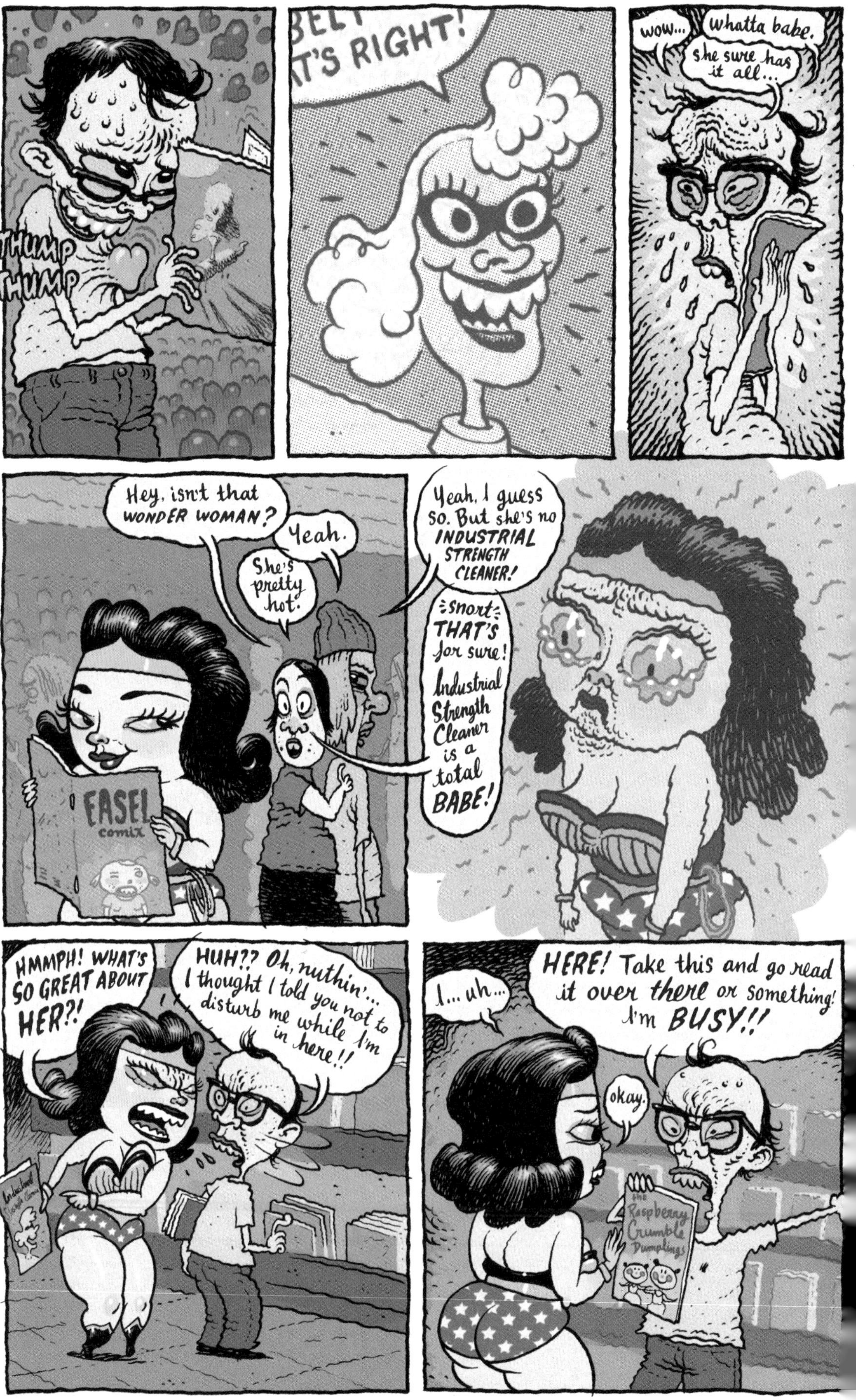
THUMP THUMP
BELT
AT'S RIGHT!
wow...
whatta babe.
she sure has it all...
Hey, isn't that WONDER WOMAN?
Yeah.
She's pretty hot.
Yeah, I guess so. But she's no INDUSTRIAL STRENGTH CLEANER!
snort THAT'S for sure! Industrial Strength Cleaner is a total BABE!
EASEL comix
HMMPH! WHAT'S SO GREAT ABOUT HER?!
HUH?? Oh, nuthin'... I thought I told you not to disturb me while I'm in here!!
I... uh...
HERE! Take this and go read it over there or something! I'm BUSY!!
okay.
the Raspberry Crumble Dumplings

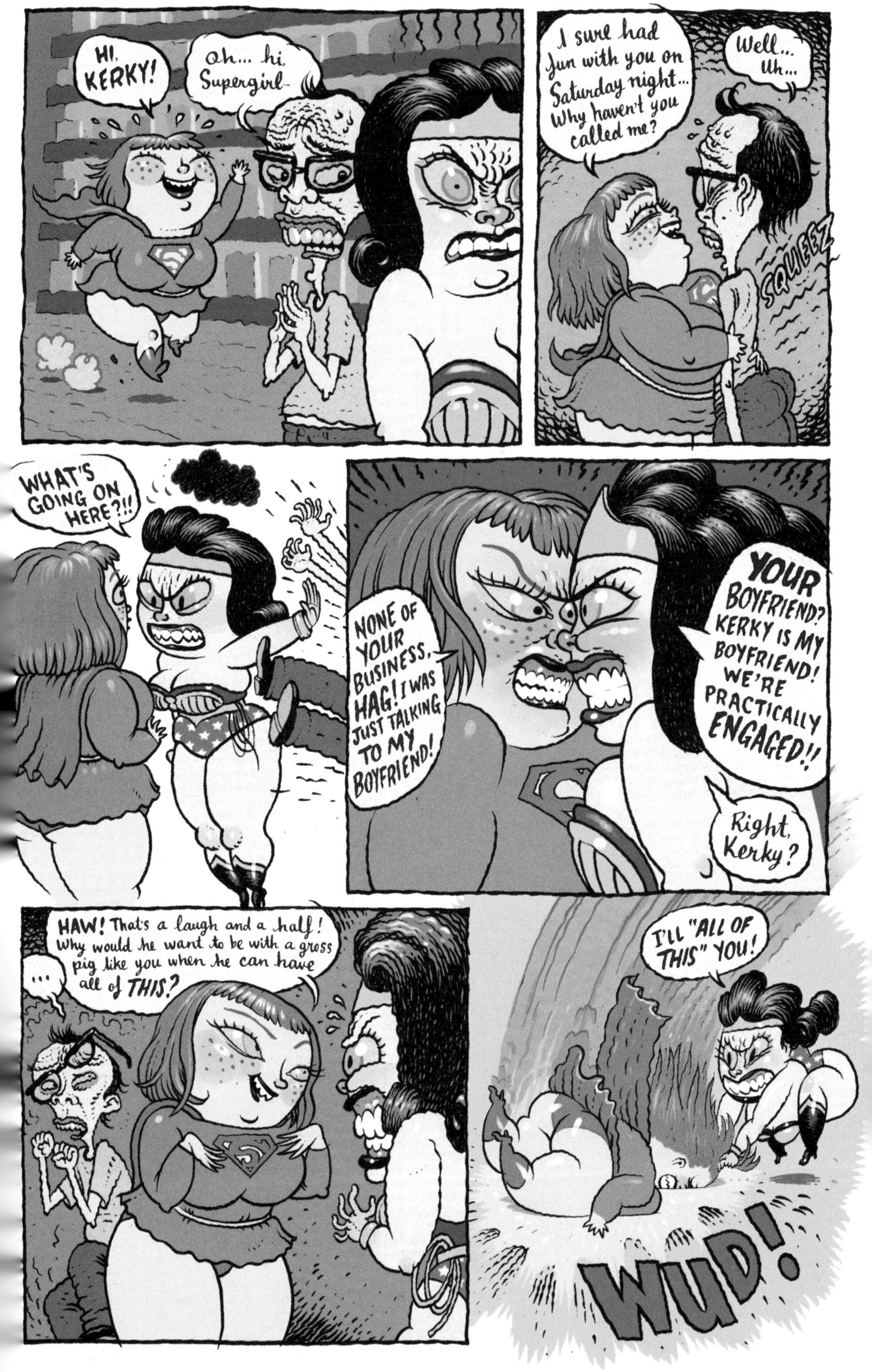

HI, KERKY!
Oh... hi, Supergirl...
I sure had fun with you on Saturday night... Why haven't you called me?
Well... Uh...
SQUEEZ
WHAT'S GOING ON HERE?!!
NONE OF YOUR BUSINESS, HAG! I WAS JUST TALKING TO MY BOYFRIEND!
YOUR BOYFRIEND? KERKY IS MY BOYFRIEND! WE'RE PRACTICALLY ENGAGED!!
Right, Kerky?
HAW! That's a laugh and a half! Why would he want to be with a gross pig like you when he can have all of THIS?
...
I'LL "ALL OF THIS" YOU!
WUD!

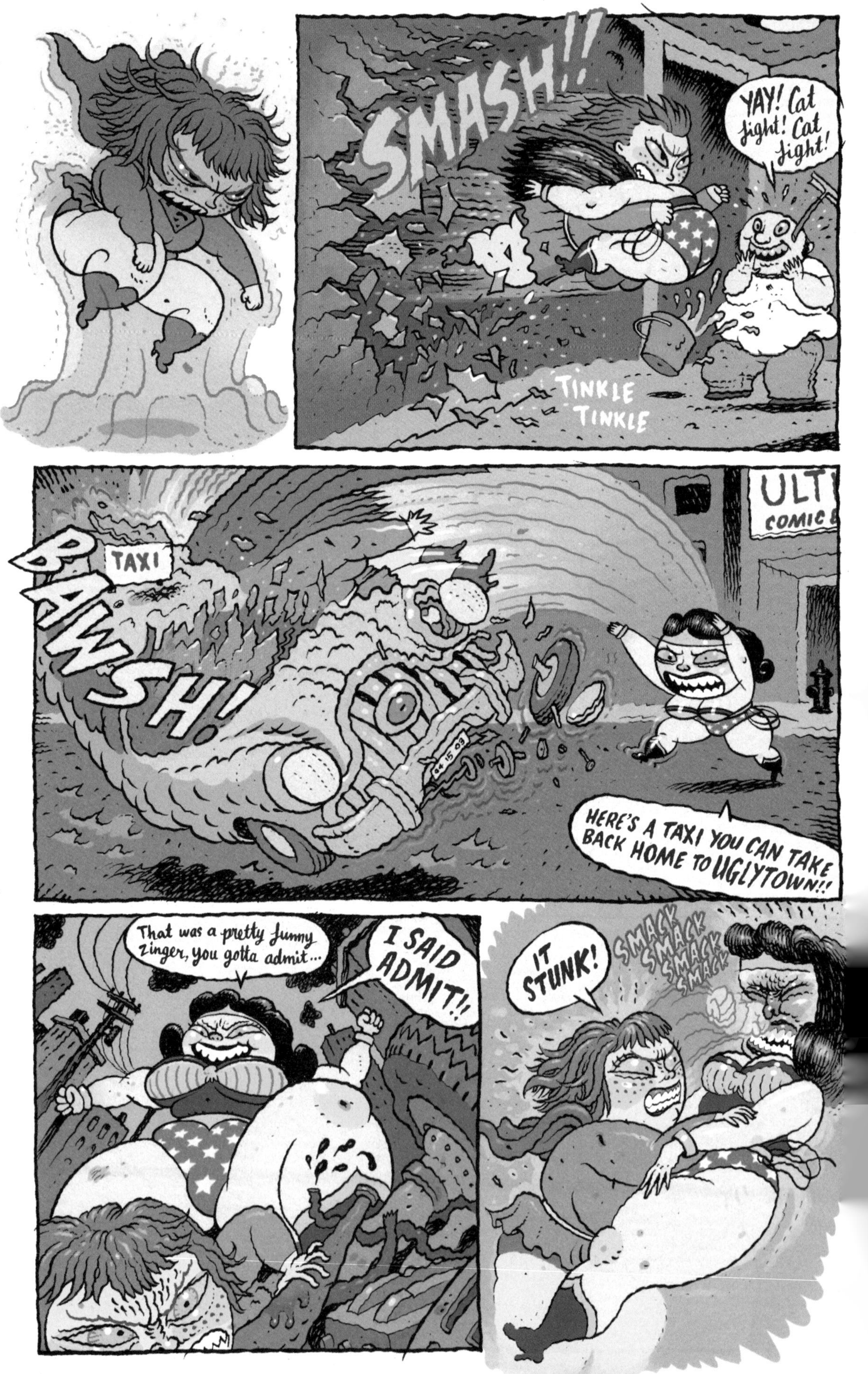
SMASH!!
YAY! Cat fight! Cat fight!
TINKLE TINKLE
TAXI
ULT
COMIC
BAWSH!
HERE'S A TAXI YOU CAN TAKE BACK HOME TO UGLYTOWN!!
That was a pretty funny zinger, you gotta admit...
I SAID ADMIT!!
IT STUNK!
SMACK SMACK SMACK SMACK

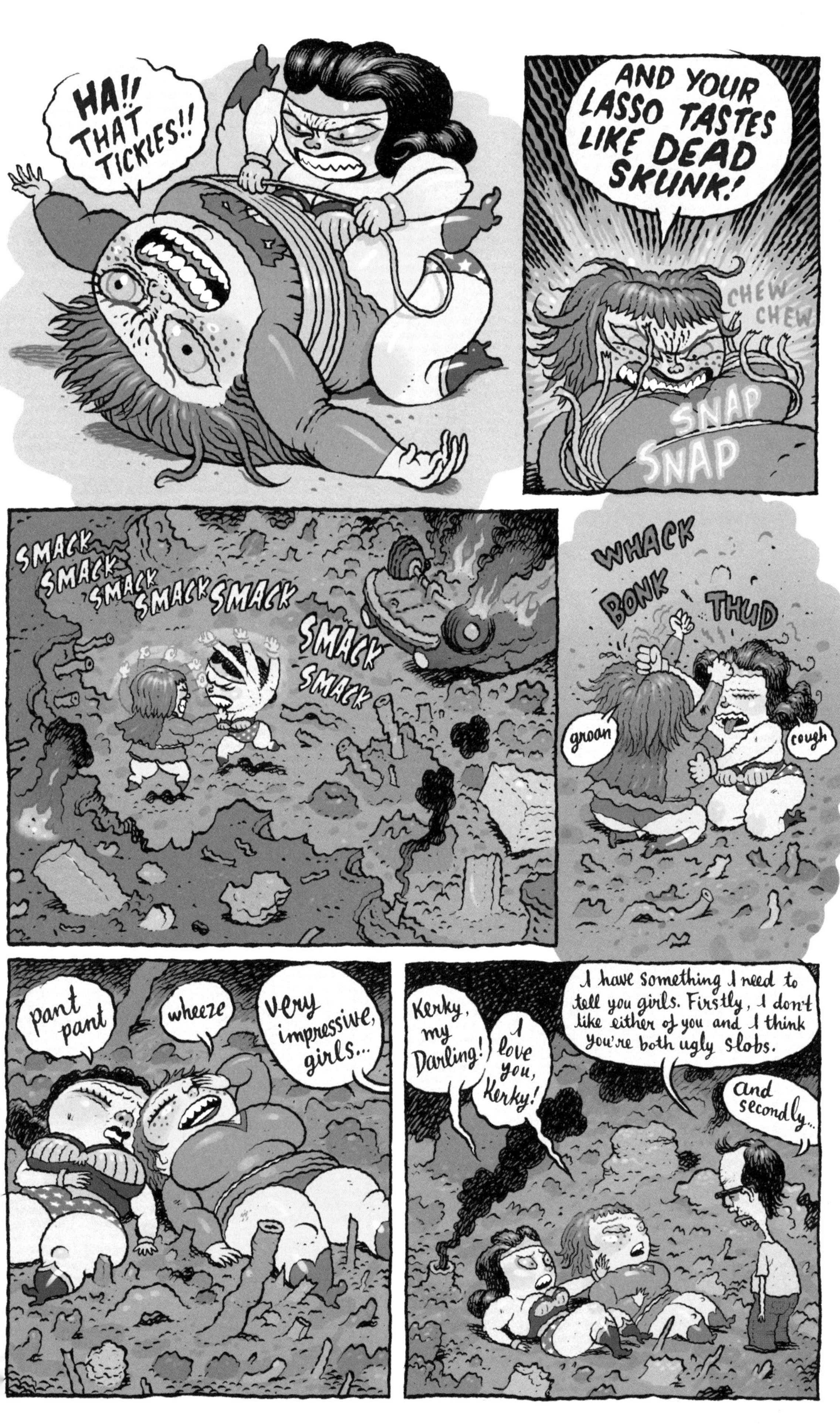

HA!! THAT TICKLES!!
AND YOUR LASSO TASTES LIKE DEAD SKUNK!
CHEW CHEW
SNAP SNAP
SMACK SMACK SMACK SMACK SMACK
SMACK SMACK
WHACK
BONK
THUD
groan
cough
pant pant
wheeze
Very impressive, girls...
Kerky, my Darling!
I love you, Kerky!
I have something I need to tell you girls. Firstly, I don't like either of you and I think you're both ugly slobs.
And secondly...

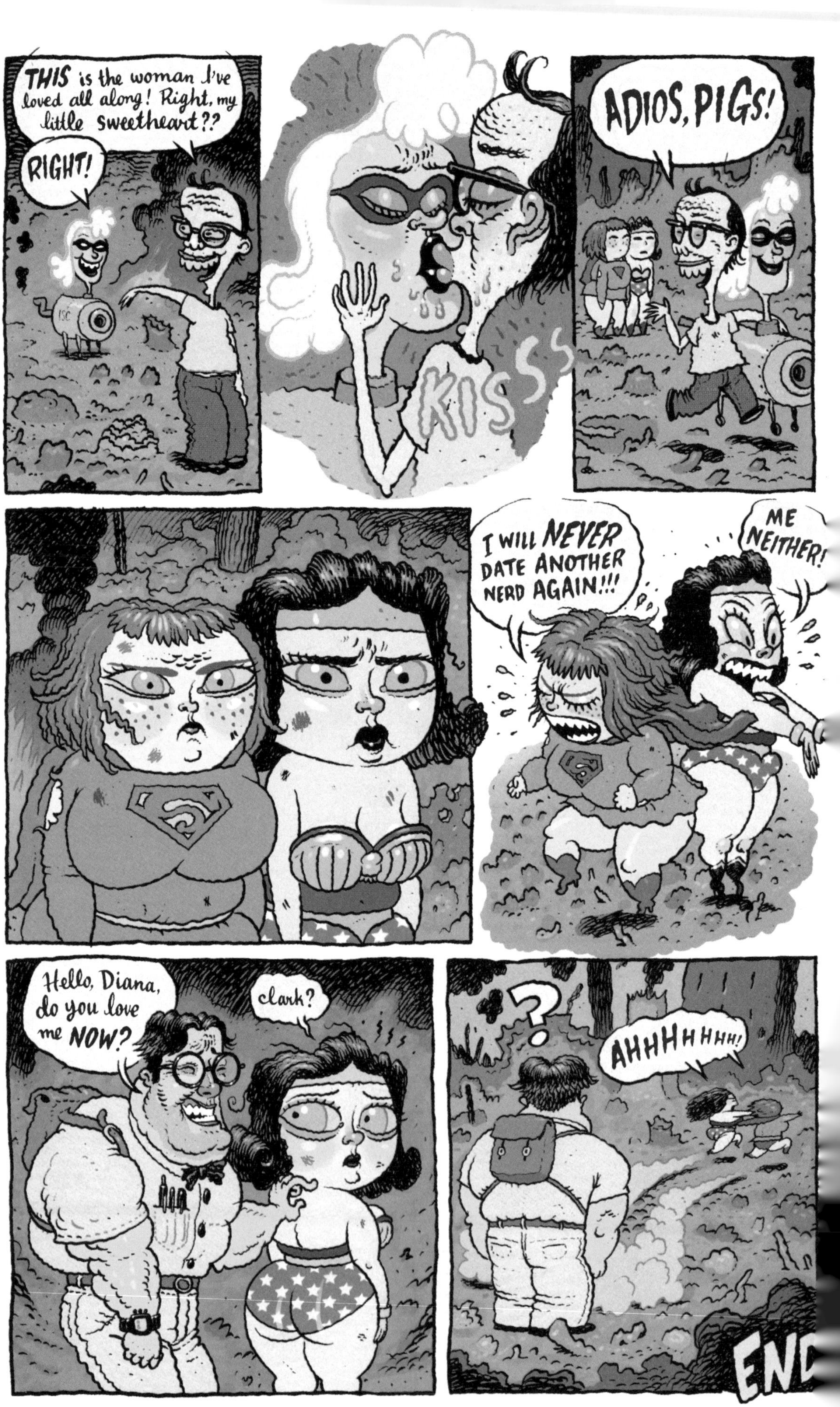
THIS is the woman I've loved all along! Right, my little sweetheart??
RIGHT!
KISSS
ADIOS, PIGS!
I WILL NEVER DATE ANOTHER NERD AGAIN!!!
ME NEITHER!
Hello, Diana, do you love me NOW?
clark?
?
AHHHHHHH!
END

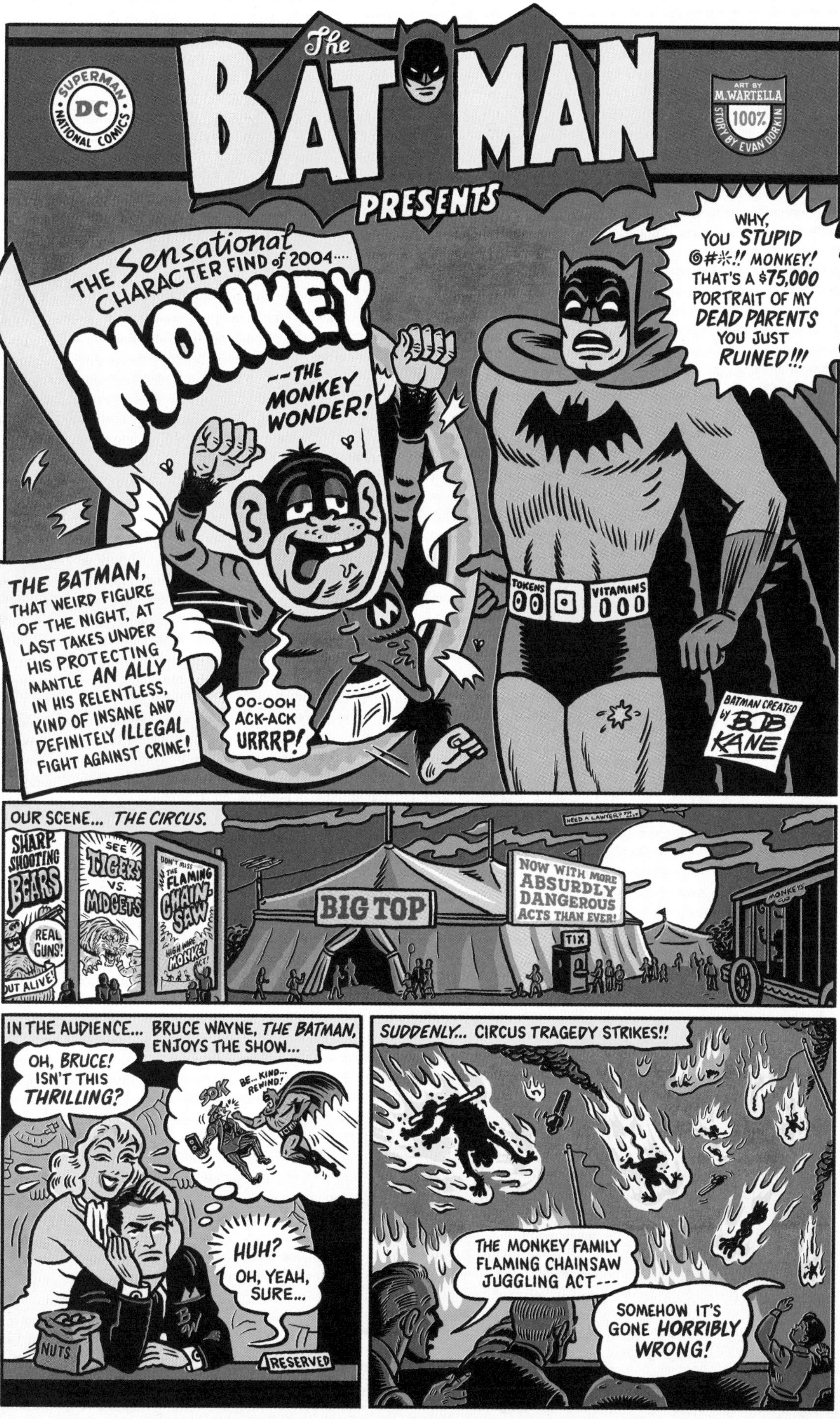

SUPERMAN DC NATIONAL COMICS
The BATMAN PRESENTS
ART BY M. WARTELLA 100% STORY BY EVAN DORKIN
THE Sensational CHARACTER FIND of 2004....
MONKEY --THE MONKEY WONDER!
WHY, YOU STUPID @#*!! MONKEY! THAT'S A $75,000 PORTRAIT OF MY DEAD PARENTS YOU JUST RUINED!!!
TOKENS VITAMINS
THE BATMAN, THAT WEIRD FIGURE OF THE NIGHT, AT LAST TAKES UNDER HIS PROTECTING MANTLE AN ALLY IN HIS RELENTLESS, KIND OF INSANE AND DEFINITELY ILLEGAL FIGHT AGAINST CRIME!
OO-OOH ACK-ACK URRRP!
BATMAN CREATED by BOB KANE
OUR SCENE... THE CIRCUS.
SHARP-SHOOTING BEARS REAL GUNS! OUT ALIVE!
SEE TIGERS VS. MIDGETS
DON'T MISS THE FLAMING CHAIN-SAW HIGH WIRE MONKEY ACT!
BIG TOP
NOW WITH MORE ABSURDLY DANGEROUS ACTS THAN EVER!
TIX
MONKEYS
NEED A LAWYER?
IN THE AUDIENCE... BRUCE WAYNE, THE BATMAN, ENJOYS THE SHOW...
OH, BRUCE! ISN'T THIS THRILLING?
SOK
BE... KIND... REWIND!
HUH? OH, YEAH, SURE...
NUTS
RESERVED
SUDDENLY... CIRCUS TRAGEDY STRIKES!!
THE MONKEY FAMILY FLAMING CHAINSAW JUGGLING ACT---
SOMEHOW IT'S GONE HORRIBLY WRONG!

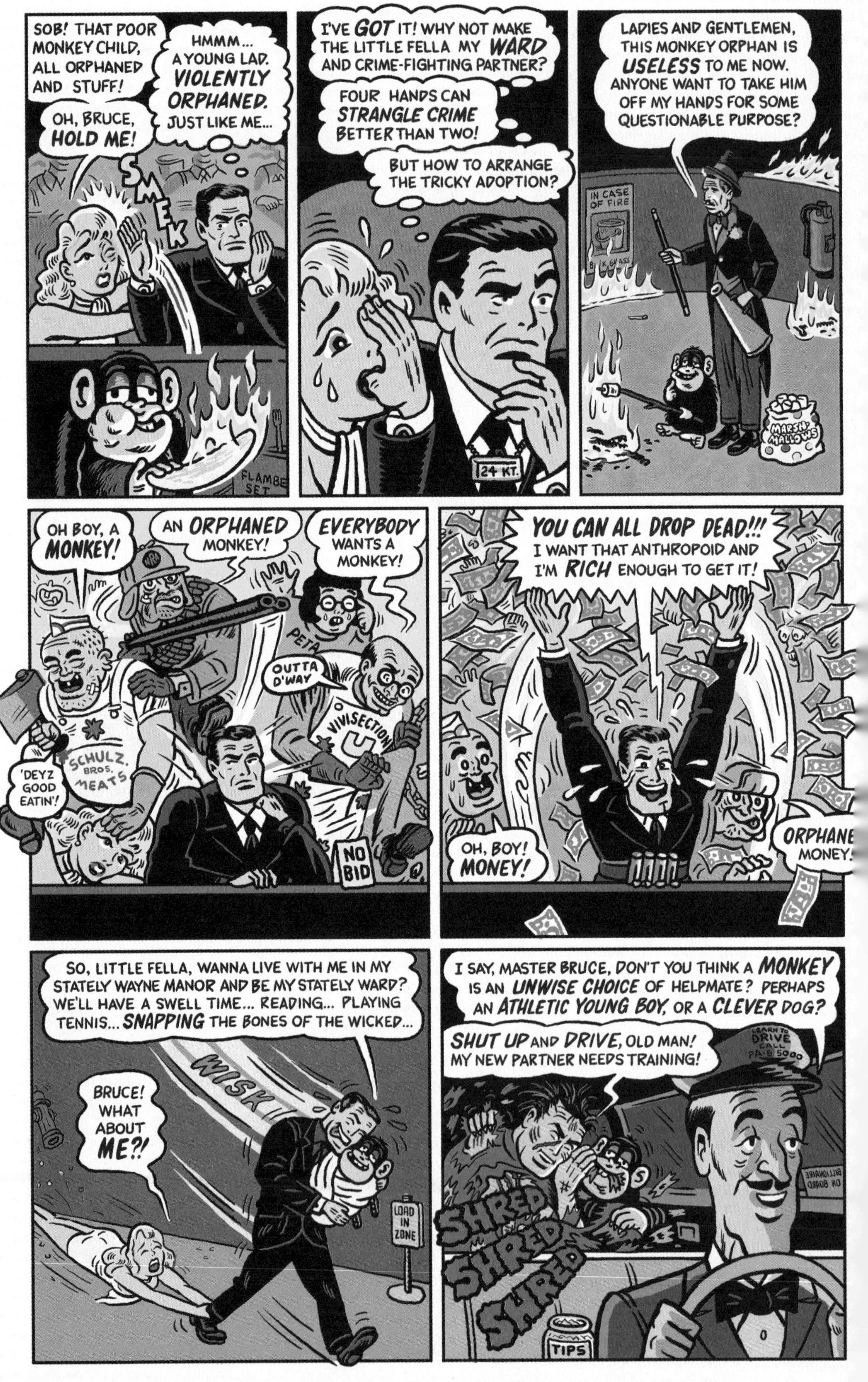

SOB! THAT POOR MONKEY CHILD, ALL ORPHANED AND STUFF!
HMMM... A YOUNG LAD. VIOLENTLY ORPHANED. JUST LIKE ME...
OH, BRUCE, HOLD ME!
SMEK
FLAMBE SET
I'VE GOT IT! WHY NOT MAKE THE LITTLE FELLA MY WARD AND CRIME-FIGHTING PARTNER?
FOUR HANDS CAN STRANGLE CRIME BETTER THAN TWO!
BUT HOW TO ARRANGE THE TRICKY ADOPTION?
24 KT.
LADIES AND GENTLEMEN, THIS MONKEY ORPHAN IS USELESS TO ME NOW. ANYONE WANT TO TAKE HIM OFF MY HANDS FOR SOME QUESTIONABLE PURPOSE?
IN CASE OF FIRE
MARSH-MALLOWS
OH BOY, A MONKEY!
AN ORPHANED MONKEY!
EVERYBODY WANTS A MONKEY!
PETA
OUTTA D'WAY
VIVISECTION U
SCHULZ BROS. MEATS
'DEYZ GOOD EATIN'!
NO BID
YOU CAN ALL DROP DEAD!!! I WANT THAT ANTHROPOID AND I'M RICH ENOUGH TO GET IT!
OH, BOY! MONEY!
ORPHANE MONEY!
SO, LITTLE FELLA, WANNA LIVE WITH ME IN MY STATELY WAYNE MANOR AND BE MY STATELY WARD? WE'LL HAVE A SWELL TIME... READING... PLAYING TENNIS... SNAPPING THE BONES OF THE WICKED...
WISK
BRUCE! WHAT ABOUT ME?!
LOAD IN ZONE
I SAY, MASTER BRUCE, DON'T YOU THINK A MONKEY IS AN UNWISE CHOICE OF HELPMATE? PERHAPS AN ATHLETIC YOUNG BOY, OR A CLEVER DOG?
SHUT UP AND DRIVE, OLD MAN! MY NEW PARTNER NEEDS TRAINING!
LEARN TO DRIVE CALL PA-6 5000
SHRED SHRED SHRED
TIPS

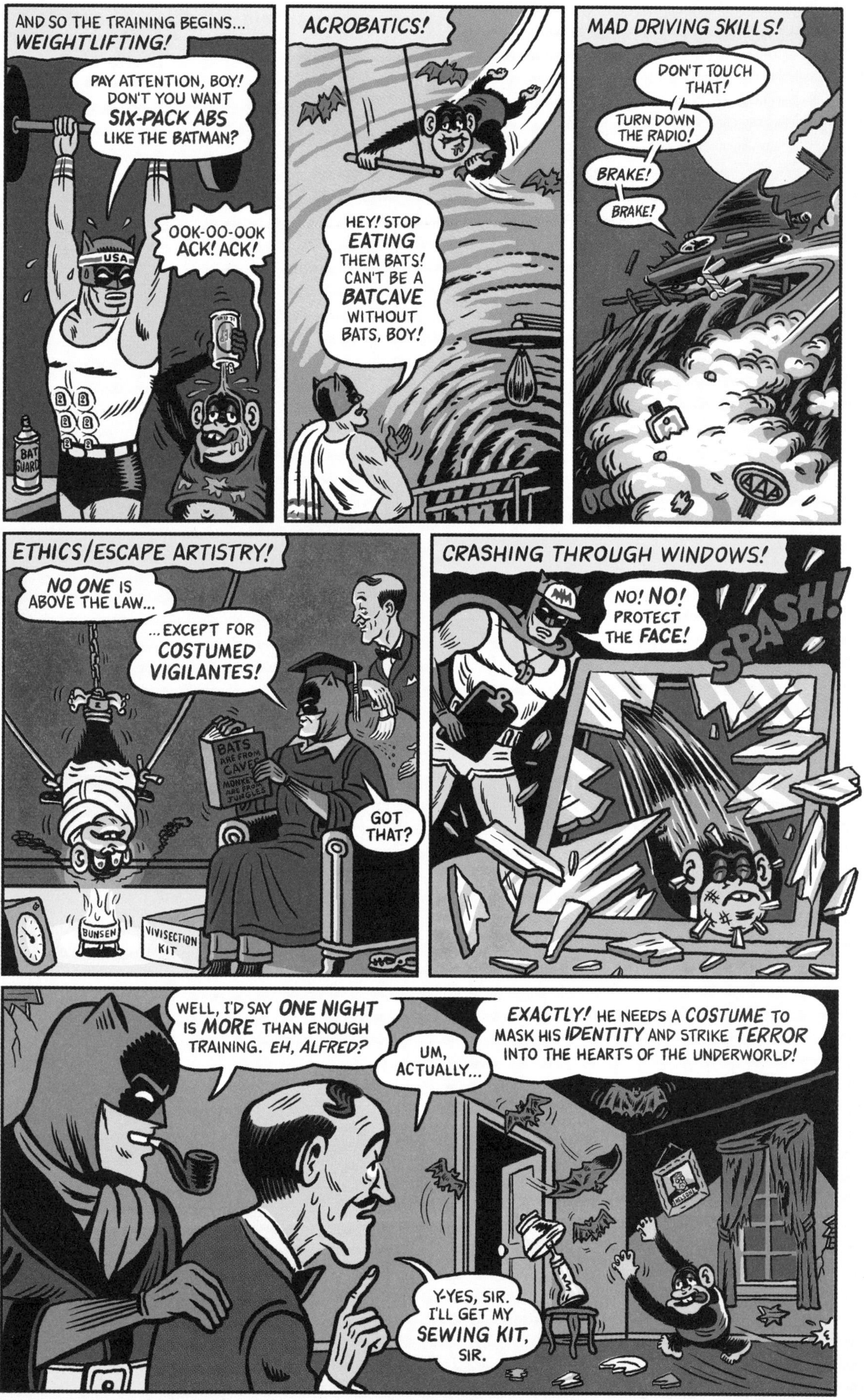
AND SO THE TRAINING BEGINS... WEIGHTLIFTING!
PAY ATTENTION, BOY! DON'T YOU WANT SIX-PACK ABS LIKE THE BATMAN?
OOK-OO-OOK ACK! ACK!
USA
BAT GUARD
ACROBATICS!
HEY! STOP EATING THEM BATS! CAN'T BE A BATCAVE WITHOUT BATS, BOY!
MAD DRIVING SKILLS!
DON'T TOUCH THAT!
TURN DOWN THE RADIO!
BRAKE!
BRAKE!
AAA
ETHICS/ESCAPE ARTISTRY!
NO ONE IS ABOVE THE LAW...
...EXCEPT FOR COSTUMED VIGILANTES!
BATS ARE FROM CAVES MONKEYS ARE FROM JUNGLES
GOT THAT?
BUNSEN
VIVISECTION KIT
CRASHING THROUGH WINDOWS!
NO! NO! PROTECT THE FACE!
SPASH!
WELL, I'D SAY ONE NIGHT IS MORE THAN ENOUGH TRAINING. EH, ALFRED?
UM, ACTUALLY...
EXACTLY! HE NEEDS A COSTUME TO MASK HIS IDENTITY AND STRIKE TERROR INTO THE HEARTS OF THE UNDERWORLD!
Y-YES, SIR. I'LL GET MY SEWING KIT, SIR.

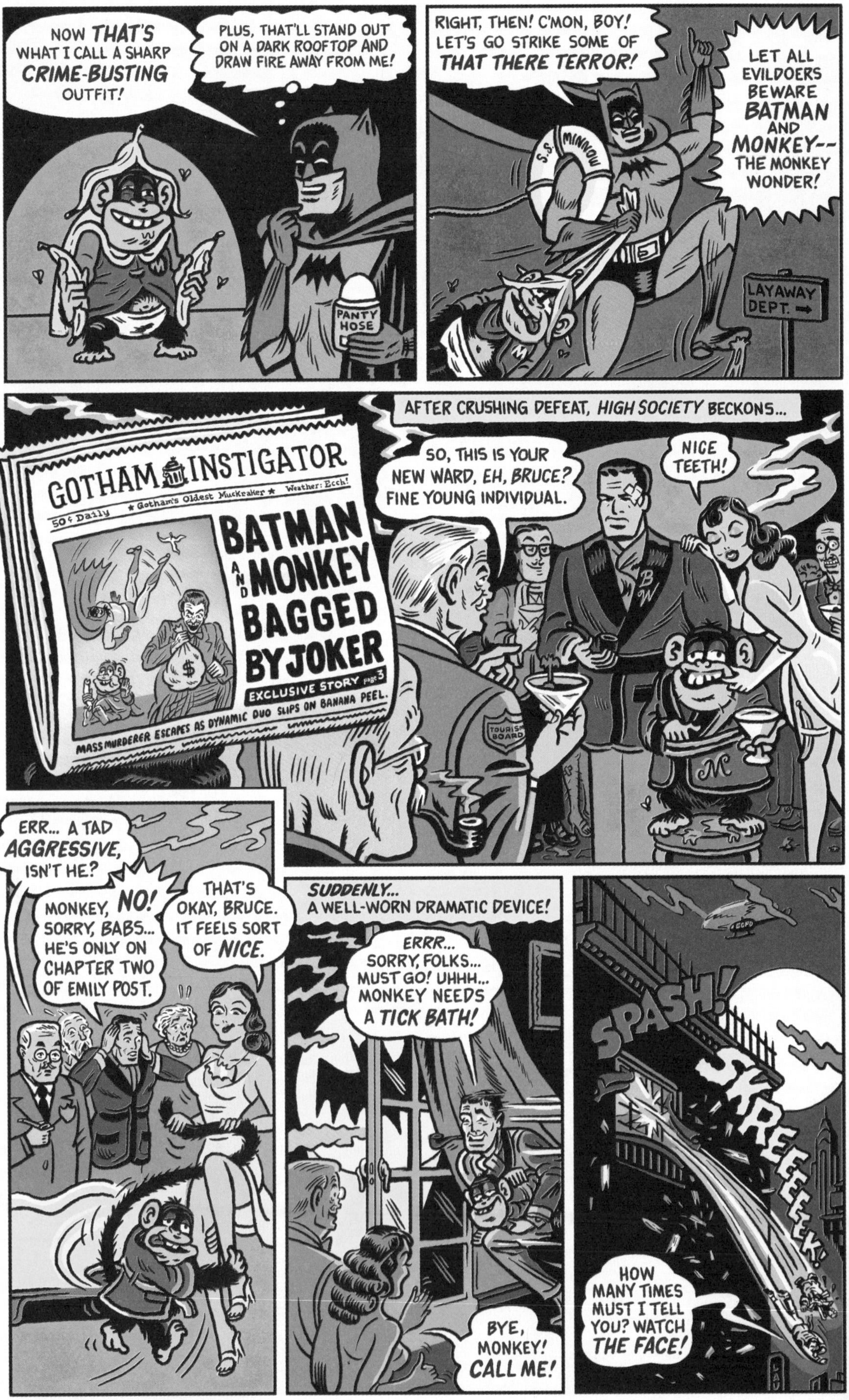
NOW THAT'S WHAT I CALL A SHARP CRIME-BUSTING OUTFIT!
PLUS, THAT'LL STAND OUT ON A DARK ROOFTOP AND DRAW FIRE AWAY FROM ME!
PANTY HOSE
RIGHT, THEN! C'MON, BOY! LET'S GO STRIKE SOME OF THAT THERE TERROR!
LET ALL EVILDOERS BEWARE BATMAN AND MONKEY-- THE MONKEY WONDER!
S.S. MINNOW
LAYAWAY DEPT. →
AFTER CRUSHING DEFEAT, HIGH SOCIETY BECKONS...
GOTHAM INSTIGATOR
50¢ Daily ★ Gotham's Oldest Muckraker ★ Weather: Ecch!
BATMAN AND MONKEY BAGGED BY JOKER
EXCLUSIVE STORY page 3
MASS MURDERER ESCAPES AS DYNAMIC DUO SLIPS ON BANANA PEEL.
SO, THIS IS YOUR NEW WARD, EH, BRUCE? FINE YOUNG INDIVIDUAL.
NICE TEETH!
TOURISM BOARD
ERR... A TAD AGGRESSIVE, ISN'T HE?
MONKEY, NO! SORRY, BABS... HE'S ONLY ON CHAPTER TWO OF EMILY POST.
THAT'S OKAY, BRUCE. IT FEELS SORT OF NICE.
SUDDENLY... A WELL-WORN DRAMATIC DEVICE!
ERRR... SORRY, FOLKS... MUST GO! UHHH... MONKEY NEEDS A TICK BATH!
BYE, MONKEY! CALL ME!
SPASH!
SKREEEEK!
HOW MANY TIMES MUST I TELL YOU? WATCH THE FACE!

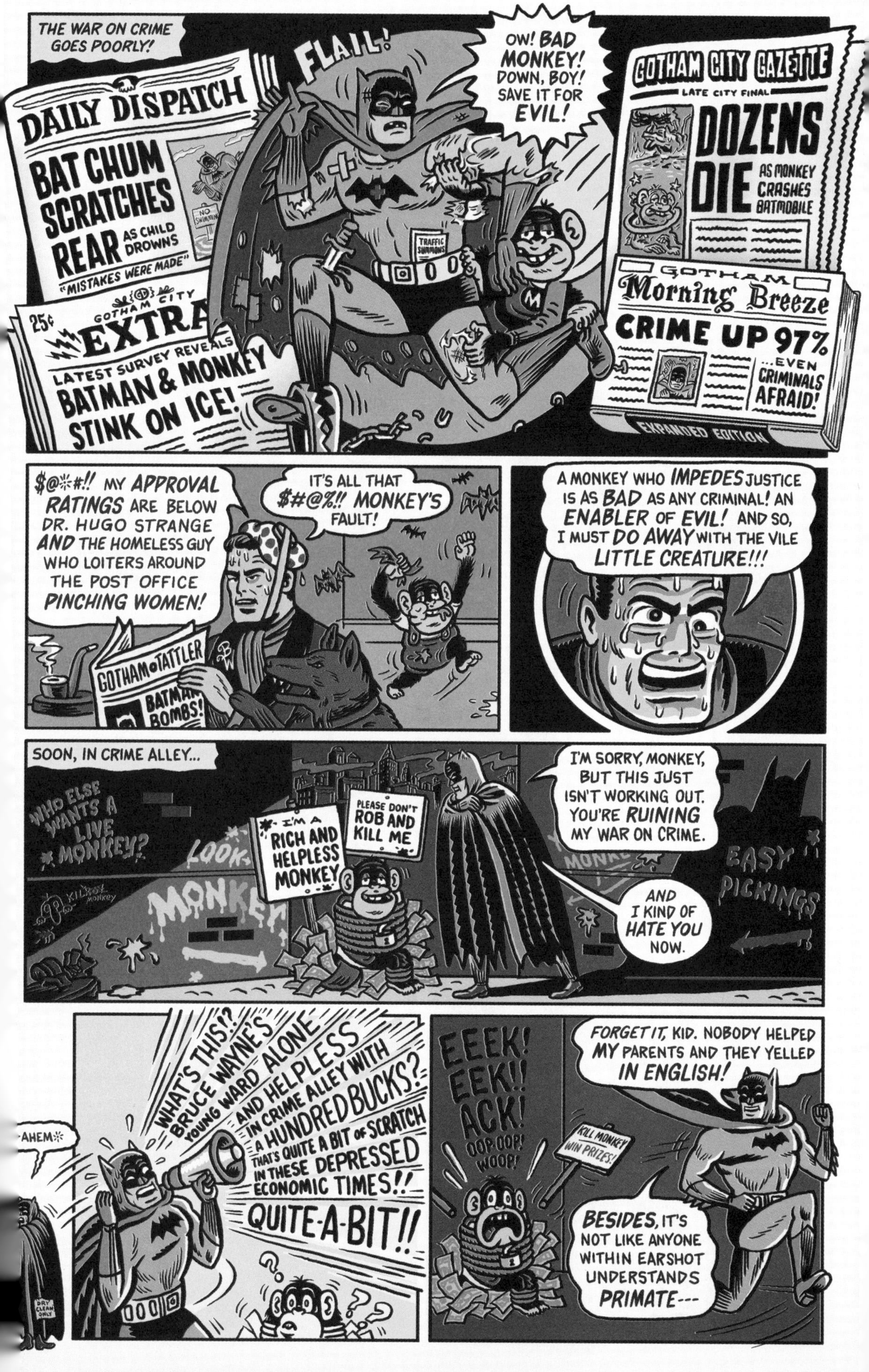

THE WAR ON CRIME GOES POORLY!
DAILY DISPATCH
BAT CHUM SCRATCHES REAR AS CHILD DROWNS
"MISTAKES WERE MADE"
NO SWIMMING
FLAIL!
OW! BAD MONKEY! DOWN, BOY! SAVE IT FOR EVIL!
TRAFFIC SUMMONS
GOTHAM CITY GAZETTE
LATE CITY FINAL
DOZENS DIE AS MONKEY CRASHES BATMOBILE
25¢
GOTHAM CITY EXTRA
LATEST SURVEY REVEALS BATMAN & MONKEY STINK ON ICE!
GOTHAM Morning Breeze
CRIME UP 97%
...EVEN CRIMINALS AFRAID!
EXPANDED EDITION
$@*#!! MY APPROVAL RATINGS ARE BELOW DR. HUGO STRANGE AND THE HOMELESS GUY WHO LOITERS AROUND THE POST OFFICE PINCHING WOMEN!
IT'S ALL THAT $#@%!! MONKEY'S FAULT!
GOTHAM TATTLER
BATMAN BOMBS!
A MONKEY WHO IMPEDES JUSTICE IS AS BAD AS ANY CRIMINAL! AN ENABLER OF EVIL! AND SO, I MUST DO AWAY WITH THE VILE LITTLE CREATURE!!!
SOON, IN CRIME ALLEY...
WHO ELSE WANTS A LIVE MONKEY?
LOOK
MONKEY
KILROY monkey
I'M A RICH AND HELPLESS MONKEY
PLEASE DON'T ROB AND KILL ME
I'M SORRY, MONKEY, BUT THIS JUST ISN'T WORKING OUT. YOU'RE RUINING MY WAR ON CRIME.
AND I KIND OF HATE YOU NOW.
EASY PICKINGS
AHEM
WHAT'S THIS!? BRUCE WAYNE'S YOUNG WARD ALONE AND HELPLESS IN CRIME ALLEY WITH A HUNDRED BUCKS? THAT'S QUITE A BIT OF SCRATCH IN THESE DEPRESSED ECONOMIC TIMES!!
QUITE-A-BIT!!
DRY CLEAN ONLY
EEEK! EEK!! ACK! OOP OOP! WOOP!
KILL MONKEY WIN PRIZES!
FORGET IT, KID. NOBODY HELPED MY PARENTS AND THEY YELLED IN ENGLISH!
BESIDES, IT'S NOT LIKE ANYONE WITHIN EARSHOT UNDERSTANDS PRIMATE---

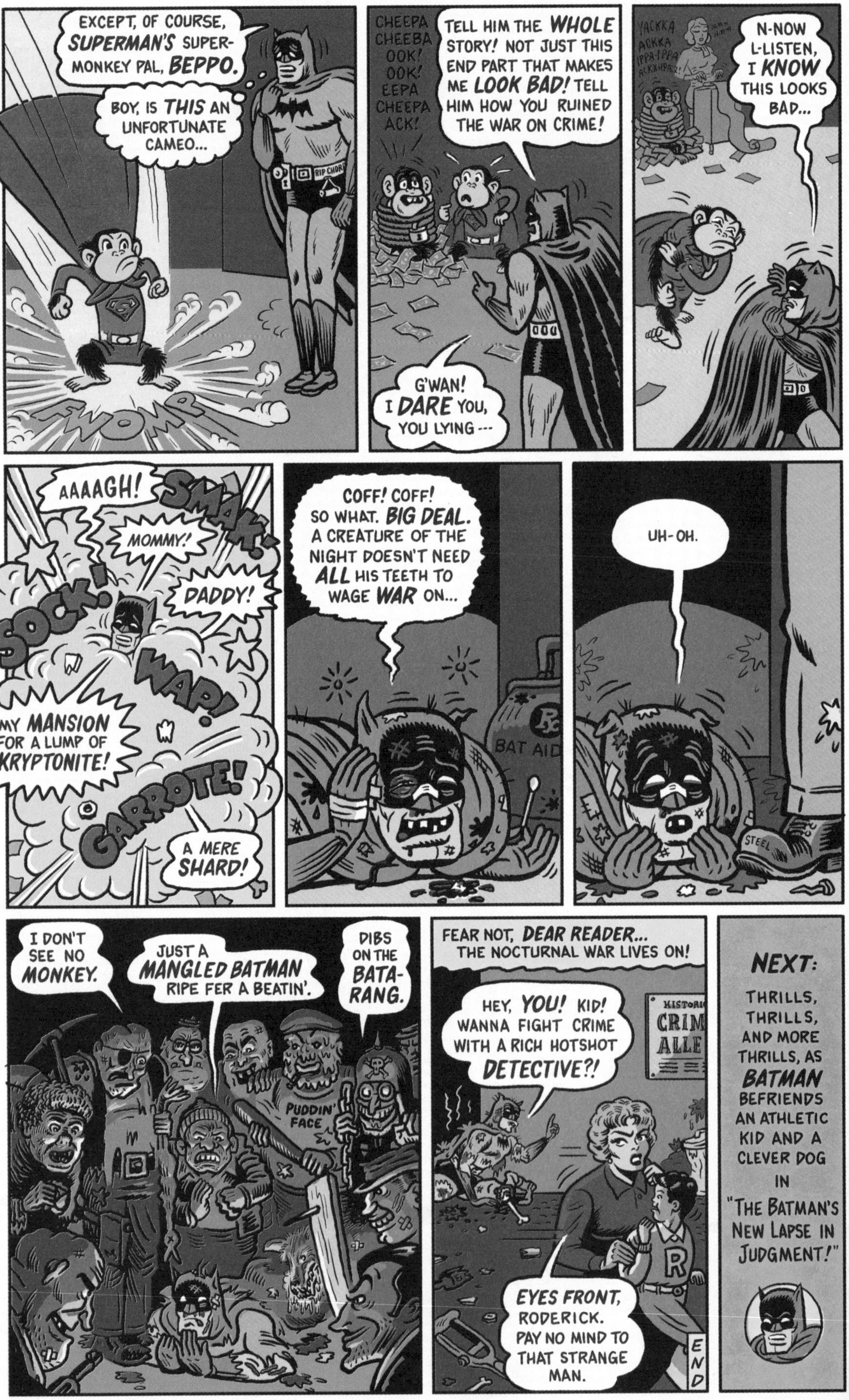

EXCEPT, OF COURSE, SUPERMAN'S SUPER-MONKEY PAL, BEPPO.
BOY, IS THIS AN UNFORTUNATE CAMEO...
RIP CHORD
FWOMP
CHEEPA CHEEBA OOK! OOK! EEPA CHEEPA ACK!
TELL HIM THE WHOLE STORY! NOT JUST THIS END PART THAT MAKES ME LOOK BAD! TELL HIM HOW YOU RUINED THE WAR ON CRIME!
G'WAN! I DARE YOU, YOU LYING ---
YACKKA ACKKA IPPA-IPPA ACKKHPPA!!
N-NOW L-LISTEN, I KNOW THIS LOOKS BAD...
AAAAGH!
SMAK!
MOMMY!
SOCK!
DADDY!
WAP!
MY MANSION FOR A LUMP OF KRYPTONITE!
GARROTE!
A MERE SHARD!
COFF! COFF! SO WHAT. BIG DEAL. A CREATURE OF THE NIGHT DOESN'T NEED ALL HIS TEETH TO WAGE WAR ON...
BAT AID
UH-OH.
STEEL
I DON'T SEE NO MONKEY.
JUST A MANGLED BATMAN RIPE FER A BEATIN'.
DIBS ON THE BATA-RANG.
PUDDIN' FACE
FEAR NOT, DEAR READER... THE NOCTURNAL WAR LIVES ON!
HEY, YOU! KID! WANNA FIGHT CRIME WITH A RICH HOTSHOT DETECTIVE?!
HISTORIC CRIM ALLE
EYES FRONT, RODERICK. PAY NO MIND TO THAT STRANGE MAN.
END
NEXT: THRILLS, THRILLS, AND MORE THRILLS, AS BATMAN BEFRIENDS AN ATHLETIC KID AND A CLEVER DOG IN "THE BATMAN'S NEW LAPSE IN JUDGMENT!"

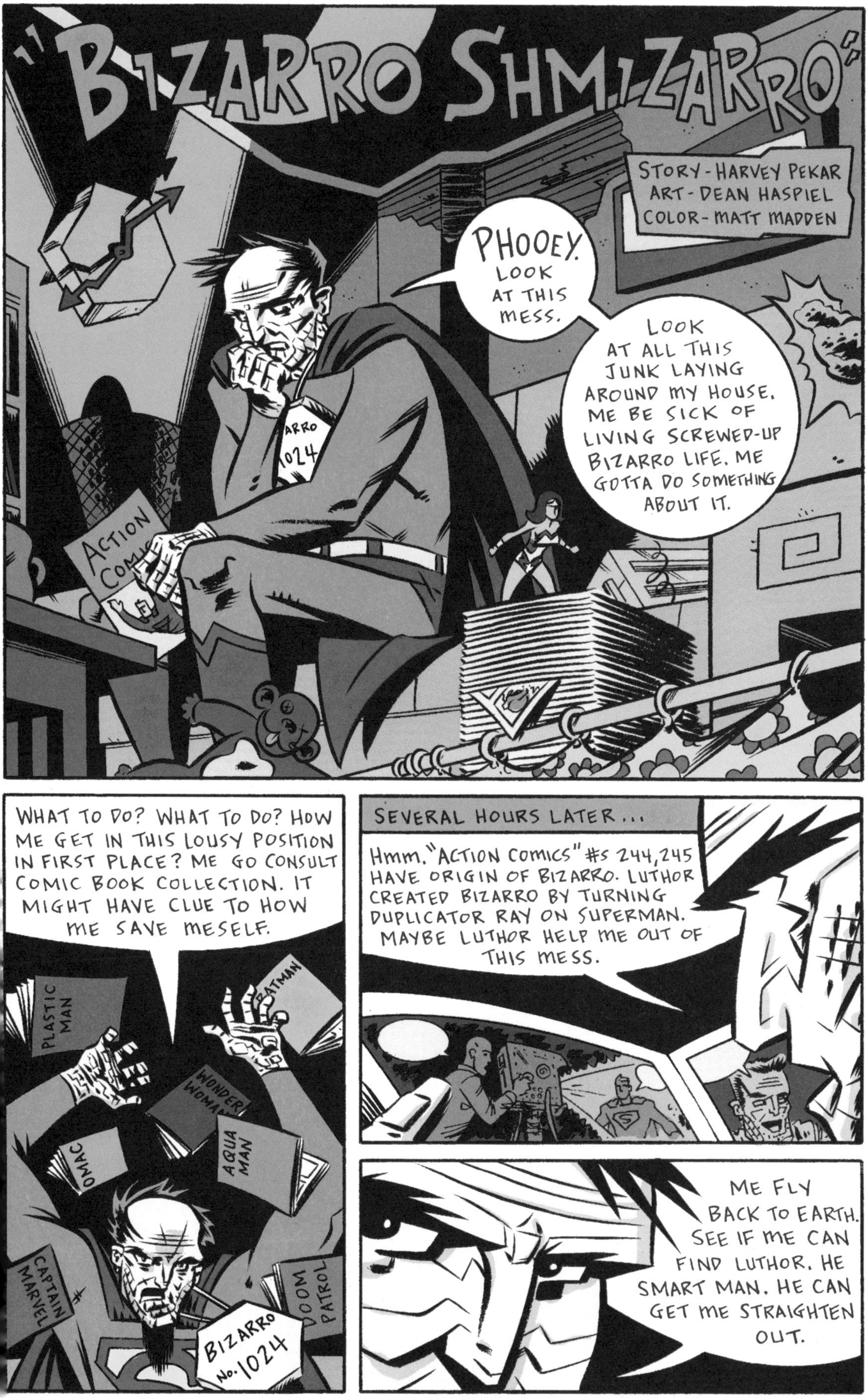
"BIZARRO SHMIZARRO"
STORY - HARVEY PEKAR
ART - DEAN HASPIEL
COLOR - MATT MADDEN
PHOOEY. LOOK AT THIS MESS.
LOOK AT ALL THIS JUNK LAYING AROUND MY HOUSE. ME BE SICK OF LIVING SCREWED-UP BIZARRO LIFE. ME GOTTA DO SOMETHING ABOUT IT.
ACTION COMICS
WHAT TO DO? WHAT TO DO? HOW ME GET IN THIS LOUSY POSITION IN FIRST PLACE? ME GO CONSULT COMIC BOOK COLLECTION. IT MIGHT HAVE CLUE TO HOW ME SAVE MESELF.
PLASTIC MAN
BATMAN
WONDER WOMAN
OMAC
AQUA MAN
CAPTAIN MARVEL
DOOM PATROL
BIZARRO No. 1024
SEVERAL HOURS LATER...
Hmm. "ACTION COMICS" #s 244, 245 HAVE ORIGIN OF BIZARRO. LUTHOR CREATED BIZARRO BY TURNING DUPLICATOR RAY ON SUPERMAN. MAYBE LUTHOR HELP ME OUT OF THIS MESS.
ME FLY BACK TO EARTH. SEE IF ME CAN FIND LUTHOR. HE SMART MAN. HE CAN GET ME STRAIGHTEN OUT.

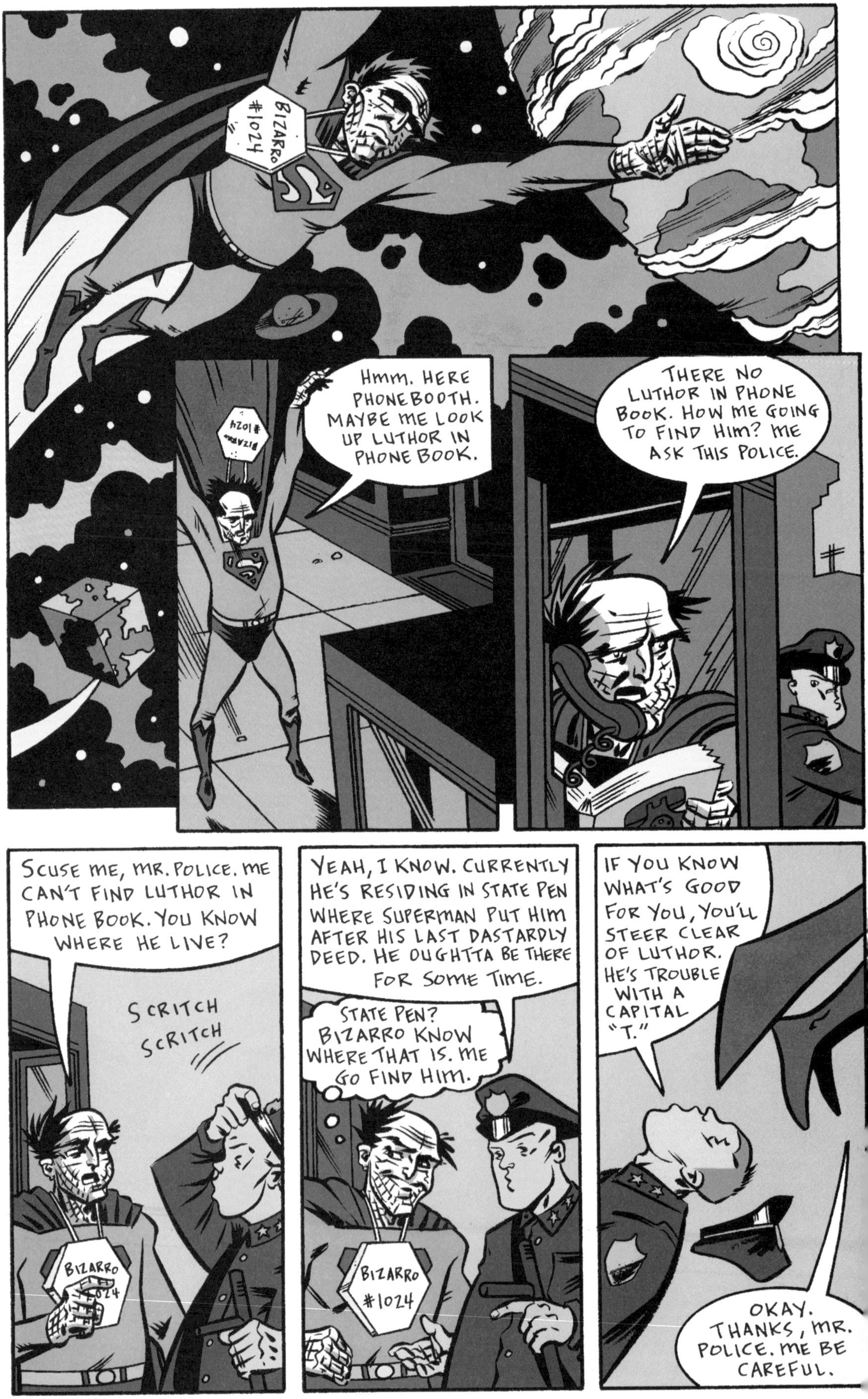
BIZARRO #1024
Hmm. HERE PHONEBOOTH. MAYBE ME LOOK UP LUTHOR IN PHONE BOOK.
THERE NO LUTHOR IN PHONE BOOK. HOW ME GOING TO FIND HIM? ME ASK THIS POLICE.
SCUSE ME, MR. POLICE. ME CAN'T FIND LUTHOR IN PHONE BOOK. YOU KNOW WHERE HE LIVE?
SCRITCH SCRITCH
BIZARRO #1024
YEAH, I KNOW. CURRENTLY HE'S RESIDING IN STATE PEN WHERE SUPERMAN PUT HIM AFTER HIS LAST DASTARDLY DEED. HE OUGHTTA BE THERE FOR SOME TIME.
STATE PEN? BIZARRO KNOW WHERE THAT IS. ME GO FIND HIM.
BIZARRO #1024
IF YOU KNOW WHAT'S GOOD FOR YOU, YOU'LL STEER CLEAR OF LUTHOR. HE'S TROUBLE WITH A CAPITAL "T."
OKAY. THANKS, MR. POLICE. ME BE CAREFUL.

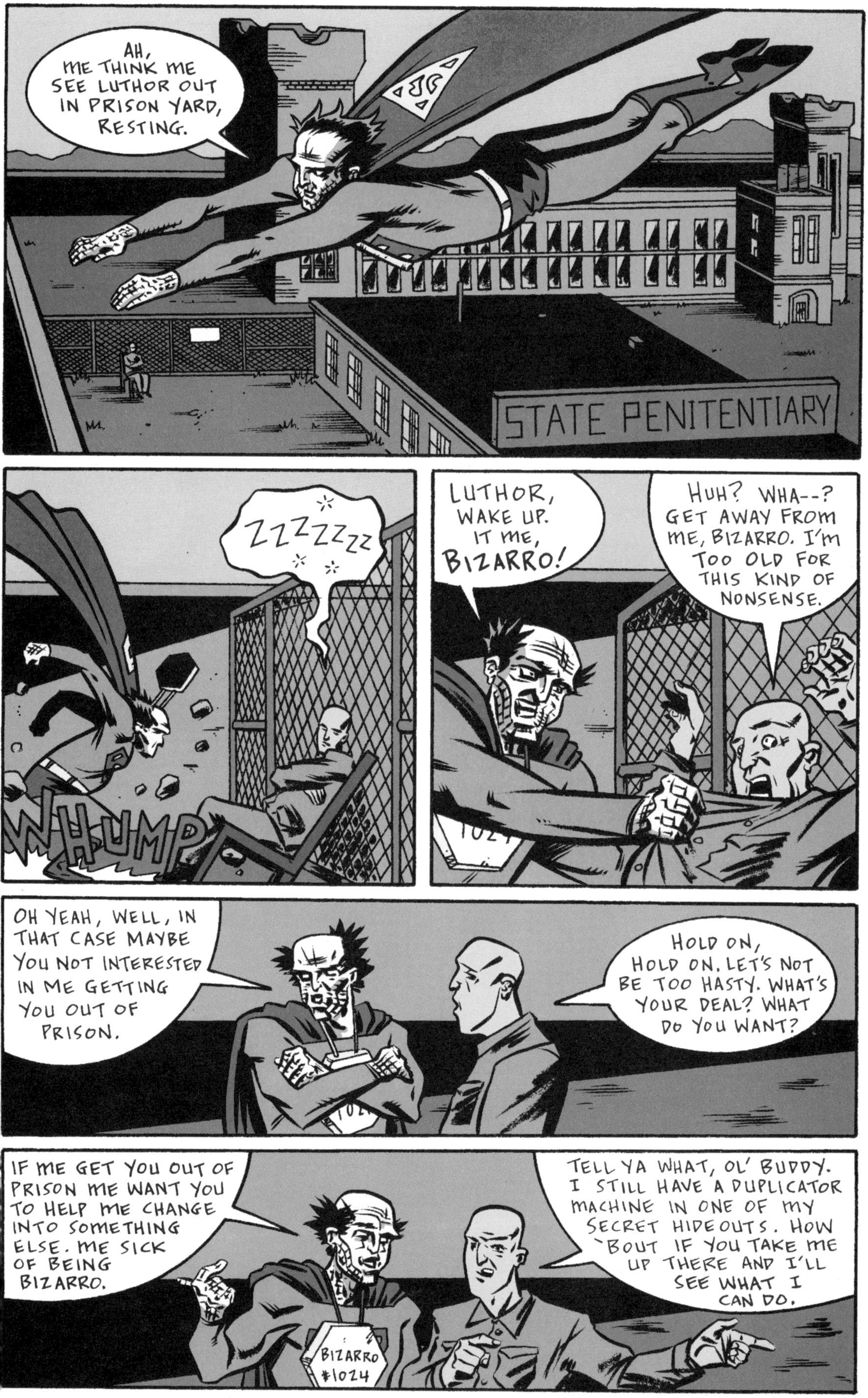
AH, ME THINK ME SEE LUTHOR OUT IN PRISON YARD, RESTING.
STATE PENITENTIARY
ZZZZZZZ
WHUMP
LUTHOR, WAKE UP. IT ME, BIZARRO!
HUH? WHA--? GET AWAY FROM ME, BIZARRO. I'M TOO OLD FOR THIS KIND OF NONSENSE.
OH YEAH, WELL, IN THAT CASE MAYBE YOU NOT INTERESTED IN ME GETTING YOU OUT OF PRISON.
HOLD ON, HOLD ON. LET'S NOT BE TOO HASTY. WHAT'S YOUR DEAL? WHAT DO YOU WANT?
IF ME GET YOU OUT OF PRISON ME WANT YOU TO HELP ME CHANGE INTO SOMETHING ELSE. ME SICK OF BEING BIZARRO.
TELL YA WHAT, OL' BUDDY. I STILL HAVE A DUPLICATOR MACHINE IN ONE OF MY SECRET HIDEOUTS. HOW 'BOUT IF YOU TAKE ME UP THERE AND I'LL SEE WHAT I CAN DO.
BIZARRO #1024

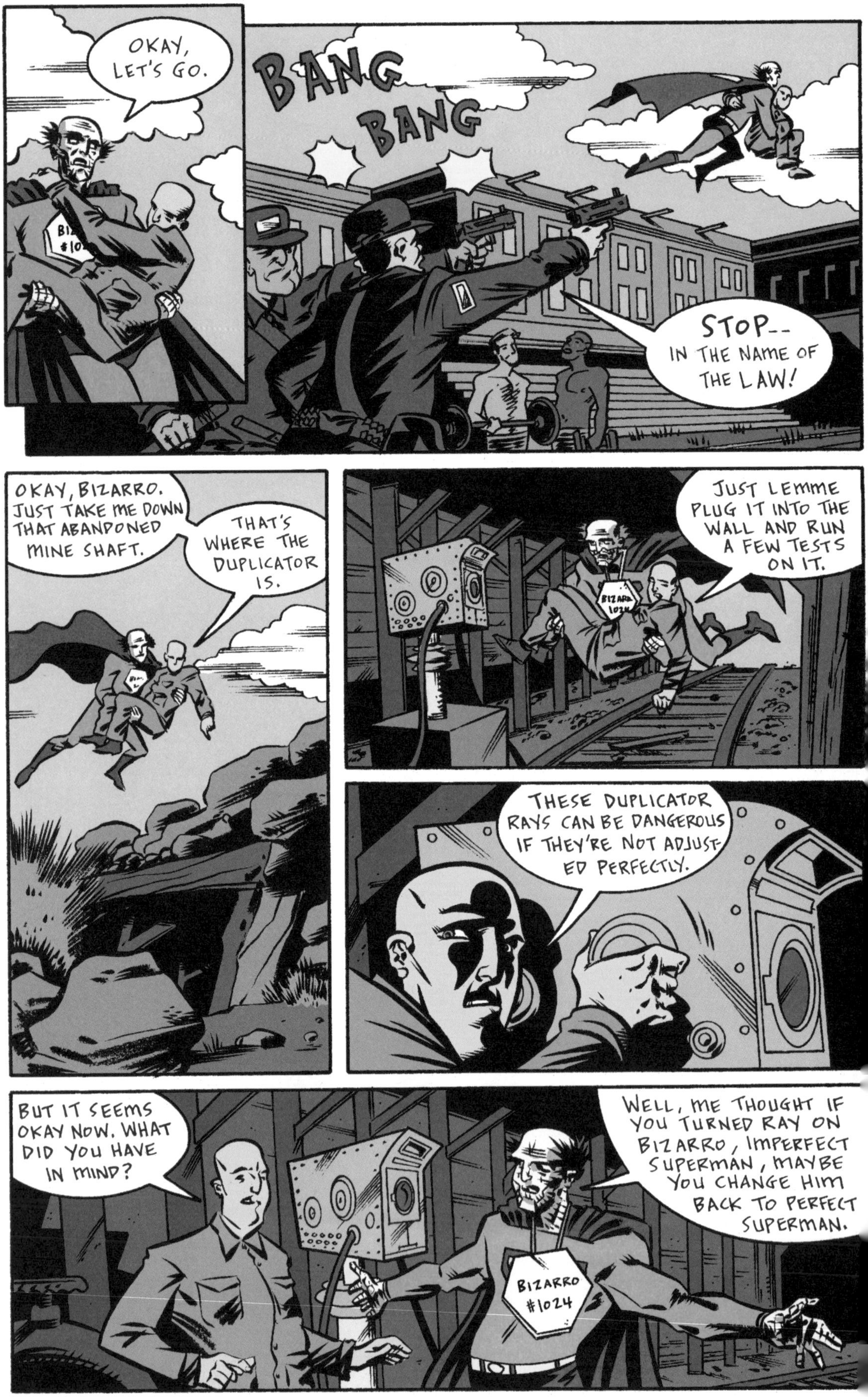
OKAY, LET'S GO.
BANG BANG
STOP-- IN THE NAME OF THE LAW!
OKAY, BIZARRO. JUST TAKE ME DOWN THAT ABANDONED MINE SHAFT.
THAT'S WHERE THE DUPLICATOR IS.
JUST LEMME PLUG IT INTO THE WALL AND RUN A FEW TESTS ON IT.
THESE DUPLICATOR RAYS CAN BE DANGEROUS IF THEY'RE NOT ADJUSTED PERFECTLY.
BUT IT SEEMS OKAY NOW. WHAT DID YOU HAVE IN MIND?
WELL, ME THOUGHT IF YOU TURNED RAY ON BIZARRO, IMPERFECT SUPERMAN, MAYBE YOU CHANGE HIM BACK TO PERFECT SUPERMAN.
BIZARRO #1024

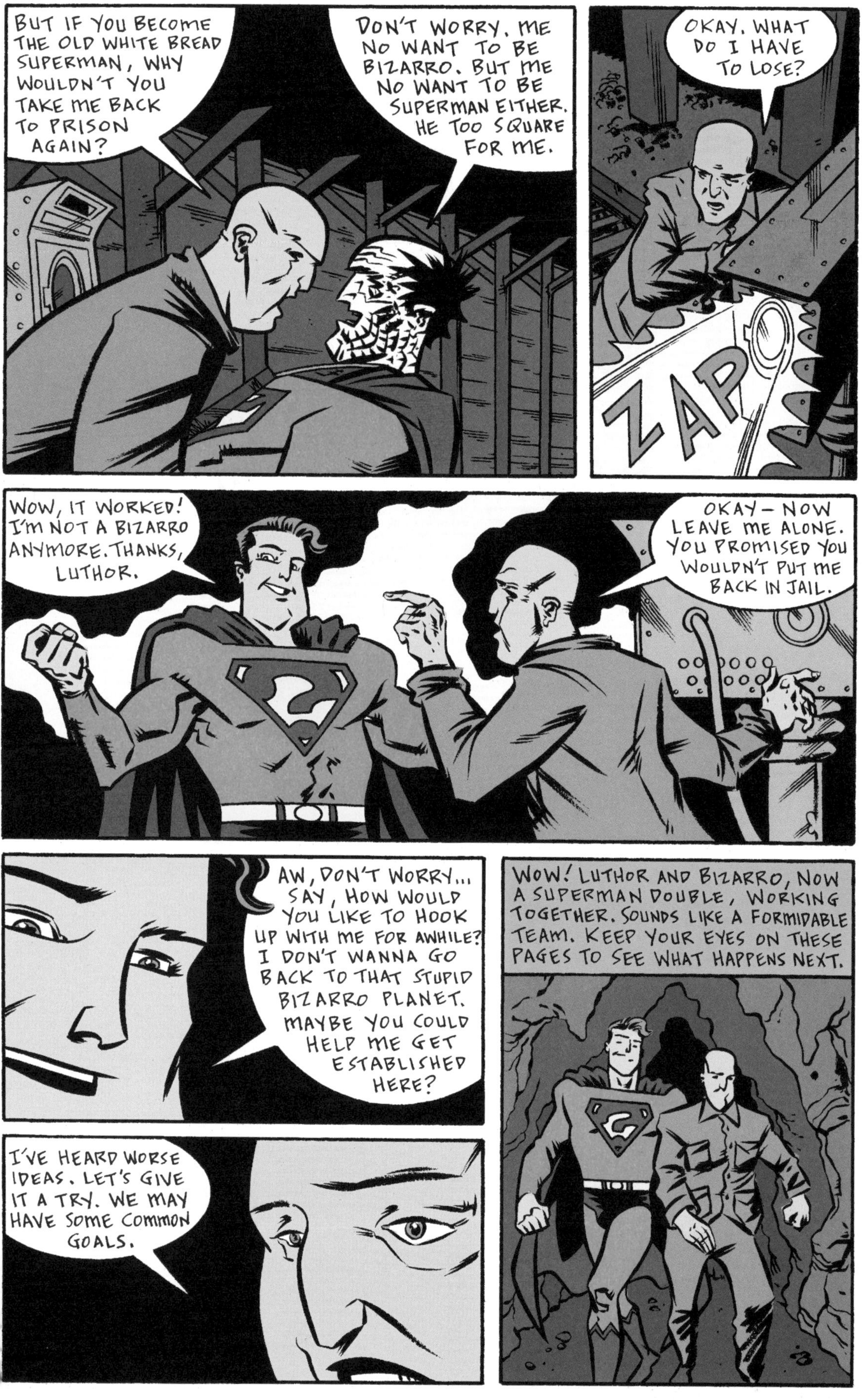

BUT IF YOU BECOME THE OLD WHITE BREAD SUPERMAN, WHY WOULDN'T YOU TAKE ME BACK TO PRISON AGAIN?
DON'T WORRY. ME NO WANT TO BE BIZARRO. BUT ME NO WANT TO BE SUPERMAN EITHER. HE TOO SQUARE FOR ME.
OKAY. WHAT DO I HAVE TO LOSE?
ZAP
WOW, IT WORKED! I'M NOT A BIZARRO ANYMORE. THANKS, LUTHOR.
OKAY—NOW LEAVE ME ALONE. YOU PROMISED YOU WOULDN'T PUT ME BACK IN JAIL.
AW, DON'T WORRY... SAY, HOW WOULD YOU LIKE TO HOOK UP WITH ME FOR AWHILE? I DON'T WANNA GO BACK TO THAT STUPID BIZARRO PLANET. MAYBE YOU COULD HELP ME GET ESTABLISHED HERE?
WOW! LUTHOR AND BIZARRO, NOW A SUPERMAN DOUBLE, WORKING TOGETHER. SOUNDS LIKE A FORMIDABLE TEAM. KEEP YOUR EYES ON THESE PAGES TO SEE WHAT HAPPENS NEXT.
I'VE HEARD WORSE IDEAS. LET'S GIVE IT A TRY. WE MAY HAVE SOME COMMON GOALS.

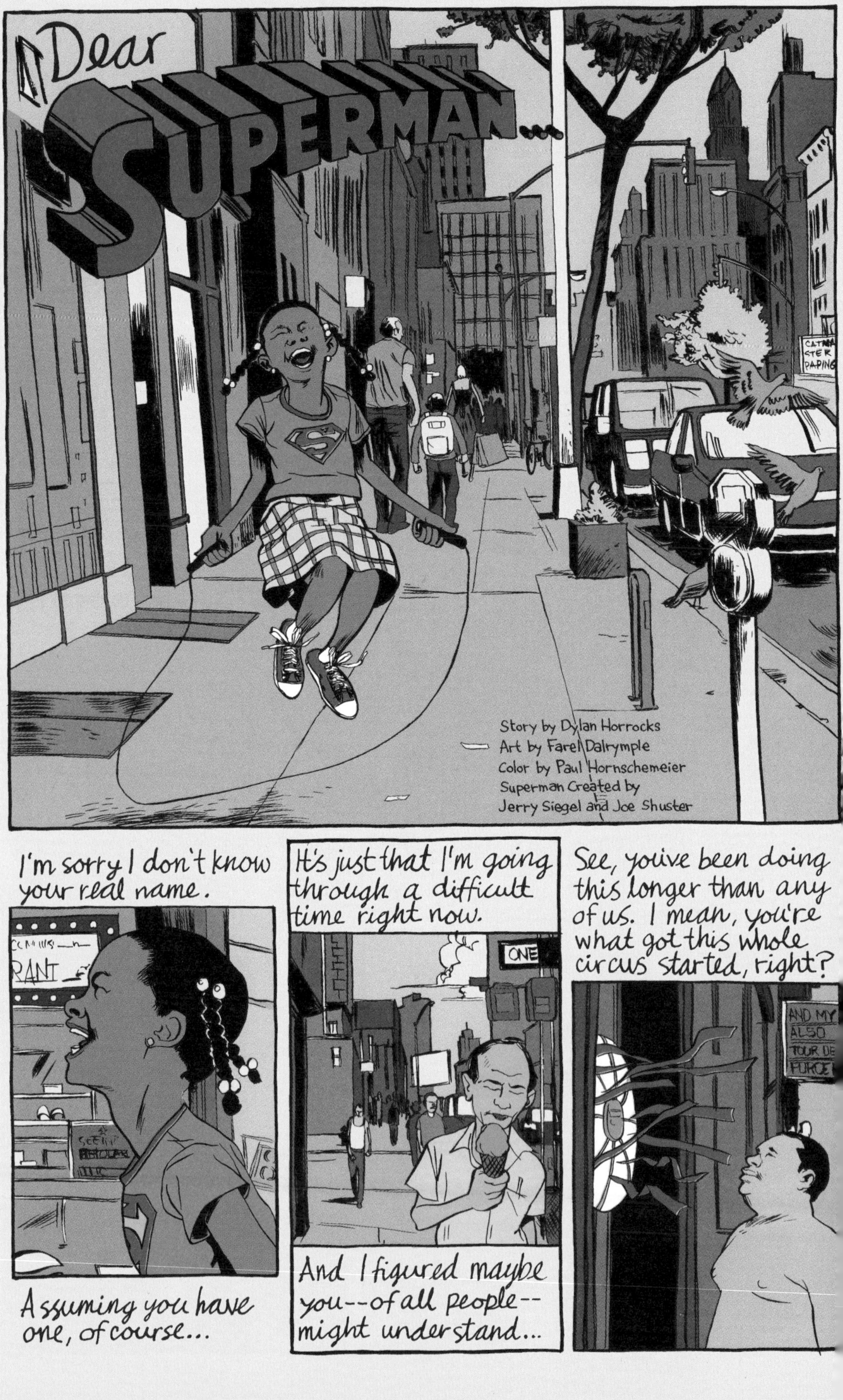
Dear
SUPERMAN...
Story by Dylan Horrocks
Art by Farel Dalrymple
Color by Paul Hornschemeier
Superman Created by
Jerry Siegel and Joe Shuster
I'm sorry I don't know your real name.
Assuming you have one, of course...
It's just that I'm going through a difficult time right now.
ONE
And I figured maybe you--of all people--might understand...
See, you've been doing this longer than any of us. I mean, you're what got this whole circus started, right?

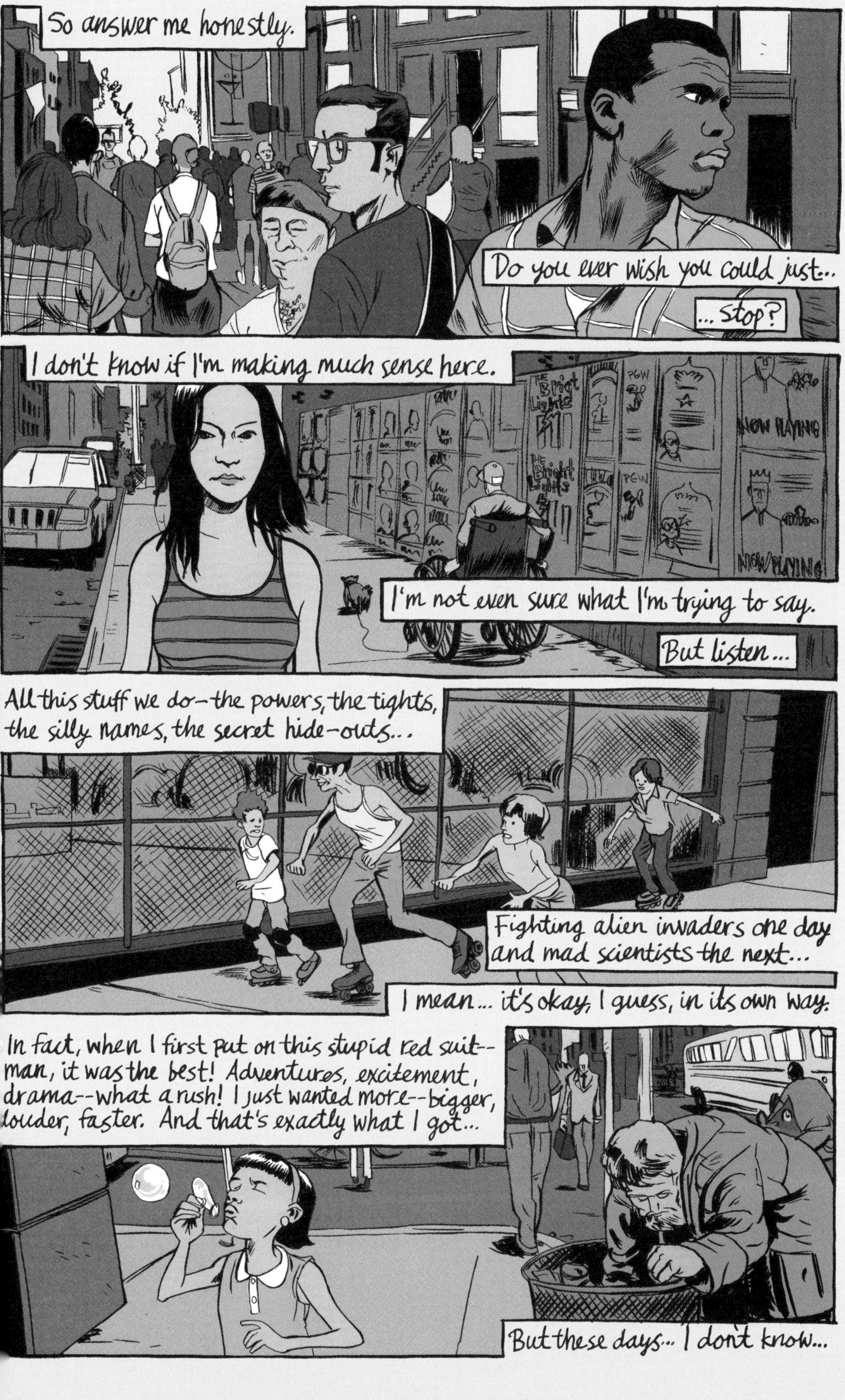
So answer me honestly.
Do you ever wish you could just...
...Stop?
I don't know if I'm making much sense here.
NOW PLAYING
NOW PLAYING
I'm not even sure what I'm trying to say.
But listen...
All this stuff we do—the powers, the tights, the silly names, the secret hide-outs...
Fighting alien invaders one day and mad scientists the next...
I mean... it's okay, I guess, in its own way.
In fact, when I first put on this stupid red suit--man, it was the best! Adventures, excitement, drama--what a rush! I just wanted more--bigger, louder, faster. And that's exactly what I got...
But these days... I don't know...

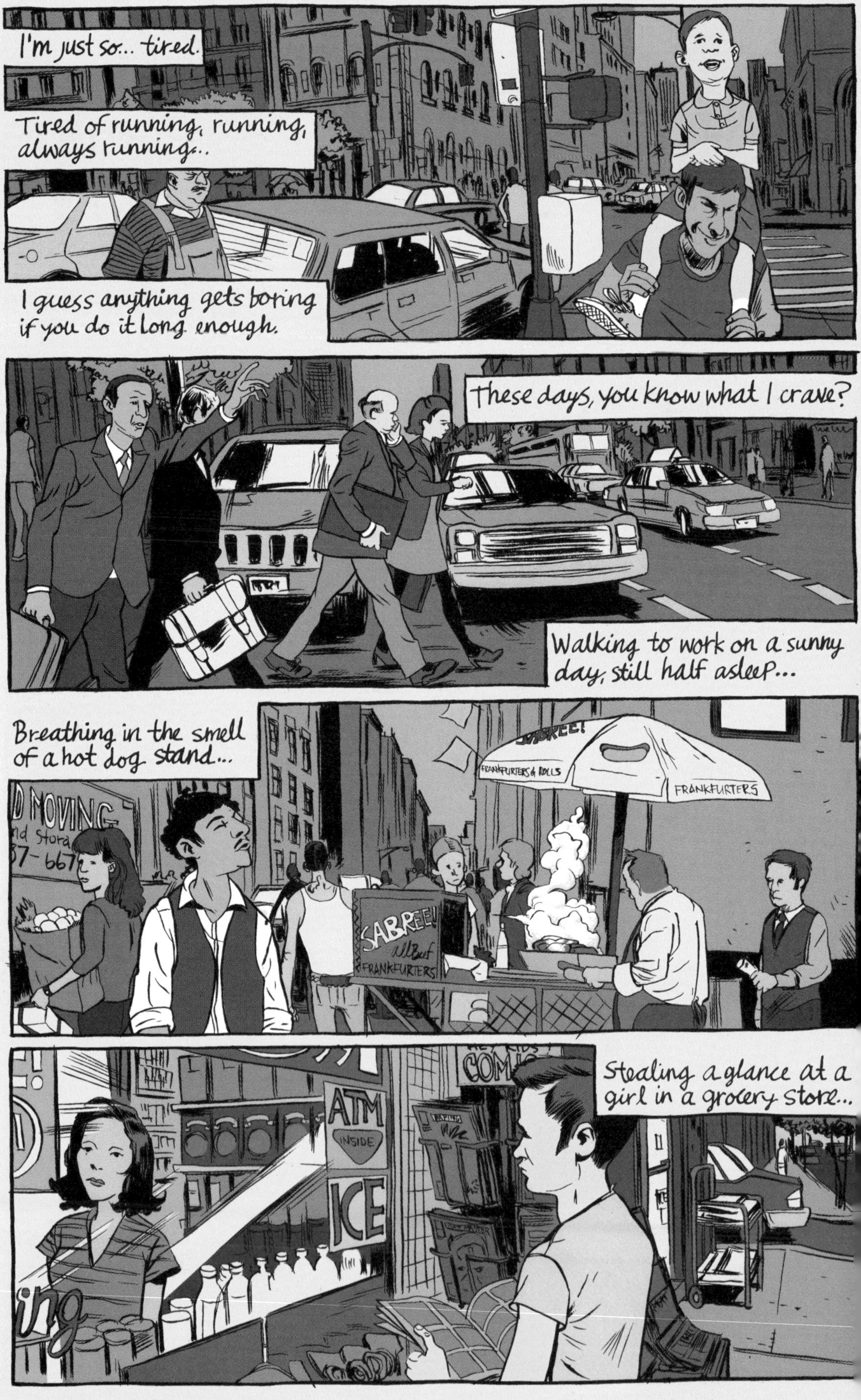
I'm just so... tired.
Tired of running, running, always running...
I guess anything gets boring if you do it long enough.
These days, you know what I crave?
Walking to work on a sunny day, still half asleep...
Breathing in the smell of a hot dog stand...
FRANKFURTERS & ROLLS
FRANKFURTERS
SABREE!
FRANKFURTERS
Stealing a glance at a girl in a grocery store...
ATM
INSIDE
ICE

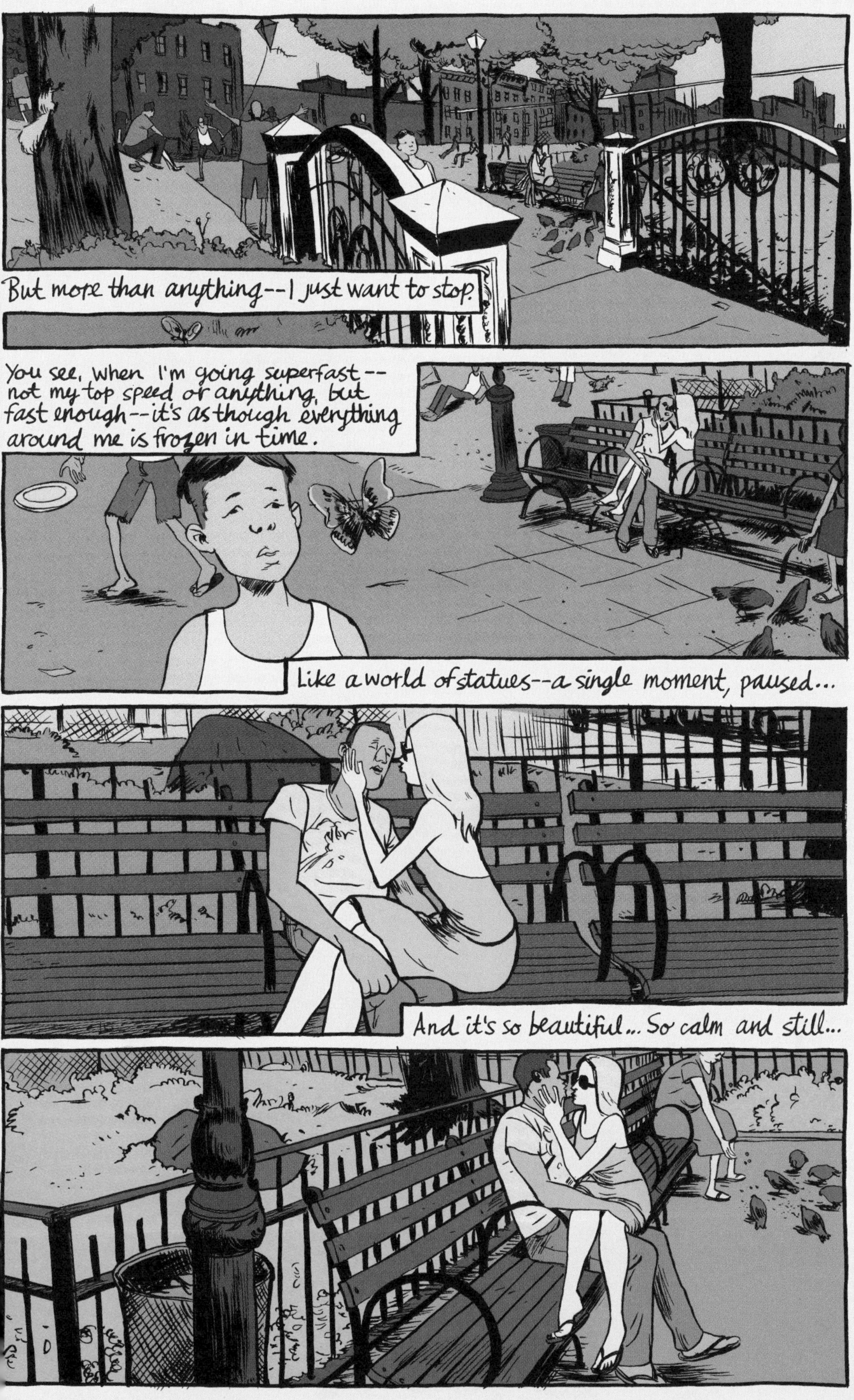
But more than anything--I just want to stop.
You see, when I'm going superfast--not my top speed or anything, but fast enough--it's as though everything around me is frozen in time.
Like a world of statues--a single moment, paused...
And it's so beautiful... So calm and still...

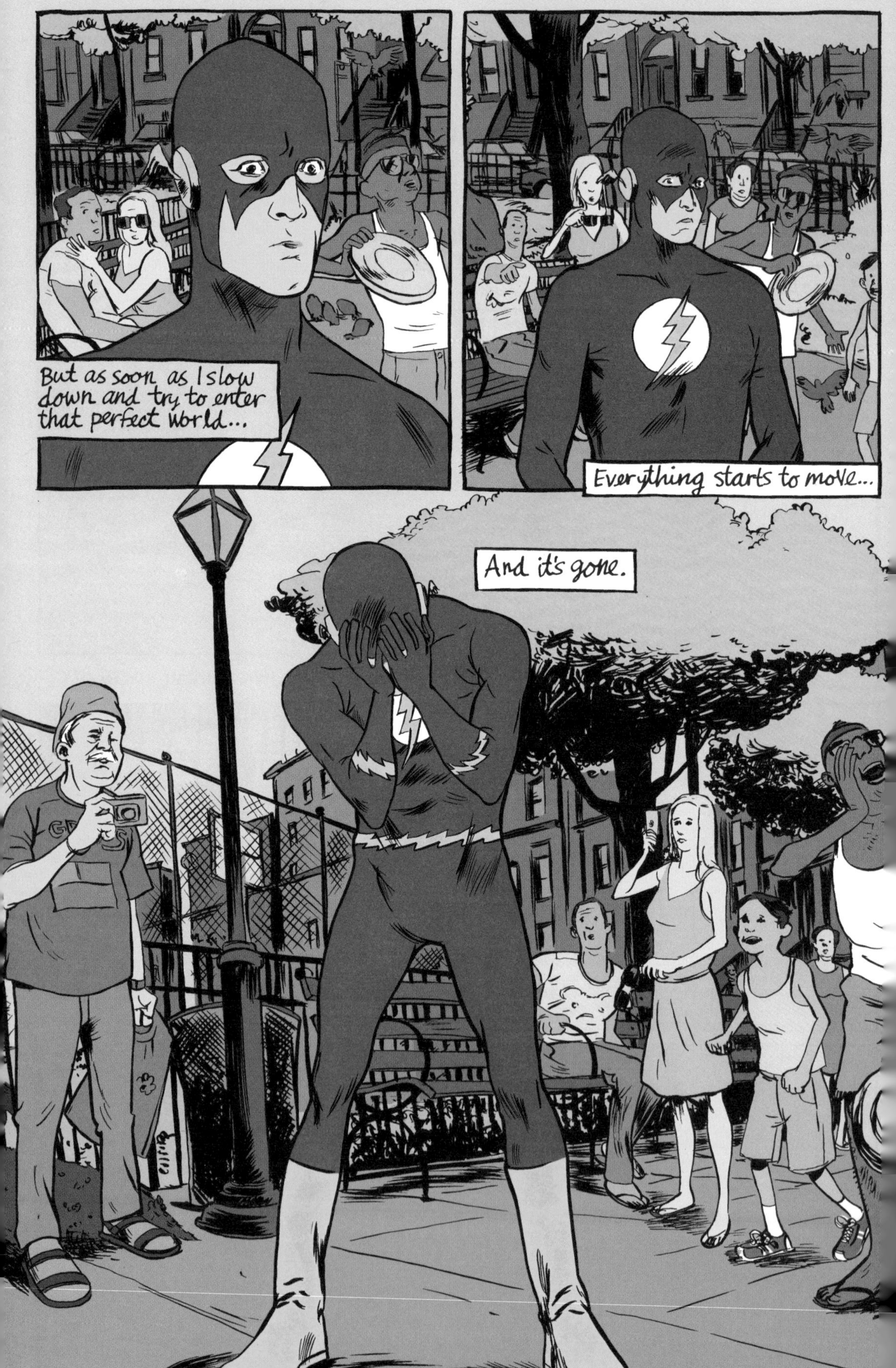
But as soon as I slow down and try to enter that perfect world...
Everything starts to move...
And it's gone.

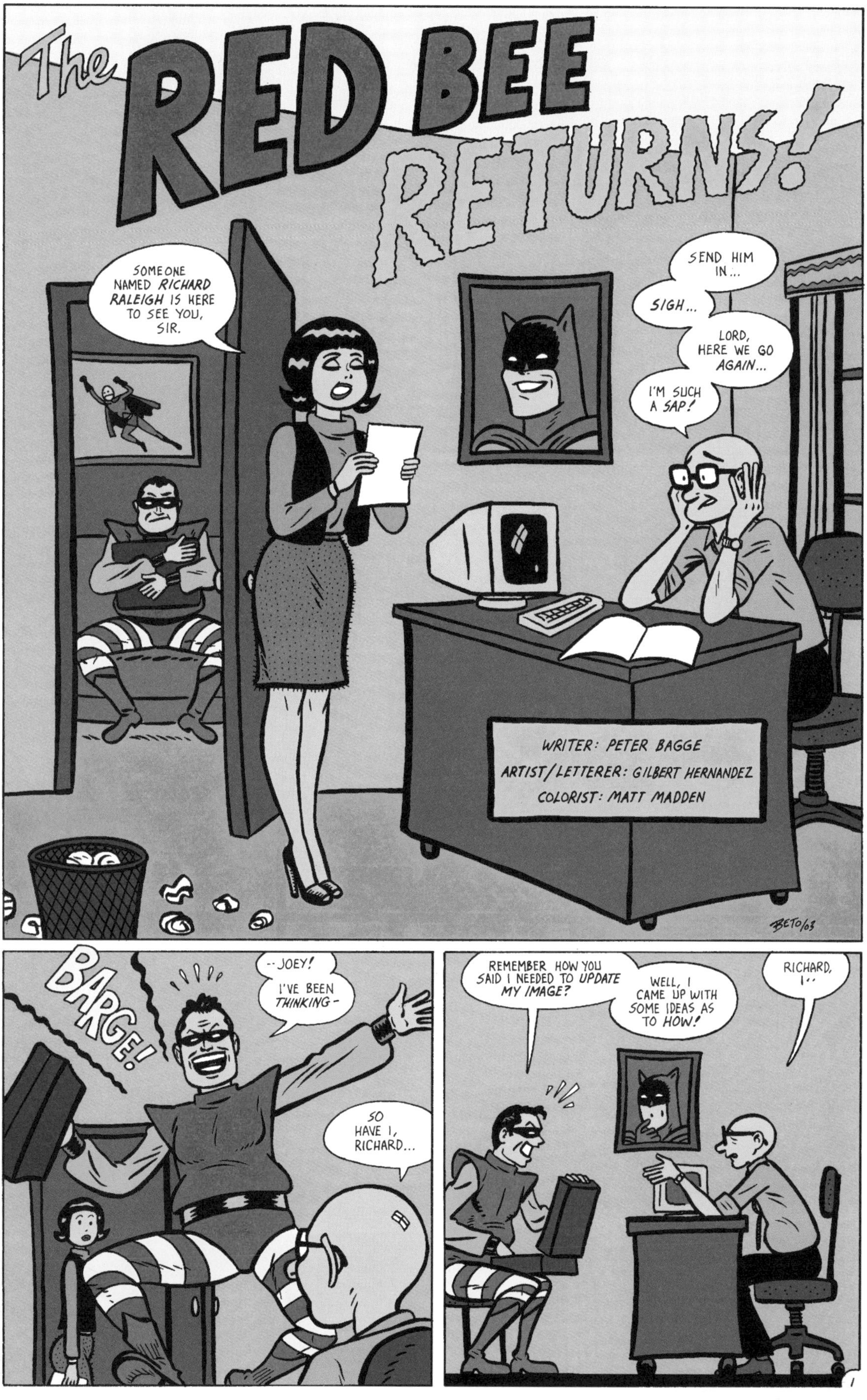
The RED BEE RETURNS!
SOMEONE NAMED RICHARD RALEIGH IS HERE TO SEE YOU, SIR.
SEND HIM IN...
SIGH...
LORD, HERE WE GO AGAIN...
I'M SUCH A SAP!
WRITER: PETER BAGGE
ARTIST/LETTERER: GILBERT HERNANDEZ
COLORIST: MATT MADDEN
BETO/03
BARGE!
--JOEY!
I'VE BEEN THINKING-
SO HAVE I, RICHARD...
REMEMBER HOW YOU SAID I NEEDED TO UPDATE MY IMAGE?
WELL, I CAME UP WITH SOME IDEAS AS TO HOW!
RICHARD, I--

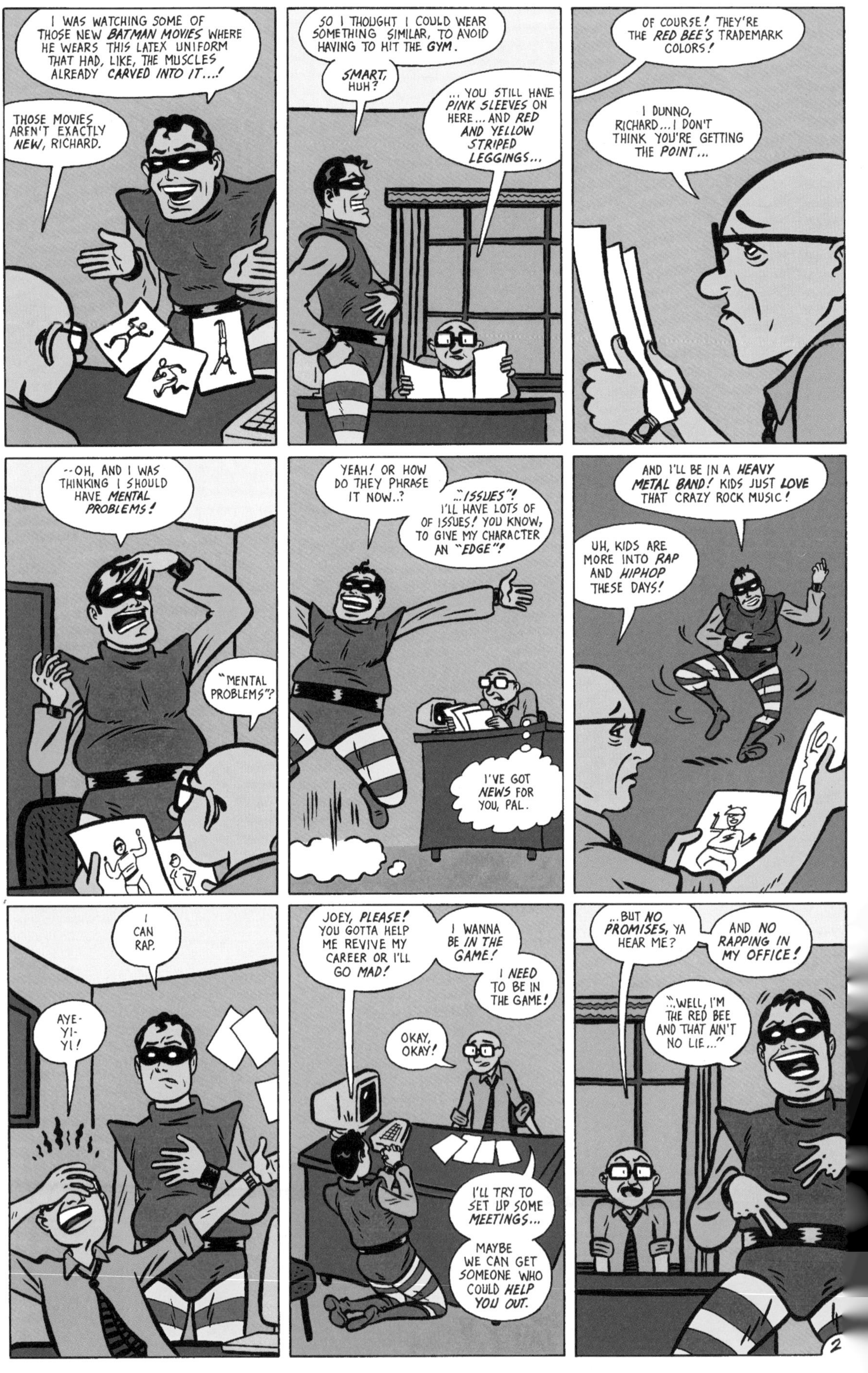

I WAS WATCHING SOME OF THOSE NEW BATMAN MOVIES WHERE HE WEARS THIS LATEX UNIFORM THAT HAD, LIKE, THE MUSCLES ALREADY CARVED INTO IT....!
THOSE MOVIES AREN'T EXACTLY NEW, RICHARD.
SO I THOUGHT I COULD WEAR SOMETHING SIMILAR, TO AVOID HAVING TO HIT THE GYM.
SMART, HUH?
... YOU STILL HAVE PINK SLEEVES ON HERE... AND RED AND YELLOW STRIPED LEGGINGS...
OF COURSE! THEY'RE THE RED BEE'S TRADEMARK COLORS!
I DUNNO, RICHARD... I DON'T THINK YOU'RE GETTING THE POINT...
--OH, AND I WAS THINKING I SHOULD HAVE MENTAL PROBLEMS!
"MENTAL PROBLEMS"?
YEAH! OR HOW DO THEY PHRASE IT NOW..?
..."ISSUES"! I'LL HAVE LOTS OF OF ISSUES! YOU KNOW, TO GIVE MY CHARACTER AN "EDGE"!
I'VE GOT NEWS FOR YOU, PAL.
AND I'LL BE IN A HEAVY METAL BAND! KIDS JUST LOVE THAT CRAZY ROCK MUSIC!
UH, KIDS ARE MORE INTO RAP AND HIPHOP THESE DAYS!
I CAN RAP.
AYE-YI-YI!
JOEY, PLEASE! YOU GOTTA HELP ME REVIVE MY CAREER OR I'LL GO MAD!
I WANNA BE IN THE GAME!
I NEED TO BE IN THE GAME!
OKAY, OKAY!
I'LL TRY TO SET UP SOME MEETINGS...
MAYBE WE CAN GET SOMEONE WHO COULD HELP YOU OUT.
...BUT NO PROMISES, YA HEAR ME?
AND NO RAPPING IN MY OFFICE!
"...WELL, I'M THE RED BEE AND THAT AIN'T NO LIE..."

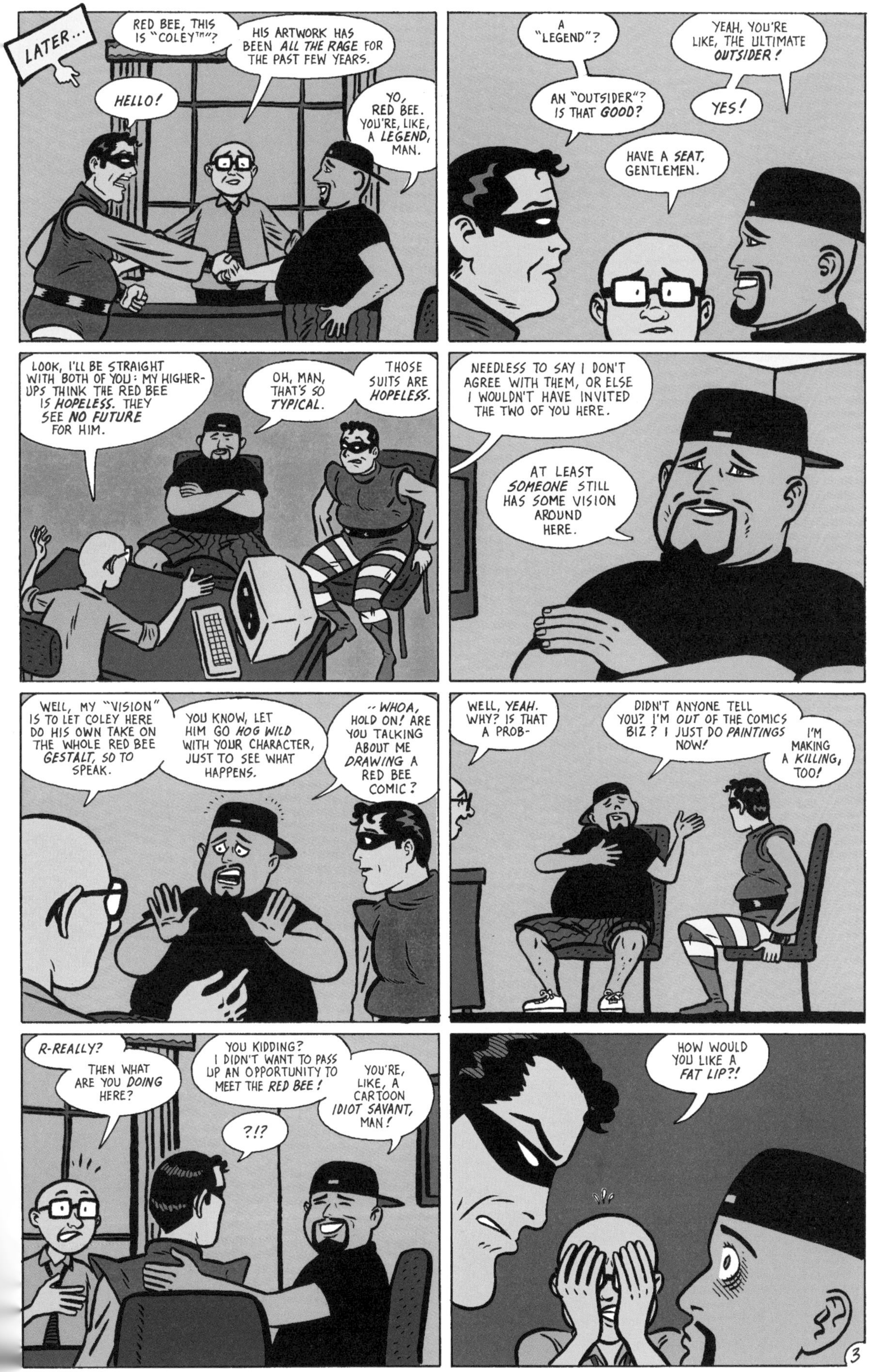
LATER...
RED BEE, THIS IS "COLEY™"?
HIS ARTWORK HAS BEEN ALL THE RAGE FOR THE PAST FEW YEARS.
HELLO!
YO, RED BEE. YOU'RE, LIKE, A LEGEND, MAN.
A "LEGEND"?
AN "OUTSIDER"? IS THAT GOOD?
YEAH, YOU'RE LIKE, THE ULTIMATE OUTSIDER!
YES!
HAVE A SEAT, GENTLEMEN.
LOOK, I'LL BE STRAIGHT WITH BOTH OF YOU: MY HIGHER-UPS THINK THE RED BEE IS HOPELESS. THEY SEE NO FUTURE FOR HIM.
OH, MAN, THAT'S SO TYPICAL.
THOSE SUITS ARE HOPELESS.
NEEDLESS TO SAY I DON'T AGREE WITH THEM, OR ELSE I WOULDN'T HAVE INVITED THE TWO OF YOU HERE.
AT LEAST SOMEONE STILL HAS SOME VISION AROUND HERE.
WELL, MY "VISION" IS TO LET COLEY HERE DO HIS OWN TAKE ON THE WHOLE RED BEE GESTALT, SO TO SPEAK.
YOU KNOW, LET HIM GO HOG WILD WITH YOUR CHARACTER, JUST TO SEE WHAT HAPPENS.
-- WHOA, HOLD ON! ARE YOU TALKING ABOUT ME DRAWING A RED BEE COMIC?
WELL, YEAH. WHY? IS THAT A PROB-
DIDN'T ANYONE TELL YOU? I'M OUT OF THE COMICS BIZ? I JUST DO PAINTINGS NOW!
I'M MAKING A KILLING, TOO!
R-REALLY?
THEN WHAT ARE YOU DOING HERE?
YOU KIDDING? I DIDN'T WANT TO PASS UP AN OPPORTUNITY TO MEET THE RED BEE!
YOU'RE, LIKE, A CARTOON IDIOT SAVANT, MAN!
?!?
HOW WOULD YOU LIKE A FAT LIP?!

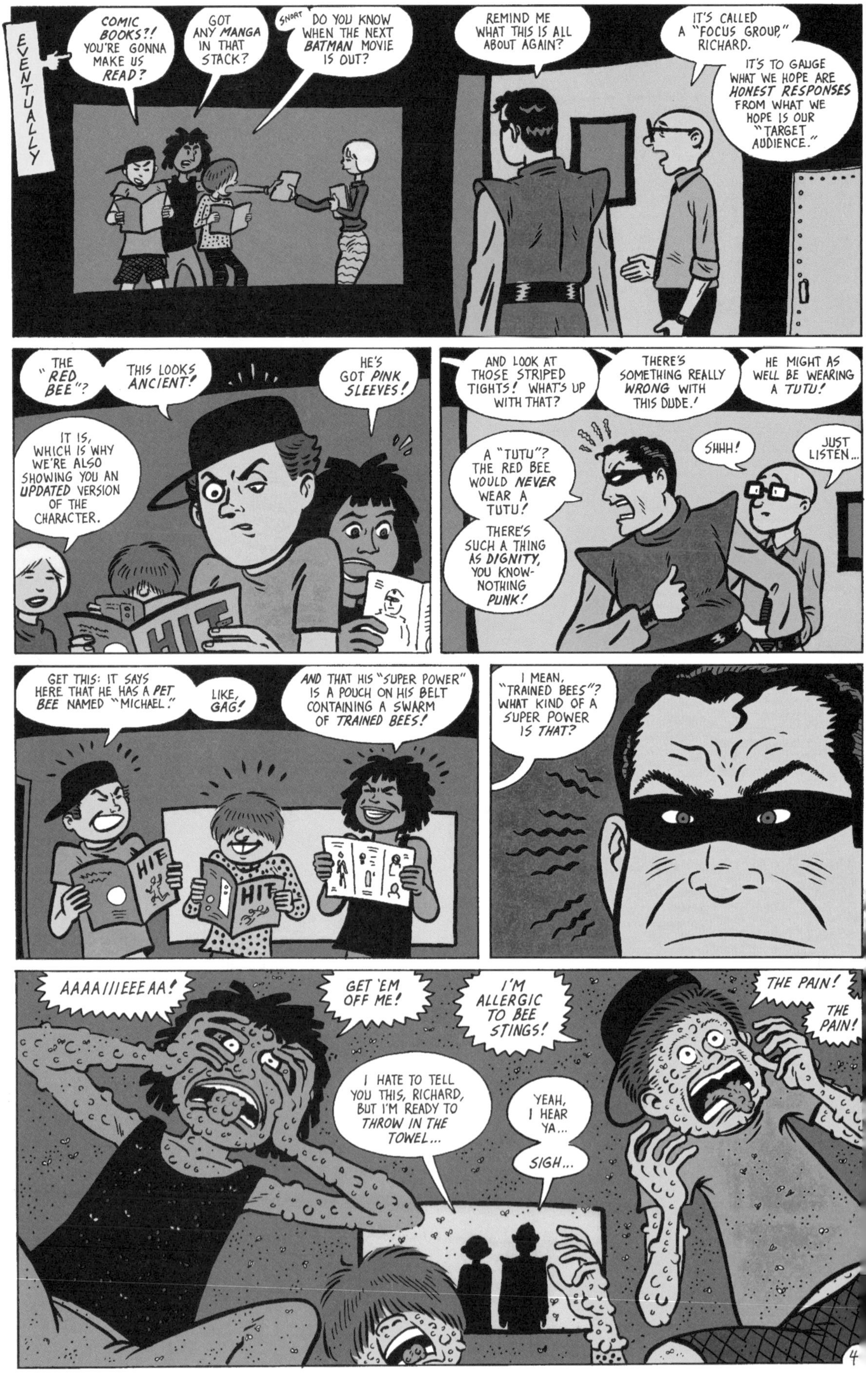
EVENTUALLY
COMIC BOOKS?! YOU'RE GONNA MAKE US READ?
GOT ANY MANGA IN THAT STACK?
SNORT
DO YOU KNOW WHEN THE NEXT BATMAN MOVIE IS OUT?
REMIND ME WHAT THIS IS ALL ABOUT AGAIN?
IT'S CALLED A "FOCUS GROUP," RICHARD.
IT'S TO GAUGE WHAT WE HOPE ARE HONEST RESPONSES FROM WHAT WE HOPE IS OUR "TARGET AUDIENCE."
"THE RED BEE"?
THIS LOOKS ANCIENT!
HE'S GOT PINK SLEEVES!
IT IS, WHICH IS WHY WE'RE ALSO SHOWING YOU AN UPDATED VERSION OF THE CHARACTER.
HIT
AND LOOK AT THOSE STRIPED TIGHTS! WHAT'S UP WITH THAT?
THERE'S SOMETHING REALLY WRONG WITH THIS DUDE!
HE MIGHT AS WELL BE WEARING A TUTU!
A "TUTU"? THE RED BEE WOULD NEVER WEAR A TUTU!
THERE'S SUCH A THING AS DIGNITY, YOU KNOW-NOTHING PUNK!
SHHH!
JUST LISTEN...
GET THIS: IT SAYS HERE THAT HE HAS A PET BEE NAMED "MICHAEL."
LIKE, GAG!
AND THAT HIS "SUPER POWER" IS A POUCH ON HIS BELT CONTAINING A SWARM OF TRAINED BEES!
HIT
HIT
I MEAN, "TRAINED BEES"? WHAT KIND OF A SUPER POWER IS THAT?
AAAAIIIEEEAA!
GET 'EM OFF ME!
I'M ALLERGIC TO BEE STINGS!
THE PAIN! THE PAIN!
I HATE TO TELL YOU THIS, RICHARD, BUT I'M READY TO THROW IN THE TOWEL...
YEAH, I HEAR YA...
SIGH...
4

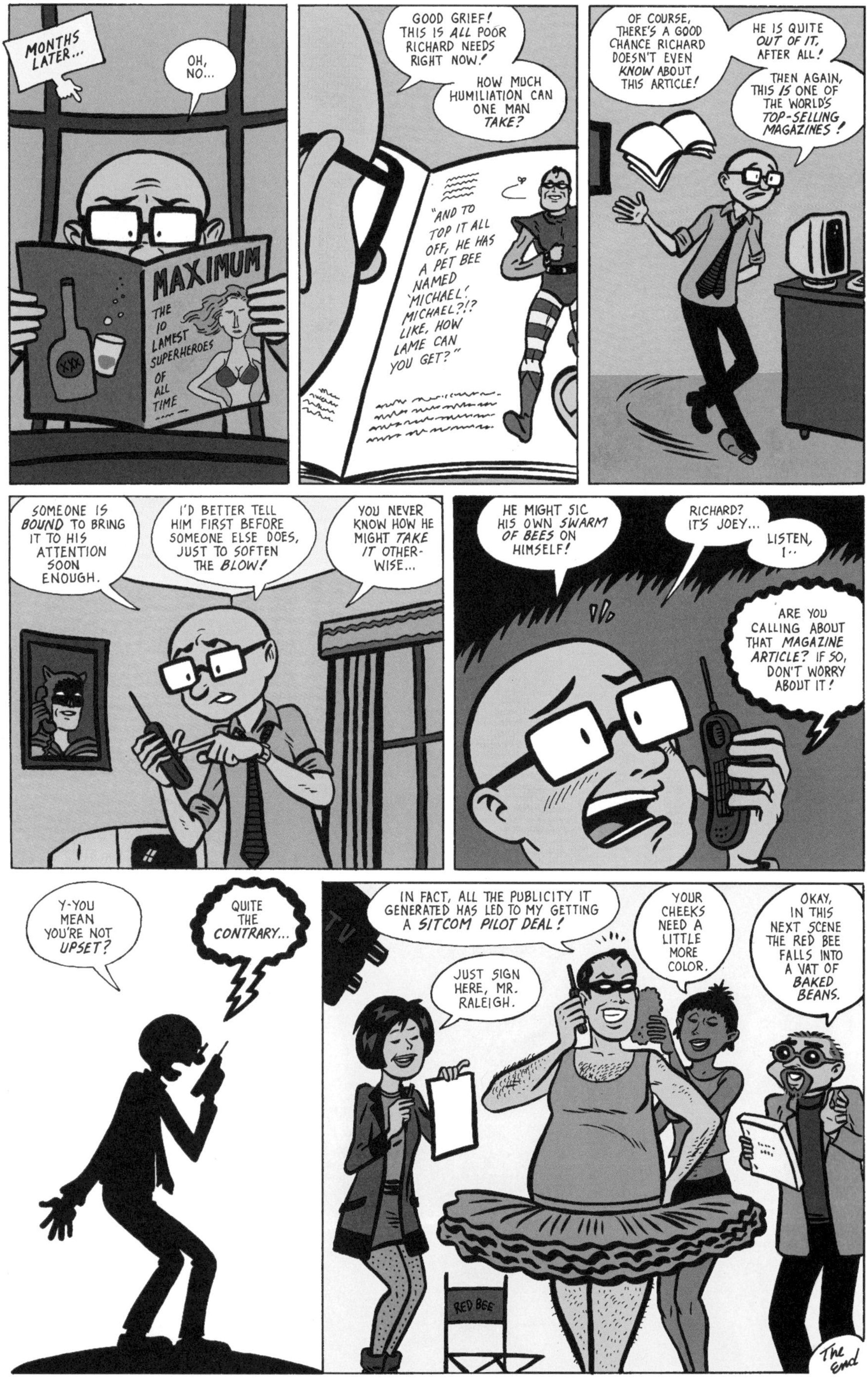

MONTHS LATER...
OH, NO...
MAXIMUM
THE 10 LAMEST SUPERHEROES OF ALL TIME
XXX
GOOD GRIEF! THIS IS ALL POOR RICHARD NEEDS RIGHT NOW!
HOW MUCH HUMILIATION CAN ONE MAN TAKE?
"AND TO TOP IT ALL OFF, HE HAS A PET BEE NAMED 'MICHAEL.' MICHAEL?!? LIKE, HOW LAME CAN YOU GET?"
OF COURSE, THERE'S A GOOD CHANCE RICHARD DOESN'T EVEN KNOW ABOUT THIS ARTICLE!
HE IS QUITE OUT OF IT, AFTER ALL!
THEN AGAIN, THIS IS ONE OF THE WORLD'S TOP-SELLING MAGAZINES!
SOMEONE IS BOUND TO BRING IT TO HIS ATTENTION SOON ENOUGH.
I'D BETTER TELL HIM FIRST BEFORE SOMEONE ELSE DOES, JUST TO SOFTEN THE BLOW!
YOU NEVER KNOW HOW HE MIGHT TAKE IT OTHER-WISE...
HE MIGHT SIC HIS OWN SWARM OF BEES ON HIMSELF!
RICHARD? IT'S JOEY...
LISTEN, I..
ARE YOU CALLING ABOUT THAT MAGAZINE ARTICLE? IF SO, DON'T WORRY ABOUT IT!
Y-YOU MEAN YOU'RE NOT UPSET?
QUITE THE CONTRARY...
IN FACT, ALL THE PUBLICITY IT GENERATED HAS LED TO MY GETTING A SITCOM PILOT DEAL!
JUST SIGN HERE, MR. RALEIGH.
YOUR CHEEKS NEED A LITTLE MORE COLOR.
OKAY, IN THIS NEXT SCENE THE RED BEE FALLS INTO A VAT OF BAKED BEANS.
TV
RED BEE
The End

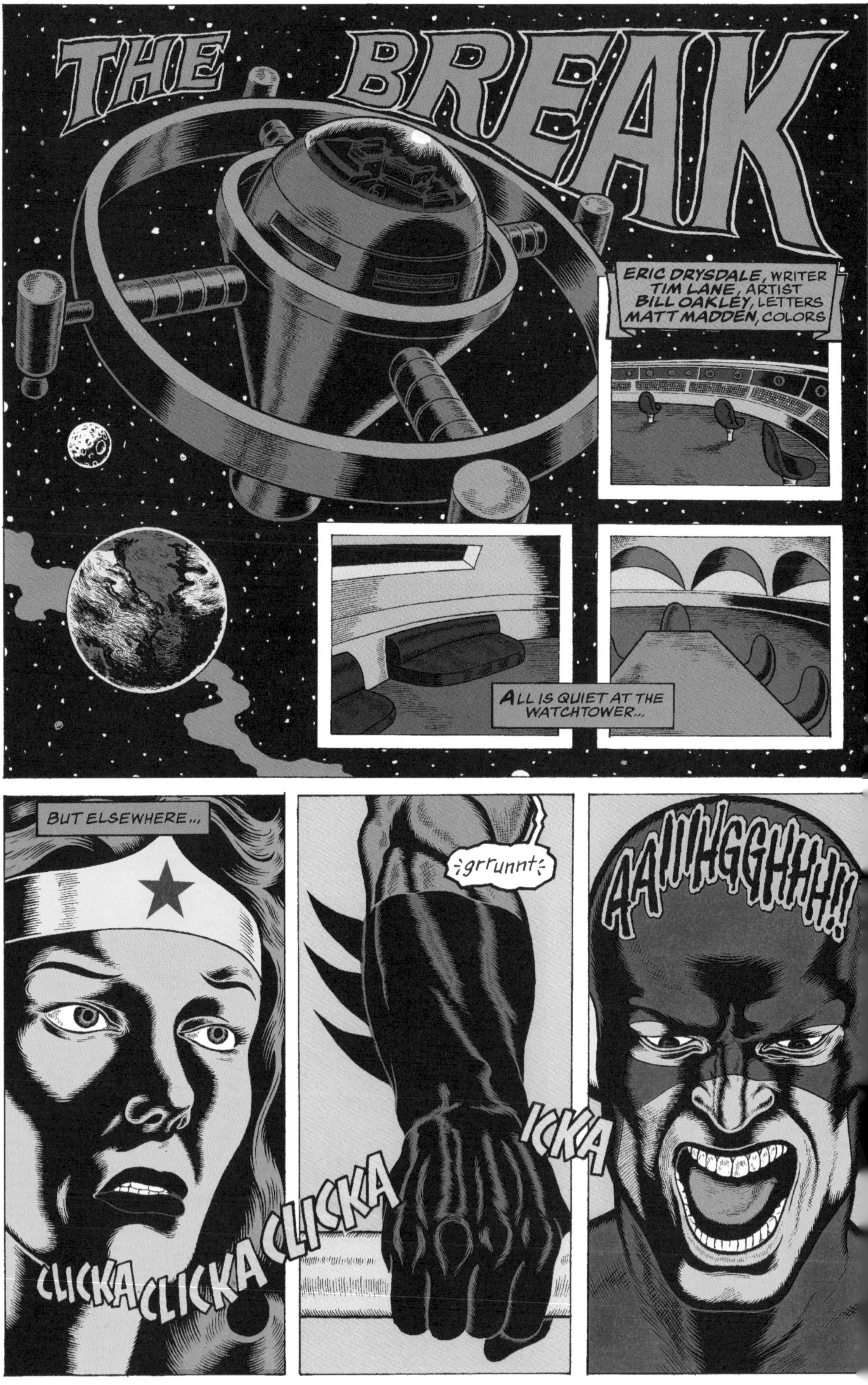
THE BREAK
ERIC DRYSDALE, WRITER
TIM LANE, ARTIST
BILL OAKLEY, LETTERS
MATT MADDEN, COLORS
ALL IS QUIET AT THE WATCHTOWER...
BUT ELSEWHERE...
grrunnt
AAIIIHGGHHH!!
CLICKACLICKACLICKA
ICKA

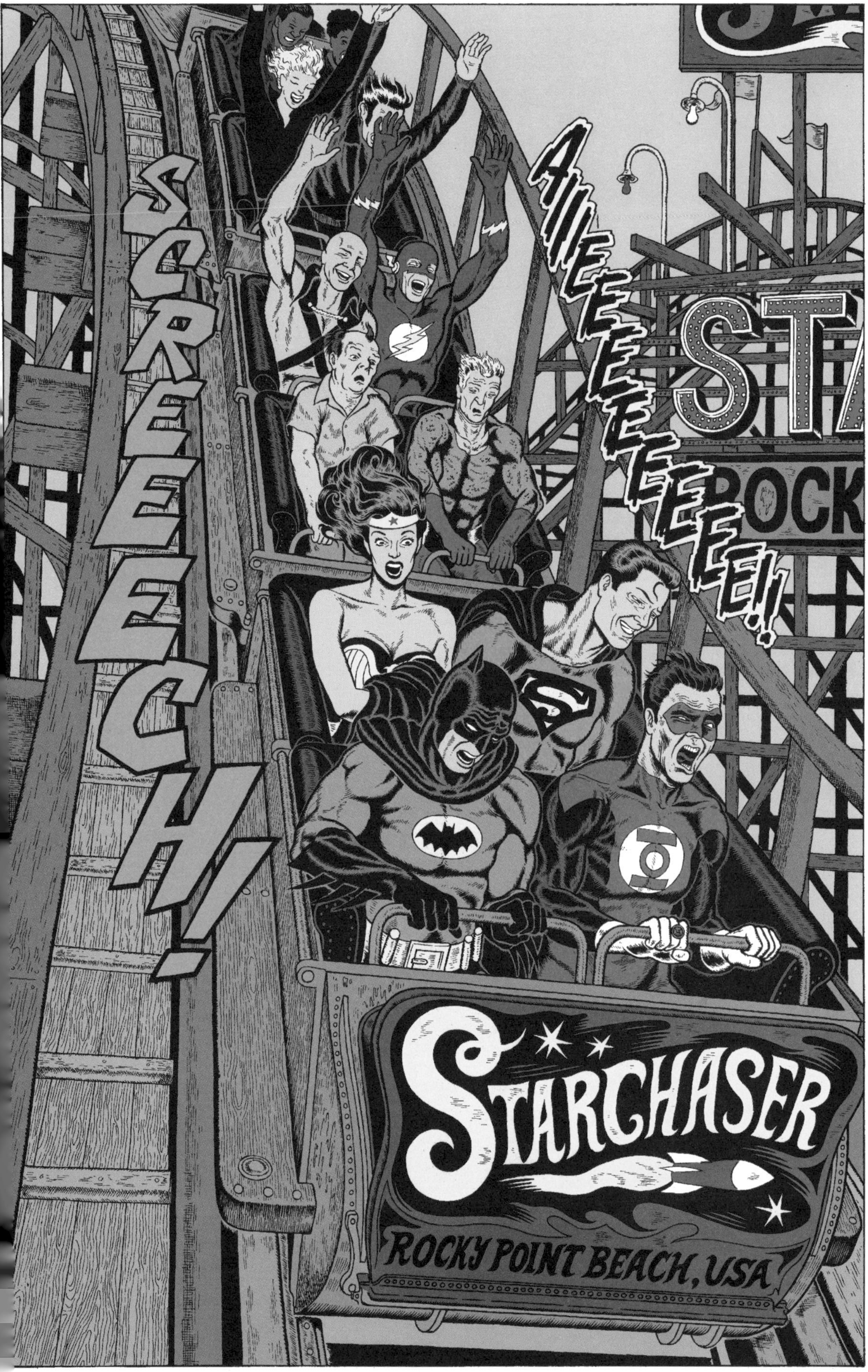
SCREEECH!
AIIEEEEEEEEEEE!!
STA
ROCK
STARCHASER
ROCKY POINT BEACH, USA

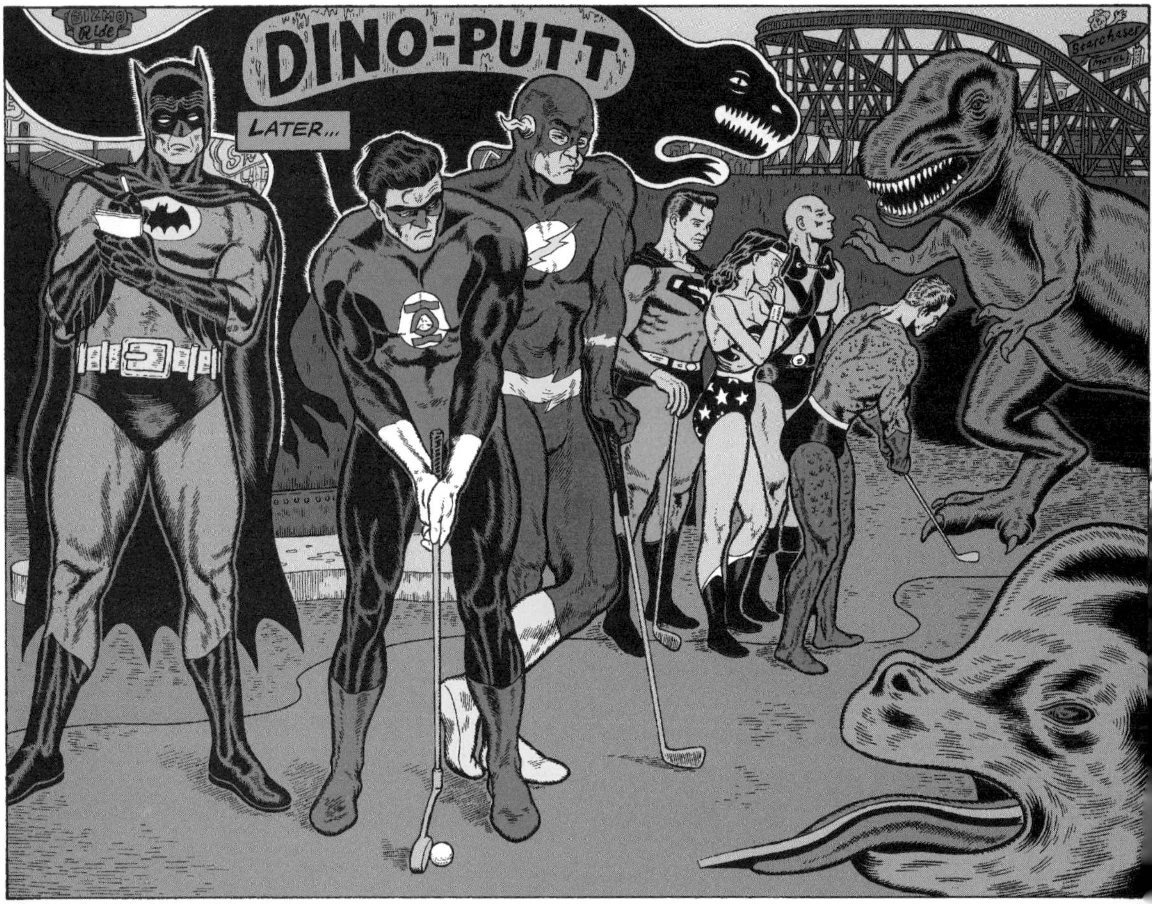
GIZMO Ride
DINO-PUTT
LATER...

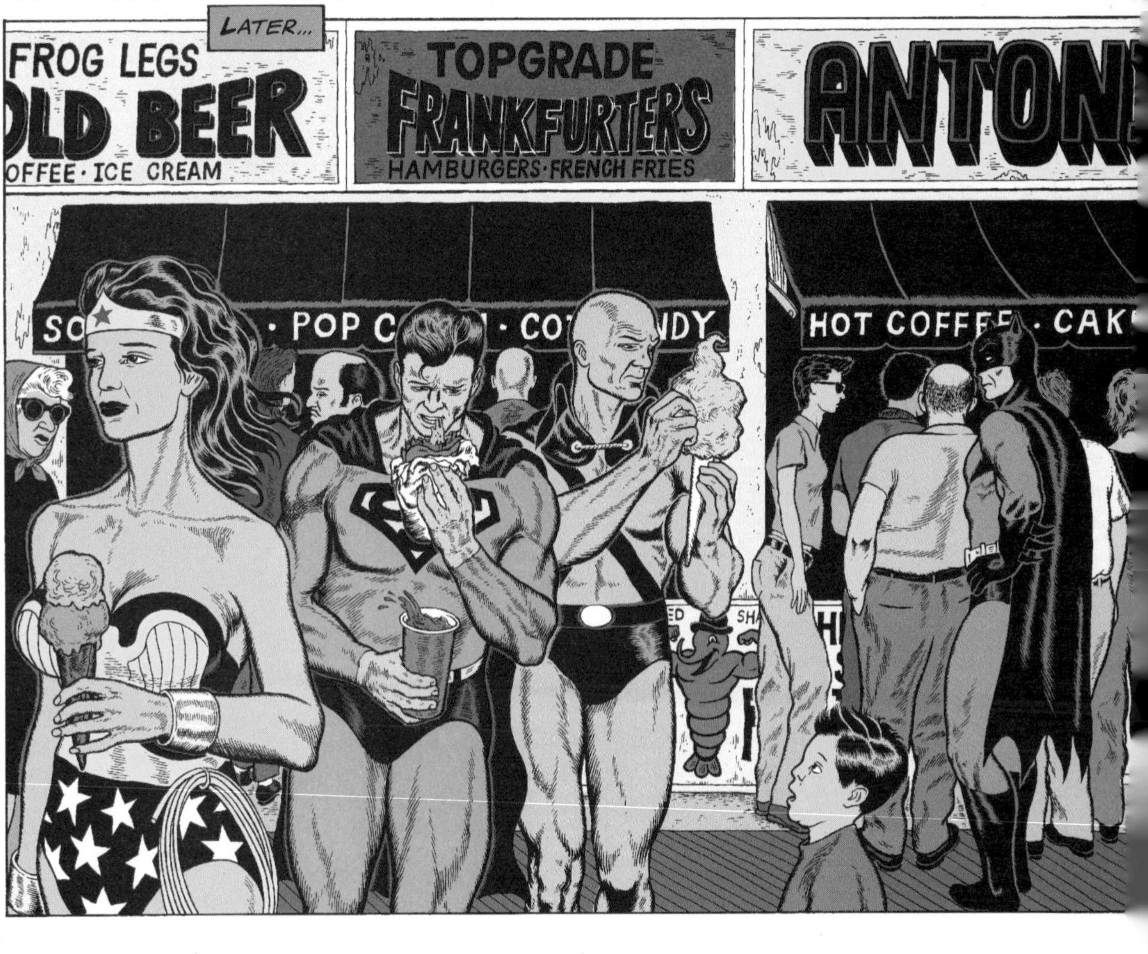
LATER...
FROG LEGS
OLD BEER
OFFEE · ICE CREAM
TOPGRADE
FRANKFURTERS
HAMBURGERS · FRENCH FRIES
ANTON
· POP C
HOT COFF

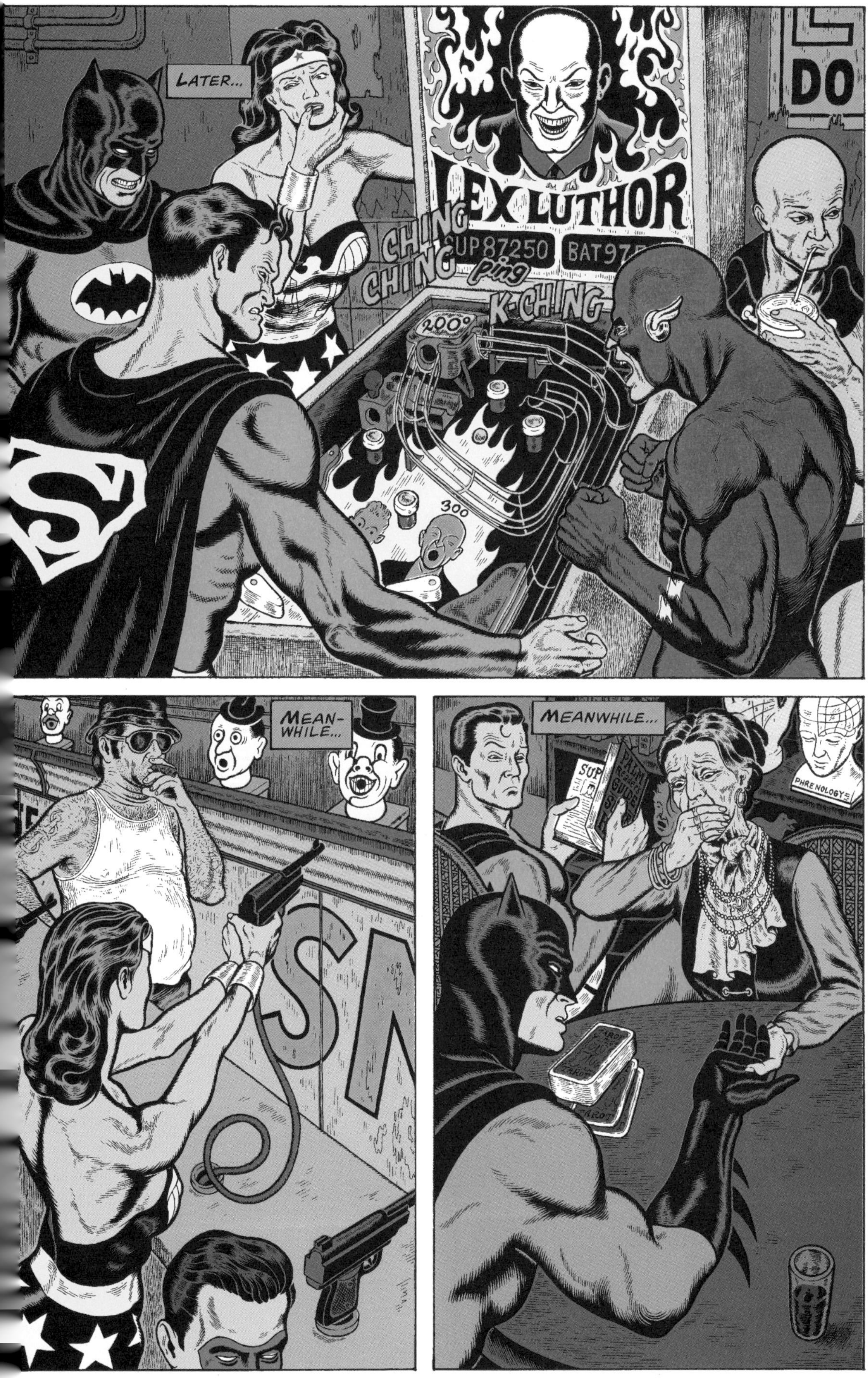

LATER...
DO
LEX LUTHOR
SUP 87250
CHING
CHING
ping
K-CHING
200
300
MEAN-WHILE...
MEANWHILE...
PHRENOLOGY
TAROT

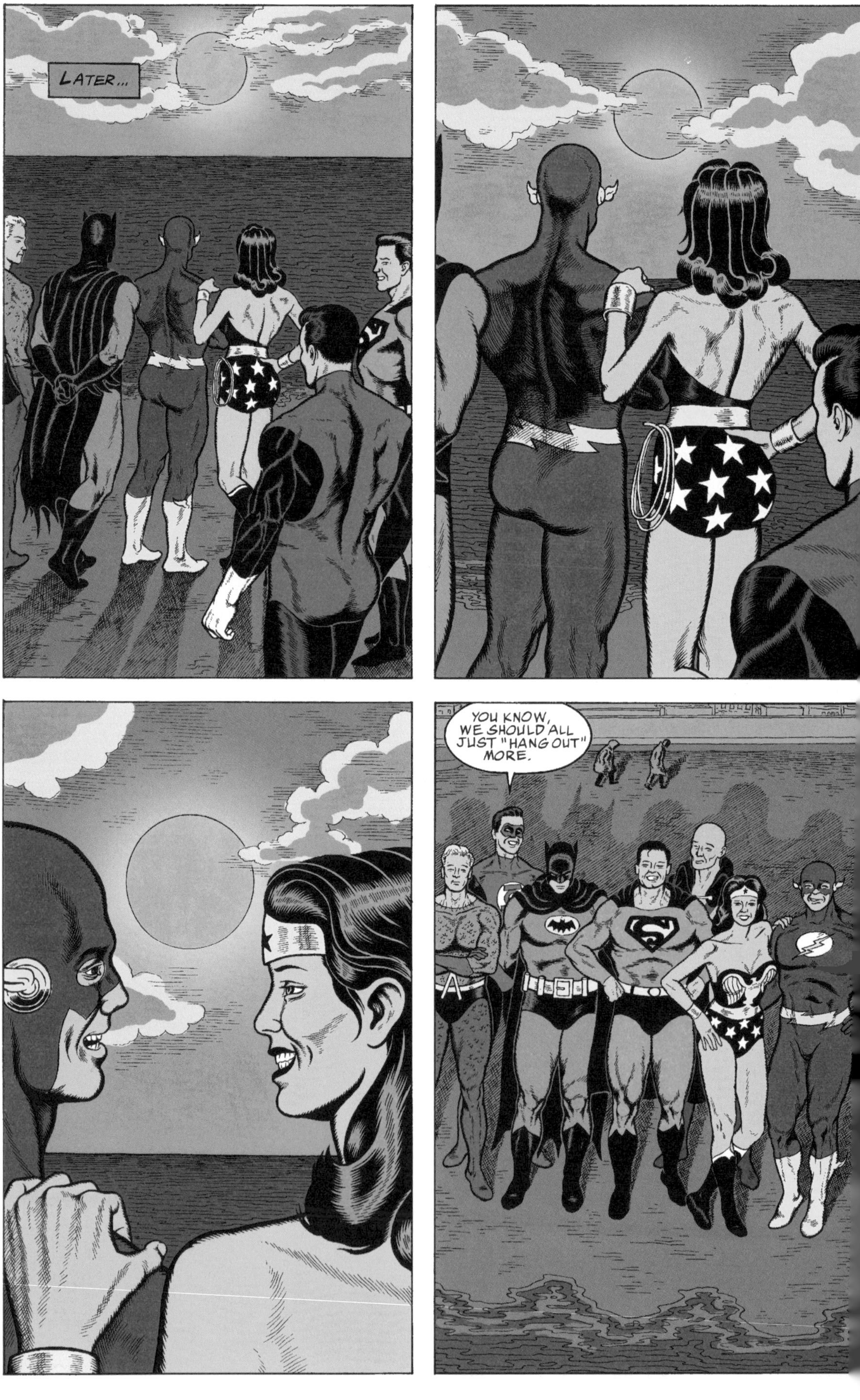
LATER...
YOU KNOW, WE SHOULD ALL JUST "HANG OUT" MORE.

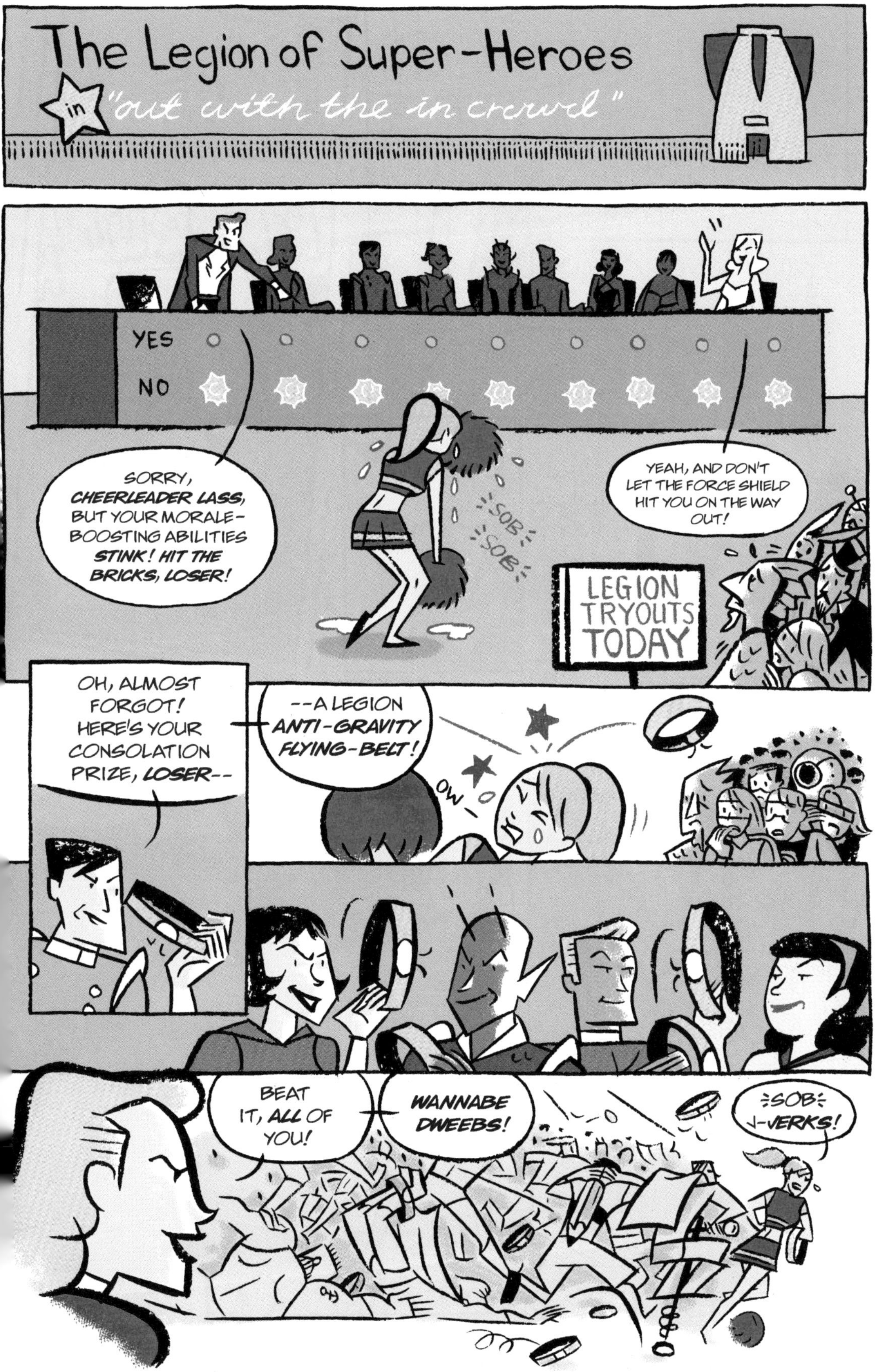

The Legion of Super-Heroes
in "out with the in crowd"
YES
NO
SORRY, CHEERLEADER LASS, BUT YOUR MORALE-BOOSTING ABILITIES STINK! HIT THE BRICKS, LOSER!
SOB SOB
YEAH, AND DON'T LET THE FORCE SHIELD HIT YOU ON THE WAY OUT!
LEGION TRYOUTS TODAY
OH, ALMOST FORGOT! HERE'S YOUR CONSOLATION PRIZE, LOSER--
--A LEGION ANTI-GRAVITY FLYING-BELT!
OW
BEAT IT, ALL OF YOU!
WANNABE DWEEBS!
SOB J-JERKS!

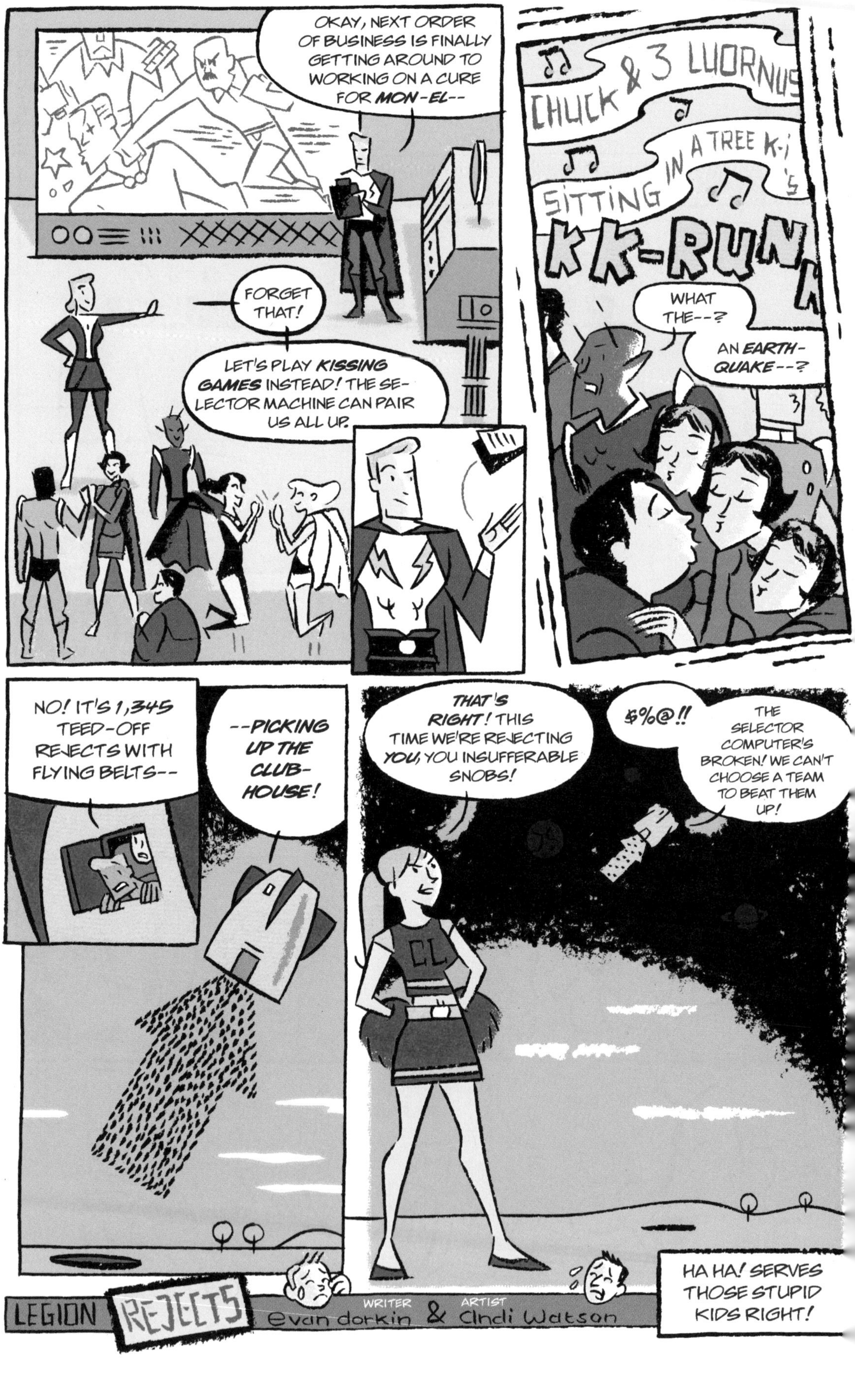
OKAY, NEXT ORDER OF BUSINESS IS FINALLY GETTING AROUND TO WORKING ON A CURE FOR MON-EL--
FORGET THAT!
LET'S PLAY KISSING GAMES INSTEAD! THE SELECTOR MACHINE CAN PAIR US ALL UP.
CHUCK & 3 LUORNUS
SITTING IN A TREE K-I
KK-RUNK
WHAT THE--?
AN EARTHQUAKE--?
NO! IT'S 1,345 TEED-OFF REJECTS WITH FLYING BELTS--
--PICKING UP THE CLUBHOUSE!
THAT'S RIGHT! THIS TIME WE'RE REJECTING YOU, YOU INSUFFERABLE SNOBS!
$%@!!
THE SELECTOR COMPUTER'S BROKEN! WE CAN'T CHOOSE A TEAM TO BEAT THEM UP!
CL
LEGION REJECTS
WRITER evan dorkin & ARTIST andi watson
HA HA! SERVES THOSE STUPID KIDS RIGHT!

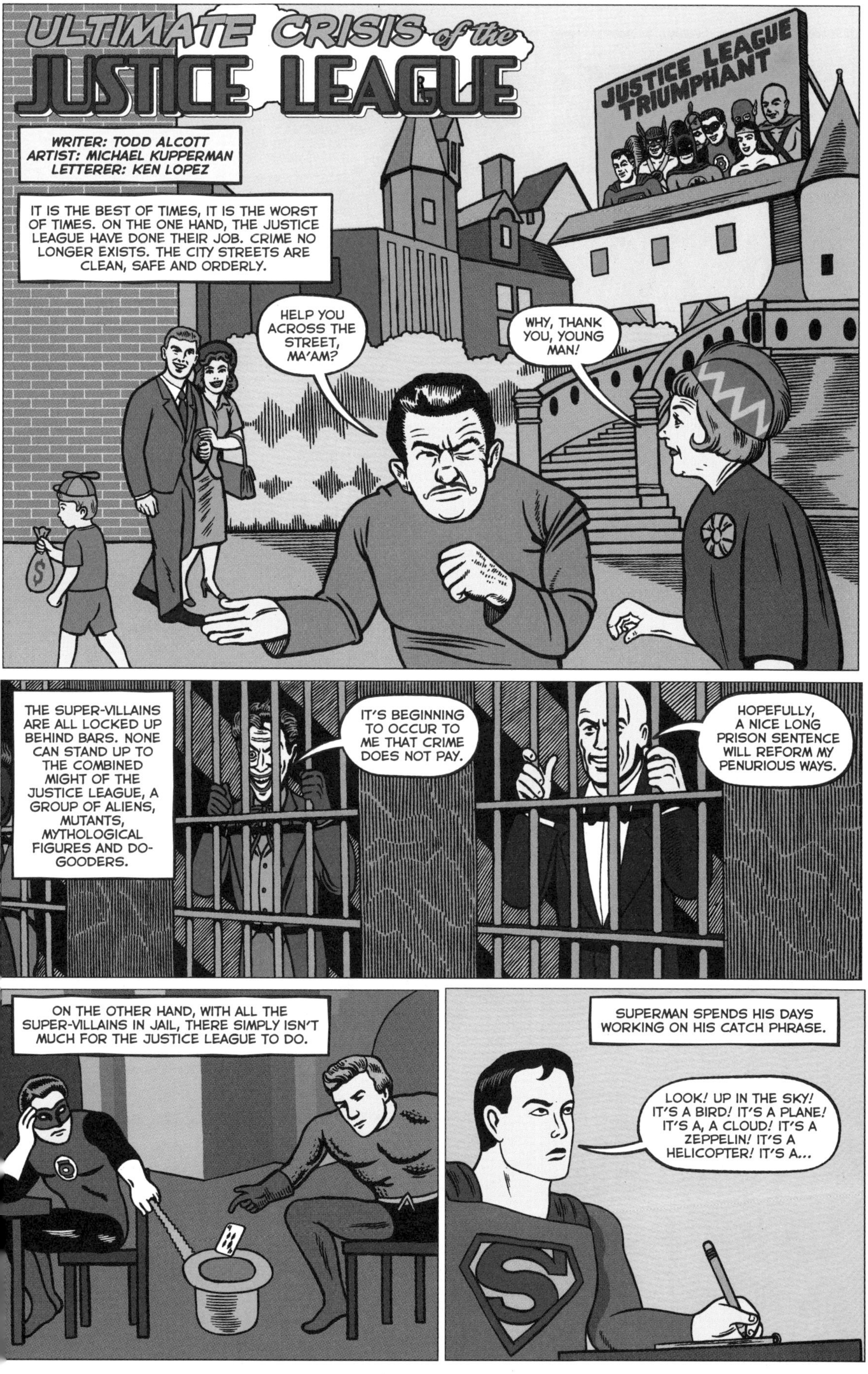
ULTIMATE CRISIS of the JUSTICE LEAGUE
WRITER: TODD ALCOTT
ARTIST: MICHAEL KUPPERMAN
LETTERER: KEN LOPEZ
JUSTICE LEAGUE TRIUMPHANT
IT IS THE BEST OF TIMES, IT IS THE WORST OF TIMES. ON THE ONE HAND, THE JUSTICE LEAGUE HAVE DONE THEIR JOB. CRIME NO LONGER EXISTS. THE CITY STREETS ARE CLEAN, SAFE AND ORDERLY.
HELP YOU ACROSS THE STREET, MA'AM?
WHY, THANK YOU, YOUNG MAN!
THE SUPER-VILLAINS ARE ALL LOCKED UP BEHIND BARS. NONE CAN STAND UP TO THE COMBINED MIGHT OF THE JUSTICE LEAGUE, A GROUP OF ALIENS, MUTANTS, MYTHOLOGICAL FIGURES AND DO-GOODERS.
IT'S BEGINNING TO OCCUR TO ME THAT CRIME DOES NOT PAY.
HOPEFULLY, A NICE LONG PRISON SENTENCE WILL REFORM MY PENURIOUS WAYS.
ON THE OTHER HAND, WITH ALL THE SUPER-VILLAINS IN JAIL, THERE SIMPLY ISN'T MUCH FOR THE JUSTICE LEAGUE TO DO.
SUPERMAN SPENDS HIS DAYS WORKING ON HIS CATCH PHRASE.
LOOK! UP IN THE SKY! IT'S A BIRD! IT'S A PLANE! IT'S A, A CLOUD! IT'S A ZEPPELIN! IT'S A HELICOPTER! IT'S A...

BATMAN WORKS ON HIS THEME SONG.

NO, IT SHOULD BE SIMPLE AND CATCHY, AND A GOOD DRIVING SONG, LIKE THAT BEATLES THING, "TAXMAN!"

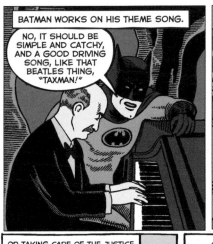

WONDER WOMAN SPENDS A LOT OF TIME WITH HER PATENT ATTORNEY.

FORTY MILLION? THAT'S OUR BEST OFFER? WE'RE TALKING ABOUT *AN INVISIBLE PLANE!* HAVE YOU TALKED TO THE PENTAGON YET?

J'ONN J'ONZZ, THE MARTIAN MANHUNTER, IS LEFT IN CHARGE, TO TAKE CARE OF MENIAL TASKS. FOR INSTANCE, CARING FOR KRYPTO, SUPERMAN'S DOG...

OR TAKING CARE OF THE JUSTICE LEAGUE'S BANK ACCOUNTS...

SORRY, MARS BOY, THIS ATM IS FOR EARTHLINGS ONLY.

TEE HEE!

...OR TIDYING UP THE HALL OF JUSTICE.

I AM A *SUPERHERO!* I AM A *SUPERHERO!*

THE FACT IS, THE MARTIAN MANHUNTER GETS NO RESPECT.

OOH, LOOK, GREEN ARROW HAS AN ARROW WITH A BOXING GLOVE ON THE END!

HE IS CURSED WITH A BACKSTORY SIMILAR TO SUPERMAN'S, BUT WITHOUT THE BENEFIT OF NOVELTY OR GOOD LOOKS.

SO, YOU SAY YOU'RE THE LAST SURVIVING MEMBER OF YOUR RACE, EH? THAT'S TRULY FASCINATING.

NEXT, WE HAVE A MAN WHO TRAINS GOPHERS TO FETCH GOLF BALLS!

WITH NO TRUE SUPER-VILLAINS LEFT, A NEW BREED OF *PETTY SUPER-VILLAINS* RISES UP TO TAKE THEIR PLACES. SUCH AS: THE SMOKER!

HEE HEE HEE! WITH *MY SECONDHAND SMOKE*, I WILL INCREASE, TO A TINY DEGREE, THE POPULATION'S RISK OF LUNG CANCER AND EMPHYSEMA!

OR THE NEFARIOUS BAND OF *JAYWALKERS!*

HA HA! THE *JAYWALKERS* DELAY THE COMMUTE OF ANOTHER HANDFUL OF WORKERS, THUS SOMEWHAT DAMAGING, IN AN UNMEASURABLE WAY, THE GROSS NATIONAL PRODUCT!

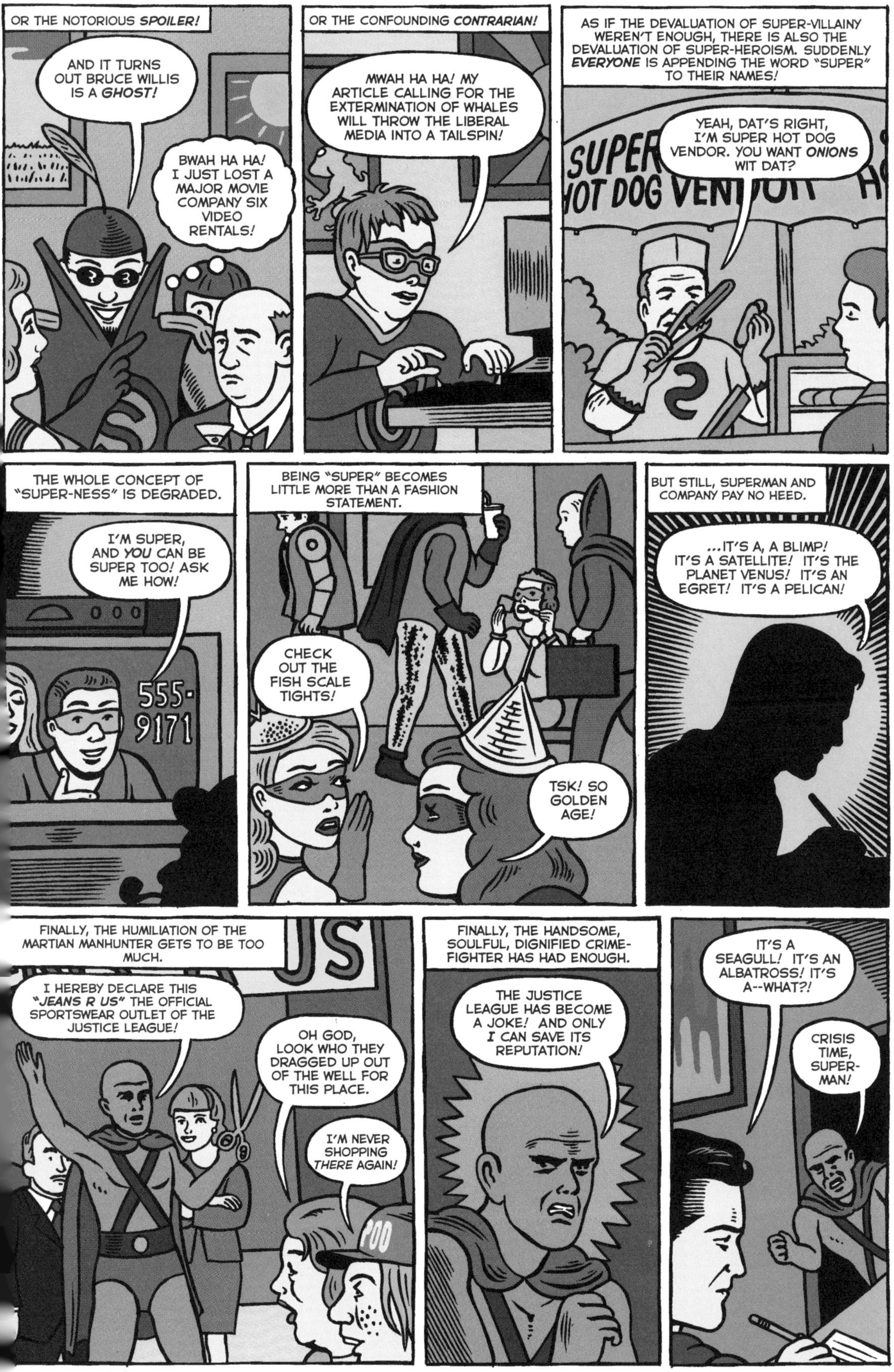
OR THE NOTORIOUS SPOILER!
AND IT TURNS OUT BRUCE WILLIS IS A GHOST!
BWAH HA HA! I JUST LOST A MAJOR MOVIE COMPANY SIX VIDEO RENTALS!
OR THE CONFOUNDING CONTRARIAN!
MWAH HA HA! MY ARTICLE CALLING FOR THE EXTERMINATION OF WHALES WILL THROW THE LIBERAL MEDIA INTO A TAILSPIN!
AS IF THE DEVALUATION OF SUPER-VILLAINY WEREN'T ENOUGH, THERE IS ALSO THE DEVALUATION OF SUPER-HEROISM. SUDDENLY EVERYONE IS APPENDING THE WORD "SUPER" TO THEIR NAMES!
YEAH, DAT'S RIGHT, I'M SUPER HOT DOG VENDOR. YOU WANT ONIONS WIT DAT?
THE WHOLE CONCEPT OF "SUPER-NESS" IS DEGRADED.
I'M SUPER, AND YOU CAN BE SUPER TOO! ASK ME HOW!
555-9171
BEING "SUPER" BECOMES LITTLE MORE THAN A FASHION STATEMENT.
CHECK OUT THE FISH SCALE TIGHTS!
TSK! SO GOLDEN AGE!
BUT STILL, SUPERMAN AND COMPANY PAY NO HEED.
...IT'S A, A BLIMP! IT'S A SATELLITE! IT'S THE PLANET VENUS! IT'S AN EGRET! IT'S A PELICAN!
FINALLY, THE HUMILIATION OF THE MARTIAN MANHUNTER GETS TO BE TOO MUCH.
I HEREBY DECLARE THIS "JEANS R US" THE OFFICIAL SPORTSWEAR OUTLET OF THE JUSTICE LEAGUE!
OH GOD, LOOK WHO THEY DRAGGED UP OUT OF THE WELL FOR THIS PLACE.
I'M NEVER SHOPPING THERE AGAIN!
FINALLY, THE HANDSOME, SOULFUL, DIGNIFIED CRIME-FIGHTER HAS HAD ENOUGH.
THE JUSTICE LEAGUE HAS BECOME A JOKE! AND ONLY I CAN SAVE ITS REPUTATION!
IT'S A SEAGULL! IT'S AN ALBATROSS! IT'S A--WHAT?!
CRISIS TIME, SUPER-MAN!

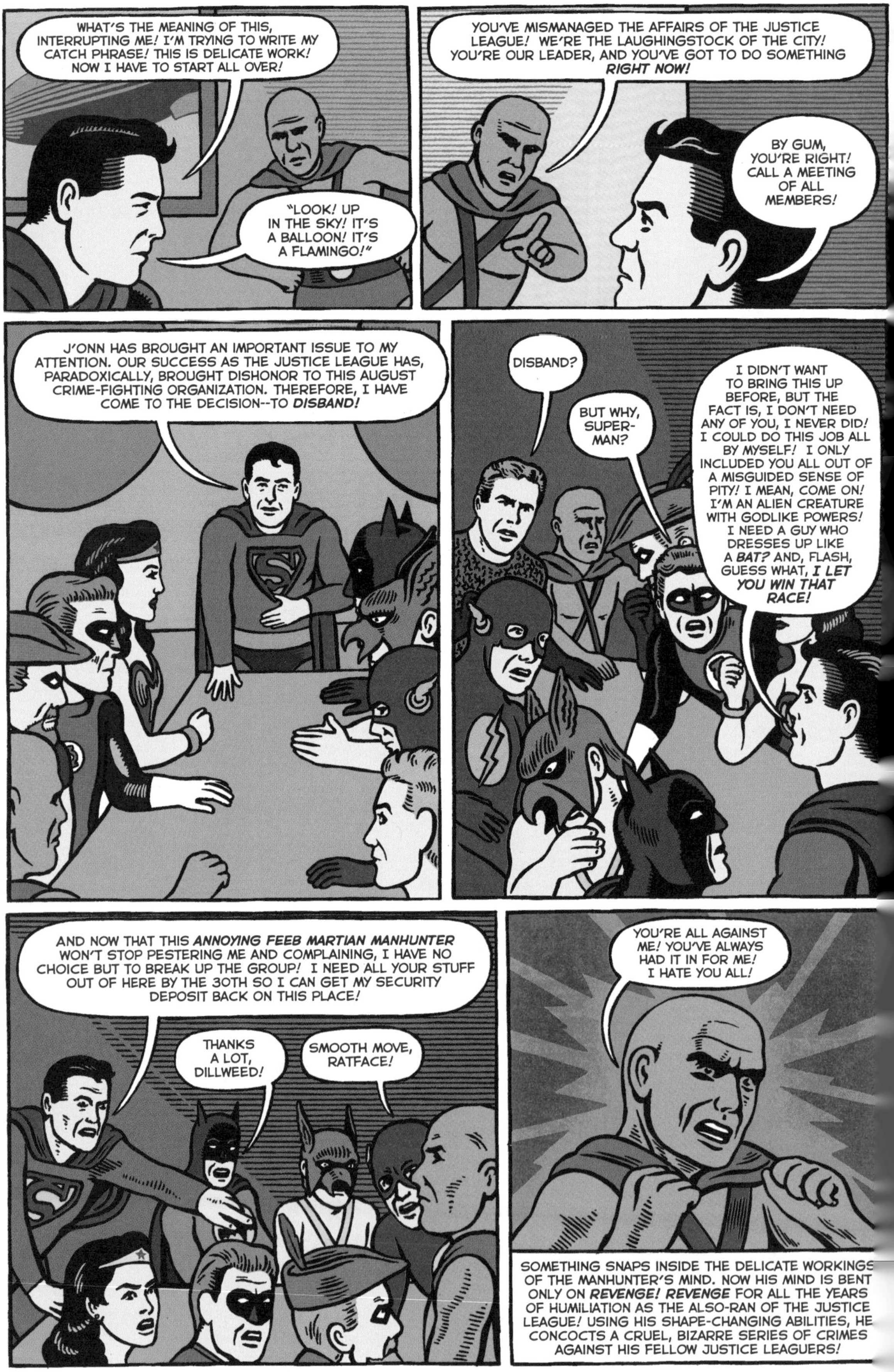
WHAT'S THE MEANING OF THIS, INTERRUPTING ME! I'M TRYING TO WRITE MY CATCH PHRASE! THIS IS DELICATE WORK! NOW I HAVE TO START ALL OVER!
"LOOK! UP IN THE SKY! IT'S A BALLOON! IT'S A FLAMINGO!"
YOU'VE MISMANAGED THE AFFAIRS OF THE JUSTICE LEAGUE! WE'RE THE LAUGHINGSTOCK OF THE CITY! YOU'RE OUR LEADER, AND YOU'VE GOT TO DO SOMETHING RIGHT NOW!
BY GUM, YOU'RE RIGHT! CALL A MEETING OF ALL MEMBERS!
J'ONN HAS BROUGHT AN IMPORTANT ISSUE TO MY ATTENTION. OUR SUCCESS AS THE JUSTICE LEAGUE HAS, PARADOXICALLY, BROUGHT DISHONOR TO THIS AUGUST CRIME-FIGHTING ORGANIZATION. THEREFORE, I HAVE COME TO THE DECISION--TO DISBAND!
DISBAND?
BUT WHY, SUPER-MAN?
I DIDN'T WANT TO BRING THIS UP BEFORE, BUT THE FACT IS, I DON'T NEED ANY OF YOU, I NEVER DID! I COULD DO THIS JOB ALL BY MYSELF! I ONLY INCLUDED YOU ALL OUT OF A MISGUIDED SENSE OF PITY! I MEAN, COME ON! I'M AN ALIEN CREATURE WITH GODLIKE POWERS! I NEED A GUY WHO DRESSES UP LIKE A BAT? AND, FLASH, GUESS WHAT, I LET YOU WIN THAT RACE!
AND NOW THAT THIS ANNOYING FEEB MARTIAN MANHUNTER WON'T STOP PESTERING ME AND COMPLAINING, I HAVE NO CHOICE BUT TO BREAK UP THE GROUP! I NEED ALL YOUR STUFF OUT OF HERE BY THE 30TH SO I CAN GET MY SECURITY DEPOSIT BACK ON THIS PLACE!
THANKS A LOT, DILLWEED!
SMOOTH MOVE, RATFACE!
YOU'RE ALL AGAINST ME! YOU'VE ALWAYS HAD IT IN FOR ME! I HATE YOU ALL!
SOMETHING SNAPS INSIDE THE DELICATE WORKINGS OF THE MANHUNTER'S MIND. NOW HIS MIND IS BENT ONLY ON REVENGE! REVENGE FOR ALL THE YEARS OF HUMILIATION AS THE ALSO-RAN OF THE JUSTICE LEAGUE! USING HIS SHAPE-CHANGING ABILITIES, HE CONCOCTS A CRUEL, BIZARRE SERIES OF CRIMES AGAINST HIS FELLOW JUSTICE LEAGUERS!

POSING AS THE LEADER OF AN ORNITHOLOGICAL SOCIETY, HE KIDNAPS *HAWKMAN!*

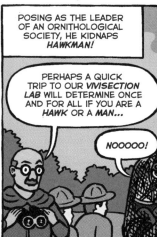

PERHAPS A QUICK TRIP TO OUR *VIVISECTION LAB* WILL DETERMINE ONCE AND FOR ALL IF YOU ARE A *HAWK* OR A *MAN...*

NOOOOO!

POSING AS A JUVENILE DELINQUENT, HE SNATCHES AWAY *BATMAN'S COWL* IN BROAD DAYLIGHT!

HEY, LOOK, EVERYBODY!

GOOD LORD! IT'S MILLIONAIRE *BRUCE WAYNE!*

A MILLIONAIRE WHO DRESSES LIKE A *BAT?*

I'M CALLING THE INSANE ASYLUM!

POSING AS AN UNSCRUPULOUS *PAWNBROKER,* HE CHEATS *GREEN LANTERN* OUT OF HIS ALL-POWERFUL RING!

THIS THING? CHEAP GLASS, SOME KIND OF ALLOY. FACE IT, PAL, WITHOUT THE BATTERY, YOU'RE JUST A GUY WITH A RING!

POSING AS A *MECHANIC,* HE DOES A POOR JOB OF REPAIRING *WONDER WOMAN'S* INVISIBLE PLANE!

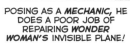

SUFFERING SAPPHO! A SPARK IN MY CENTRAL FUEL TANK!

POSING AS A *HUNTER,* HE MISTAKES SUPERMAN FOR A DEER AND SHOOTS HIM WITH A *KRYPTONITE BULLET!*

LOOK, A TEN-POINTER!

ARRGH! I BREATHE MY LAST!

HA HA HA! FINALLY, VICTORY IS MINE! NO LONGER WILL THE LAST SON OF KRYPTON TAKE THE *MARTIAN MAN-HUNTER* FOR GRANTED!

DON'T SAVOR YOUR VICTORY QUITE YET, J'ONN!

WHA--YOU'RE NOT DEAD!

AND WHO ARE YOU?

ALLOW ME TO INTRODUCE MYSELF! I AM DR. JULIUS OSGOOD, AND YOU HAVE JUST GREATLY BENEFITED THE CAUSE OF MENTAL HEALTH!

YOU SEE, I'M PROMOTING MY NEW BOOK *"PUSHED TOO FAR: WHEN GOOD PEOPLE GO BAD,"* AND THE JUSTICE LEAGUE WAS NICE ENOUGH TO HELP OUT WITH A TEST CASE! ALL THAT YOU HAVE BEEN EXPERIENCING HAS BEEN STAGED BY US, WITH THE HELP OF ACTORS AND ROBOTS, TO HELP ILLUSTRATE MY THEORIES OF RAGE TRANSFERENCE! MY BOOK WILL HELP MILLIONS UNDER-STAND THEIR FEELINGS OF ANGER AND IMPOTENCE, AND YOU WILL HAVE HELPED THEM!

SO, YOU DON'T REALLY HATE ME?

HATE YOU? YOU'RE ONE OF US!

HEY, DON'T GET ALL BLUBBERY ON US, NOW!

KICK ME

AMY SHALINGER, NINE YEARS OLD, HAS BEEN IN A COMA FOR THE LAST SIX MONTHS.

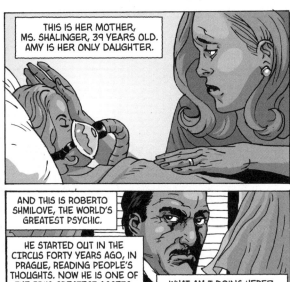

THIS IS HER MOTHER, MS. SHALINGER, 39 YEARS OLD. AMY IS HER ONLY DAUGHTER.

AND THIS IS ROBERTO SHMILOVE, THE WORLD'S GREATEST PSYCHIC.

HE STARTED OUT IN THE CIRCUS FORTY YEARS AGO, IN PRAGUE, READING PEOPLE'S THOUGHTS. NOW HE IS ONE OF THE FBI'S GREATEST ASSETS.

WHAT AM I DOING HERE? I'M NOT SURE YET. ROBERTO SAID I'M THE MAN MOST SUITED FOR THIS.

WHEN I ASKED HIM, "SUITED FOR WHAT?" HE SAID, "CONFRONTING FEAR."

HE USED TO DO THIS TRICK BACK IN HIS CIRCUS DAYS. HE WOULD HOLD TWO PEOPLE'S HANDS AND SOMEHOW JOIN THEIR CONSCIOUSNESS.

AS THE YEARS PASSED, HE MANAGED TO CONTROL THIS PSYCHIC ABILITY.

NOW HE CAN MAKE ONE PERSON ENTER ANOTHER ONE'S MIND.

YOU CAN IMAGINE WHY THE F.B.I. HIRED THE GUY.

STORY AND ART BY TOMER AND ASAF HANUKA   COLOR BY JIM CAMPBELL   LETTERING BY KEN LOPEZ
BATMAN CREATED BY BOB KANE

SIX MONTHS AGO, THE JOKER DISAPPEARED FROM ARKHAM.

AT THE SAME TIME, AMY FELL INTO A COMA. COINCIDENCE? COMMISSIONER GORDON DIDN'T THINK SO. HE CALLED THE FBI, WHO CALLED SHMILOVE. IT TOOK HIM ONE LOOK AT THE GIRL TO KNOW SHE WAS DEEPLY TROUBLED.

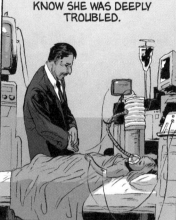

THEN THEY CALLED ME.

SHMILOVE WAS RIGHT. I KNOW FEAR.

I AM LOST.

I LOST MY MOM.

AMY, I AM HERE TO HELP YOU.

DON'T BE SCARED--

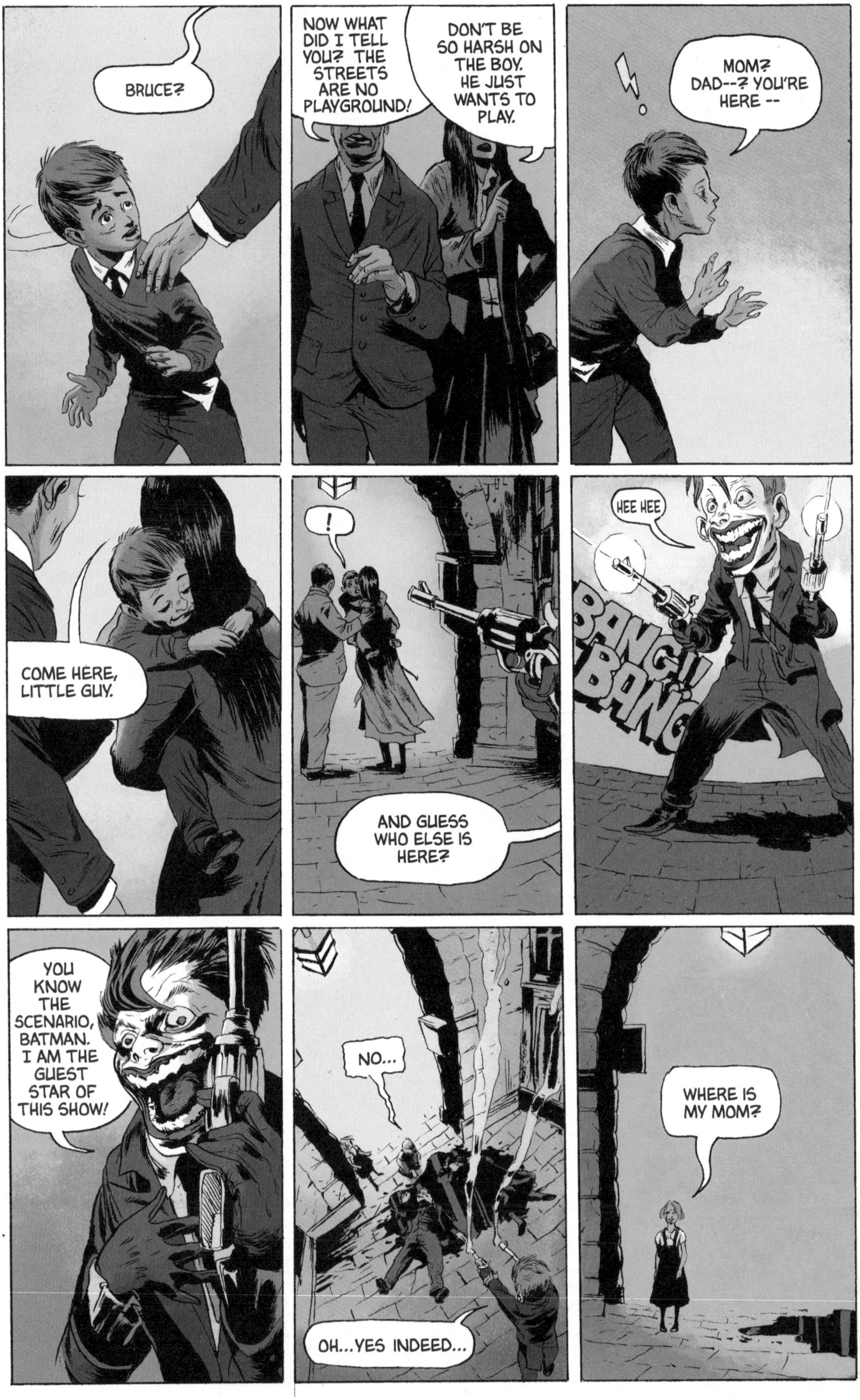
BRUCE?
NOW WHAT DID I TELL YOU? THE STREETS ARE NO PLAYGROUND!
DON'T BE SO HARSH ON THE BOY. HE JUST WANTS TO PLAY.
MOM? DAD--? YOU'RE HERE --
COME HERE, LITTLE GUY.
!
AND GUESS WHO ELSE IS HERE?
HEE HEE
BANG!! BANG
YOU KNOW THE SCENARIO, BATMAN. I AM THE GUEST STAR OF THIS SHOW!
NO...
OH...YES INDEED...
WHERE IS MY MOM?

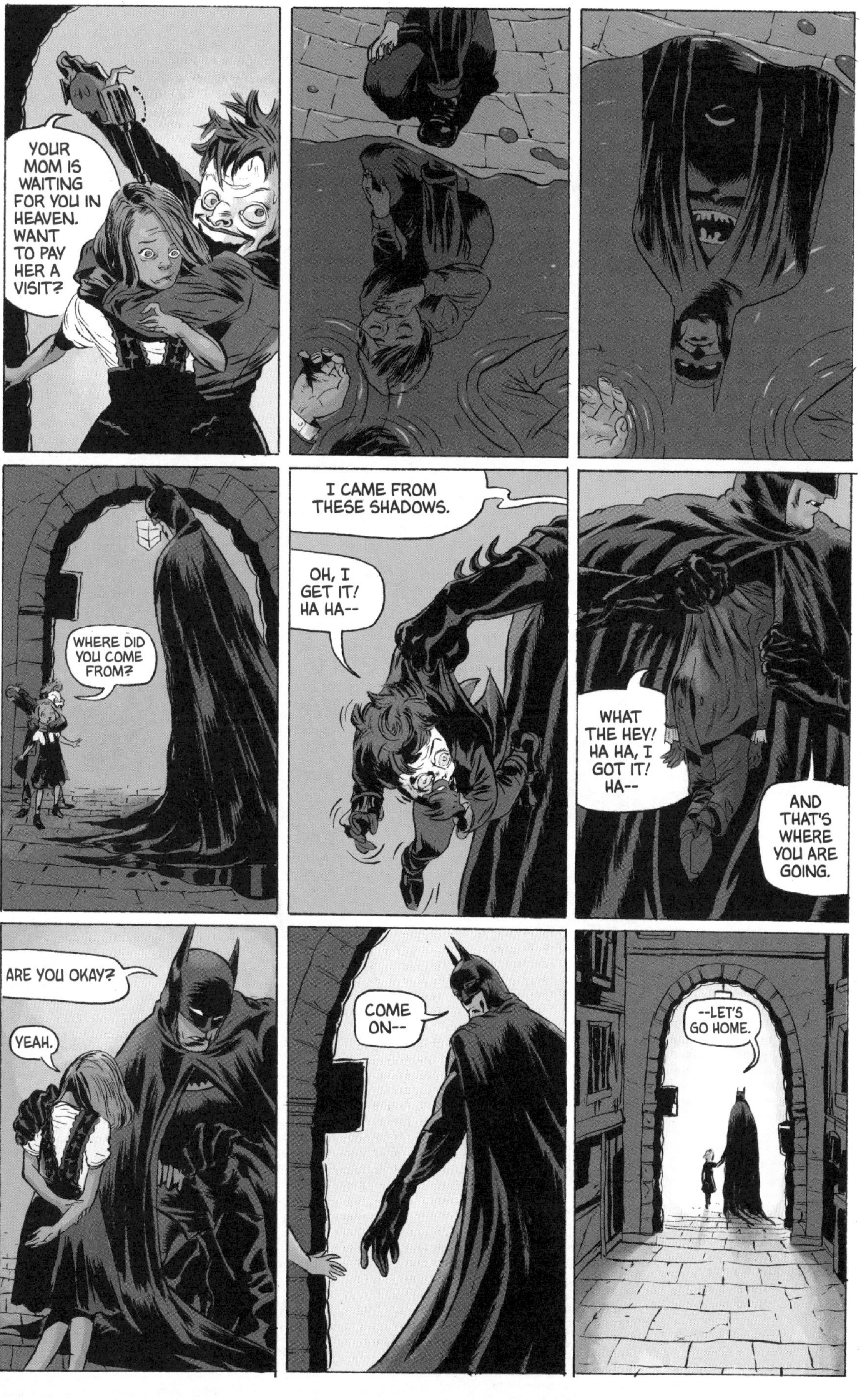
YOUR MOM IS WAITING FOR YOU IN HEAVEN. WANT TO PAY HER A VISIT?
WHERE DID YOU COME FROM?
I CAME FROM THESE SHADOWS.
OH, I GET IT! HA HA--
WHAT THE HEY! HA HA, I GOT IT! HA--
AND THAT'S WHERE YOU ARE GOING.
ARE YOU OKAY?
YEAH.
COME ON--
--LET'S GO HOME.

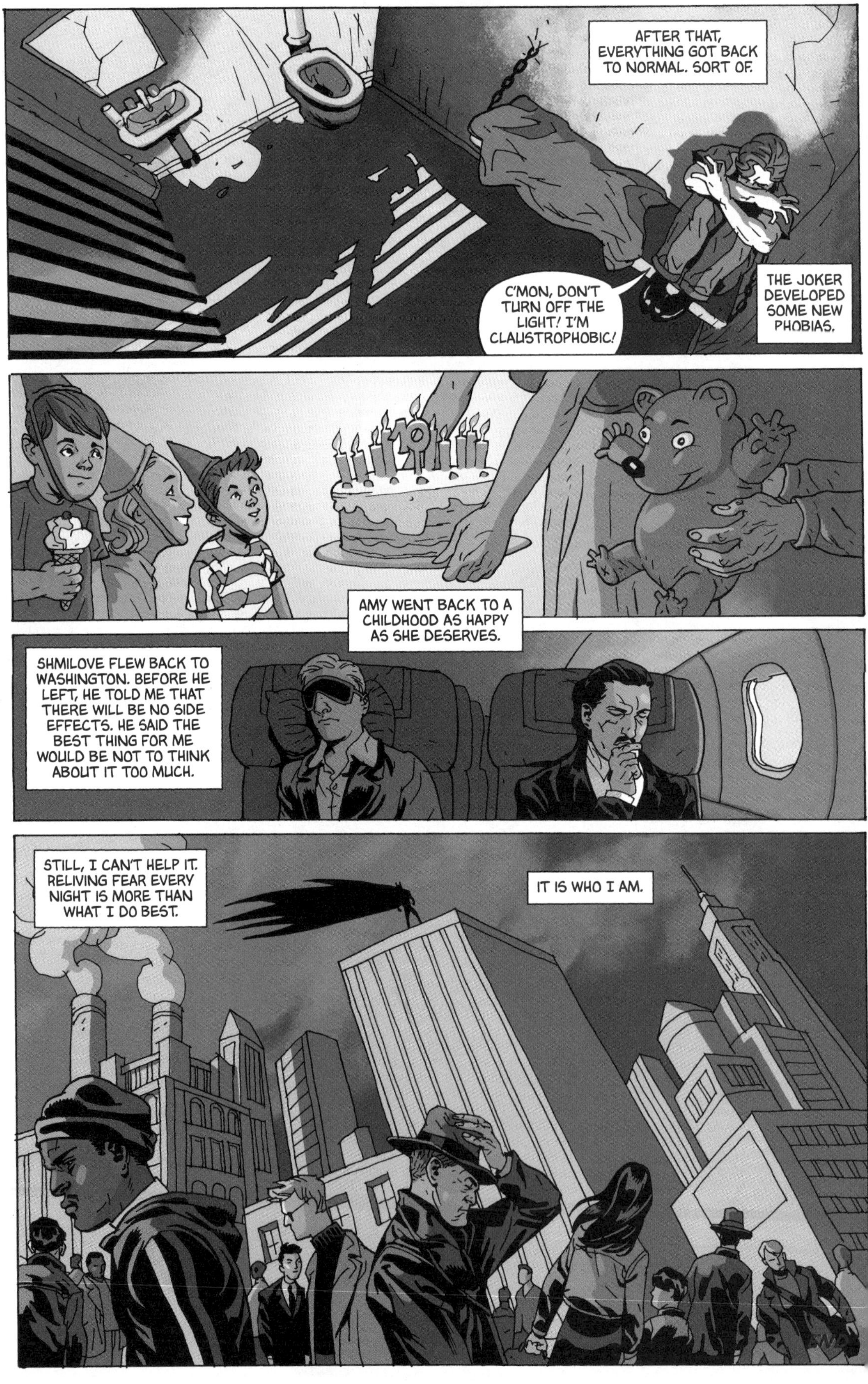
AFTER THAT, EVERYTHING GOT BACK TO NORMAL. SORT OF.
C'MON, DON'T TURN OFF THE LIGHT! I'M CLAUSTROPHOBIC!
THE JOKER DEVELOPED SOME NEW PHOBIAS.
AMY WENT BACK TO A CHILDHOOD AS HAPPY AS SHE DESERVES.
SHMILOVE FLEW BACK TO WASHINGTON. BEFORE HE LEFT, HE TOLD ME THAT THERE WILL BE NO SIDE EFFECTS. HE SAID THE BEST THING FOR ME WOULD BE NOT TO THINK ABOUT IT TOO MUCH.
STILL, I CAN'T HELP IT. RELIVING FEAR EVERY NIGHT IS MORE THAN WHAT I DO BEST.
IT IS WHO I AM.

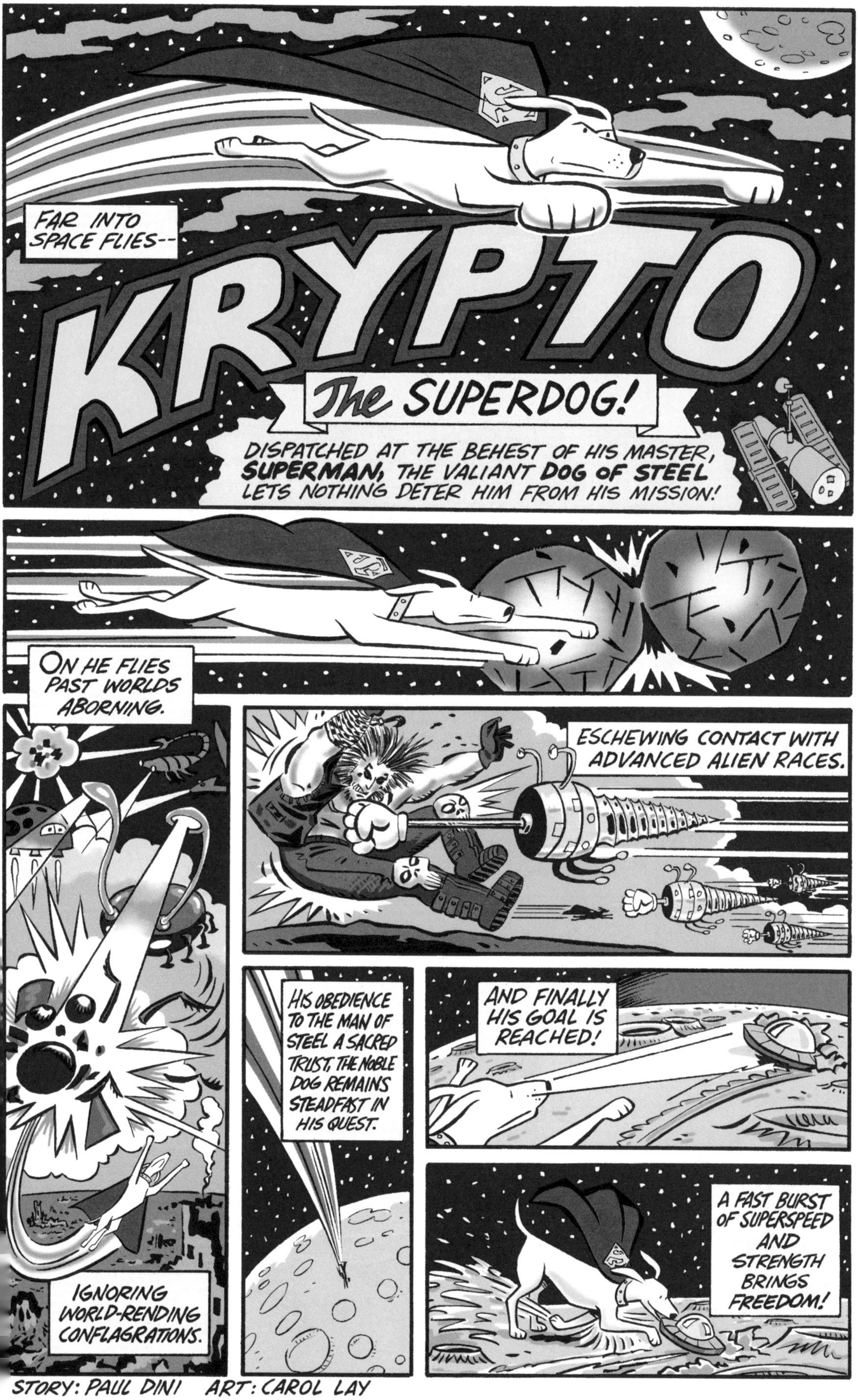

FAR INTO SPACE FLIES--
KRYPTO
The SUPERDOG!
DISPATCHED AT THE BEHEST OF HIS MASTER, SUPERMAN, THE VALIANT DOG OF STEEL LETS NOTHING DETER HIM FROM HIS MISSION!
ON HE FLIES PAST WORLDS ABORNING.
IGNORING WORLD-RENDING CONFLAGRATIONS.
ESCHEWING CONTACT WITH ADVANCED ALIEN RACES.
HIS OBEDIENCE TO THE MAN OF STEEL A SACRED TRUST, THE NOBLE DOG REMAINS STEADFAST IN HIS QUEST.
AND FINALLY HIS GOAL IS REACHED!
A FAST BURST OF SUPERSPEED AND STRENGTH BRINGS FREEDOM!

STORY: PAUL DINI   ART: CAROL LAY

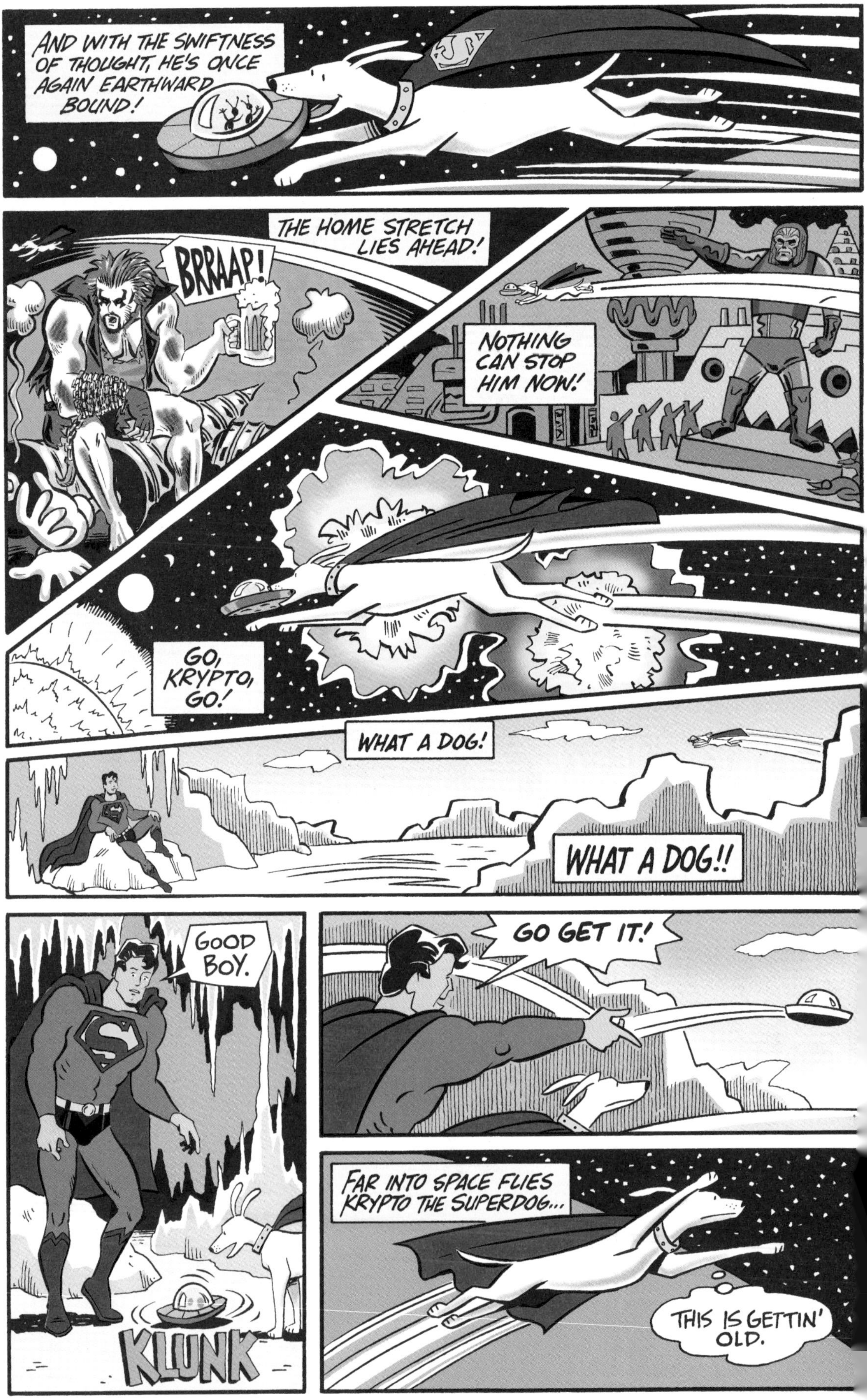
AND WITH THE SWIFTNESS OF THOUGHT, HE'S ONCE AGAIN EARTHWARD BOUND!
THE HOME STRETCH LIES AHEAD!
BRRAAP!
NOTHING CAN STOP HIM NOW!
GO, KRYPTO, GO!
WHAT A DOG!
WHAT A DOG!!
GOOD BOY.
KLUNK
GO GET IT!
FAR INTO SPACE FLIES KRYPTO THE SUPERDOG...
THIS IS GETTIN' OLD.

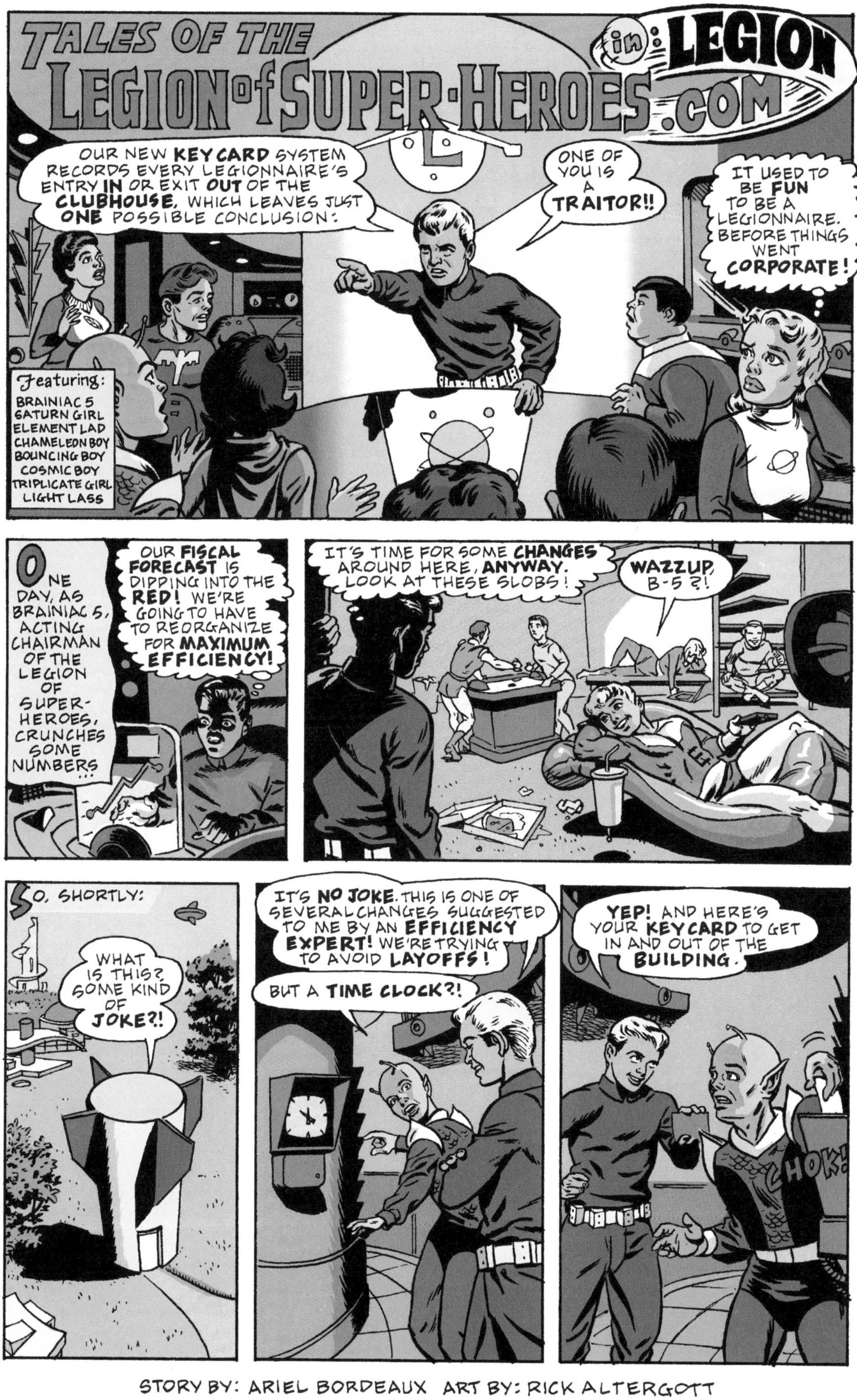
TALES OF THE LEGION of SUPER-HEROES in: LEGION .COM
OUR NEW KEYCARD SYSTEM RECORDS EVERY LEGIONNAIRE'S ENTRY IN OR EXIT OUT OF THE CLUBHOUSE, WHICH LEAVES JUST ONE POSSIBLE CONCLUSION:
ONE OF YOU IS A TRAITOR!!
IT USED TO BE FUN TO BE A LEGIONNAIRE. BEFORE THINGS WENT CORPORATE!
Featuring: BRAINIAC 5 SATURN GIRL ELEMENT LAD CHAMELEON BOY BOUNCING BOY COSMIC BOY TRIPLICATE GIRL LIGHT LASS
ONE DAY, AS BRAINIAC 5, ACTING CHAIRMAN OF THE LEGION OF SUPER-HEROES, CRUNCHES SOME NUMBERS...
OUR FISCAL FORECAST IS DIPPING INTO THE RED! WE'RE GOING TO HAVE TO REORGANIZE FOR MAXIMUM EFFICIENCY!
IT'S TIME FOR SOME CHANGES AROUND HERE, ANYWAY. LOOK AT THESE SLOBS!
WAZZUP, B-5 ?!
SO, SHORTLY:
WHAT IS THIS? SOME KIND OF JOKE?!
IT'S NO JOKE. THIS IS ONE OF SEVERAL CHANGES SUGGESTED TO ME BY AN EFFICIENCY EXPERT! WE'RE TRYING TO AVOID LAYOFFS!
BUT A TIME CLOCK?!
YEP! AND HERE'S YOUR KEYCARD TO GET IN AND OUT OF THE BUILDING.
CHOK!

STORY BY: ARIEL BORDEAUX ART BY: RICK ALTERGOTT

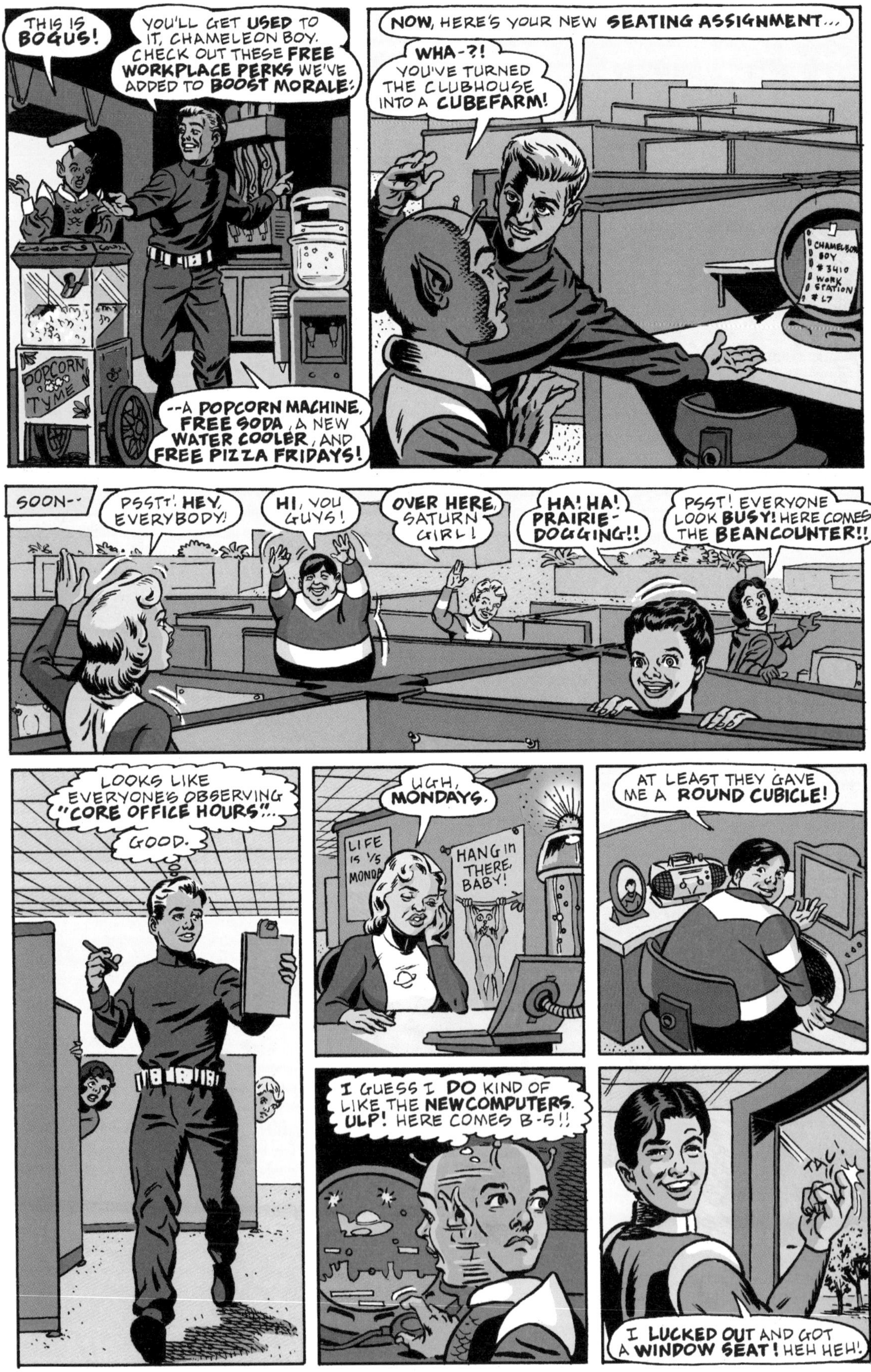
THIS IS BOGUS!
YOU'LL GET USED TO IT, CHAMELEON BOY. CHECK OUT THESE FREE WORKPLACE PERKS WE'VE ADDED TO BOOST MORALE:
POPCORN TYME
--A POPCORN MACHINE, FREE SODA, A NEW WATER COOLER, AND FREE PIZZA FRIDAYS!
NOW, HERE'S YOUR NEW SEATING ASSIGNMENT...
WHA-?! YOU'VE TURNED THE CLUBHOUSE INTO A CUBEFARM!
CHAMELEON BOY #3410 WORK STATION #L7
SOON--
PSSST! HEY, EVERYBODY!
HI, YOU GUYS!
OVER HERE, SATURN GIRL!
HA! HA! PRAIRIE-DOGGING!!
PSST! EVERYONE LOOK BUSY! HERE COMES THE BEANCOUNTER!!
LOOKS LIKE EVERYONE'S OBSERVING "CORE OFFICE HOURS"...
GOOD.
UGH, MONDAYS.
LIFE IS 1/5 MONDA
HANG in THERE, BABY!
AT LEAST THEY GAVE ME A ROUND CUBICLE!
I GUESS I DO KIND OF LIKE THE NEW COMPUTERS. ULP! HERE COMES B-5!!
I LUCKED OUT AND GOT A WINDOW SEAT! HEH HEH!

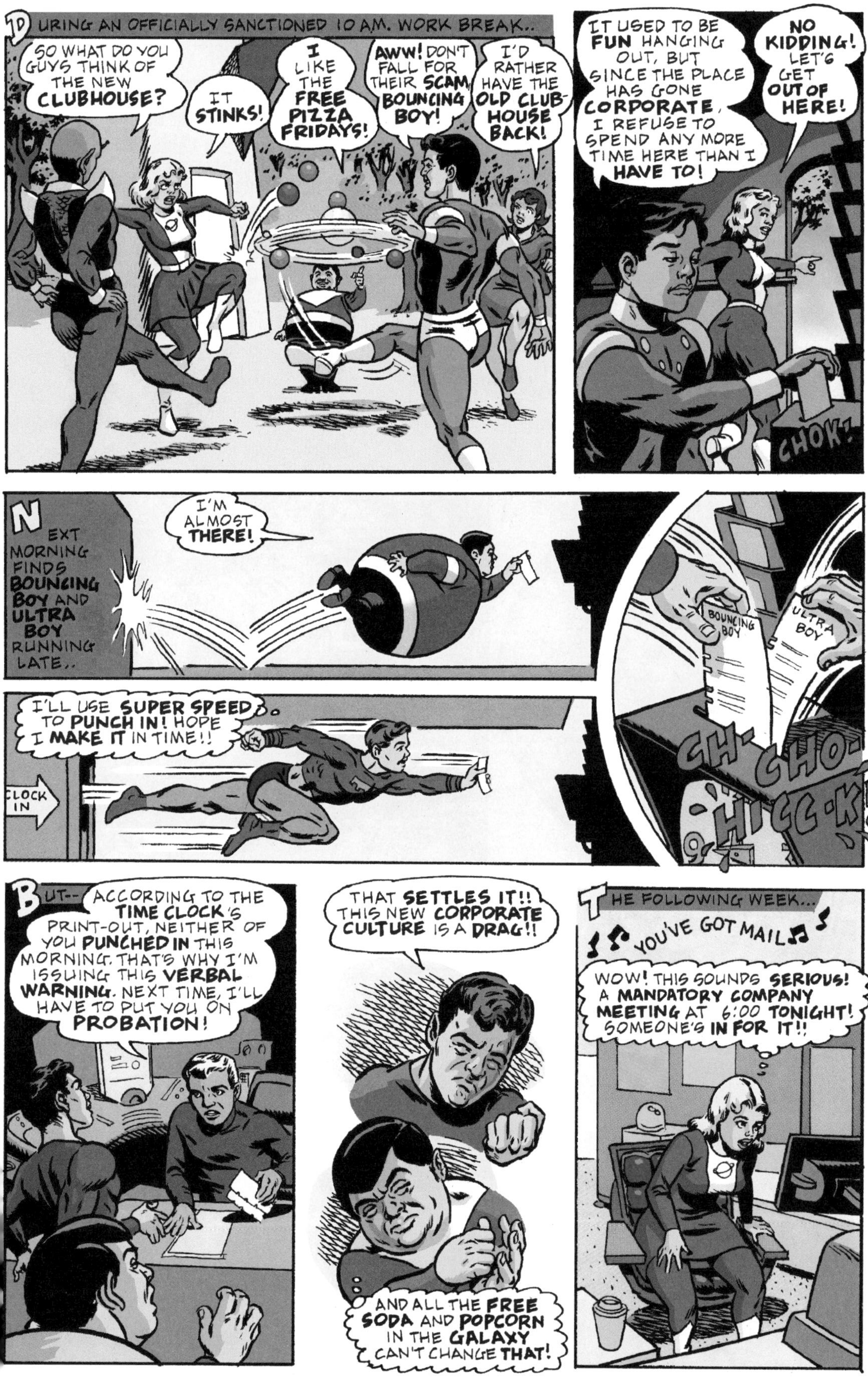
DURING AN OFFICIALLY SANCTIONED 10 A.M. WORK BREAK..
SO WHAT DO YOU GUYS THINK OF THE NEW CLUBHOUSE?
IT STINKS!
I LIKE THE FREE PIZZA FRIDAYS!
AWW! DON'T FALL FOR THEIR SCAM, BOUNCING BOY!
I'D RATHER HAVE THE OLD CLUB-HOUSE BACK!
IT USED TO BE FUN HANGING OUT, BUT SINCE THE PLACE HAS GONE CORPORATE, I REFUSE TO SPEND ANY MORE TIME HERE THAN I HAVE TO!
NO KIDDING! LET'S GET OUT OF HERE!
CHOK!
NEXT MORNING FINDS BOUNCING BOY AND ULTRA BOY RUNNING LATE..
I'M ALMOST THERE!
I'LL USE SUPER SPEED TO PUNCH IN! HOPE I MAKE IT IN TIME!!
CLOCK IN
BOUNCING BOY
ULTRA BOY
CH-CHO-HICC-K!
BUT-- ACCORDING TO THE TIME CLOCK'S PRINT-OUT, NEITHER OF YOU PUNCHED IN THIS MORNING. THAT'S WHY I'M ISSUING THIS VERBAL WARNING. NEXT TIME, I'LL HAVE TO PUT YOU ON PROBATION!
THAT SETTLES IT!! THIS NEW CORPORATE CULTURE IS A DRAG!!
AND ALL THE FREE SODA AND POPCORN IN THE GALAXY CAN'T CHANGE THAT!
THE FOLLOWING WEEK...
YOU'VE GOT MAIL
WOW! THIS SOUNDS SERIOUS! A MANDATORY COMPANY MEETING AT 6:00 TONIGHT! SOMEONE'S IN FOR IT!!

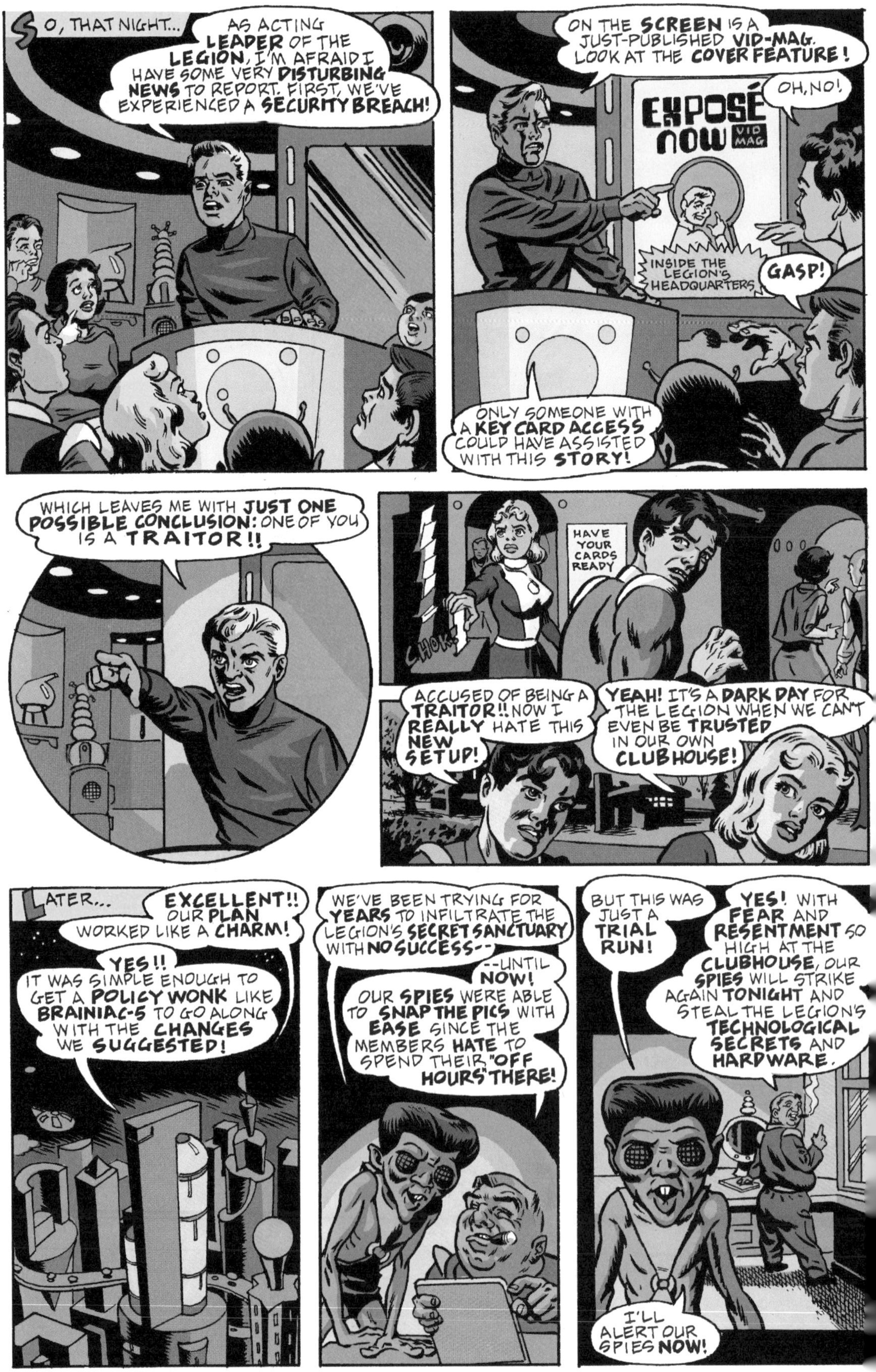
SO, THAT NIGHT...
AS ACTING LEADER OF THE LEGION, I'M AFRAID I HAVE SOME VERY DISTURBING NEWS TO REPORT. FIRST, WE'VE EXPERIENCED A SECURITY BREACH!
ON THE SCREEN IS A JUST-PUBLISHED VID-MAG. LOOK AT THE COVER FEATURE!
EXPOSÉ NOW VID MAG
INSIDE THE LEGION'S HEADQUARTERS
OH, NO!
GASP!
ONLY SOMEONE WITH A KEY CARD ACCESS COULD HAVE ASSISTED WITH THIS STORY!
WHICH LEAVES ME WITH JUST ONE POSSIBLE CONCLUSION: ONE OF YOU IS A TRAITOR!!
HAVE YOUR CARDS READY
CHOK!
ACCUSED OF BEING A TRAITOR!! NOW I REALLY HATE THIS NEW SETUP!
YEAH! IT'S A DARK DAY FOR THE LEGION WHEN WE CAN'T EVEN BE TRUSTED IN OUR OWN CLUBHOUSE!
LATER...
EXCELLENT!! OUR PLAN WORKED LIKE A CHARM!
YES!! IT WAS SIMPLE ENOUGH TO GET A POLICY WONK LIKE BRAINIAC-5 TO GO ALONG WITH THE CHANGES WE SUGGESTED!
WE'VE BEEN TRYING FOR YEARS TO INFILTRATE THE LEGION'S SECRET SANCTUARY WITH NO SUCCESS--
--UNTIL NOW! OUR SPIES WERE ABLE TO SNAP THE PICS WITH EASE SINCE THE MEMBERS HATE TO SPEND THEIR "OFF HOURS" THERE!
BUT THIS WAS JUST A TRIAL RUN!
YES! WITH FEAR AND RESENTMENT SO HIGH AT THE CLUBHOUSE, OUR SPIES WILL STRIKE AGAIN TONIGHT AND STEAL THE LEGION'S TECHNOLOGICAL SECRETS AND HARDWARE.
I'LL ALERT OUR SPIES NOW!

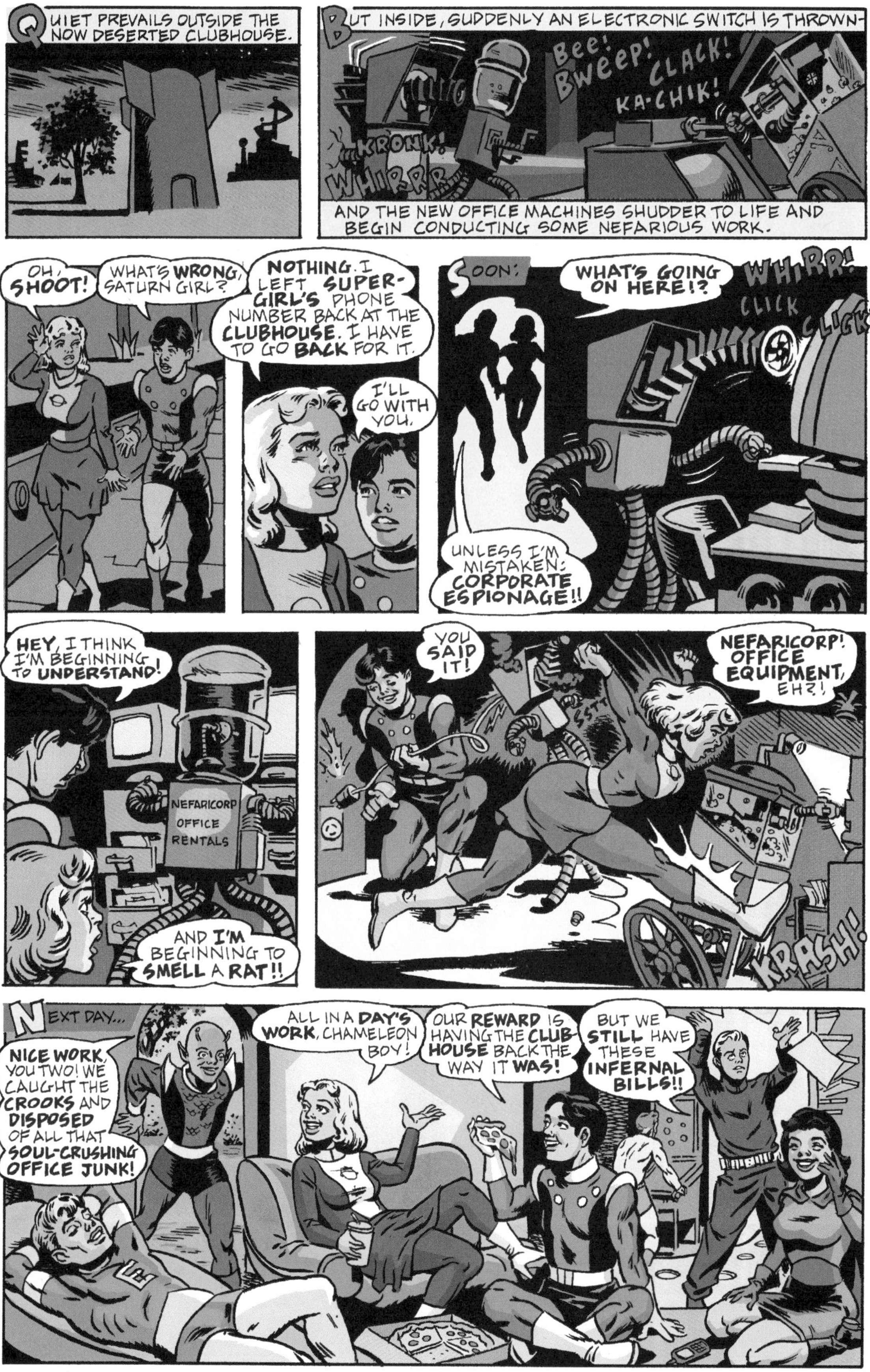
QUIET PREVAILS OUTSIDE THE NOW DESERTED CLUBHOUSE.
BUT INSIDE, SUDDENLY AN ELECTRONIC SWITCH IS THROWN-
Bee! Bweep!
CLACK!
KA-CHIK!
KRONK!
WHIRRR
AND THE NEW OFFICE MACHINES SHUDDER TO LIFE AND BEGIN CONDUCTING SOME NEFARIOUS WORK.
OH, SHOOT!
WHAT'S WRONG, SATURN GIRL?
NOTHING. I LEFT SUPER-GIRL'S PHONE NUMBER BACK AT THE CLUBHOUSE. I HAVE TO GO BACK FOR IT.
I'LL GO WITH YOU.
SOON:
WHAT'S GOING ON HERE!?
WHIRR!
CLICK
CLICK!
UNLESS I'M MISTAKEN: CORPORATE ESPIONAGE!!
HEY, I THINK I'M BEGINNING TO UNDERSTAND!
NEFARICORP OFFICE RENTALS
AND I'M BEGINNING TO SMELL A RAT!!
YOU SAID IT!
NEFARICORP! OFFICE EQUIPMENT, EH?!
KRASH!
NEXT DAY...
NICE WORK, YOU TWO! WE CAUGHT THE CROOKS AND DISPOSED OF ALL THAT SOUL-CRUSHING OFFICE JUNK!
ALL IN A DAY'S WORK, CHAMELEON BOY!
OUR REWARD IS HAVING THE CLUB-HOUSE BACK THE WAY IT WAS!
BUT WE STILL HAVE THESE INFERNAL BILLS!!

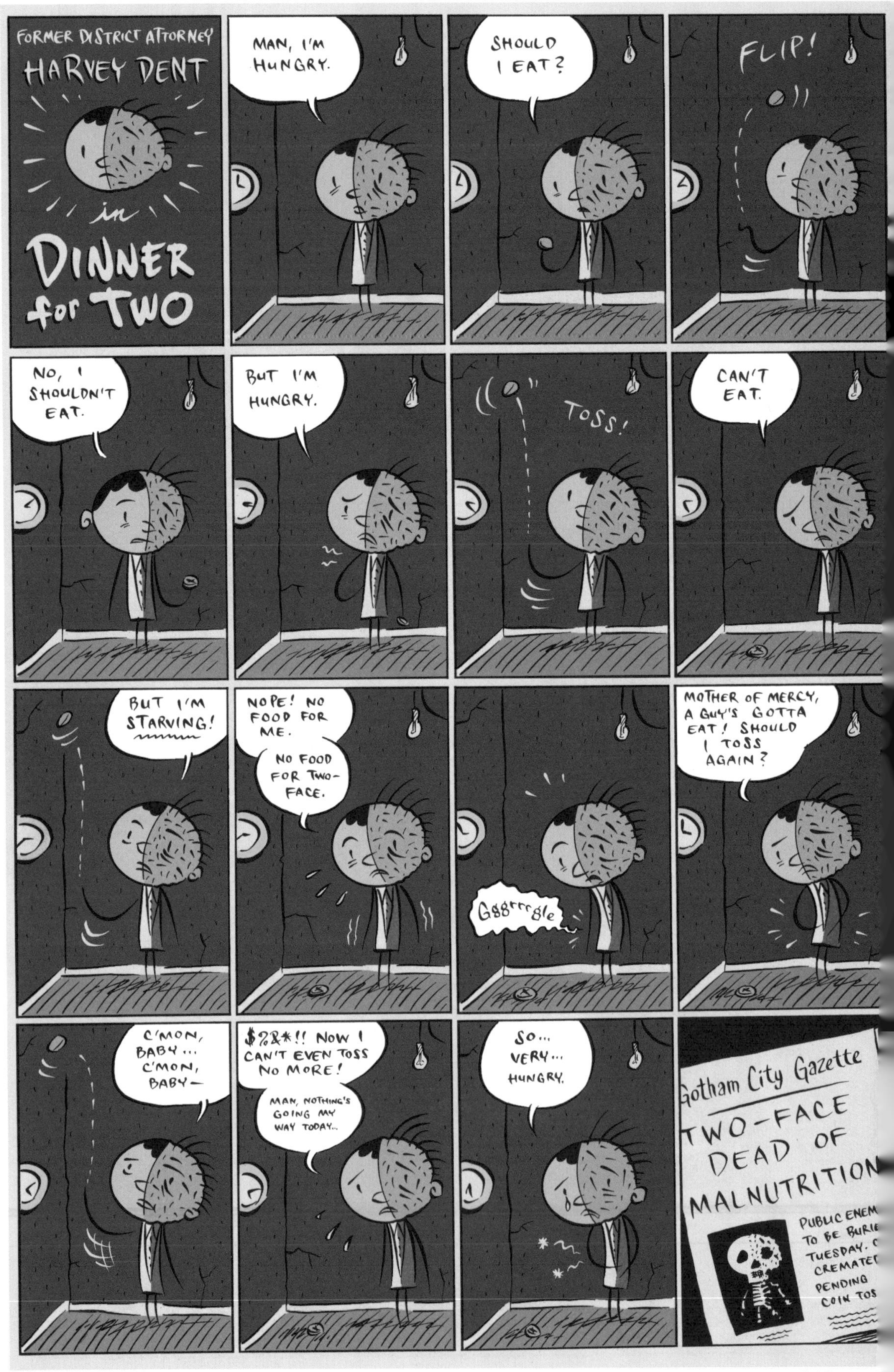

FORMER DISTRICT ATTORNEY
HARVEY DENT
in
DINNER for TWO
MAN, I'M HUNGRY.
SHOULD I EAT?
FLIP!
NO, I SHOULDN'T EAT.
BUT I'M HUNGRY.
TOSS!
CAN'T EAT.
BUT I'M STARVING!
NOPE! NO FOOD FOR ME.
NO FOOD FOR TWO-FACE.
Ggggrrrgle
MOTHER OF MERCY, A GUY'S GOTTA EAT! SHOULD I TOSS AGAIN?
C'MON, BABY... C'MON, BABY—
$%&*!! NOW I CAN'T EVEN TOSS NO MORE!
MAN, NOTHING'S GOING MY WAY TODAY...
SO... VERY... HUNGRY.
Gotham City Gazette
TWO-FACE DEAD OF MALNUTRITION
PUBLIC ENEM
TO BE BURIE
TUESDAY, O
CREMATE
PENDING
COIN TOS

WRITER: EVAN DORKIN

ARTIST: IVAN BRUNETTI

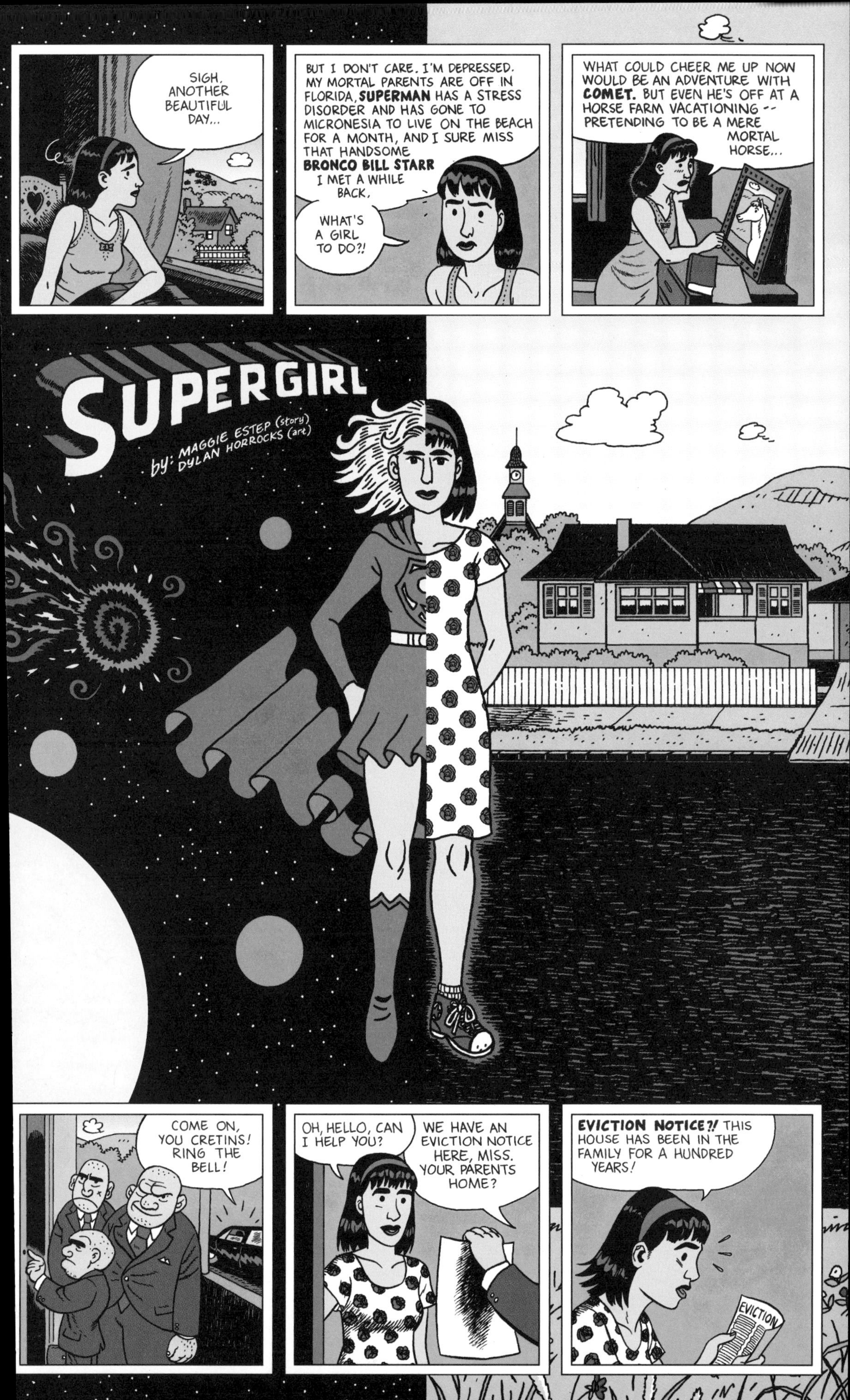
SIGH, ANOTHER BEAUTIFUL DAY...
BUT I DON'T CARE. I'M DEPRESSED. MY MORTAL PARENTS ARE OFF IN FLORIDA, SUPERMAN HAS A STRESS DISORDER AND HAS GONE TO MICRONESIA TO LIVE ON THE BEACH FOR A MONTH, AND I SURE MISS THAT HANDSOME BRONCO BILL STARR I MET A WHILE BACK,
WHAT'S A GIRL TO DO?!
WHAT COULD CHEER ME UP NOW WOULD BE AN ADVENTURE WITH COMET. BUT EVEN HE'S OFF AT A HORSE FARM VACATIONING -- PRETENDING TO BE A MERE MORTAL HORSE...
SUPERGIRL
by: MAGGIE ESTEP (story) DYLAN HORROCKS (art)
COME ON, YOU CRETINS! RING THE BELL!
OH, HELLO, CAN I HELP YOU?
WE HAVE AN EVICTION NOTICE HERE, MISS. YOUR PARENTS HOME?
EVICTION NOTICE?! THIS HOUSE HAS BEEN IN THE FAMILY FOR A HUNDRED YEARS!
EVICTION

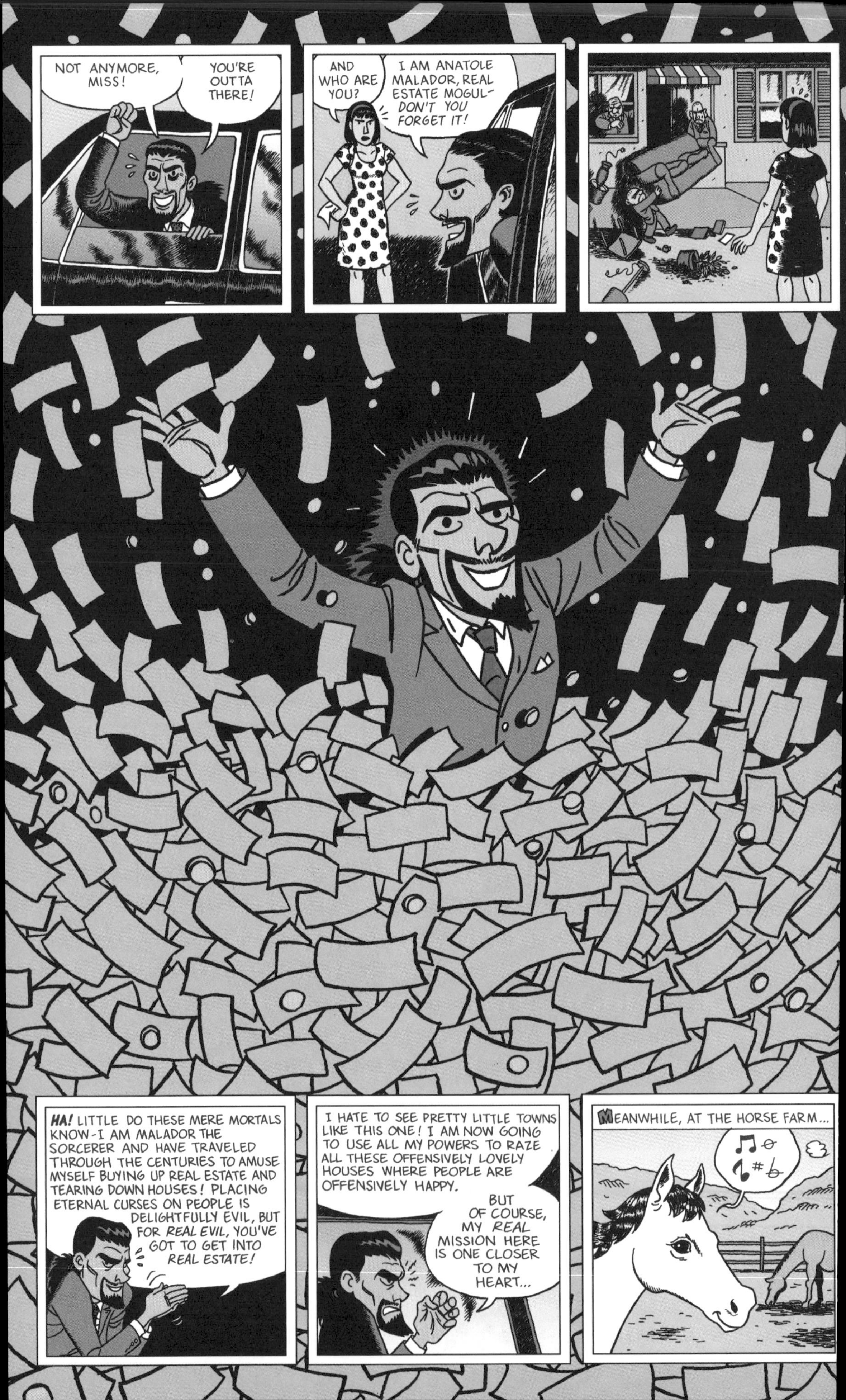
NOT ANYMORE, MISS!
YOU'RE OUTTA THERE!
AND WHO ARE YOU?
I AM ANATOLE MALADOR, REAL ESTATE MOGUL- DON'T YOU FORGET IT!
HA! LITTLE DO THESE MERE MORTALS KNOW-I AM MALADOR THE SORCERER AND HAVE TRAVELED THROUGH THE CENTURIES TO AMUSE MYSELF BUYING UP REAL ESTATE AND TEARING DOWN HOUSES! PLACING ETERNAL CURSES ON PEOPLE IS DELIGHTFULLY EVIL, BUT FOR REAL EVIL, YOU'VE GOT TO GET INTO REAL ESTATE!
I HATE TO SEE PRETTY LITTLE TOWNS LIKE THIS ONE! I AM NOW GOING TO USE ALL MY POWERS TO RAZE ALL THESE OFFENSIVELY LOVELY HOUSES WHERE PEOPLE ARE OFFENSIVELY HAPPY.
BUT OF COURSE, MY REAL MISSION HERE IS ONE CLOSER TO MY HEART...
MEANWHILE, AT THE HORSE FARM...

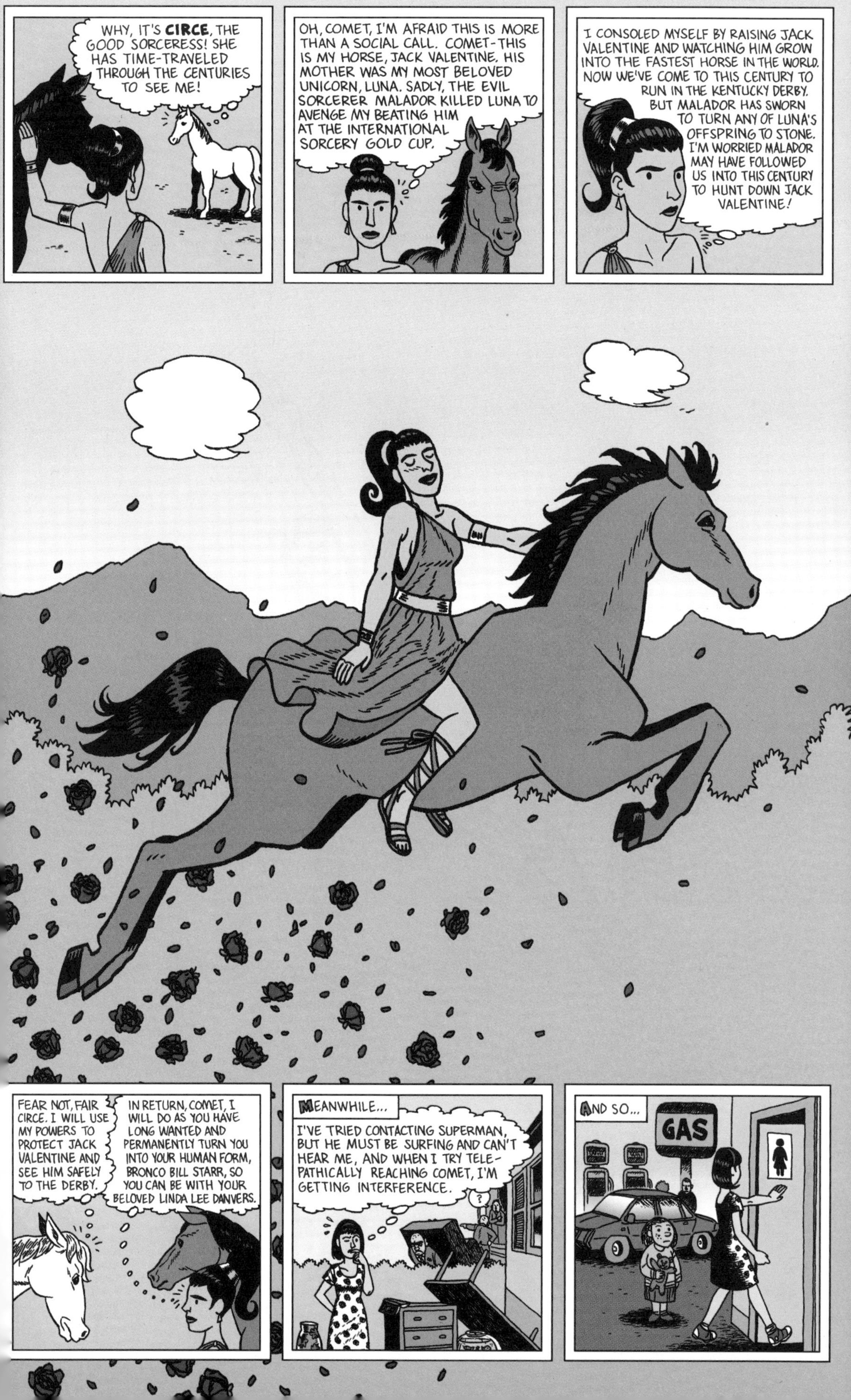

WHY, IT'S CIRCE, THE GOOD SORCERESS! SHE HAS TIME-TRAVELED THROUGH THE CENTURIES TO SEE ME!
OH, COMET, I'M AFRAID THIS IS MORE THAN A SOCIAL CALL. COMET- THIS IS MY HORSE, JACK VALENTINE. HIS MOTHER WAS MY MOST BELOVED UNICORN, LUNA. SADLY, THE EVIL SORCERER MALADOR KILLED LUNA TO AVENGE MY BEATING HIM AT THE INTERNATIONAL SORCERY GOLD CUP.
I CONSOLED MYSELF BY RAISING JACK VALENTINE AND WATCHING HIM GROW INTO THE FASTEST HORSE IN THE WORLD. NOW WE'VE COME TO THIS CENTURY TO RUN IN THE KENTUCKY DERBY. BUT MALADOR HAS SWORN TO TURN ANY OF LUNA'S OFFSPRING TO STONE. I'M WORRIED MALADOR MAY HAVE FOLLOWED US INTO THIS CENTURY TO HUNT DOWN JACK VALENTINE!
FEAR NOT, FAIR CIRCE. I WILL USE MY POWERS TO PROTECT JACK VALENTINE AND SEE HIM SAFELY TO THE DERBY.
IN RETURN, COMET, I WILL DO AS YOU HAVE LONG WANTED AND PERMANENTLY TURN YOU INTO YOUR HUMAN FORM, BRONCO BILL STARR, SO YOU CAN BE WITH YOUR BELOVED LINDA LEE DANVERS.
MEANWHILE...
I'VE TRIED CONTACTING SUPERMAN, BUT HE MUST BE SURFING AND CAN'T HEAR ME, AND WHEN I TRY TELE-PATHICALLY REACHING COMET, I'M GETTING INTERFERENCE.
?
AND SO...
GAS

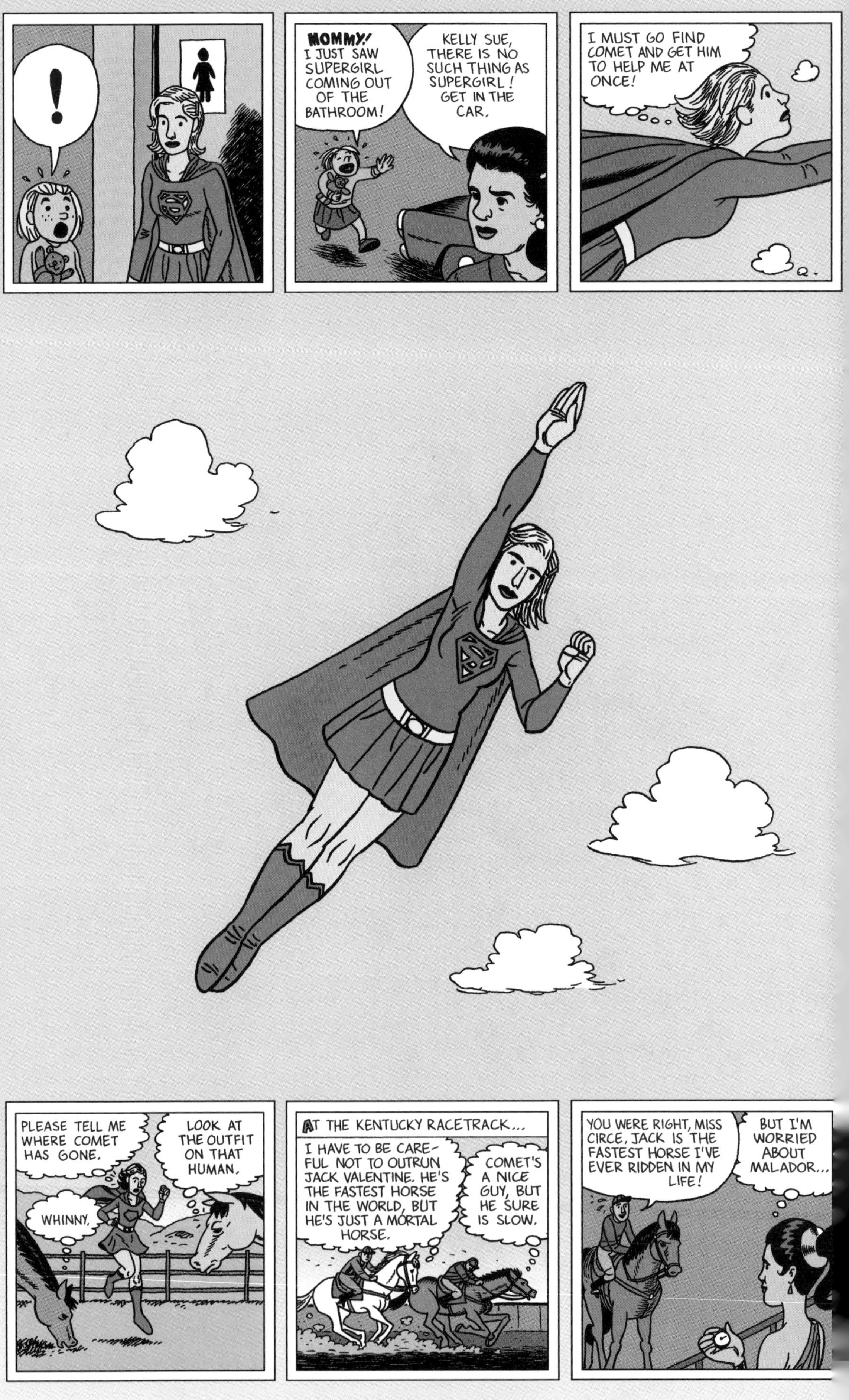
!
MOMMY! I JUST SAW SUPERGIRL COMING OUT OF THE BATHROOM!
KELLY SUE, THERE IS NO SUCH THING AS SUPERGIRL! GET IN THE CAR.
I MUST GO FIND COMET AND GET HIM TO HELP ME AT ONCE!
PLEASE TELL ME WHERE COMET HAS GONE.
LOOK AT THE OUTFIT ON THAT HUMAN.
WHINNY.
AT THE KENTUCKY RACETRACK...
I HAVE TO BE CAREFUL NOT TO OUTRUN JACK VALENTINE. HE'S THE FASTEST HORSE IN THE WORLD, BUT HE'S JUST A MORTAL HORSE.
COMET'S A NICE GUY, BUT HE SURE IS SLOW.
YOU WERE RIGHT, MISS CIRCE, JACK IS THE FASTEST HORSE I'VE EVER RIDDEN IN MY LIFE!
BUT I'M WORRIED ABOUT MALADOR...

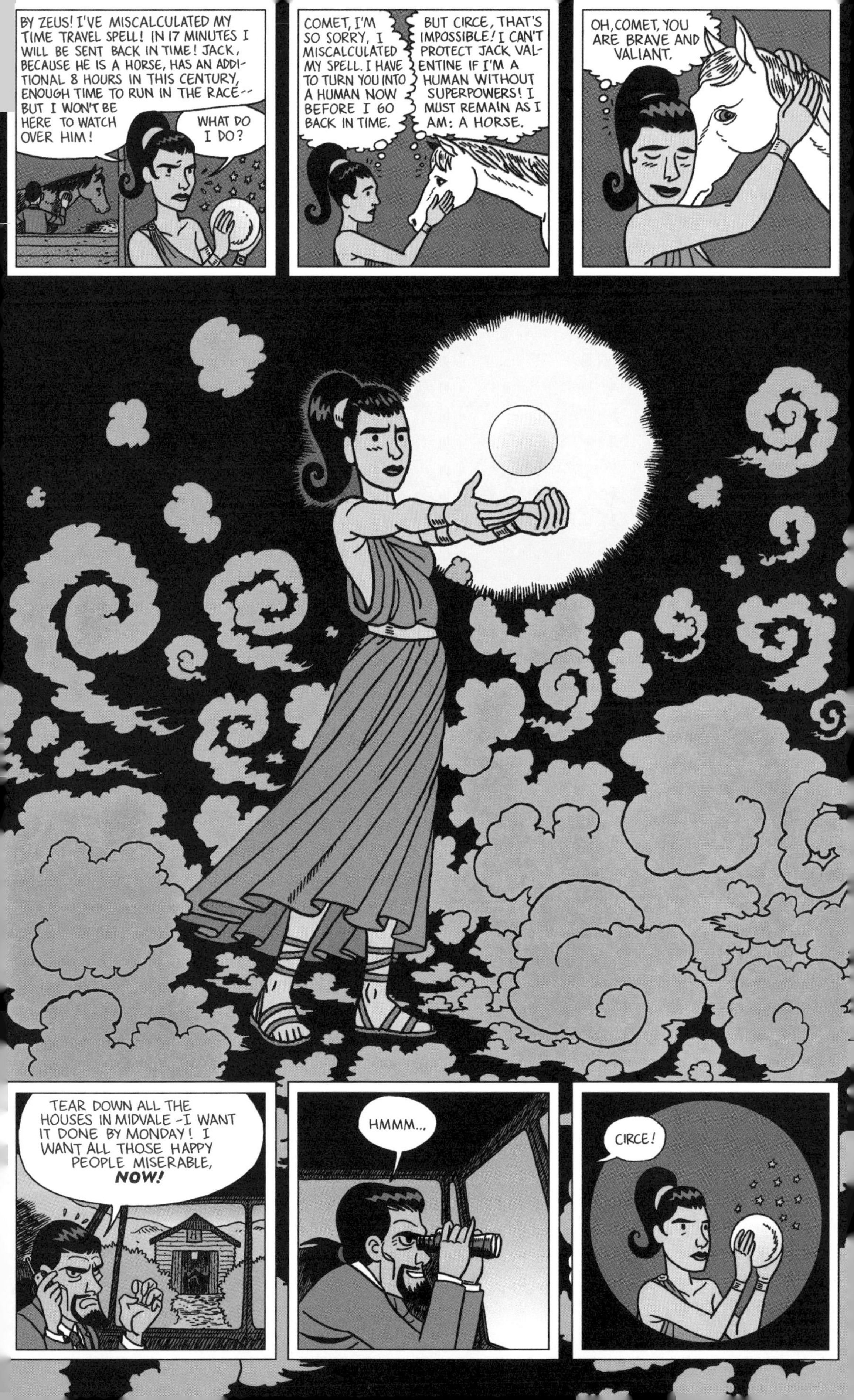
BY ZEUS! I'VE MISCALCULATED MY TIME TRAVEL SPELL! IN 17 MINUTES I WILL BE SENT BACK IN TIME! JACK, BECAUSE HE IS A HORSE, HAS AN ADDITIONAL 8 HOURS IN THIS CENTURY, ENOUGH TIME TO RUN IN THE RACE-- BUT I WON'T BE HERE TO WATCH OVER HIM!
WHAT DO I DO?
COMET, I'M SO SORRY, I MISCALCULATED MY SPELL. I HAVE TO TURN YOU INTO A HUMAN NOW BEFORE I GO BACK IN TIME.
BUT CIRCE, THAT'S IMPOSSIBLE! I CAN'T PROTECT JACK VALENTINE IF I'M A HUMAN WITHOUT SUPERPOWERS! I MUST REMAIN AS I AM: A HORSE.
OH, COMET, YOU ARE BRAVE AND VALIANT.
TEAR DOWN ALL THE HOUSES IN MIDVALE -I WANT IT DONE BY MONDAY! I WANT ALL THOSE HAPPY PEOPLE MISERABLE, **NOW!**
HMMM...
CIRCE!

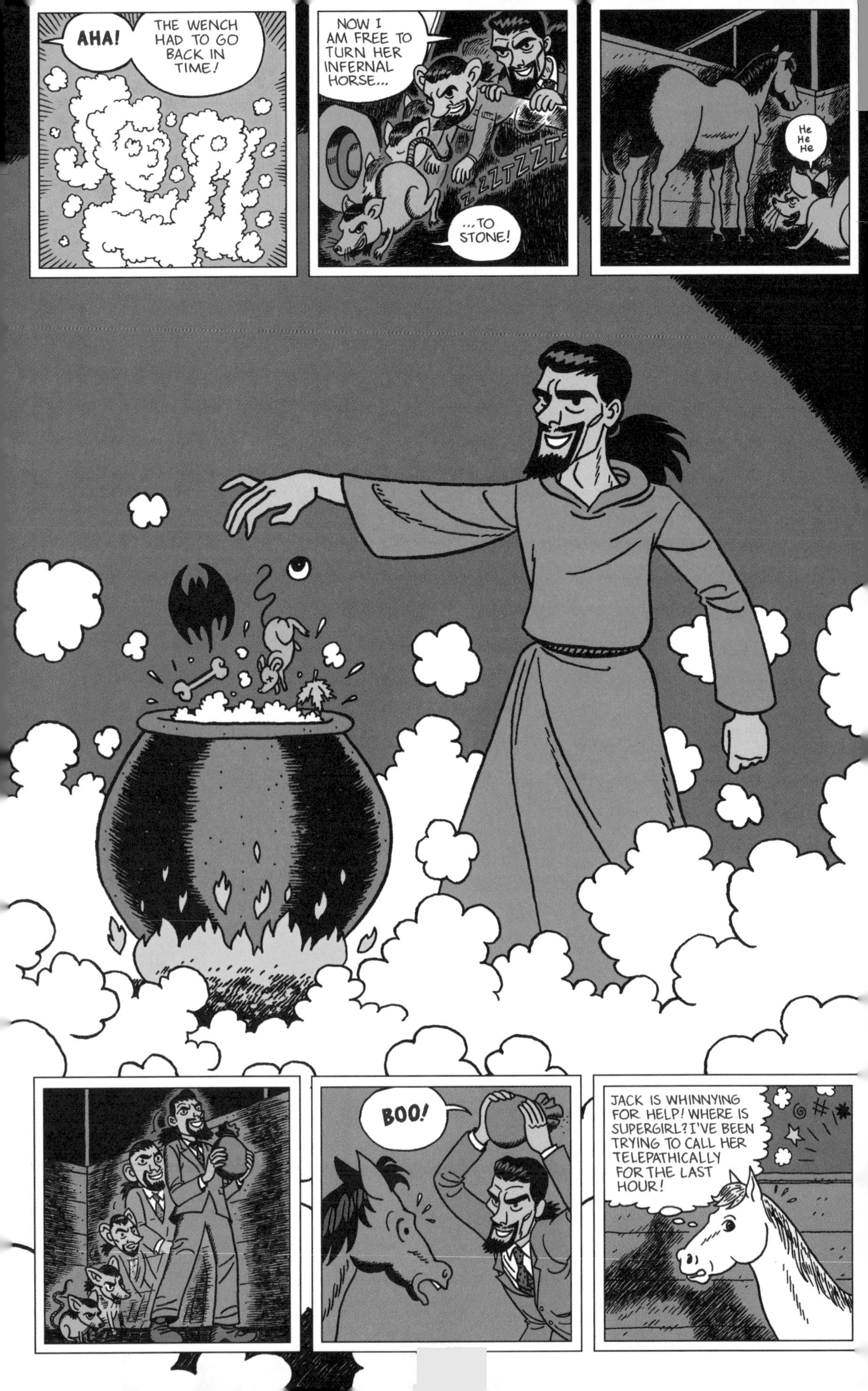
AHA!
THE WENCH HAD TO GO BACK IN TIME!
NOW I AM FREE TO TURN HER INFERNAL HORSE...
ZZZTZZZTZ
...TO STONE!
He He He
BOO!
JACK IS WHINNYING FOR HELP! WHERE IS SUPERGIRL? I'VE BEEN TRYING TO CALL HER TELEPATHICALLY FOR THE LAST HOUR!

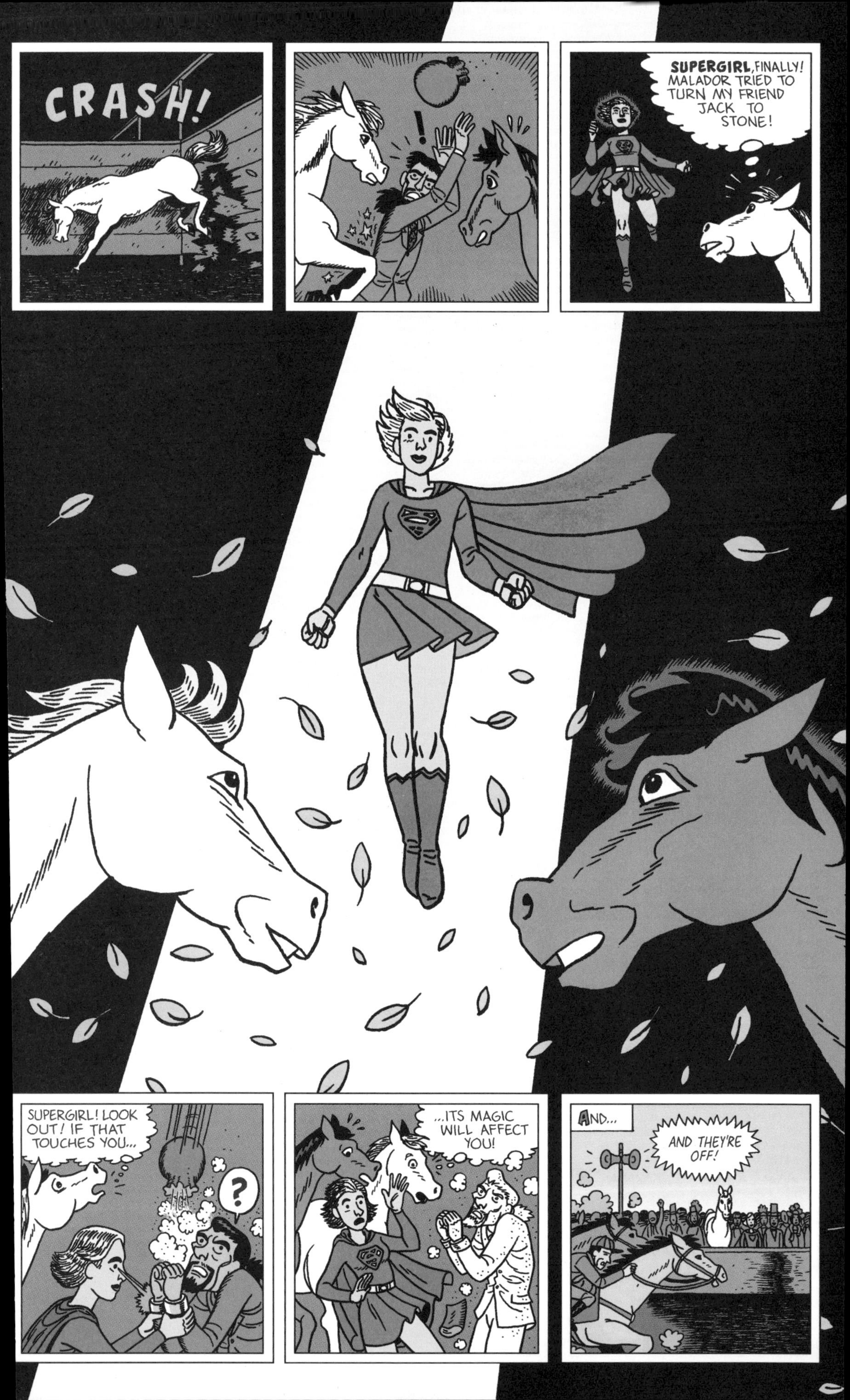
CRASH!
!
SUPERGIRL, FINALLY! MALADOR TRIED TO TURN MY FRIEND JACK TO STONE!
SUPERGIRL! LOOK OUT! IF THAT TOUCHES YOU...
?
...ITS MAGIC WILL AFFECT YOU!
AND...
AND THEY'RE OFF!

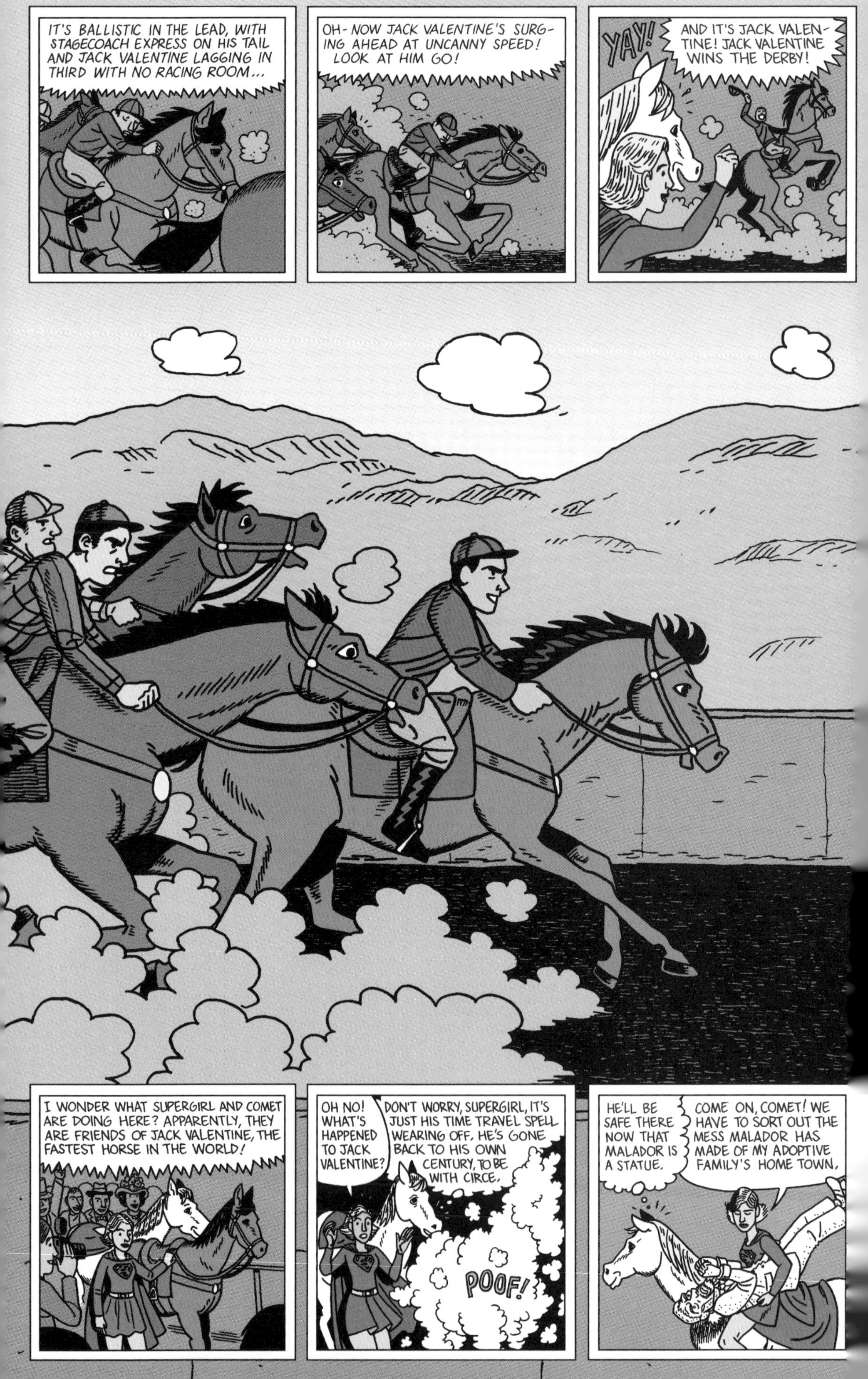

IT'S BALLISTIC IN THE LEAD, WITH STAGECOACH EXPRESS ON HIS TAIL AND JACK VALENTINE LAGGING IN THIRD WITH NO RACING ROOM...
OH- NOW JACK VALENTINE'S SURGING AHEAD AT UNCANNY SPEED! LOOK AT HIM GO!
YAY!
AND IT'S JACK VALENTINE! JACK VALENTINE WINS THE DERBY!
I WONDER WHAT SUPERGIRL AND COMET ARE DOING HERE? APPARENTLY, THEY ARE FRIENDS OF JACK VALENTINE, THE FASTEST HORSE IN THE WORLD!
OH NO! WHAT'S HAPPENED TO JACK VALENTINE?
DON'T WORRY, SUPERGIRL, IT'S JUST HIS TIME TRAVEL SPELL WEARING OFF. HE'S GONE BACK TO HIS OWN CENTURY, TO BE WITH CIRCE.
POOF!
HE'LL BE SAFE THERE NOW THAT MALADOR IS A STATUE.
COME ON, COMET! WE HAVE TO SORT OUT THE MESS MALADOR HAS MADE OF MY ADOPTIVE FAMILY'S HOME TOWN.

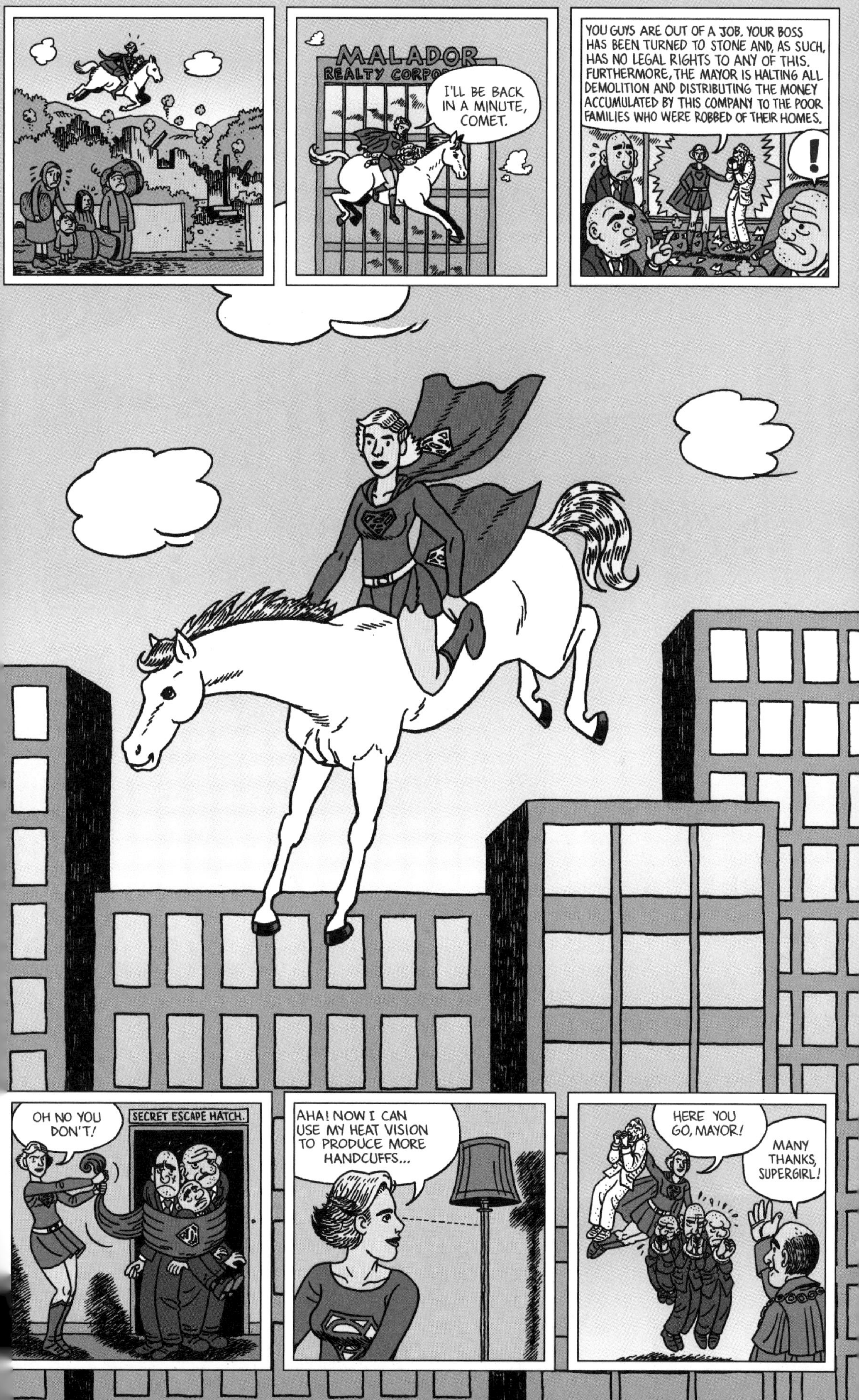
MALADOR
REALTY CORPOR
I'LL BE BACK IN A MINUTE, COMET.
YOU GUYS ARE OUT OF A JOB. YOUR BOSS HAS BEEN TURNED TO STONE AND, AS SUCH, HAS NO LEGAL RIGHTS TO ANY OF THIS. FURTHERMORE, THE MAYOR IS HALTING ALL DEMOLITION AND DISTRIBUTING THE MONEY ACCUMULATED BY THIS COMPANY TO THE POOR FAMILIES WHO WERE ROBBED OF THEIR HOMES.
!
OH NO YOU DON'T!
SECRET ESCAPE HATCH.
AHA! NOW I CAN USE MY HEAT VISION TO PRODUCE MORE HANDCUFFS...
HERE YOU GO, MAYOR!
MANY THANKS, SUPERGIRL!

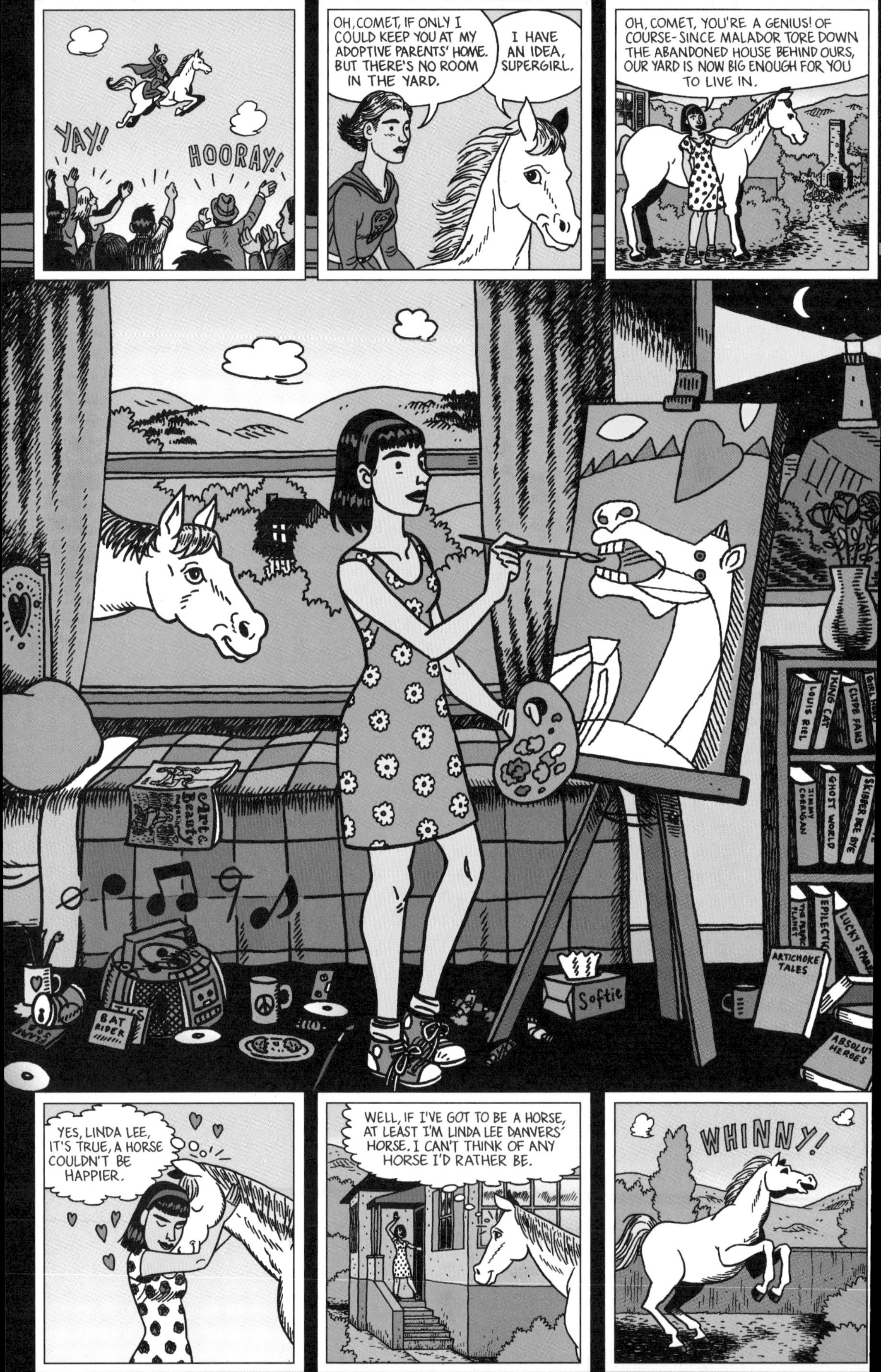
YAY!
HOORAY!
OH, COMET, IF ONLY I COULD KEEP YOU AT MY ADOPTIVE PARENTS' HOME. BUT THERE'S NO ROOM IN THE YARD.
I HAVE AN IDEA, SUPERGIRL.
OH, COMET, YOU'RE A GENIUS! OF COURSE- SINCE MALADOR TORE DOWN THE ABANDONED HOUSE BEHIND OURS, OUR YARD IS NOW BIG ENOUGH FOR YOU TO LIVE IN.
Art & Beauty
LOUIS RIEL
KING CAT
CLYDE FANS
JIMMY CORRIGAN
GHOST WORLD
SKIBBER DEE BYE
EPILECTIC
ARTICHOKE TALES
Softie
BAT RIDER
YES, LINDA LEE, IT'S TRUE, A HORSE COULDN'T BE HAPPIER.
WELL, IF I'VE GOT TO BE A HORSE, AT LEAST I'M LINDA LEE DANVERS' HORSE. I CAN'T THINK OF ANY HORSE I'D RATHER BE.
WHINNY!

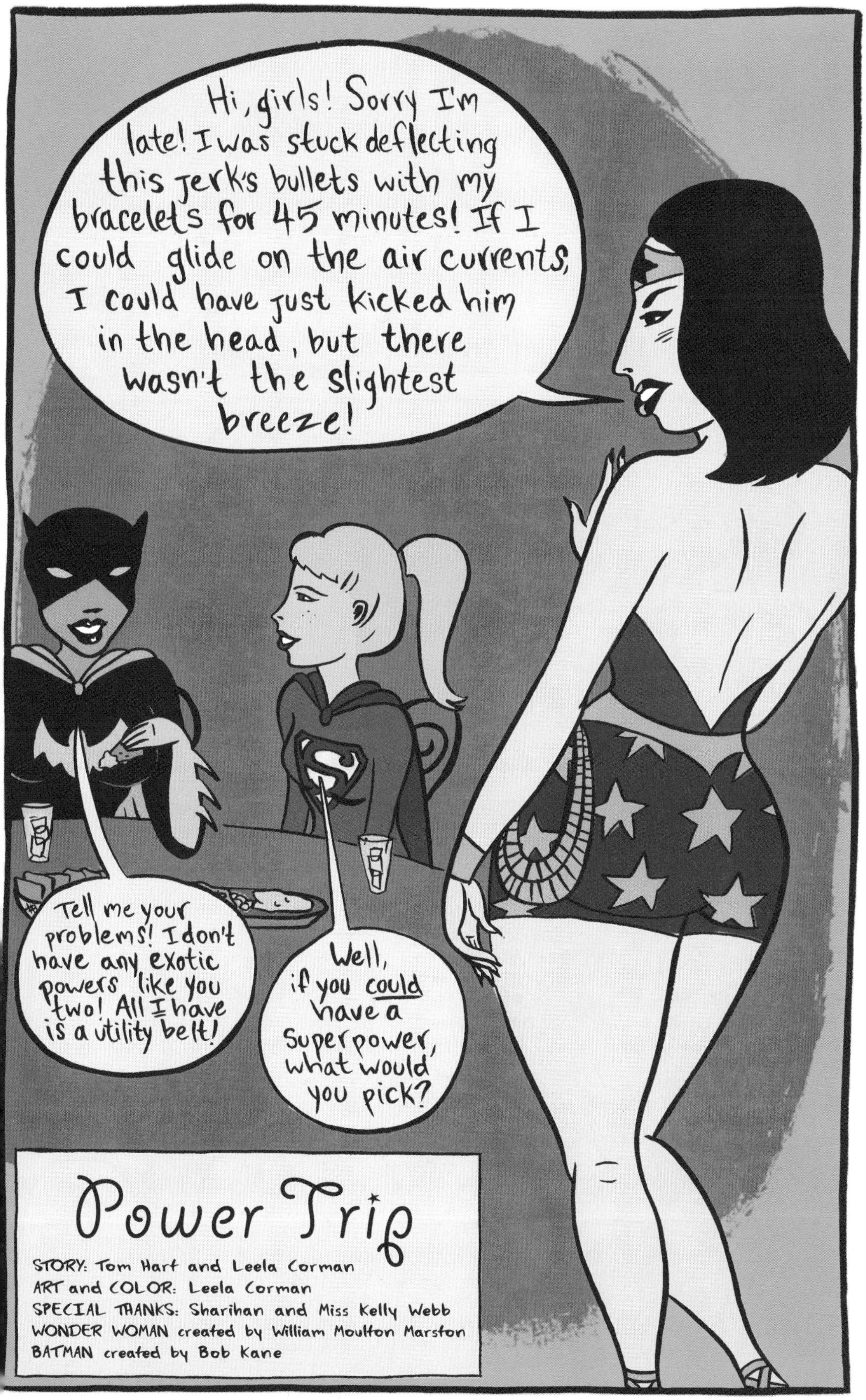
Hi, girls! Sorry I'm late! I was stuck deflecting this jerk's bullets with my bracelets for 45 minutes! If I could glide on the air currents, I could have just kicked him in the head, but there wasn't the slightest breeze!
Tell me your problems! I don't have any exotic powers like you two! All I have is a utility belt!
Well, if you could have a superpower, what would you pick?

Power Trip

STORY: Tom Hart and Leela Corman
ART and COLOR: Leela Corman
SPECIAL THANKS: Sharihan and Miss Kelly Webb
WONDER WOMAN created by William Moulton Marston
BATMAN created by Bob Kane

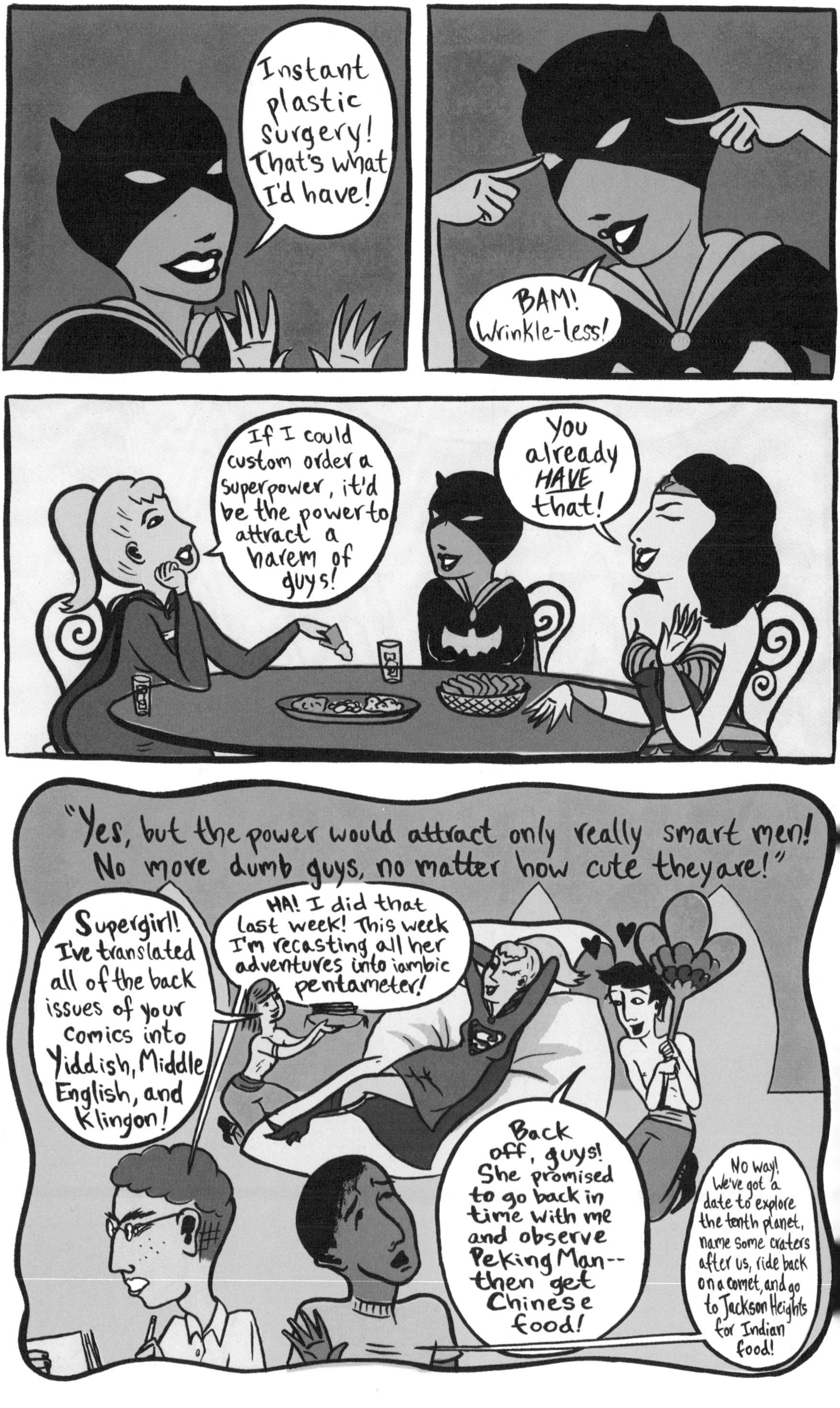
Instant plastic surgery! That's what I'd have!
BAM! Wrinkle-less!
If I could custom order a superpower, it'd be the power to attract a harem of guys!
You already HAVE that!
"Yes, but the power would attract only really smart men! No more dumb guys, no matter how cute they are!"
Supergirl! I've translated all of the back issues of your comics into Yiddish, Middle English, and Klingon!
HA! I did that last week! This week I'm recasting all her adventures into iambic pentameter!
Back off, guys! She promised to go back in time with me and observe Peking Man-- then get Chinese food!
No way! We've got a date to explore the tenth planet, name some craters after us, ride back on a comet, and go to Jackson Heights for Indian food!

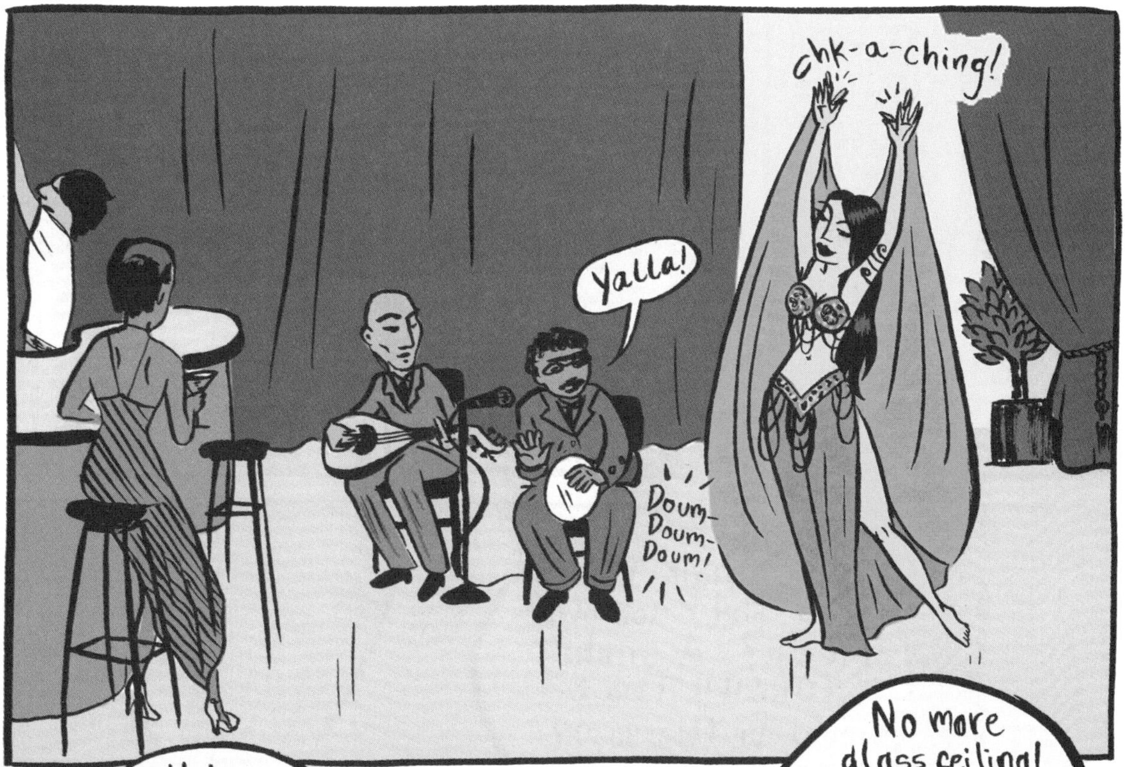
chk-a-ching!
Yalla!
Doum-Doum-Doum!

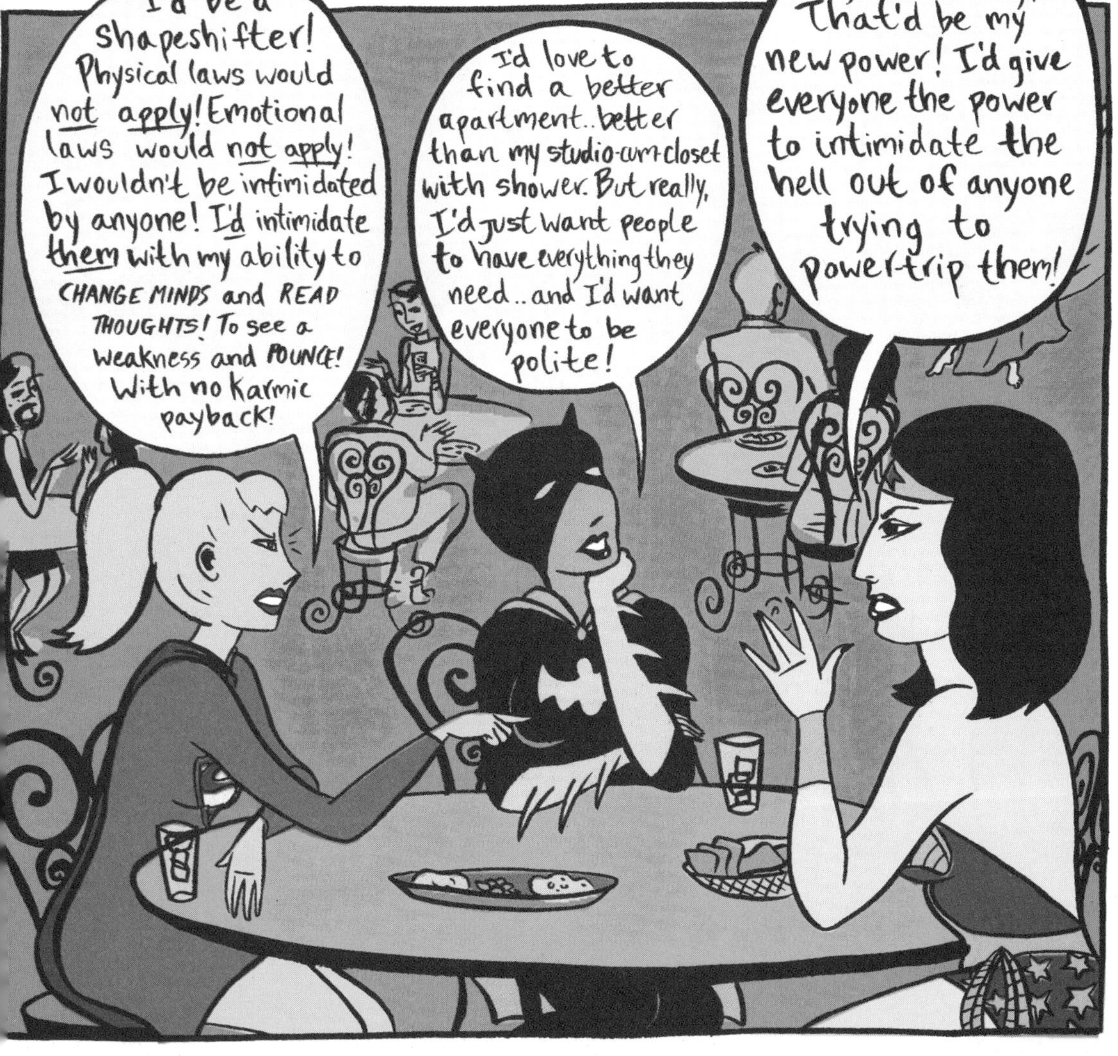
I'd be a Shapeshifter! Physical laws would not apply! Emotional laws would not apply! I wouldn't be intimidated by anyone! I'd intimidate them with my ability to CHANGE MINDS and READ THOUGHTS! To see a weakness and POUNCE! With no Karmic payback!
I'd love to find a better apartment.. better than my studio-cum-closet with shower. But really, I'd just want people to have everything they need.. and I'd want everyone to be polite!
No more glass ceiling! That'd be my new power! I'd give everyone the power to intimidate the hell out of anyone trying to power-trip them!

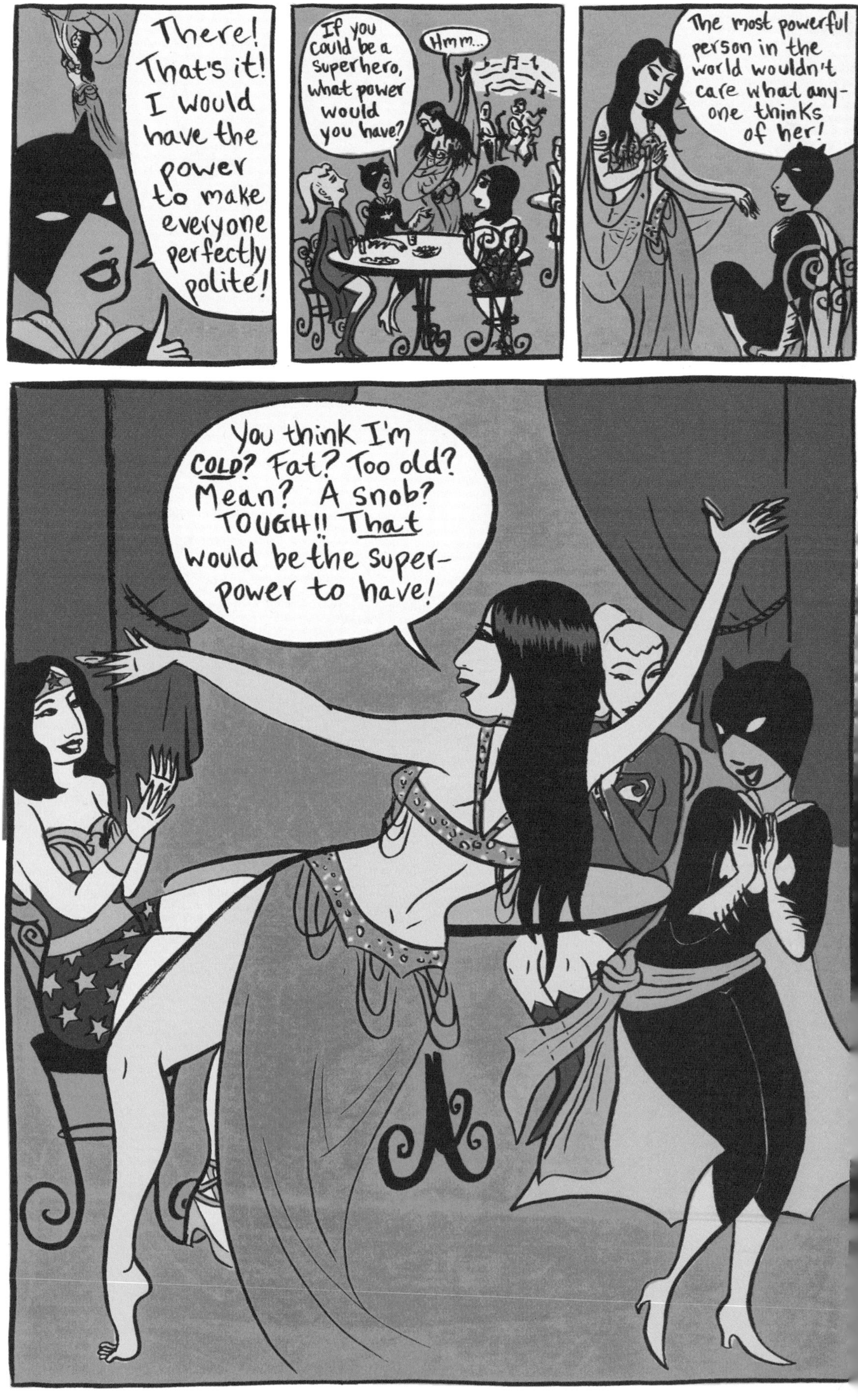
There! That's it! I would have the power to make everyone perfectly polite!
If you could be a superhero, what power would you have?
Hmm...
The most powerful person in the world wouldn't care what any-one thinks of her!
You think I'm COLD? Fat? Too old? Mean? A snob? TOUGH!! That would be the super-power to have!

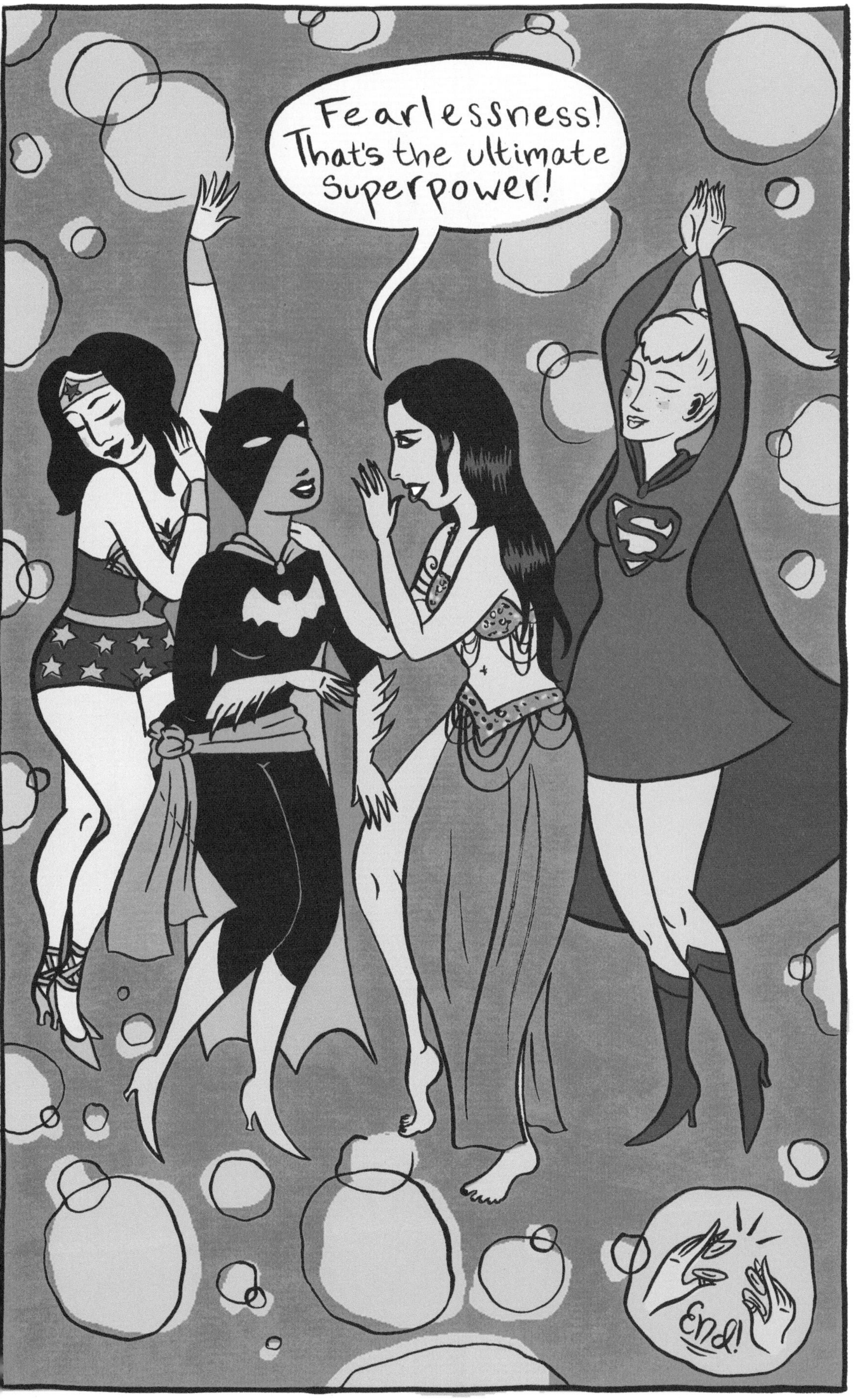
Fearlessness! That's the ultimate Superpower!
End!

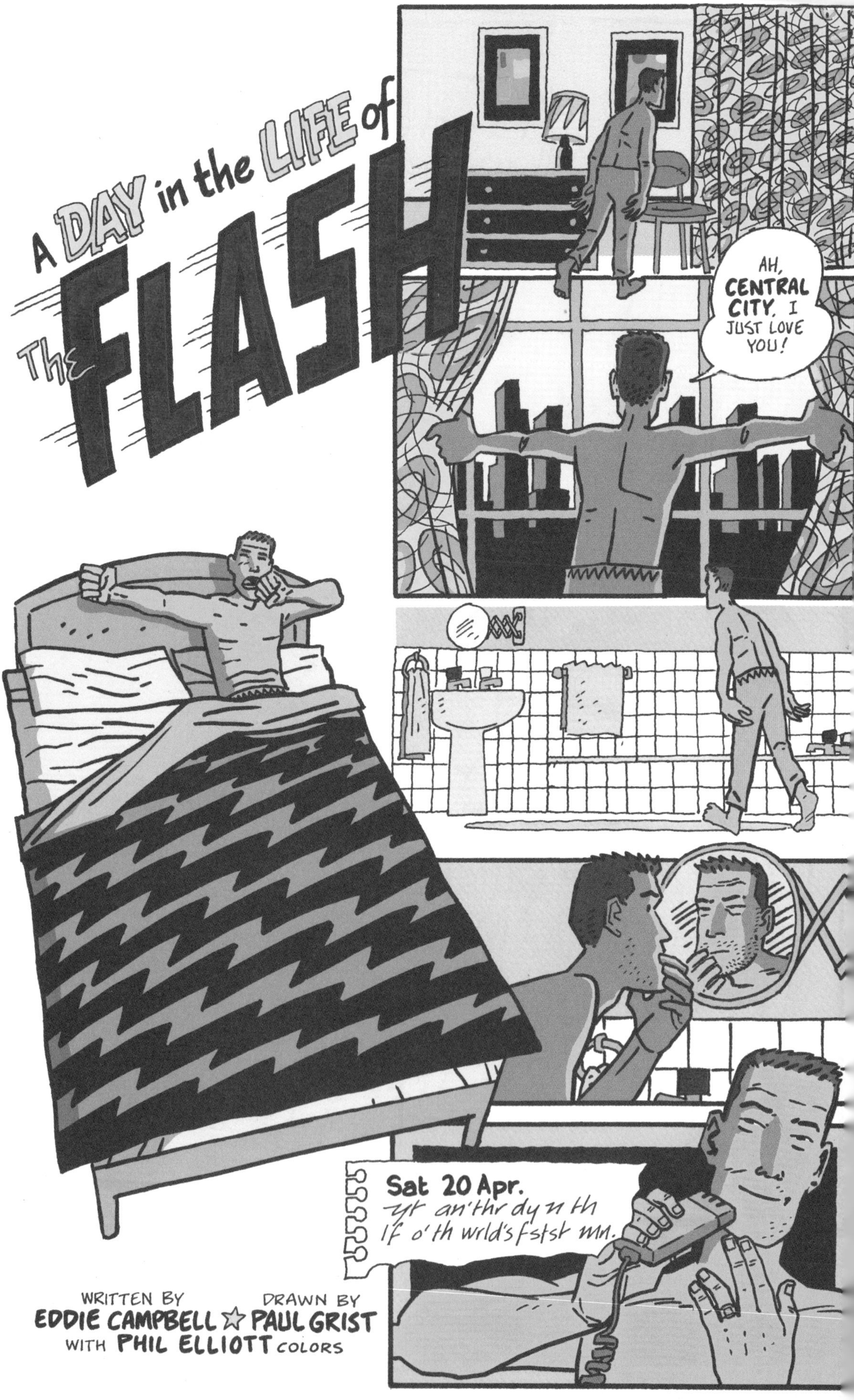
A DAY in the LIFE of The FLASH
AH, CENTRAL CITY, I JUST LOVE YOU!
Sat 20 Apr.
yt an'thr dy n th lf o' th wrld's fstst mn.
WRITTEN BY EDDIE CAMPBELL ☆ DRAWN BY PAUL GRIST
WITH PHIL ELLIOTT COLORS

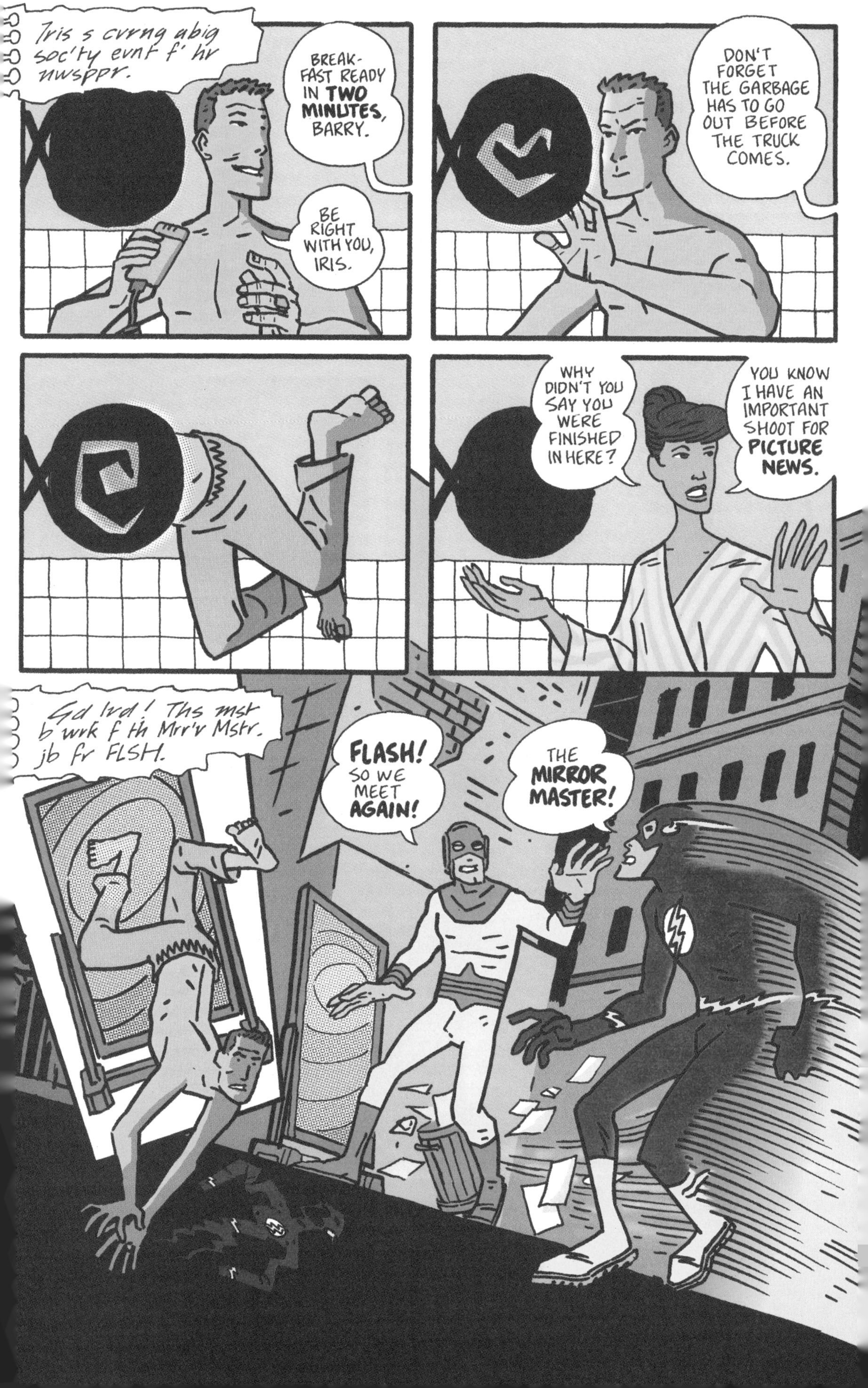
Iris s cvrng abig soc'ty evnt f' hr nwsppr.
BREAK-FAST READY IN TWO MINUTES, BARRY.
BE RIGHT WITH YOU, IRIS.
DON'T FORGET THE GARBAGE HAS TO GO OUT BEFORE THE TRUCK COMES.
WHY DIDN'T YOU SAY YOU WERE FINISHED IN HERE?
YOU KNOW I HAVE AN IMPORTANT SHOOT FOR PICTURE NEWS.
Gd lrd! Ths mst b wrk f th Mrr'r Mstr. jb fr FLSH.
FLASH! SO WE MEET AGAIN!
THE MIRROR MASTER!

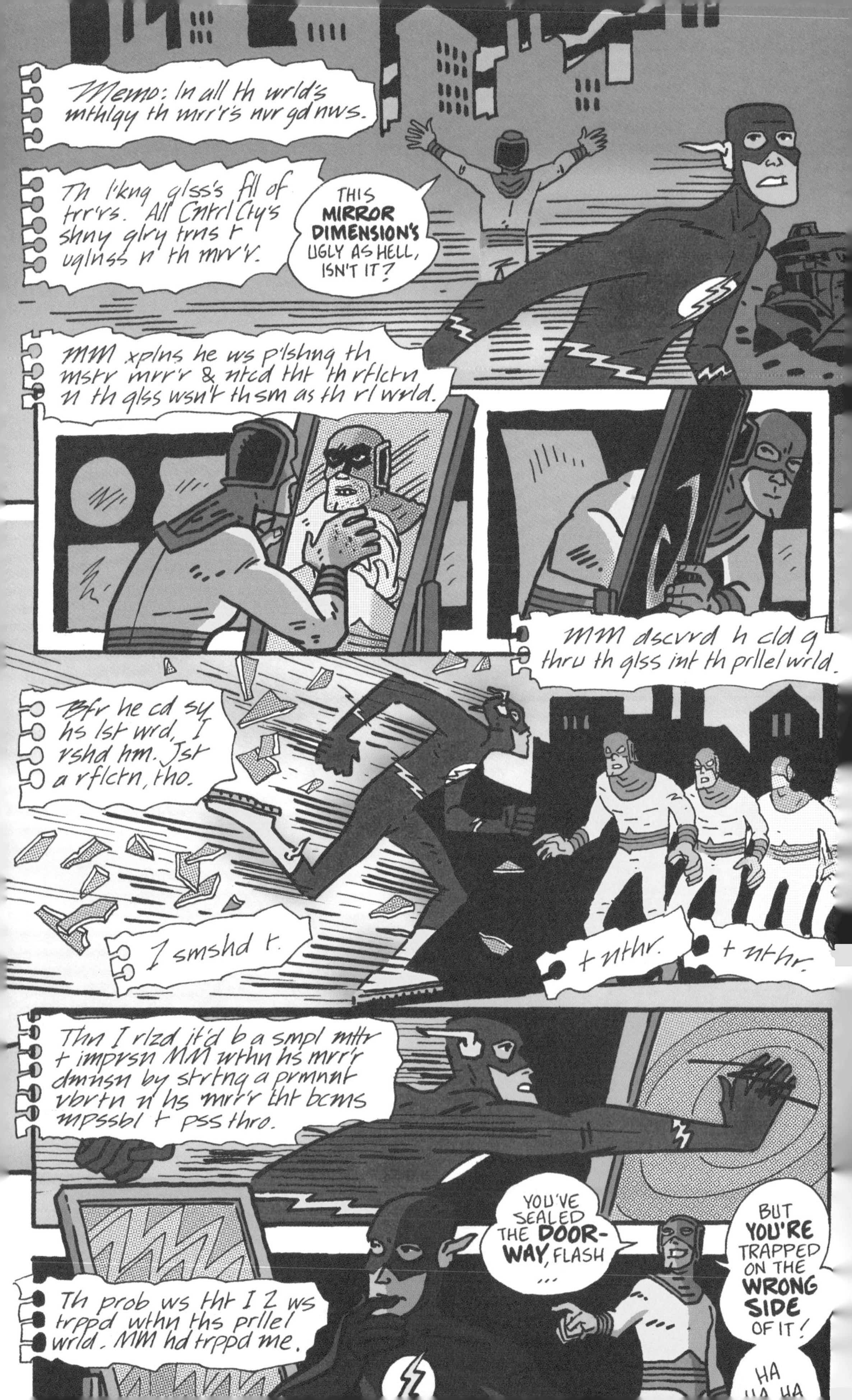
Memo: In all th wrld's mthlgy th mrr'r's nvr gd nws.
Th l'kng glss's fll of trr'rs. All Cntrl Cty's shny glry trns t uglnss n' th mrr'r.
THIS **MIRROR DIMENSION'S** UGLY AS HELL, ISN'T IT?
MM xplns he ws p'lshng th mstr mrr'r & ntcd tht th rflctn n th glss wsn't th sm as th rl wrld.
MM dscvrd h cld g thru th glss int th prllel wrld.
Bfr he cd sy hs lst wrd, I rshd hm. Jst a rflctn, tho.
I smshd t.
+ nthr.
+ nthr.
Thn I rlzd it'd b a smpl mttr t imprsn MM wthn hs mrr'r dmnsn by strtng a prmnnt vbrtn n hs mrr'r tht bcms mpssbl t pss thro.
YOU'VE SEALED THE **DOORWAY**, FLASH ...
BUT **YOU'RE** TRAPPED ON THE **WRONG SIDE** OF IT!
Th prob ws tht I 2 ws trppd wthn ths prllel wrld. MM hd trppd me.
HA

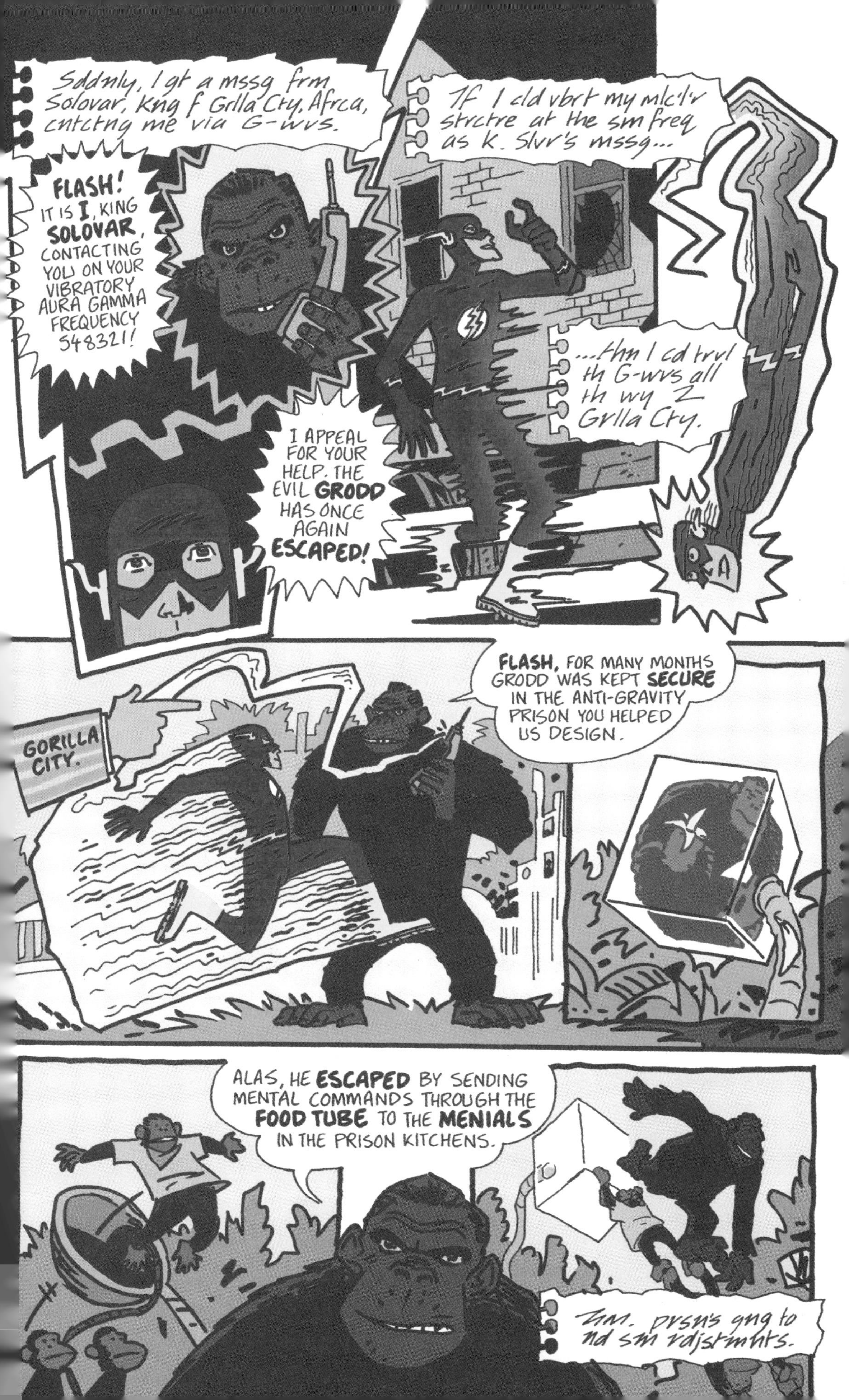

Sddnly, I gt a mssg frm Solovar, Kng f Grlla Cty, Afrca, cntctng me via G-wvs.
If I cld vbrt my mlc'lr strctre at the sm freq as K. Slvr's mssg...
FLASH! IT IS I, KING SOLOVAR, CONTACTING YOU ON YOUR VIBRATORY AURA GAMMA FREQUENCY 548321!
...thn I cd trvl th G-wvs all th wy 2 Grlla Cty.
I APPEAL FOR YOUR HELP. THE EVIL GRODD HAS ONCE AGAIN ESCAPED!
GORILLA CITY.
FLASH, FOR MANY MONTHS GRODD WAS KEPT SECURE IN THE ANTI-GRAVITY PRISON YOU HELPED US DESIGN.
ALAS, HE ESCAPED BY SENDING MENTAL COMMANDS THROUGH THE FOOD TUBE TO THE MENIALS IN THE PRISON KITCHENS.
Hm. prsn's gng to nd sm rdjstmnts.

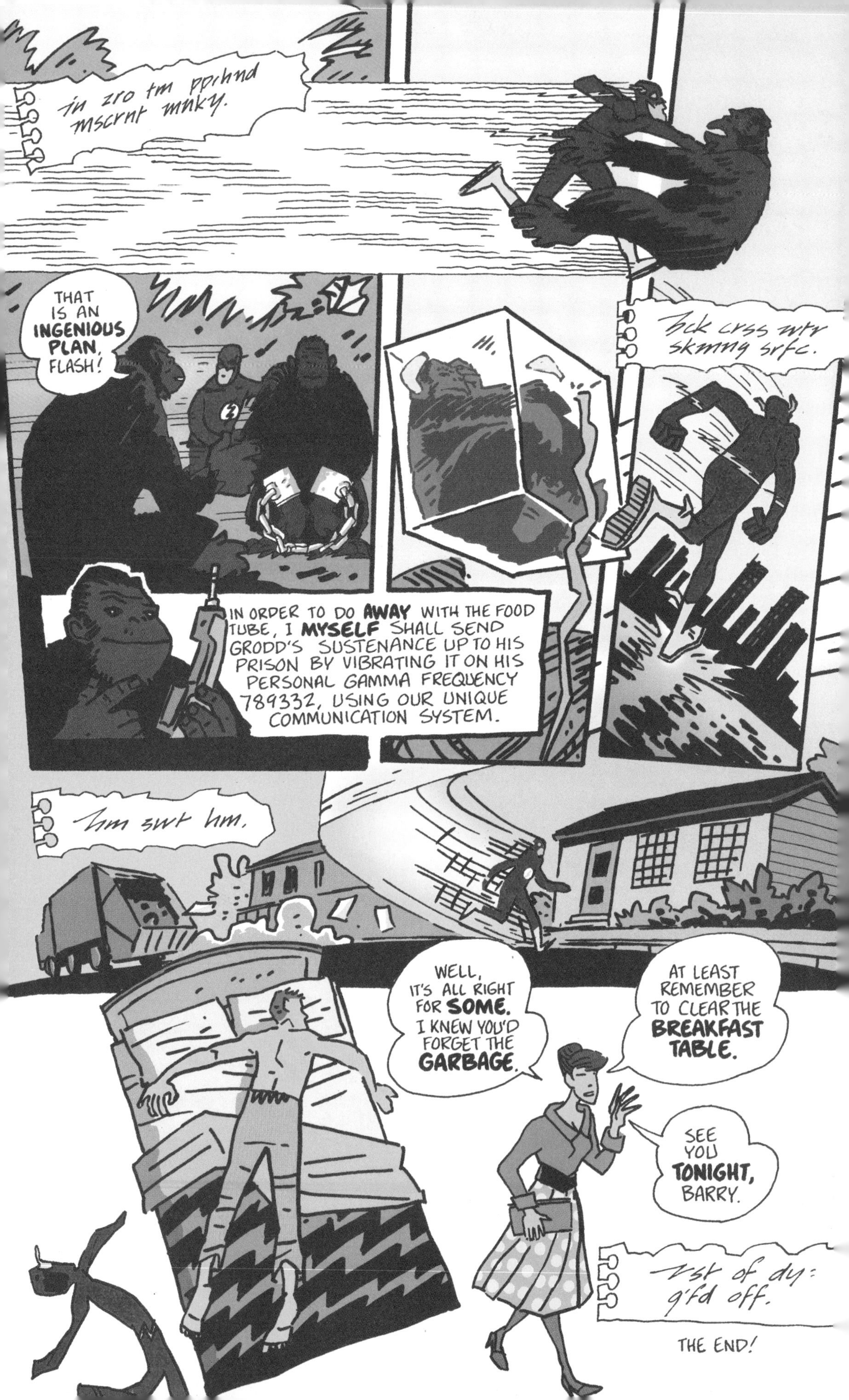

in zro tm pprhnd mscrnt mnky.
THAT IS AN INGENIOUS PLAN, FLASH!
IN ORDER TO DO AWAY WITH THE FOOD TUBE, I MYSELF SHALL SEND GRODD'S SUSTENANCE UP TO HIS PRISON BY VIBRATING IT ON HIS PERSONAL GAMMA FREQUENCY 789332, USING OUR UNIQUE COMMUNICATION SYSTEM.
bck crss wtr skmmg srfc.
hm swt hm.
WELL, IT'S ALL RIGHT FOR SOME. I KNEW YOU'D FORGET THE GARBAGE.
AT LEAST REMEMBER TO CLEAR THE BREAKFAST TABLE.
SEE YOU TONIGHT, BARRY.
rst of dy: g'fd off.
THE END!

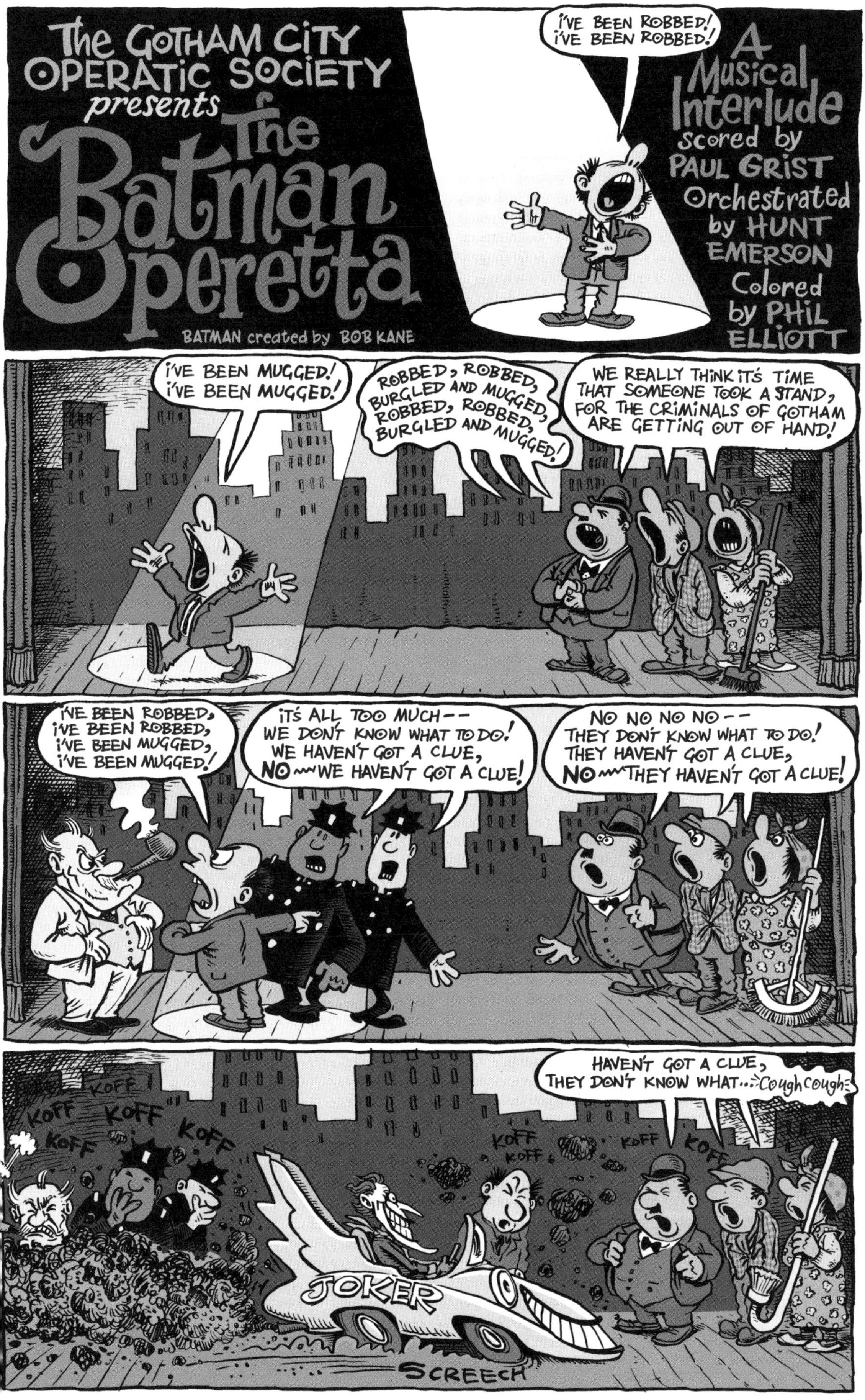
The GOTHAM CITY OPERATIC SOCIETY presents The Batman Operetta
BATMAN created by BOB KANE
i'VE BEEN ROBBED! i'VE BEEN ROBBED!
A Musical Interlude scored by PAUL GRIST Orchestrated by HUNT EMERSON Colored by PHIL ELLIOTT
i'VE BEEN MUGGED! i'VE BEEN MUGGED!
ROBBED, ROBBED, BURGLED AND MUGGED, ROBBED, ROBBED, BURGLED AND MUGGED!
WE REALLY THINK iT'S TiME THAT SOMEONE TOOK A STAND, FOR THE CRiMINALS OF GOTHAM ARE GETTiNG OUT OF HAND!
i'VE BEEN ROBBED, i'VE BEEN ROBBED, i'VE BEEN MUGGED, i'VE BEEN MUGGED!
iT'S ALL TOO MUCH-- WE DON'T KNOW WHAT TO DO! WE HAVEN'T GOT A CLUE, NO~~WE HAVEN'T GOT A CLUE!
NO NO NO NO-- THEY DON'T KNOW WHAT TO DO! THEY HAVEN'T GOT A CLUE, NO~~THEY HAVEN'T GOT A CLUE!
HAVEN'T GOT A CLUE, THEY DON'T KNOW WHAT...Cough Cough
KOFF KOFF KOFF KOFF KOFF
KOFF KOFF KOFF KOFF
JOKER
SCREECH

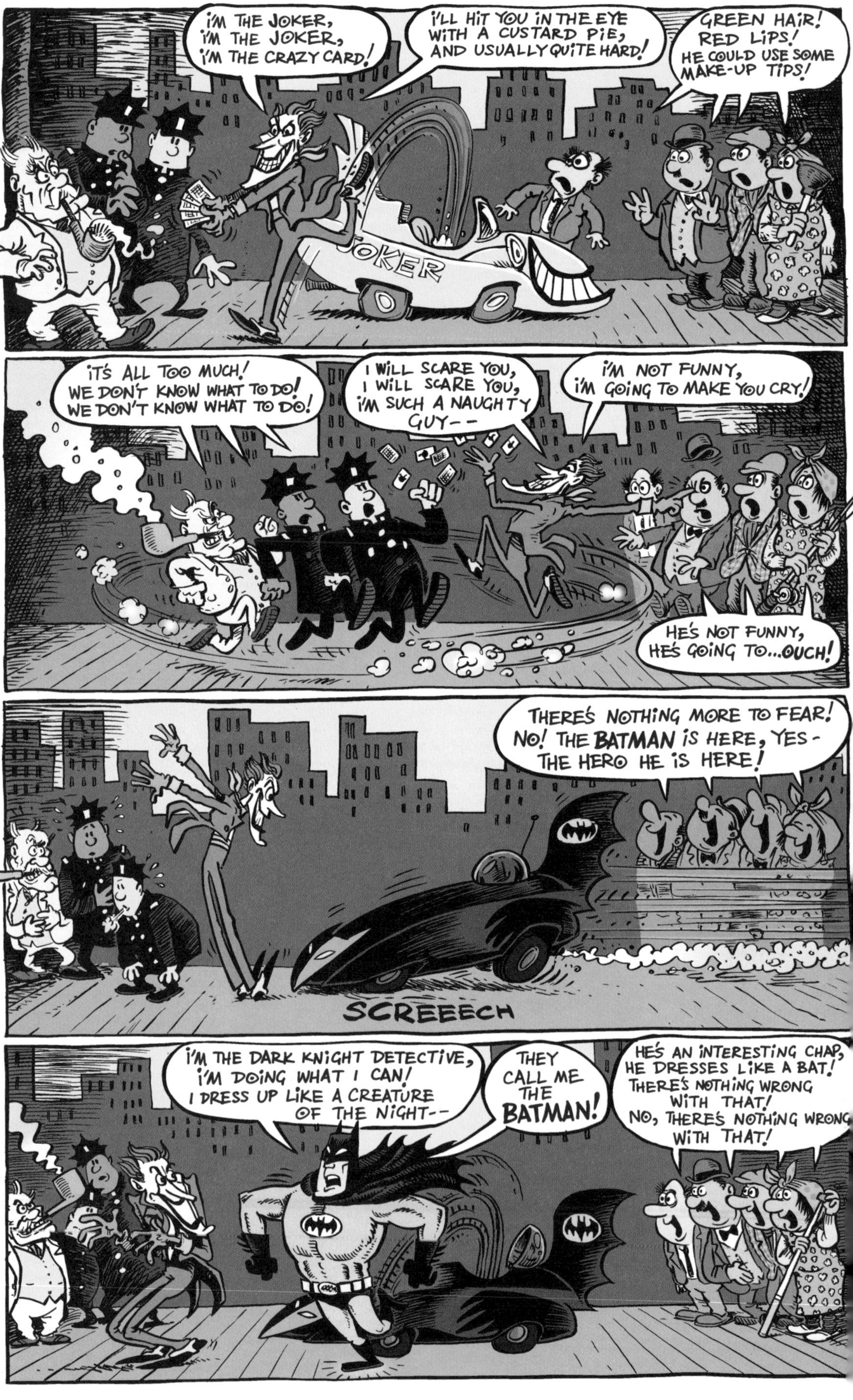

I'M THE JOKER, I'M THE JOKER, I'M THE CRAZY CARD!
I'LL HIT YOU IN THE EYE WITH A CUSTARD PIE, AND USUALLY QUITE HARD!
GREEN HAIR! RED LIPS! HE COULD USE SOME MAKE-UP TIPS!
JOKER
IT'S ALL TOO MUCH! WE DON'T KNOW WHAT TO DO! WE DON'T KNOW WHAT TO DO!
I WILL SCARE YOU, I WILL SCARE YOU, I'M SUCH A NAUGHTY GUY--
I'M NOT FUNNY, I'M GOING TO MAKE YOU CRY!
HE'S NOT FUNNY, HE'S GOING TO...OUCH!
THERE'S NOTHING MORE TO FEAR! NO! THE BATMAN IS HERE, YES - THE HERO HE IS HERE!
SCREEECH
I'M THE DARK KNIGHT DETECTIVE, I'M DOING WHAT I CAN! I DRESS UP LIKE A CREATURE OF THE NIGHT--
THEY CALL ME THE BATMAN!
HE'S AN INTERESTING CHAP, HE DRESSES LIKE A BAT! THERE'S NOTHING WRONG WITH THAT! NO, THERE'S NOTHING WRONG WITH THAT!

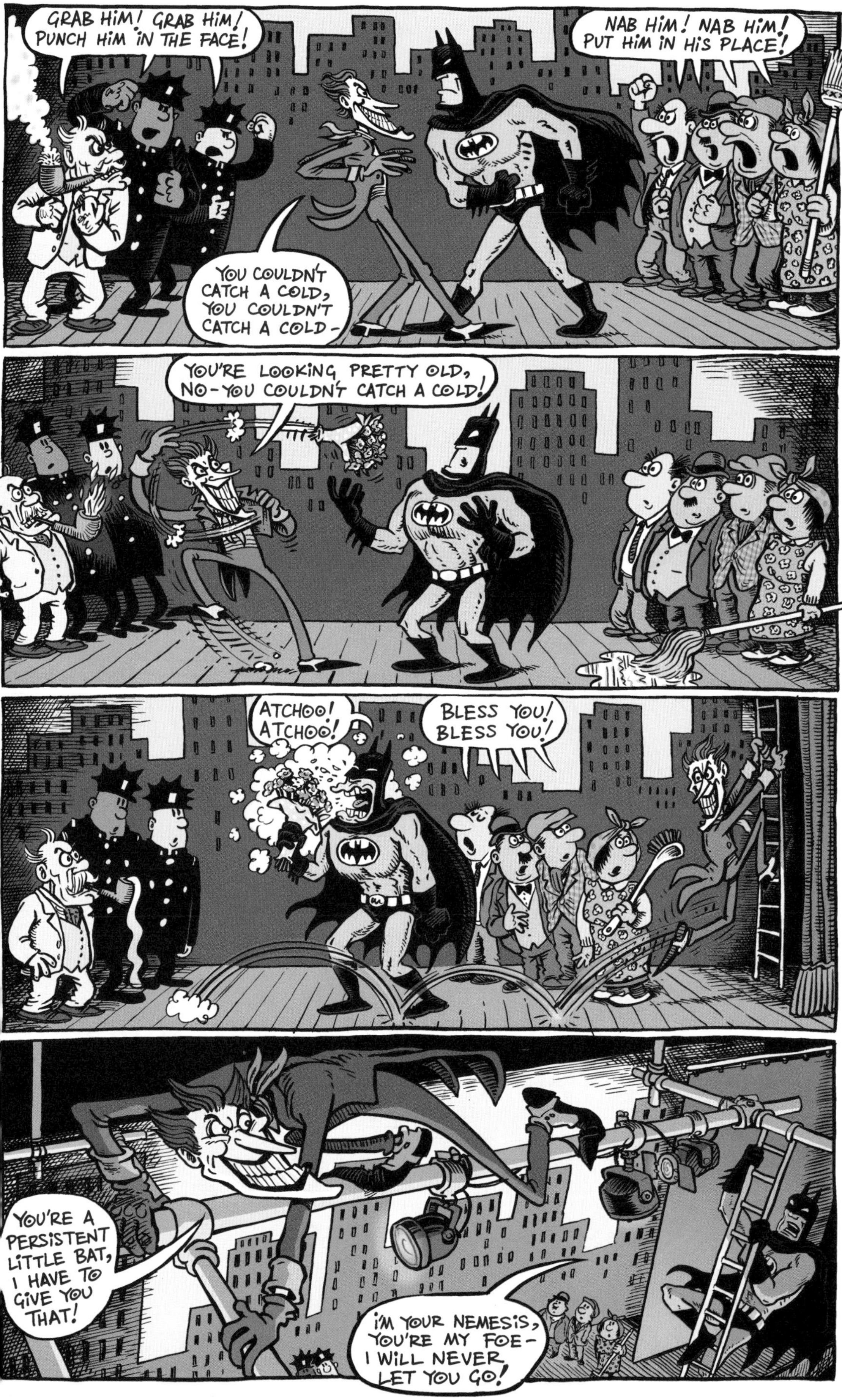
GRAB HIM! GRAB HIM! PUNCH HIM IN THE FACE!
NAB HIM! NAB HIM! PUT HIM IN HIS PLACE!
YOU COULDN'T CATCH A COLD, YOU COULDN'T CATCH A COLD-
YOU'RE LOOKING PRETTY OLD, NO-YOU COULDN'T CATCH A COLD!
ATCHOO! ATCHOO!
BLESS YOU! BLESS YOU!
YOU'RE A PERSISTENT LITTLE BAT, I HAVE TO GIVE YOU THAT!
I'M YOUR NEMESIS, YOU'RE MY FOE- I WILL NEVER LET YOU GO!

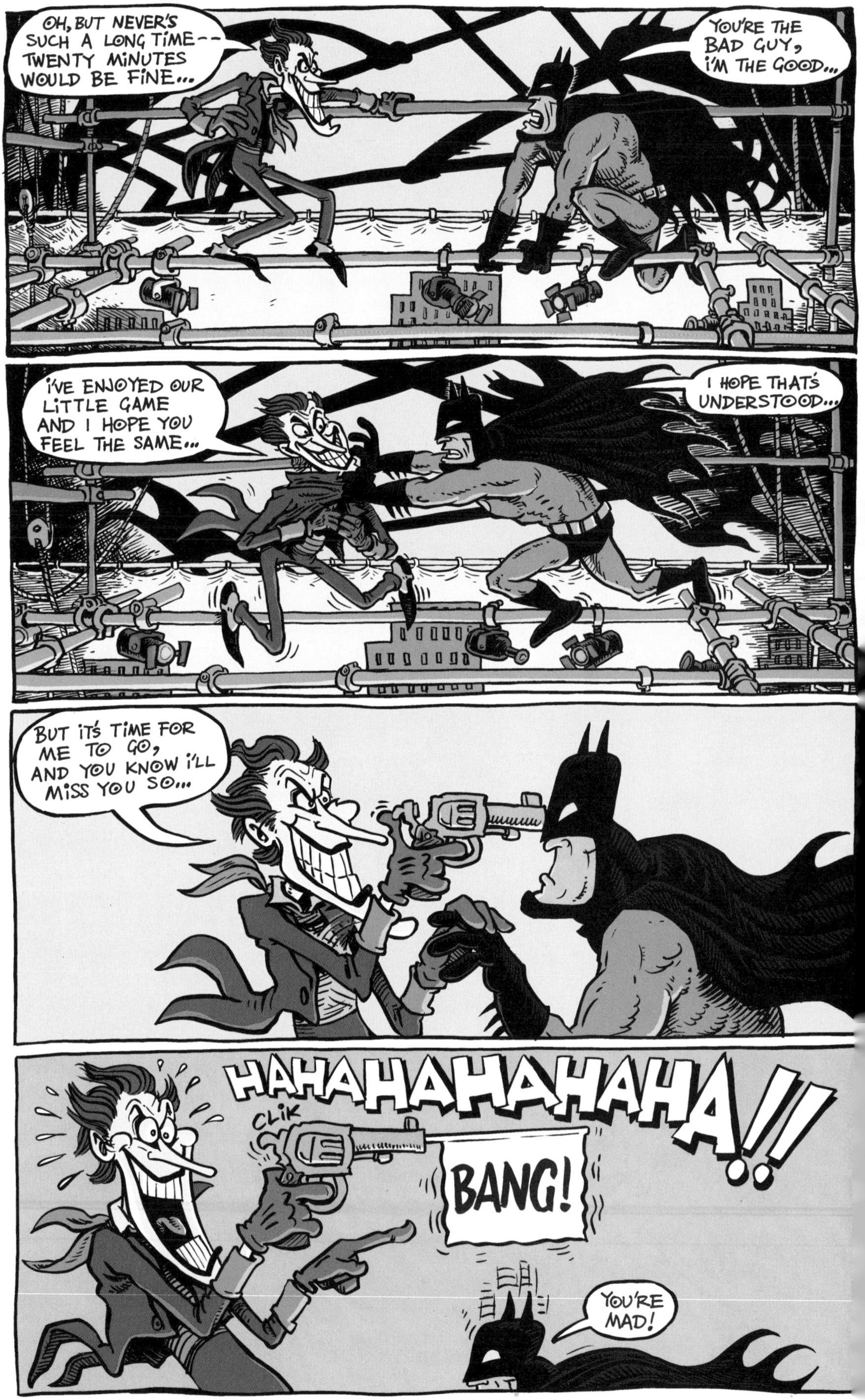
OH, BUT NEVER'S SUCH A LONG TIME-- TWENTY MINUTES WOULD BE FINE...
YOU'RE THE BAD GUY, I'M THE GOOD...
I'VE ENJOYED OUR LITTLE GAME AND I HOPE YOU FEEL THE SAME...
I HOPE THAT'S UNDERSTOOD...
BUT IT'S TIME FOR ME TO GO, AND YOU KNOW I'LL MISS YOU SO...
HAHAHAHAHAHAHA!!
CLIK
BANG!
YOU'RE MAD!

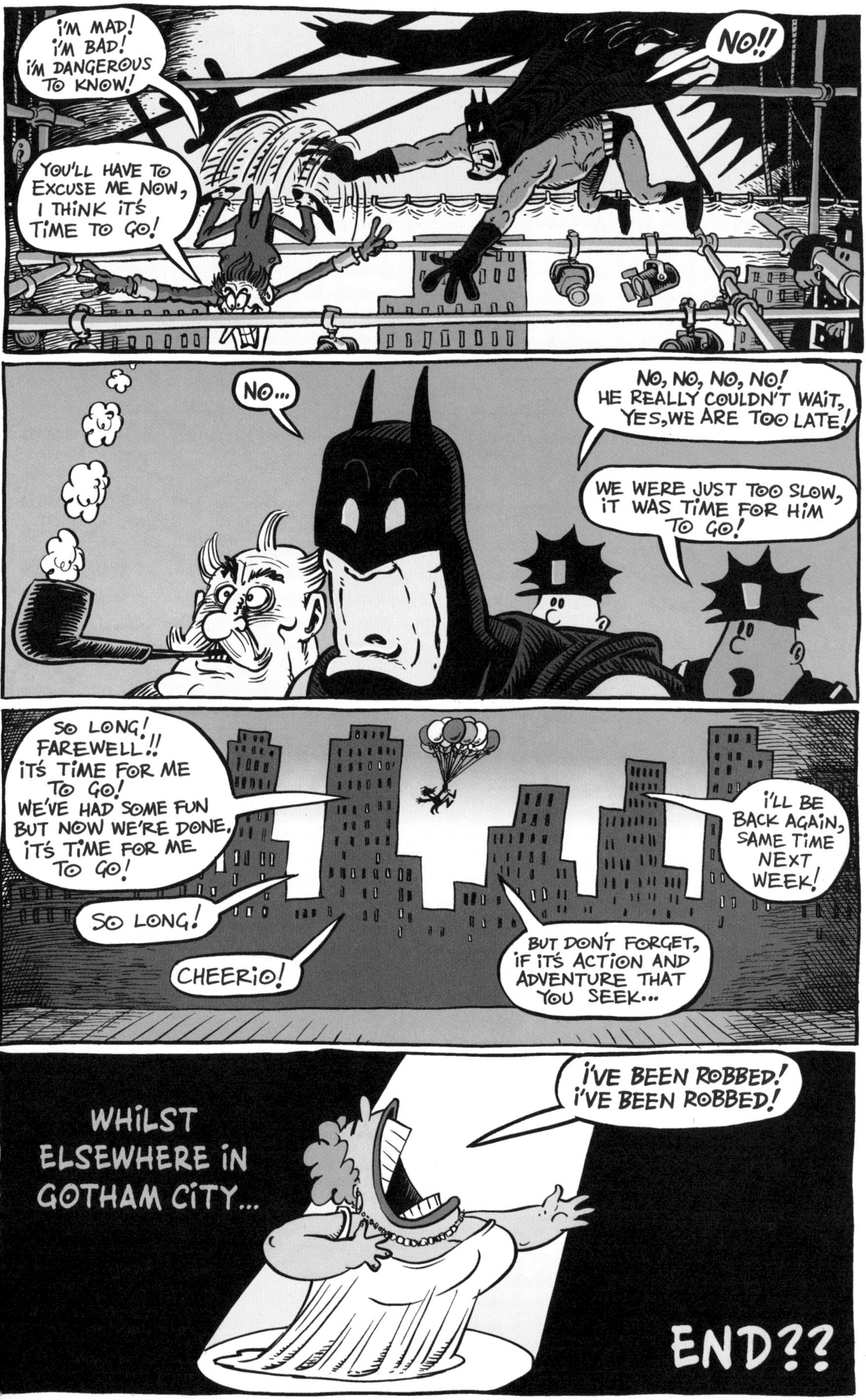

I'M MAD! I'M BAD! I'M DANGEROUS TO KNOW!
NO!!
YOU'LL HAVE TO EXCUSE ME NOW, I THINK IT'S TIME TO GO!
NO...
NO, NO, NO, NO! HE REALLY COULDN'T WAIT, YES, WE ARE TOO LATE!
WE WERE JUST TOO SLOW, IT WAS TIME FOR HIM TO GO!
SO LONG! FAREWELL!! IT'S TIME FOR ME TO GO! WE'VE HAD SOME FUN BUT NOW WE'RE DONE, IT'S TIME FOR ME TO GO!
SO LONG!
CHEERIO!
BUT DON'T FORGET, IF IT'S ACTION AND ADVENTURE THAT YOU SEEK...
I'LL BE BACK AGAIN, SAME TIME NEXT WEEK!
WHILST ELSEWHERE IN GOTHAM CITY...
I'VE BEEN ROBBED! I'VE BEEN ROBBED!
END??

HEY, ADULTS! *COMICS!*

Daily Htrae

HEY, KIDS! *ADS!*

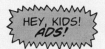

Written by Evan Dorkin

Drawn by R. Sikoryak

BIZARRO HISTORY 101

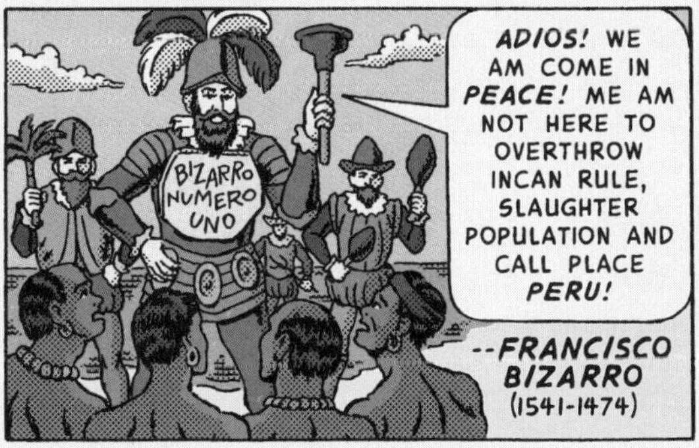
BIZARRO NUMERO UNO
ADIOS! WE AM COME IN PEACE! ME AM NOT HERE TO OVERTHROW INCAN RULE, SLAUGHTER POPULATION AND CALL PLACE PERU!
--FRANCISCO BIZARRO (1541-1474)

OF ALL THE LUCK!

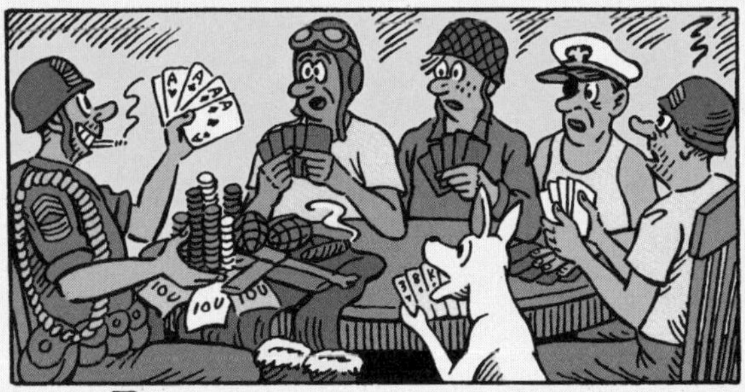
IOU
IOU
IOU

FOR SOME REASON, EVERYONE LOVED PLAYING CARDS WITH THE LOSERS.

THE "MARVEL FAMILY" CIRCUS

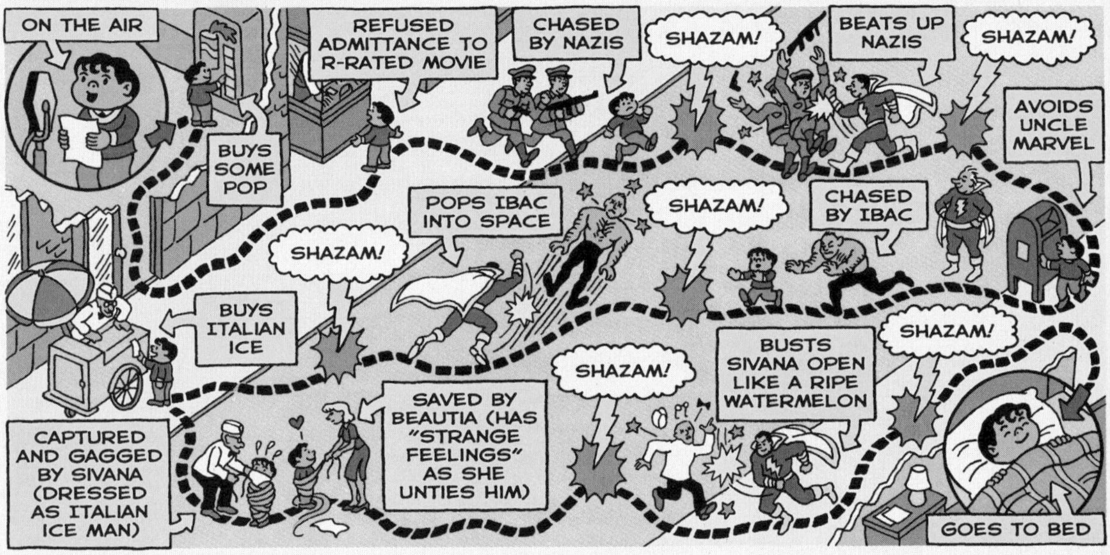
ON THE AIR
BUYS SOME POP
REFUSED ADMITTANCE TO R-RATED MOVIE
CHASED BY NAZIS
SHAZAM!
BEATS UP NAZIS
SHAZAM!
AVOIDS UNCLE MARVEL
CHASED BY IBAC
SHAZAM!
POPS IBAC INTO SPACE
SHAZAM!
BUYS ITALIAN ICE
CAPTURED AND GAGGED BY SIVANA (DRESSED AS ITALIAN ICE MAN)
SAVED BY BEAUTIA (HAS "STRANGE FEELINGS" AS SHE UNTIES HIM)
SHAZAM!
BUSTS SIVANA OPEN LIKE A RIPE WATERMELON
SHAZAM!
GOES TO BED

THE BLACK RACER

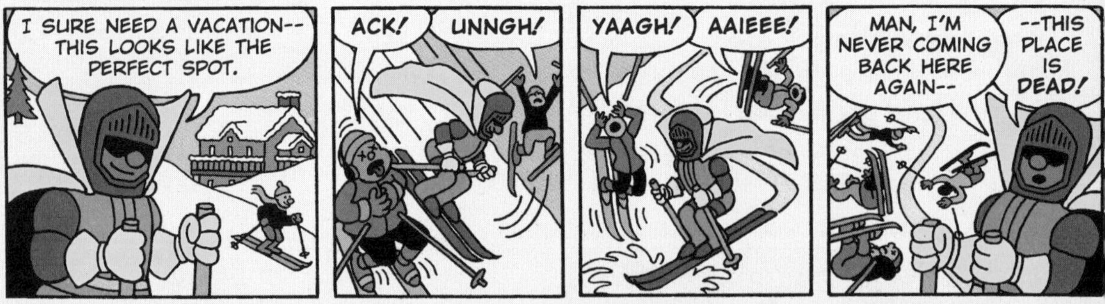
I SURE NEED A VACATION-- THIS LOOKS LIKE THE PERFECT SPOT.
ACK!
UNNGH!
YAAGH!
AAIEEE!
MAN, I'M NEVER COMING BACK HERE AGAIN--
--THIS PLACE IS DEAD!

ABNEGAZAR, RATH AND GHAST, ATTORNEYS AT LAW

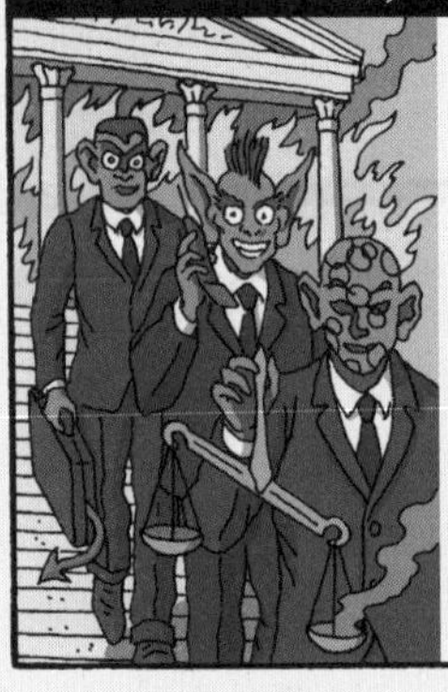

Have you been injured, through no fault of your own? Have you been injured because you're an irresponsible doofus? Y'know, backyard wrestling or emulating some stunt on MTV? Whatever the case may be, somebody's to blame, and it isn't you. So call Abnegazar, Rath and Ghast. We've beaten the Justice League, and now we're beating the living bejeesus out of the justice system. And we have made a sacred vow never to let something as confusing and insubstantial as justice stand in the way of getting our clients big cash settlements for their injuries no matter how specious their claims may be. That's a pact you can count on.

We do it all: Accident, Personal Injury, Impersonal Injury, Wrongful Death, A Lot of Wrongful Death, War Crimes, Mass Destruction, Divorce, Paternity suits, File Sharing.

We ♥ frivolous lawsuits! Jury tampering our specialty! And we accept all major credit cards, blood types, souls and first born.

Now with locations on three physical planes, operators hovering by to take your call, tachyon message, subconscious or telepathic plea.

Abnegazar, Rath and Ghast. We give you real power of attorney.

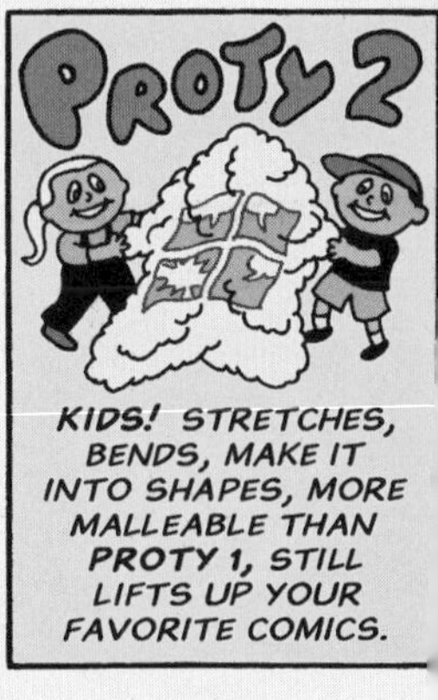
PROTY 2
KIDS! STRETCHES, BENDS, MAKE IT INTO SHAPES, MORE MALLEABLE THAN PROTY 1, STILL LIFTS UP YOUR FAVORITE COMICS.

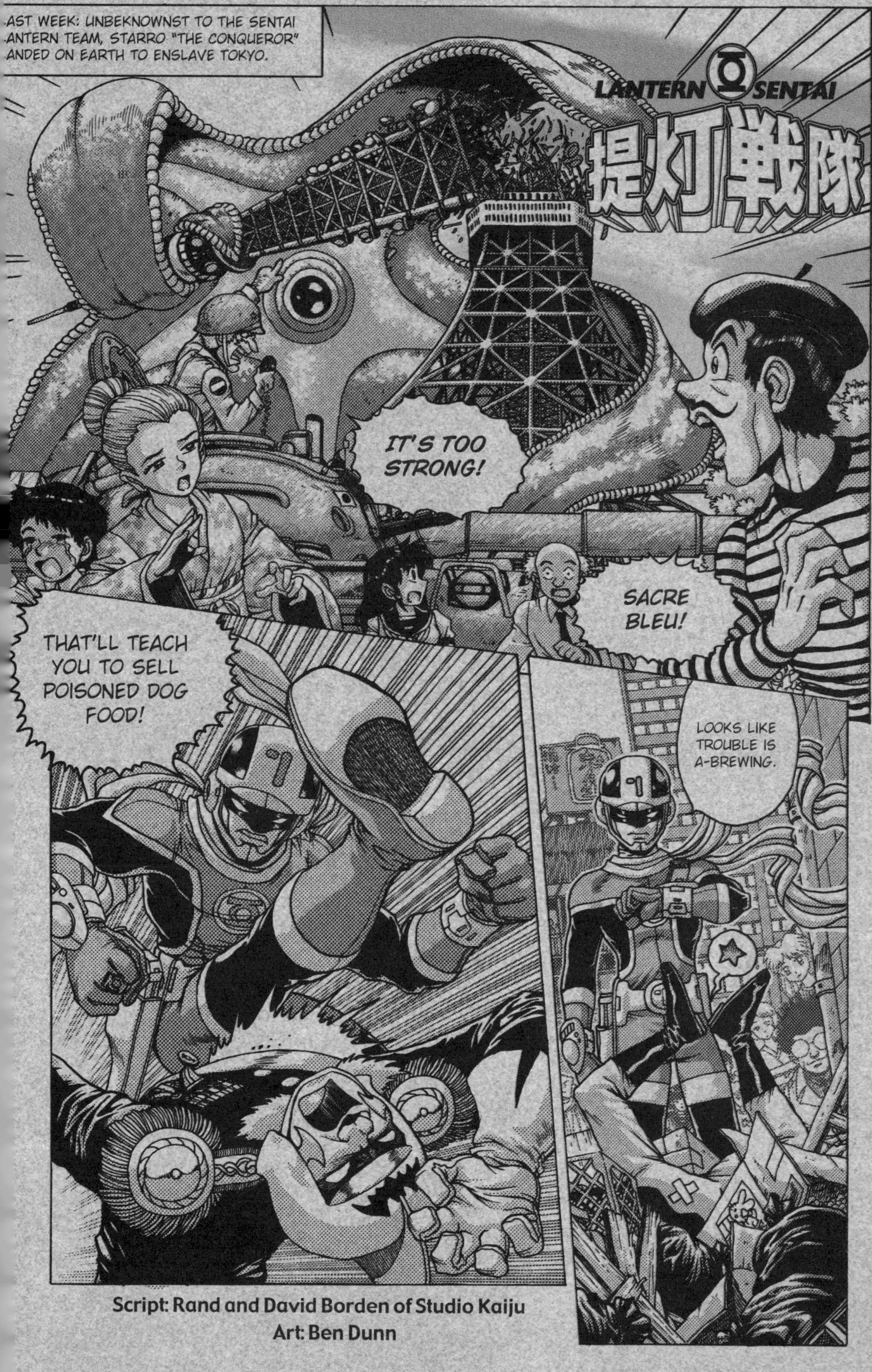
-AST WEEK: UNBEKNOWNST TO THE SENTAI
-ANTERN TEAM, STARRO "THE CONQUEROR"
-ANDED ON EARTH TO ENSLAVE TOKYO.
LANTERN SENTAI
提灯戦隊
IT'S TOO STRONG!
SACRE BLEU!
THAT'LL TEACH YOU TO SELL POISONED DOG FOOD!
LOOKS LIKE TROUBLE IS A-BREWING.

Script: Rand and David Borden of Studio Kaiju
Art: Ben Dunn

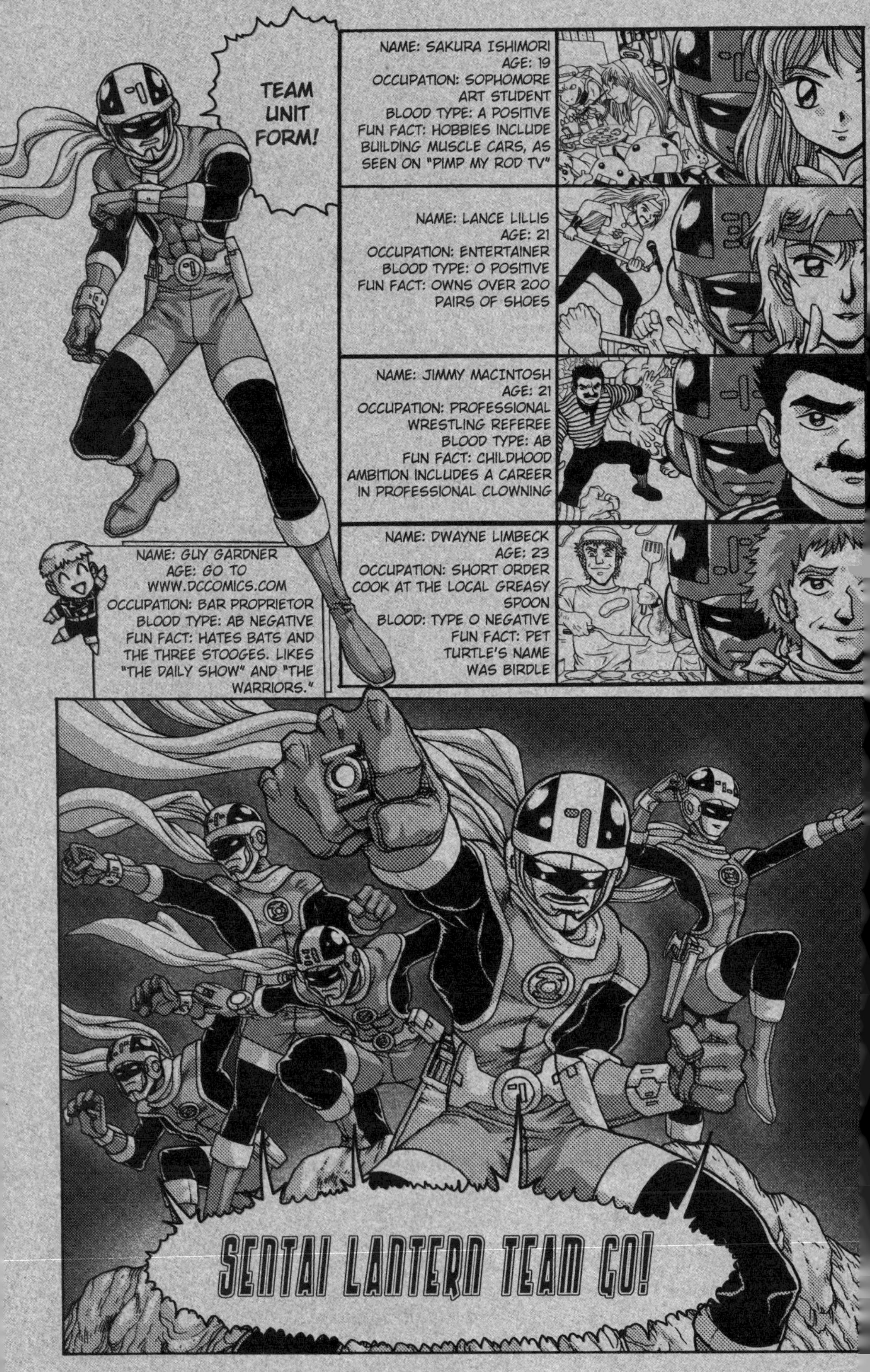
TEAM UNIT FORM!
NAME: SAKURA ISHIMORI
AGE: 19
OCCUPATION: SOPHOMORE ART STUDENT
BLOOD TYPE: A POSITIVE
FUN FACT: HOBBIES INCLUDE BUILDING MUSCLE CARS, AS SEEN ON "PIMP MY ROD TV"
NAME: LANCE LILLIS
AGE: 21
OCCUPATION: ENTERTAINER
BLOOD TYPE: O POSITIVE
FUN FACT: OWNS OVER 200 PAIRS OF SHOES
NAME: JIMMY MACINTOSH
AGE: 21
OCCUPATION: PROFESSIONAL WRESTLING REFEREE
BLOOD TYPE: AB
FUN FACT: CHILDHOOD AMBITION INCLUDES A CAREER IN PROFESSIONAL CLOWNING
NAME: DWAYNE LIMBECK
AGE: 23
OCCUPATION: SHORT ORDER COOK AT THE LOCAL GREASY SPOON
BLOOD: TYPE O NEGATIVE
FUN FACT: PET TURTLE'S NAME WAS BIRDLE
NAME: GUY GARDNER
AGE: GO TO WWW.DCCOMICS.COM
OCCUPATION: BAR PROPRIETOR
BLOOD TYPE: AB NEGATIVE
FUN FACT: HATES BATS AND THE THREE STOOGES. LIKES "THE DAILY SHOW" AND "THE WARRIORS."
SENTAI LANTERN TEAM GO!

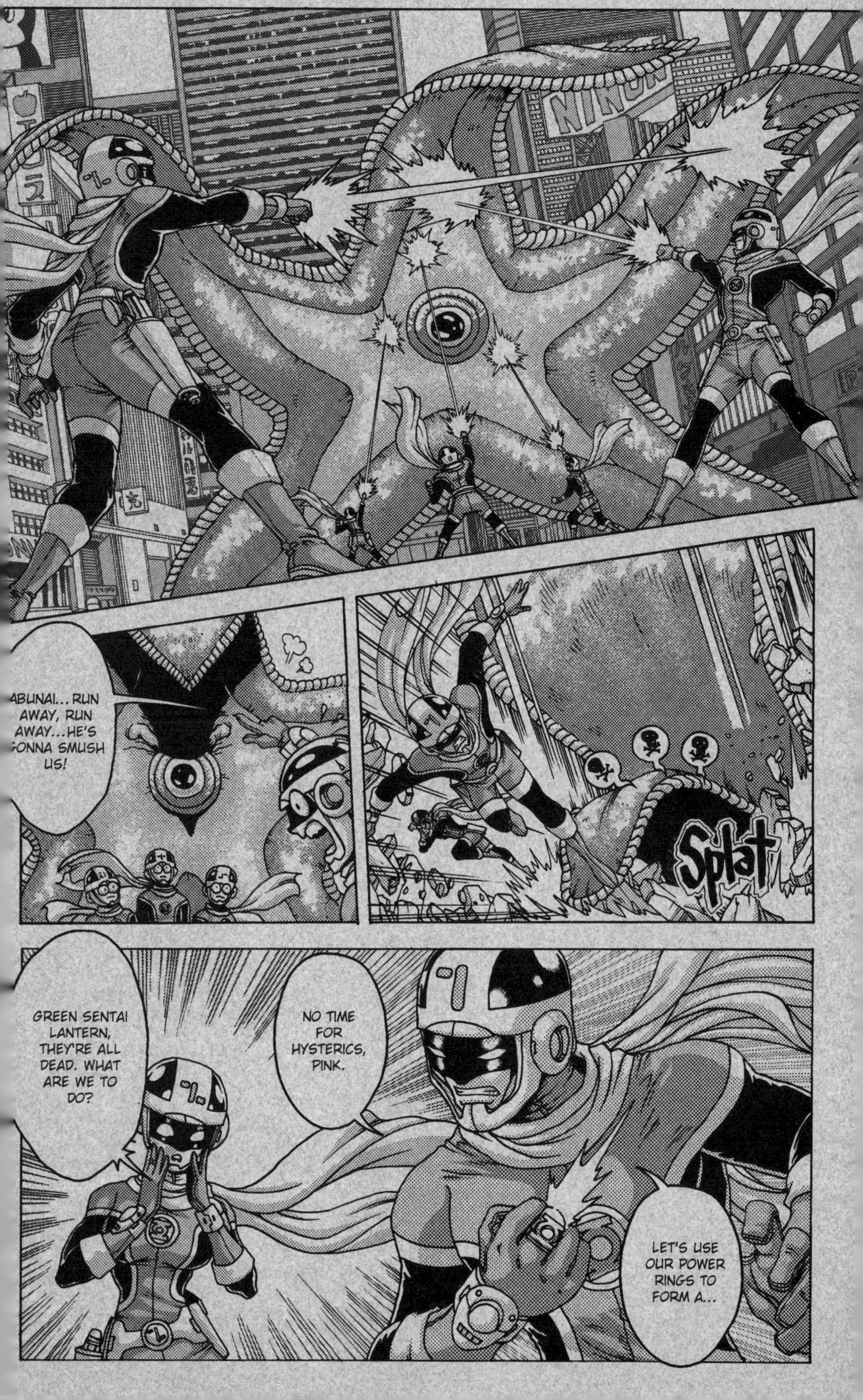

ABUNAI... RUN AWAY, RUN AWAY...HE'S GONNA SMUSH US!
Splat
GREEN SENTAI LANTERN, THEY'RE ALL DEAD. WHAT ARE WE TO DO?
NO TIME FOR HYSTERICS, PINK.
LET'S USE OUR POWER RINGS TO FORM A...

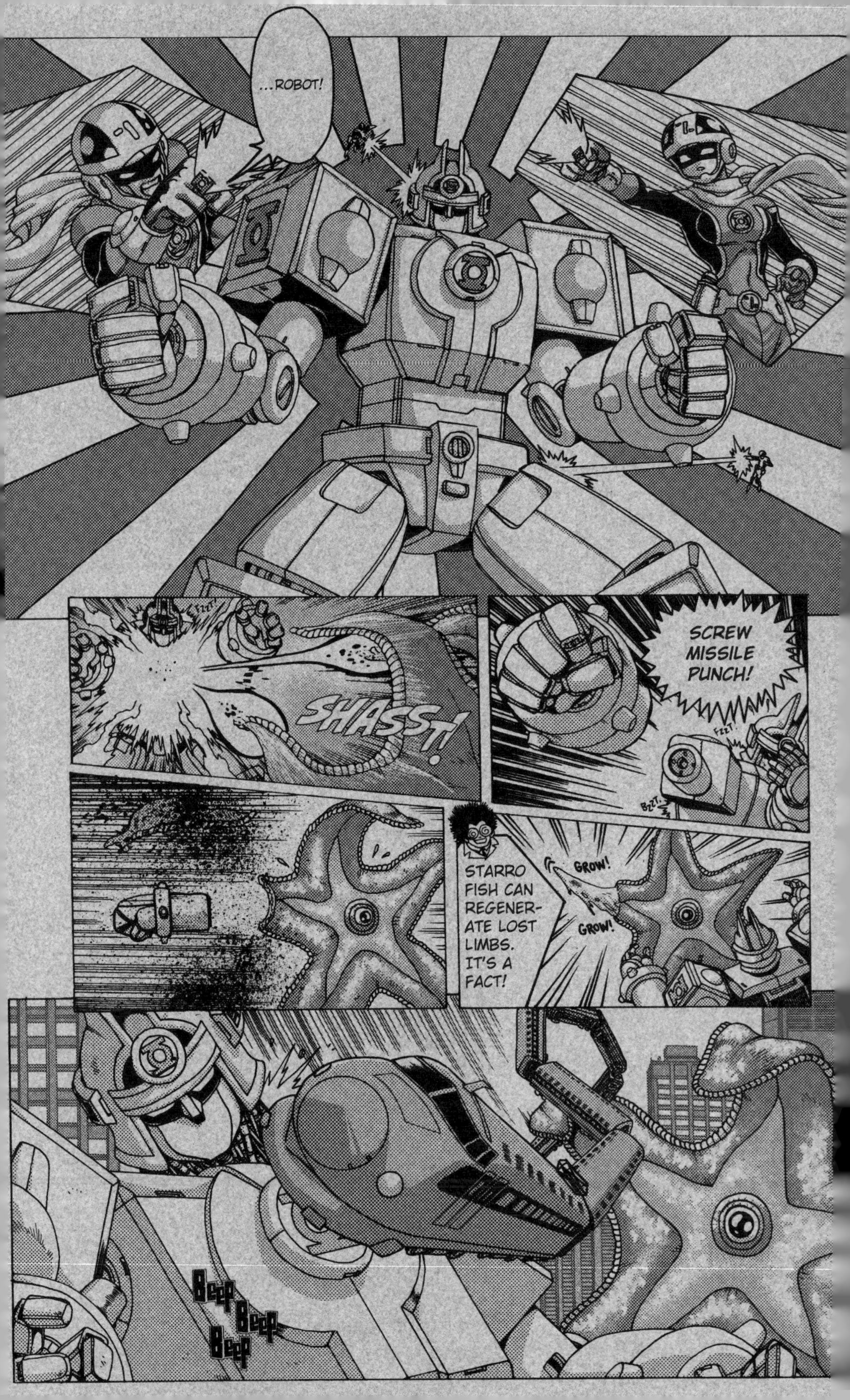
...ROBOT!
FZZT!
SHASST!
SCREW MISSILE PUNCH!
FZZT.
BZZT.
STARRO FISH CAN REGENERATE LOST LIMBS. IT'S A FACT!
GROW!
GROW!
Beep Beep Beep

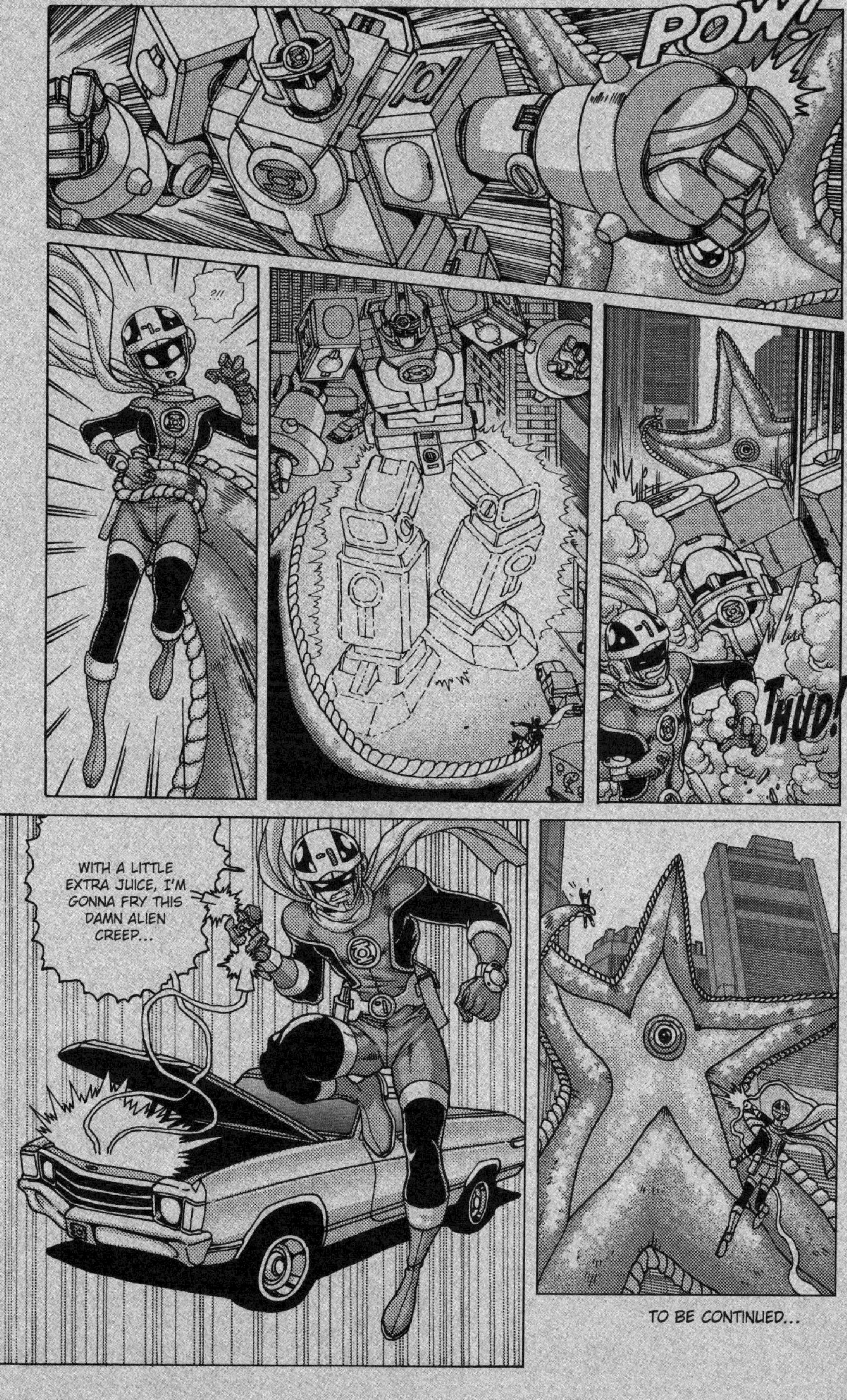
POW!
?!!
THUD!
WITH A LITTLE EXTRA JUICE, I'M GONNA FRY THIS DAMN ALIEN CREEP...
TO BE CONTINUED...

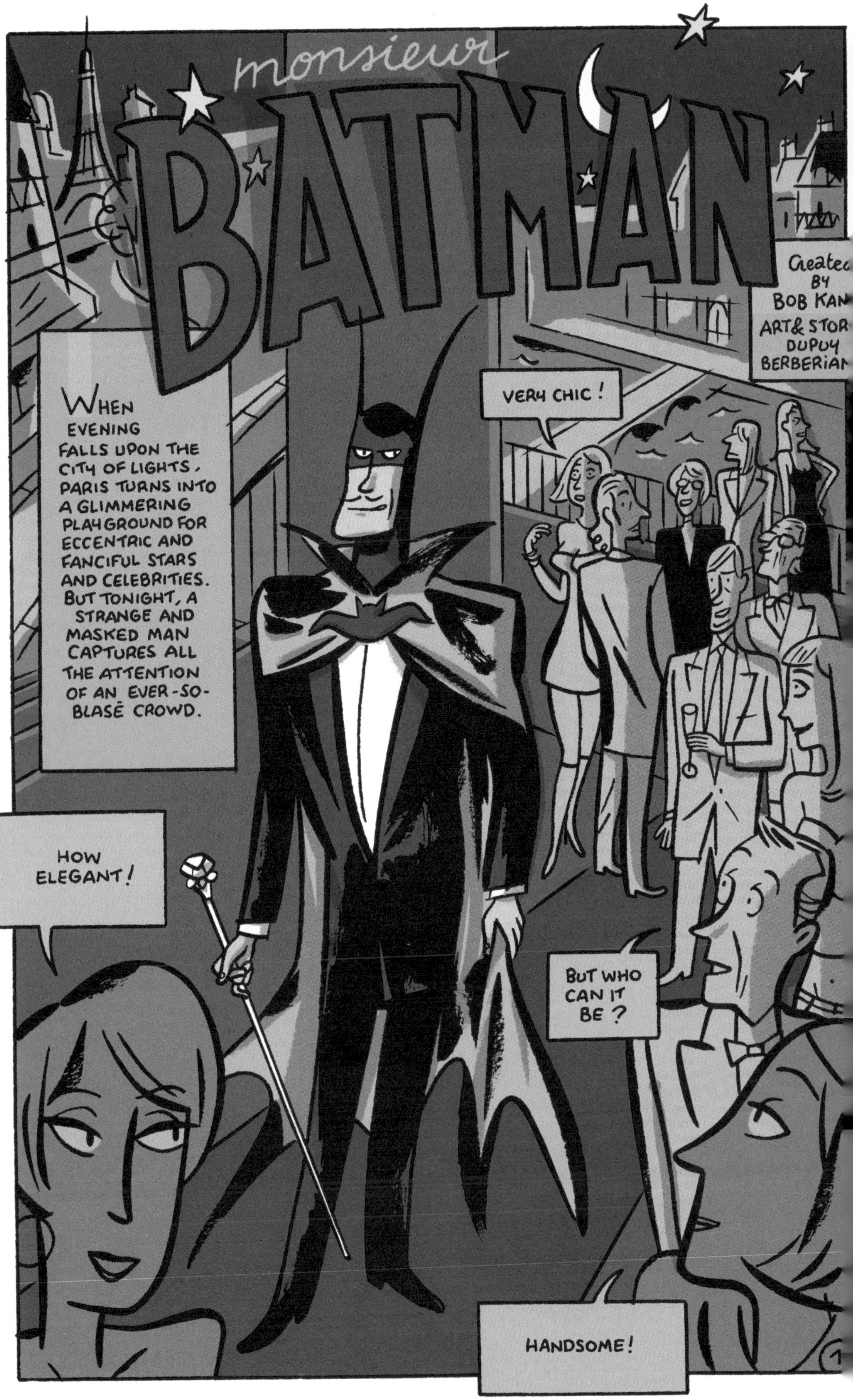
monsieur
BATMAN
Created BY BOB KAN
ART& STOR
DUPUY
BERBERIAN
WHEN EVENING FALLS UPON THE CITY OF LIGHTS, PARIS TURNS INTO A GLIMMERING PLAYGROUND FOR ECCENTRIC AND FANCIFUL STARS AND CELEBRITIES. BUT TONIGHT, A STRANGE AND MASKED MAN CAPTURES ALL THE ATTENTION OF AN EVER-SO-BLASÉ CROWD.
VERY CHIC!
HOW ELEGANT!
BUT WHO CAN IT BE?
HANDSOME!

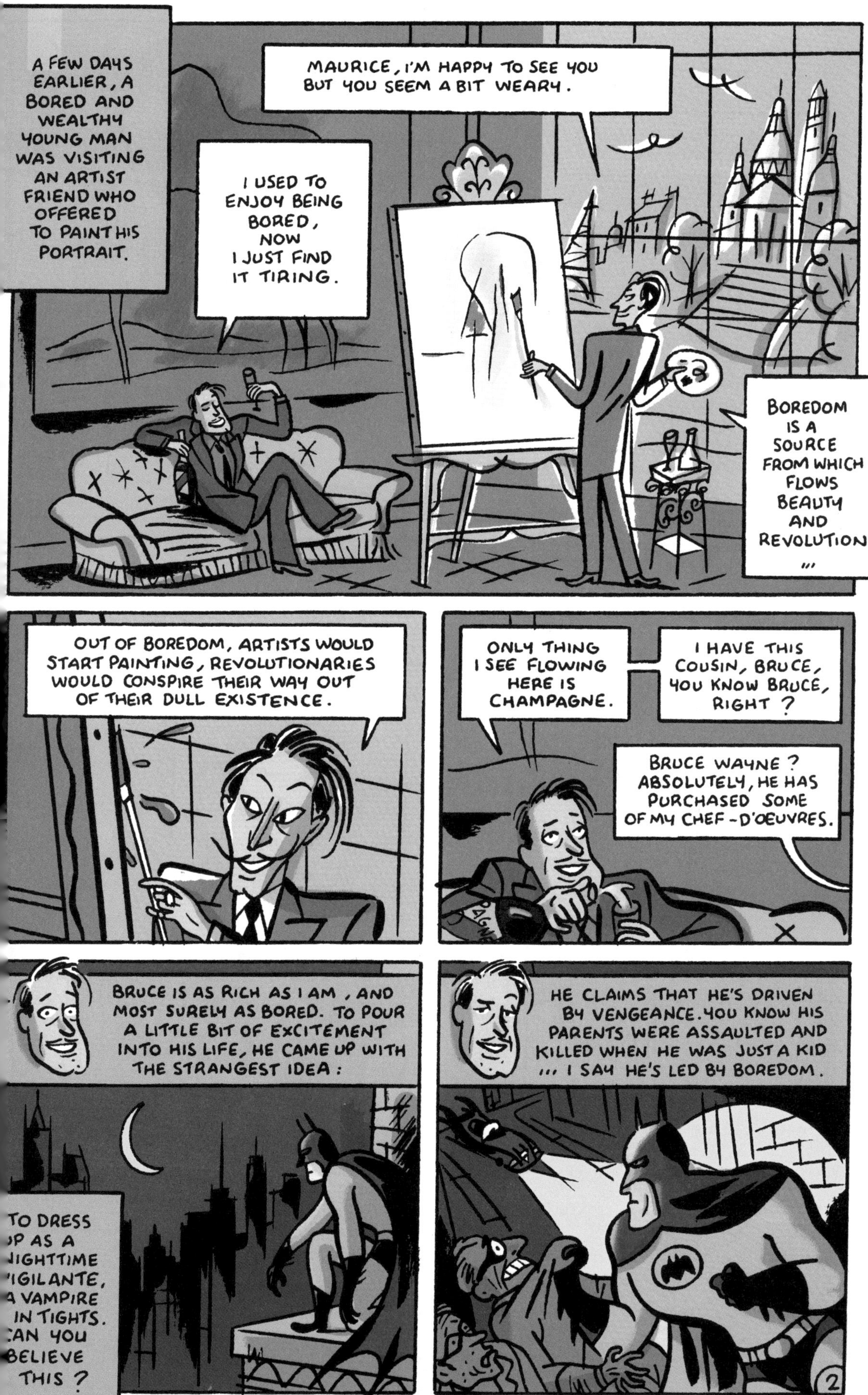
A FEW DAYS EARLIER, A BORED AND WEALTHY YOUNG MAN WAS VISITING AN ARTIST FRIEND WHO OFFERED TO PAINT HIS PORTRAIT.
MAURICE, I'M HAPPY TO SEE YOU BUT YOU SEEM A BIT WEARY.
I USED TO ENJOY BEING BORED, NOW I JUST FIND IT TIRING.
BOREDOM IS A SOURCE FROM WHICH FLOWS BEAUTY AND REVOLUTION ...
OUT OF BOREDOM, ARTISTS WOULD START PAINTING, REVOLUTIONARIES WOULD CONSPIRE THEIR WAY OUT OF THEIR DULL EXISTENCE.
ONLY THING I SEE FLOWING HERE IS CHAMPAGNE.
I HAVE THIS COUSIN, BRUCE, YOU KNOW BRUCE, RIGHT ?
BRUCE WAYNE ? ABSOLUTELY, HE HAS PURCHASED SOME OF MY CHEF-D'OEUVRES.
BRUCE IS AS RICH AS I AM, AND MOST SURELY AS BORED. TO POUR A LITTLE BIT OF EXCITEMENT INTO HIS LIFE, HE CAME UP WITH THE STRANGEST IDEA :
TO DRESS UP AS A NIGHTTIME VIGILANTE, A VAMPIRE IN TIGHTS. CAN YOU BELIEVE THIS ?
HE CLAIMS THAT HE'S DRIVEN BY VENGEANCE. YOU KNOW HIS PARENTS WERE ASSAULTED AND KILLED WHEN HE WAS JUST A KID ... I SAY HE'S LED BY BOREDOM.
2

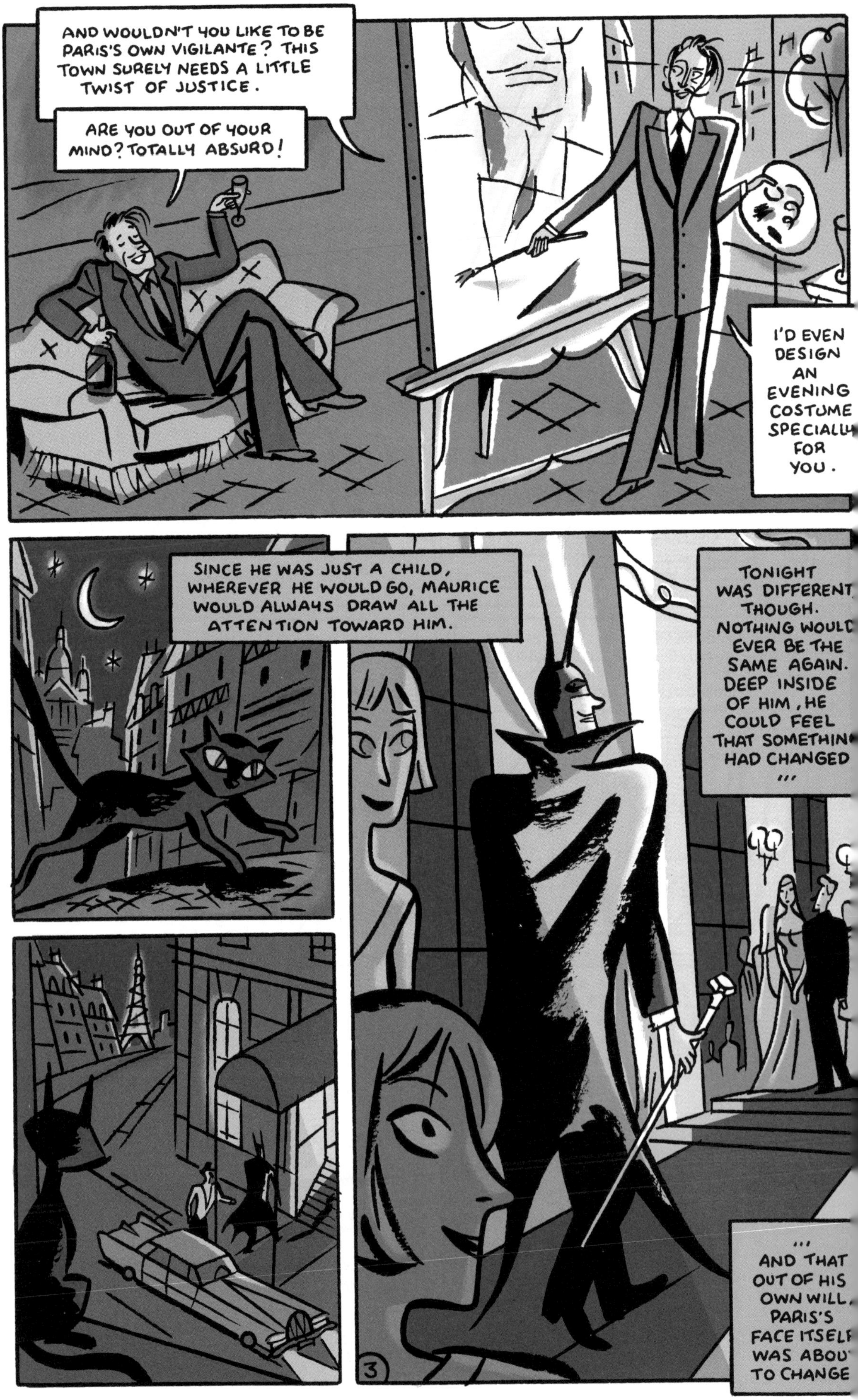

AND WOULDN'T YOU LIKE TO BE PARIS'S OWN VIGILANTE? THIS TOWN SURELY NEEDS A LITTLE TWIST OF JUSTICE.
ARE YOU OUT OF YOUR MIND? TOTALLY ABSURD!
I'D EVEN DESIGN AN EVENING COSTUME SPECIALLY FOR YOU.
SINCE HE WAS JUST A CHILD, WHEREVER HE WOULD GO, MAURICE WOULD ALWAYS DRAW ALL THE ATTENTION TOWARD HIM.
TONIGHT WAS DIFFERENT THOUGH. NOTHING WOULD EVER BE THE SAME AGAIN. DEEP INSIDE OF HIM, HE COULD FEEL THAT SOMETHING HAD CHANGED ...
... AND THAT OUT OF HIS OWN WILL, PARIS'S FACE ITSELF WAS ABOUT TO CHANGE
3

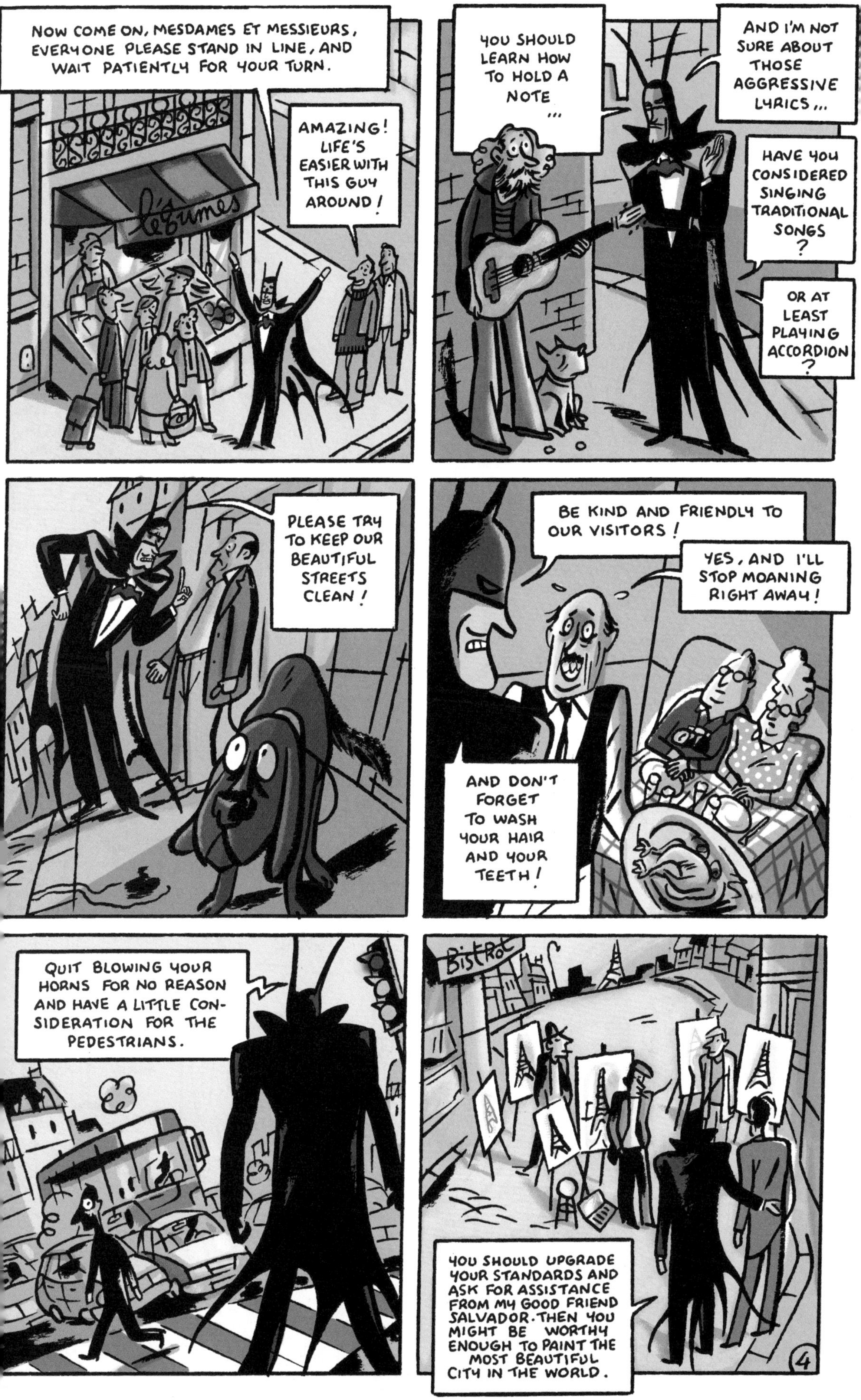
NOW COME ON, MESDAMES ET MESSIEURS, EVERYONE PLEASE STAND IN LINE, AND WAIT PATIENTLY FOR YOUR TURN.
AMAZING! LIFE'S EASIER WITH THIS GUY AROUND!
légumes
YOU SHOULD LEARN HOW TO HOLD A NOTE ...
AND I'M NOT SURE ABOUT THOSE AGGRESSIVE LYRICS...
HAVE YOU CONSIDERED SINGING TRADITIONAL SONGS?
OR AT LEAST PLAYING ACCORDION?
PLEASE TRY TO KEEP OUR BEAUTIFUL STREETS CLEAN!
BE KIND AND FRIENDLY TO OUR VISITORS!
YES, AND I'LL STOP MOANING RIGHT AWAY!
AND DON'T FORGET TO WASH YOUR HAIR AND YOUR TEETH!
QUIT BLOWING YOUR HORNS FOR NO REASON AND HAVE A LITTLE CON-SIDERATION FOR THE PEDESTRIANS.
BistRot
YOU SHOULD UPGRADE YOUR STANDARDS AND ASK FOR ASSISTANCE FROM MY GOOD FRIEND SALVADOR. THEN YOU MIGHT BE WORTHY ENOUGH TO PAINT THE MOST BEAUTIFUL CITY IN THE WORLD.

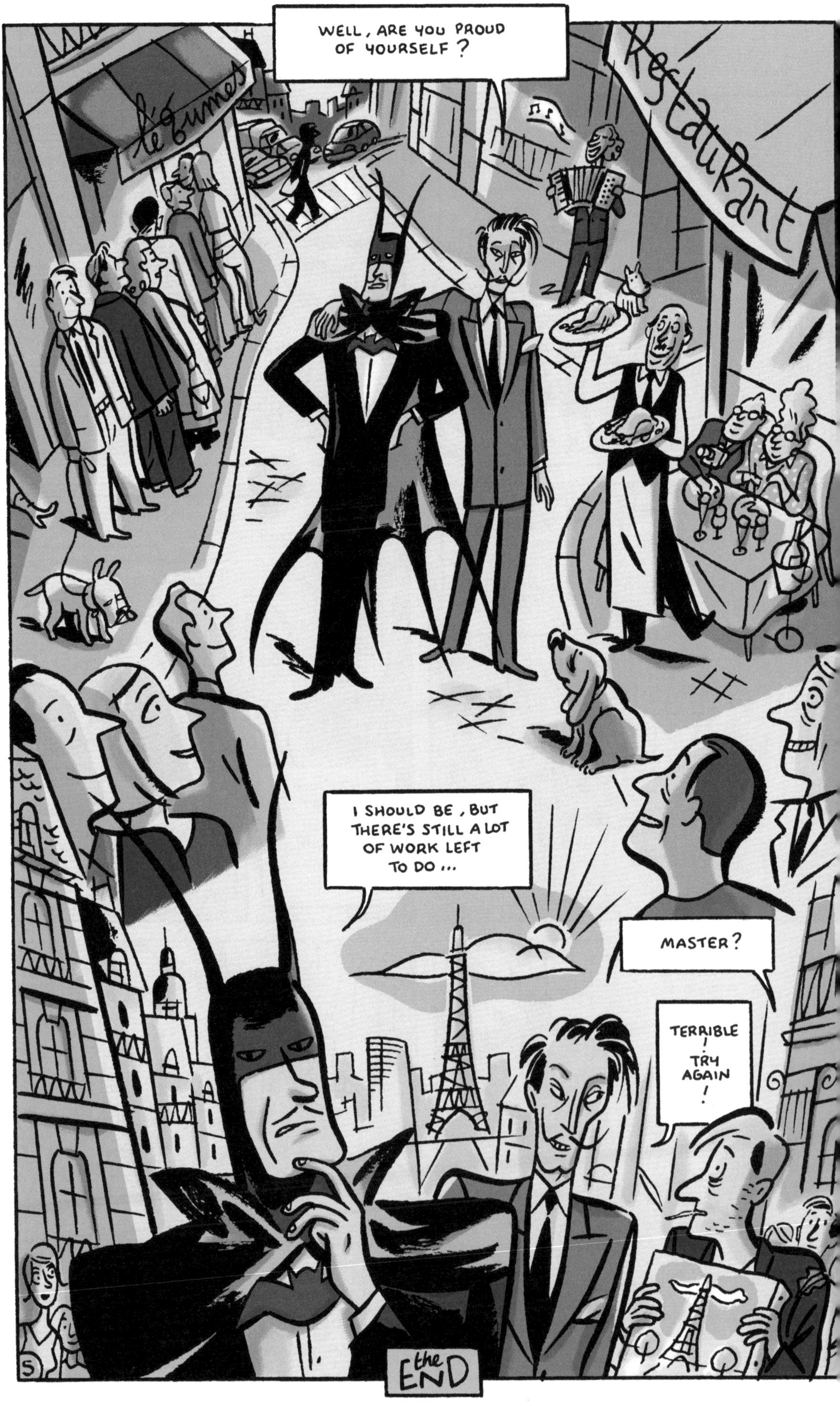
WELL, ARE YOU PROUD OF YOURSELF?
Restaurant
légumes
I SHOULD BE, BUT THERE'S STILL A LOT OF WORK LEFT TO DO...
MASTER?
TERRIBLE! TRY AGAIN!
THE END

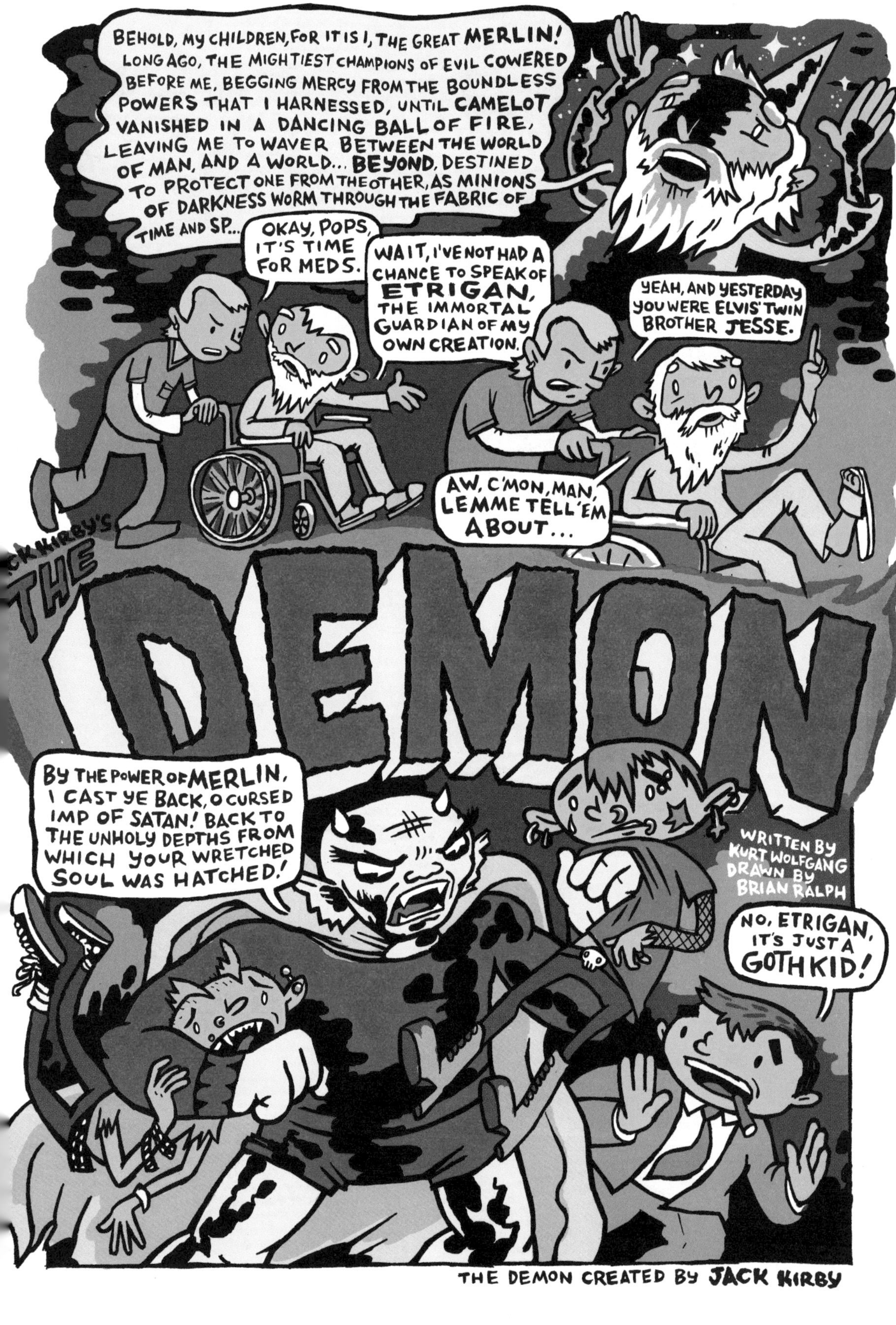
BEHOLD, MY CHILDREN, FOR IT IS I, THE GREAT MERLIN! LONG AGO, THE MIGHTIEST CHAMPIONS OF EVIL COWERED BEFORE ME, BEGGING MERCY FROM THE BOUNDLESS POWERS THAT I HARNESSED, UNTIL CAMELOT VANISHED IN A DANCING BALL OF FIRE, LEAVING ME TO WAVER BETWEEN THE WORLD OF MAN, AND A WORLD... BEYOND, DESTINED TO PROTECT ONE FROM THE OTHER, AS MINIONS OF DARKNESS WORM THROUGH THE FABRIC OF TIME AND SP...
OKAY, POPS, IT'S TIME FOR MEDS.
WAIT, I'VE NOT HAD A CHANCE TO SPEAK OF ETRIGAN, THE IMMORTAL GUARDIAN OF MY OWN CREATION.
YEAH, AND YESTERDAY YOU WERE ELVIS' TWIN BROTHER JESSE.
AW, C'MON, MAN, LEMME TELL 'EM ABOUT...
CK KIRBY'S THE DEMON
BY THE POWER OF MERLIN, I CAST YE BACK, O CURSED IMP OF SATAN! BACK TO THE UNHOLY DEPTHS FROM WHICH YOUR WRETCHED SOUL WAS HATCHED!
WRITTEN BY KURT WOLFGANG DRAWN BY BRIAN RALPH
NO, ETRIGAN, IT'S JUST A GOTH KID!

THE DEMON CREATED BY JACK KIRBY

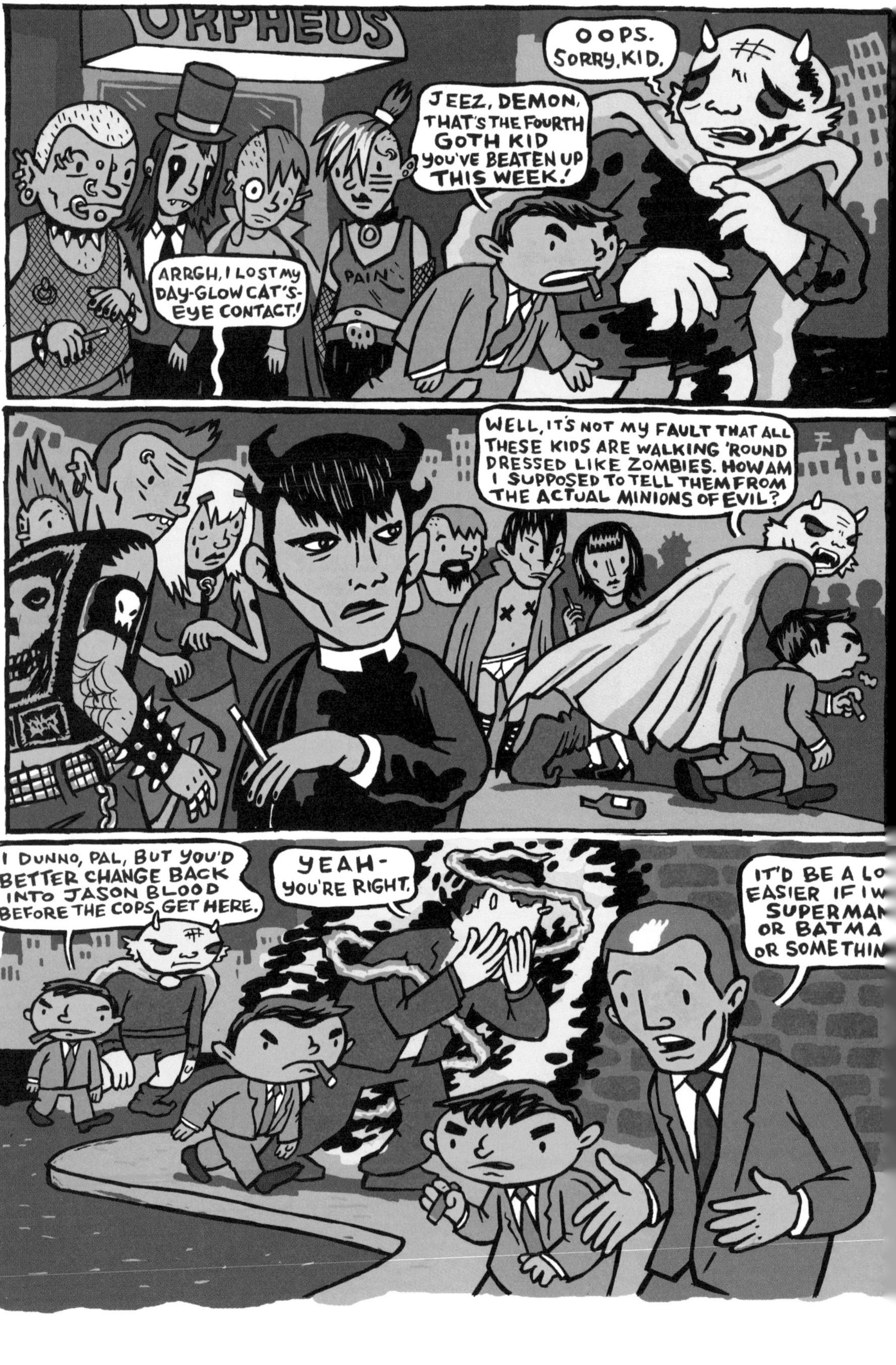
ORPHEUS
OOPS. SORRY, KID.
JEEZ, DEMON, THAT'S THE FOURTH GOTH KID YOU'VE BEATEN UP THIS WEEK!
ARRGH, I LOST MY DAY-GLOW CAT'S-EYE CONTACT!
PAIN
WELL, IT'S NOT MY FAULT THAT ALL THESE KIDS ARE WALKING 'ROUND DRESSED LIKE ZOMBIES. HOW AM I SUPPOSED TO TELL THEM FROM THE ACTUAL MINIONS OF EVIL?
I DUNNO, PAL, BUT YOU'D BETTER CHANGE BACK INTO JASON BLOOD BEFORE THE COPS GET HERE.
YEAH - YOU'RE RIGHT.

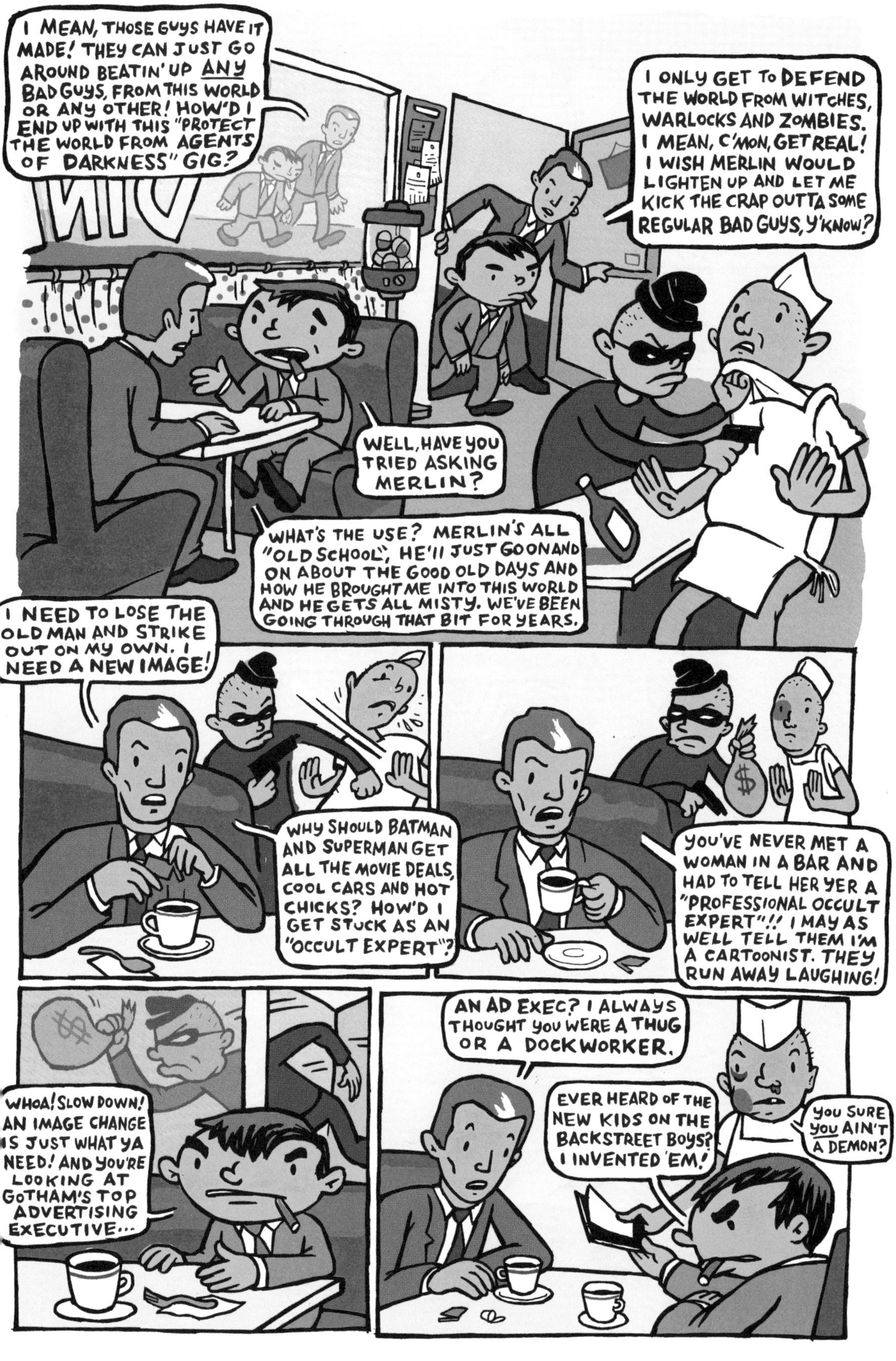
I MEAN, THOSE GUYS HAVE IT MADE! THEY CAN JUST GO AROUND BEATIN' UP ANY BAD GUYS, FROM THIS WORLD OR ANY OTHER! HOW'D I END UP WITH THIS "PROTECT THE WORLD FROM AGENTS OF DARKNESS" GIG?
I ONLY GET TO DEFEND THE WORLD FROM WITCHES, WARLOCKS AND ZOMBIES. I MEAN, C'MON, GET REAL! I WISH MERLIN WOULD LIGHTEN UP AND LET ME KICK THE CRAP OUTTA SOME REGULAR BAD GUYS, Y'KNOW?
WELL, HAVE YOU TRIED ASKING MERLIN?
WHAT'S THE USE? MERLIN'S ALL "OLD SCHOOL", HE'LL JUST GO ON AND ON ABOUT THE GOOD OLD DAYS AND HOW HE BROUGHT ME INTO THIS WORLD AND HE GETS ALL MISTY. WE'VE BEEN GOING THROUGH THAT BIT FOR YEARS.
I NEED TO LOSE THE OLD MAN AND STRIKE OUT ON MY OWN. I NEED A NEW IMAGE!
WHY SHOULD BATMAN AND SUPERMAN GET ALL THE MOVIE DEALS, COOL CARS AND HOT CHICKS? HOW'D I GET STUCK AS AN "OCCULT EXPERT"?
YOU'VE NEVER MET A WOMAN IN A BAR AND HAD TO TELL HER YER A "PROFESSIONAL OCCULT EXPERT"!! I MAY AS WELL TELL THEM I'M A CARTOONIST. THEY RUN AWAY LAUGHING!
WHOA! SLOW DOWN! AN IMAGE CHANGE IS JUST WHAT YA NEED! AND YOU'RE LOOKING AT GOTHAM'S TOP ADVERTISING EXECUTIVE...
AN AD EXEC? I ALWAYS THOUGHT YOU WERE A THUG OR A DOCKWORKER.
EVER HEARD OF THE NEW KIDS ON THE BACKSTREET BOYS? I INVENTED 'EM!
YOU SURE YOU AIN'T A DEMON?

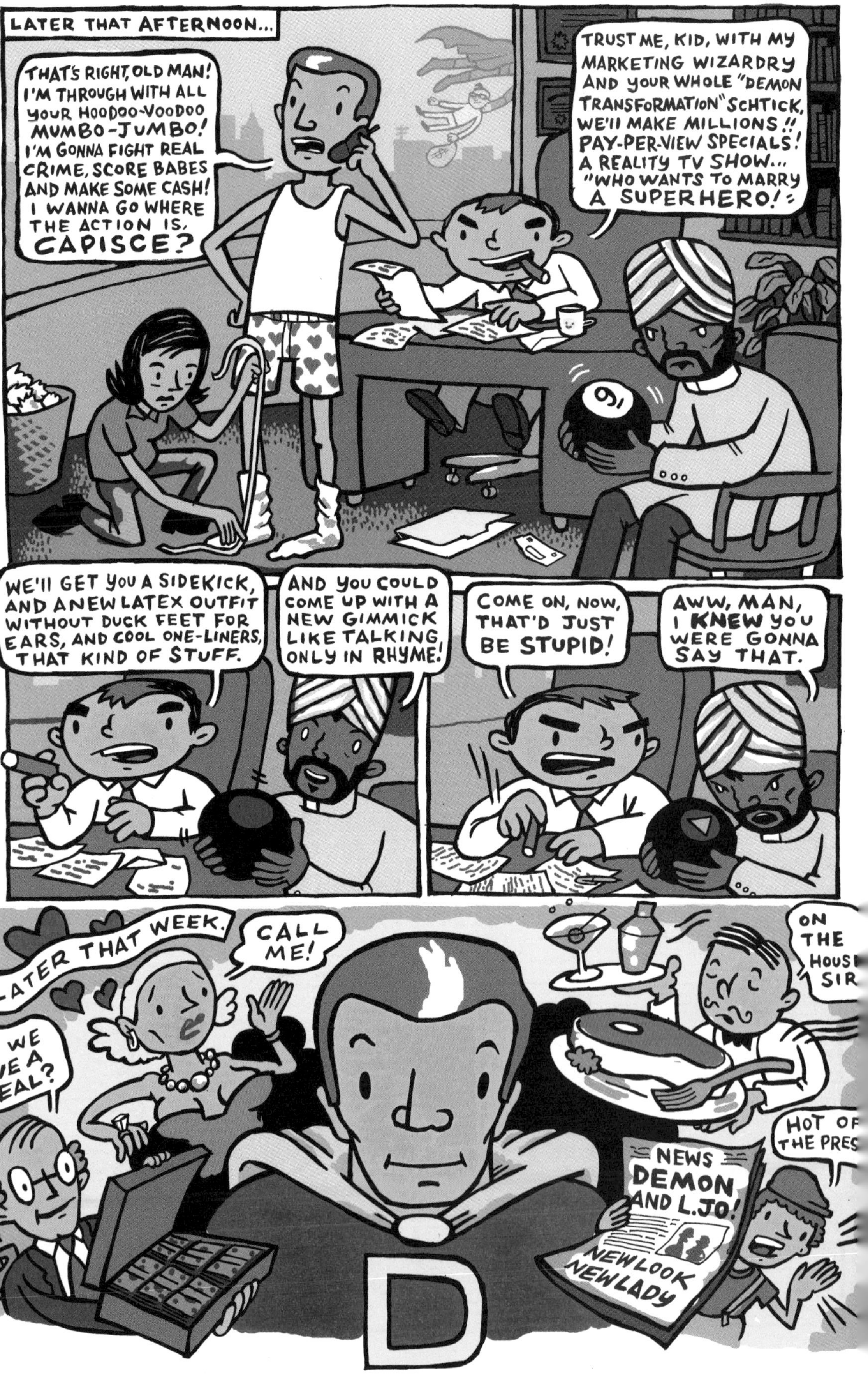
LATER THAT AFTERNOON...
THAT'S RIGHT, OLD MAN! I'M THROUGH WITH ALL YOUR HOODOO-VOODOO MUMBO-JUMBO! I'M GONNA FIGHT REAL CRIME, SCORE BABES AND MAKE SOME CASH! I WANNA GO WHERE THE ACTION IS, CAPISCE?
TRUST ME, KID, WITH MY MARKETING WIZARDRY AND YOUR WHOLE "DEMON TRANSFORMATION" SCHTICK, WE'LL MAKE MILLIONS!! PAY-PER-VIEW SPECIALS! A REALITY TV SHOW... "WHO WANTS TO MARRY A SUPERHERO!"
WE'LL GET YOU A SIDEKICK, AND A NEW LATEX OUTFIT WITHOUT DUCK FEET FOR EARS, AND COOL ONE-LINERS, THAT KIND OF STUFF.
AND YOU COULD COME UP WITH A NEW GIMMICK LIKE TALKING ONLY IN RHYME!
COME ON, NOW, THAT'D JUST BE STUPID!
AWW, MAN, I KNEW YOU WERE GONNA SAY THAT.
LATER THAT WEEK.
CALL ME!
DO WE HAVE A DEAL?
ON THE HOUS SIR
HOT OF THE PRES
NEWS
DEMON AND L.JO!
NEW LOOK NEW LADY
D

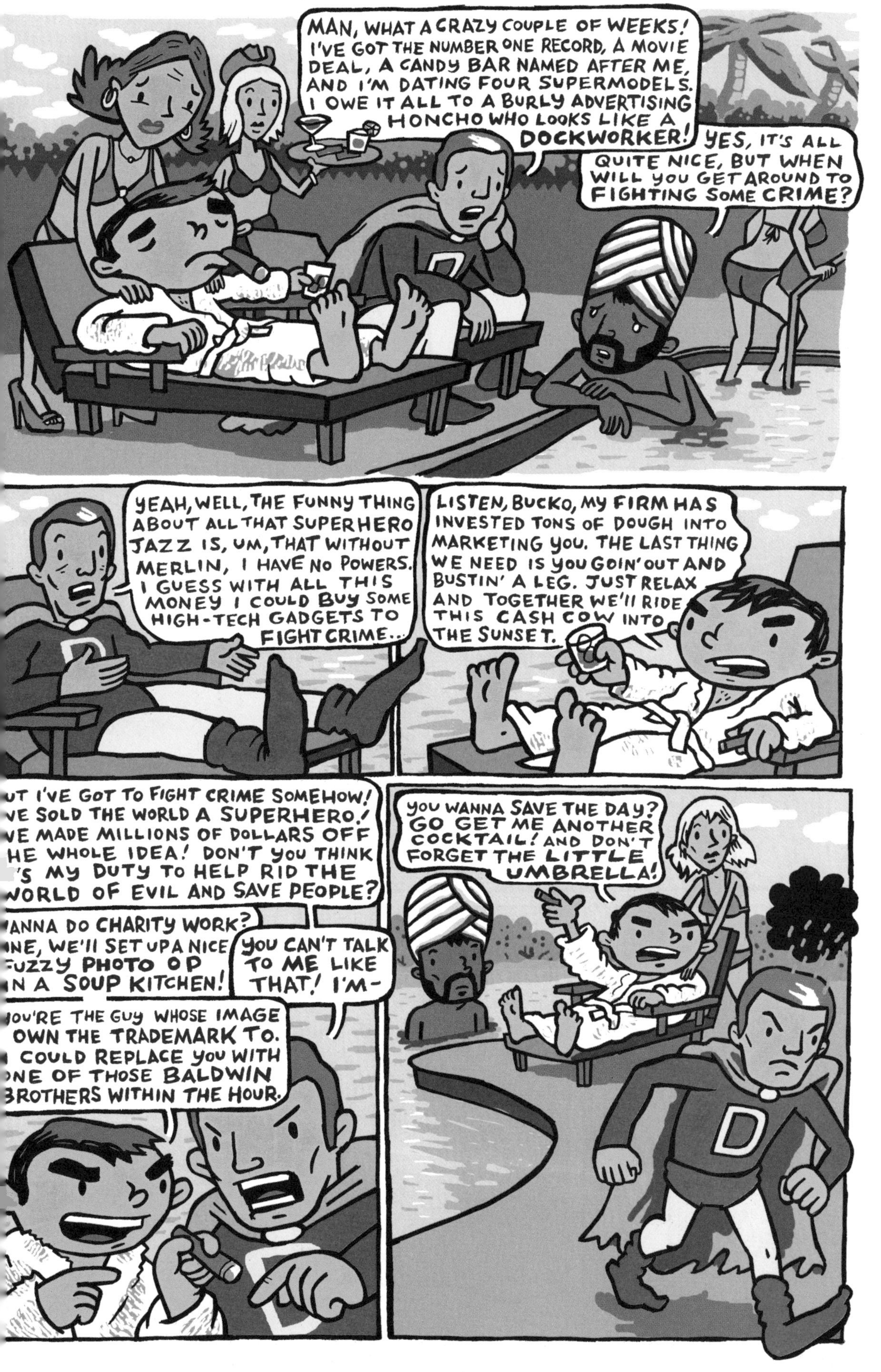
MAN, WHAT A CRAZY COUPLE OF WEEKS! I'VE GOT THE NUMBER ONE RECORD, A MOVIE DEAL, A CANDY BAR NAMED AFTER ME, AND I'M DATING FOUR SUPERMODELS. I OWE IT ALL TO A BURLY ADVERTISING HONCHO WHO LOOKS LIKE A DOCKWORKER!
YES, IT'S ALL QUITE NICE, BUT WHEN WILL YOU GET AROUND TO FIGHTING SOME CRIME?
YEAH, WELL, THE FUNNY THING ABOUT ALL THAT SUPERHERO JAZZ IS, UM, THAT WITHOUT MERLIN, I HAVE NO POWERS. I GUESS WITH ALL THIS MONEY I COULD BUY SOME HIGH-TECH GADGETS TO FIGHT CRIME...
LISTEN, BUCKO, MY FIRM HAS INVESTED TONS OF DOUGH INTO MARKETING YOU. THE LAST THING WE NEED IS YOU GOIN' OUT AND BUSTIN' A LEG. JUST RELAX AND TOGETHER WE'LL RIDE THIS CASH COW INTO THE SUNSET.
UT I'VE GOT TO FIGHT CRIME SOMEHOW! VE SOLD THE WORLD A SUPERHERO! VE MADE MILLIONS OF DOLLARS OFF HE WHOLE IDEA! DON'T YOU THINK 'S MY DUTY TO HELP RID THE WORLD OF EVIL AND SAVE PEOPLE?
ANNA DO CHARITY WORK? NE, WE'LL SET UP A NICE UZZY PHOTO OP N A SOUP KITCHEN!
YOU CAN'T TALK TO ME LIKE THAT! I'M-
OU'RE THE GUY WHOSE IMAGE OWN THE TRADEMARK TO. COULD REPLACE YOU WITH NE OF THOSE BALDWIN ROTHERS WITHIN THE HOUR.
YOU WANNA SAVE THE DAY? GO GET ME ANOTHER COCKTAIL! AND DON'T FORGET THE LITTLE UMBRELLA!

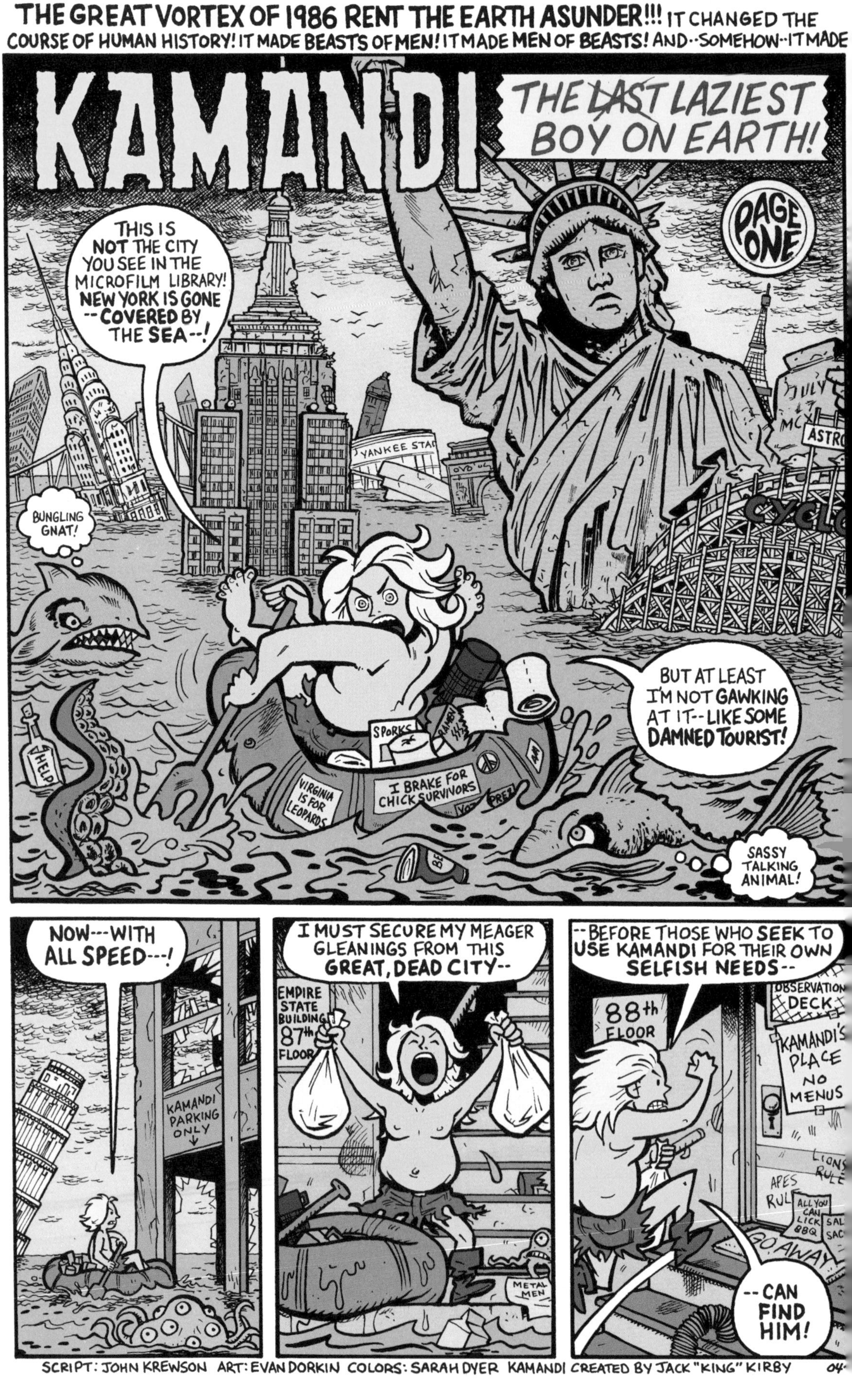
THE GREAT VORTEX OF 1986 RENT THE EARTH ASUNDER!!! IT CHANGED THE COURSE OF HUMAN HISTORY! IT MADE BEASTS OF MEN! IT MADE MEN OF BEASTS! AND--SOMEHOW--IT MADE
KAMANDI
THE LAST LAZIEST BOY ON EARTH!
PAGE ONE
THIS IS NOT THE CITY YOU SEE IN THE MICROFILM LIBRARY! NEW YORK IS GONE --COVERED BY THE SEA--!
BUNGLING GNAT!
YANKEE STA
ASTRO
CYCLO
HELP
SPORKS
RAMEN
VIRGINIA IS FOR LEOPARDS
I BRAKE FOR CHICK SURVIVORS
BUT AT LEAST I'M NOT GAWKING AT IT--LIKE SOME DAMNED TOURIST!
SASSY TALKING ANIMAL!
NOW---WITH ALL SPEED---!
KAMANDI PARKING ONLY
I MUST SECURE MY MEAGER GLEANINGS FROM THIS GREAT, DEAD CITY--
EMPIRE STATE BUILDING 87th FLOOR
METAL MEN
--BEFORE THOSE WHO SEEK TO USE KAMANDI FOR THEIR OWN SELFISH NEEDS--
OBSERVATION DECK
88th FLOOR
KAMANDI'S PLACE NO MENUS
LIONS RULE
APES RULE
ALL YOU CAN LICK BBQ
GO AWAY
--CAN FIND HIM!
SCRIPT: JOHN KREWSON ART: EVAN DORKIN COLORS: SARAH DYER KAMANDI CREATED BY JACK "KING" KIRBY
04

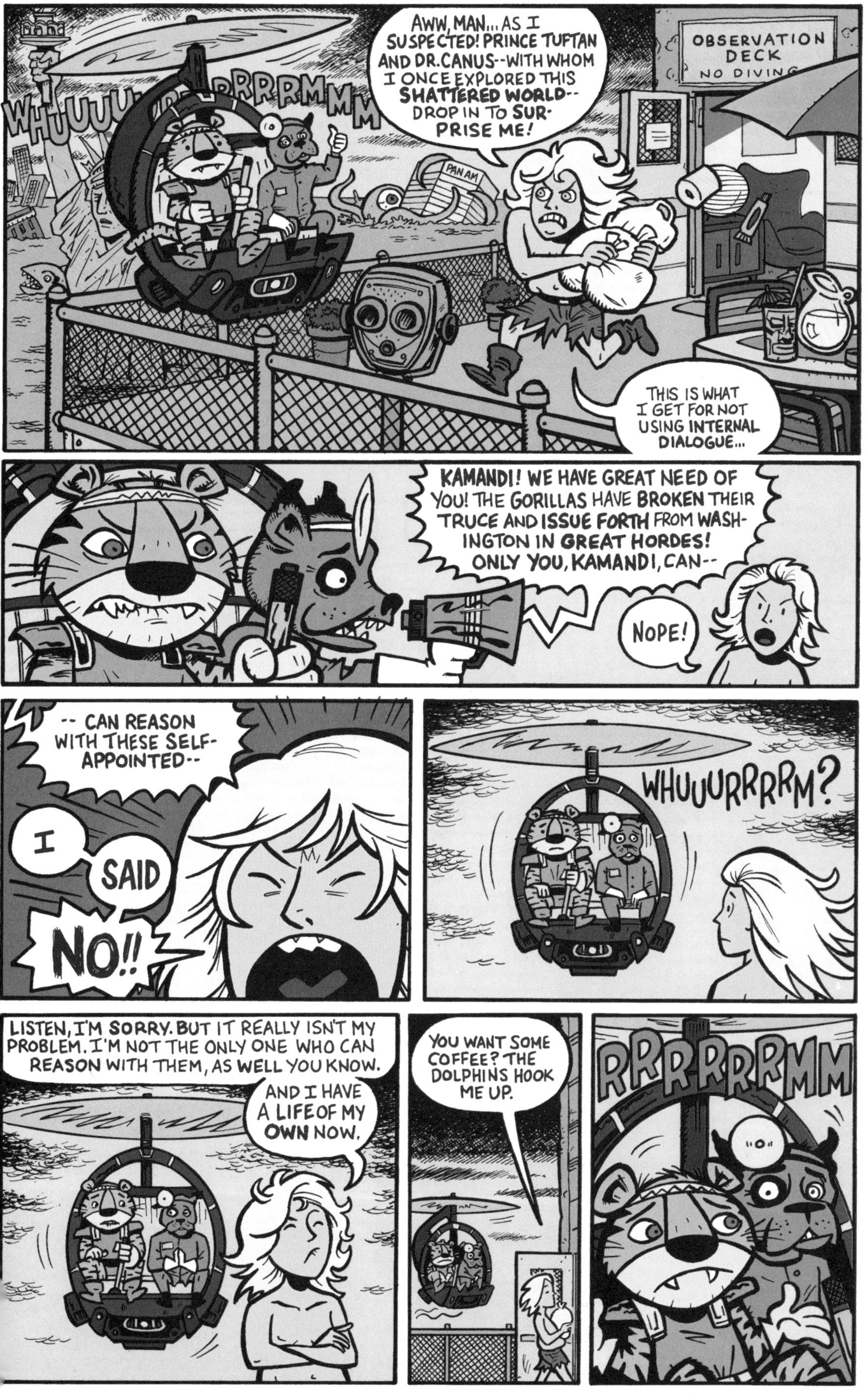
WHUUUURRRRRMMMM
AWW, MAN... AS I SUSPECTED! PRINCE TUFTAN AND DR. CANUS--WITH WHOM I ONCE EXPLORED THIS SHATTERED WORLD--DROP IN TO SURPRISE ME!
OBSERVATION DECK
NO DIVING
PAN AM
THIS IS WHAT I GET FOR NOT USING INTERNAL DIALOGUE...
KAMANDI! WE HAVE GREAT NEED OF YOU! THE GORILLAS HAVE BROKEN THEIR TRUCE AND ISSUE FORTH FROM WASHINGTON IN GREAT HORDES! ONLY YOU, KAMANDI, CAN--
NOPE!
-- CAN REASON WITH THESE SELF-APPOINTED--
I
SAID
NO!!
WHUUURRRRM?
LISTEN, I'M SORRY. BUT IT REALLY ISN'T MY PROBLEM. I'M NOT THE ONLY ONE WHO CAN REASON WITH THEM, AS WELL YOU KNOW.
AND I HAVE A LIFE OF MY OWN NOW.
YOU WANT SOME COFFEE? THE DOLPHINS HOOK ME UP.
RRRRRRMM

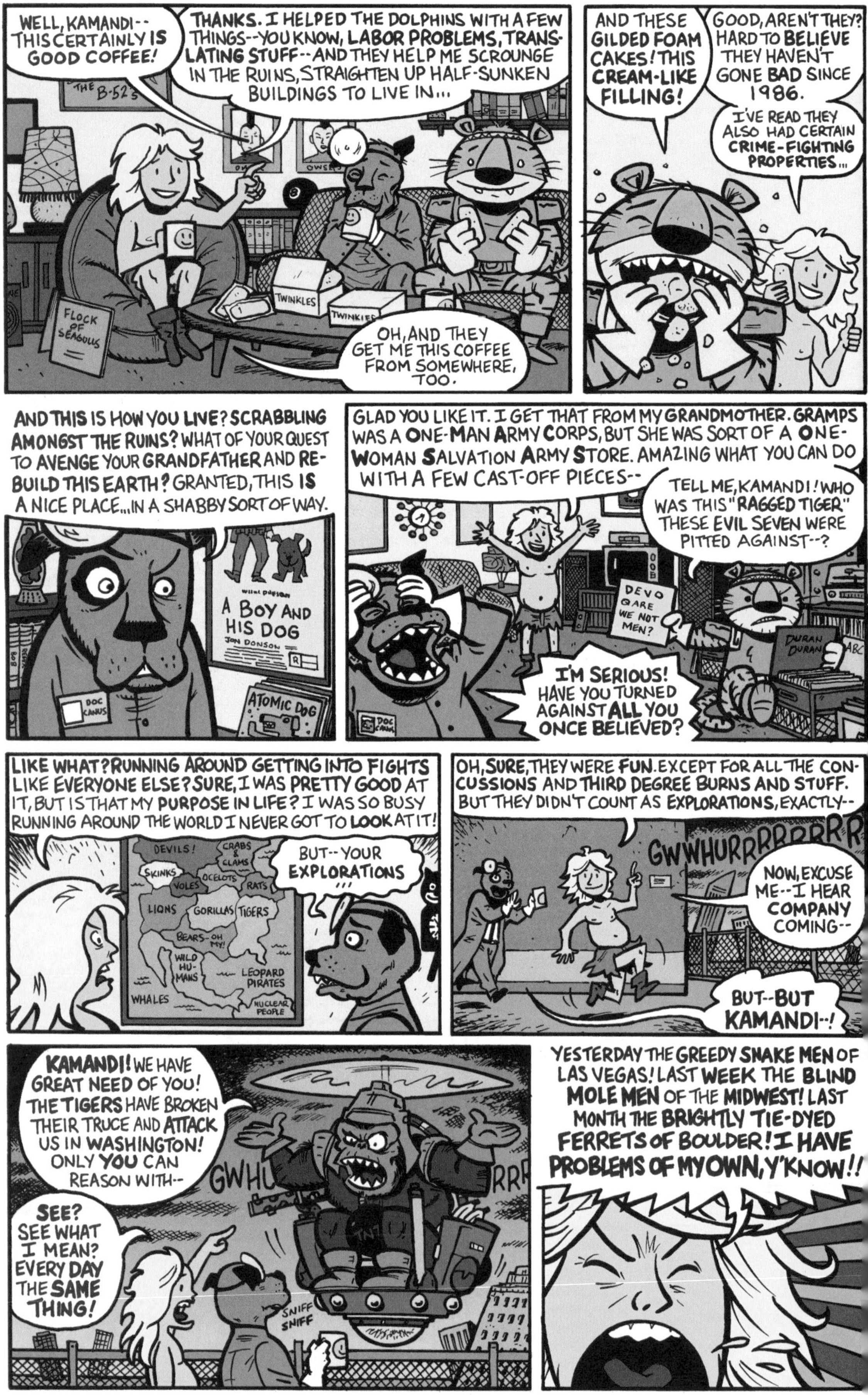
WELL, KAMANDI-- THIS CERTAINLY IS GOOD COFFEE!
THANKS. I HELPED THE DOLPHINS WITH A FEW THINGS--YOU KNOW, LABOR PROBLEMS, TRANSLATING STUFF--AND THEY HELP ME SCROUNGE IN THE RUINS, STRAIGHTEN UP HALF-SUNKEN BUILDINGS TO LIVE IN...
THE B-52's
FLOCK OF SEAGULLS
TWINKLES
TWINKIES
OH, AND THEY GET ME THIS COFFEE FROM SOMEWHERE, TOO.
AND THESE GILDED FOAM CAKES! THIS CREAM-LIKE FILLING!
GOOD, AREN'T THEY? HARD TO BELIEVE THEY HAVEN'T GONE BAD SINCE 1986.
I'VE READ THEY ALSO HAD CERTAIN CRIME-FIGHTING PROPERTIES...
AND THIS IS HOW YOU LIVE? SCRABBLING AMONGST THE RUINS? WHAT OF YOUR QUEST TO AVENGE YOUR GRANDFATHER AND REBUILD THIS EARTH? GRANTED, THIS IS A NICE PLACE...IN A SHABBY SORT OF WAY.
A BOY AND HIS DOG
JON DONSON
DOC CANUS
ATOMIC DOG
GLAD YOU LIKE IT. I GET THAT FROM MY GRANDMOTHER. GRAMPS WAS A ONE-MAN ARMY CORPS, BUT SHE WAS SORT OF A ONE-WOMAN SALVATION ARMY STORE. AMAZING WHAT YOU CAN DO WITH A FEW CAST-OFF PIECES--
TELL ME, KAMANDI! WHO WAS THIS "RAGGED TIGER" THESE EVIL SEVEN WERE PITTED AGAINST--?
DEVO Q ARE WE NOT MEN?
DURAN DURAN
ABC
I'M SERIOUS! HAVE YOU TURNED AGAINST ALL YOU ONCE BELIEVED?
LIKE WHAT? RUNNING AROUND GETTING INTO FIGHTS LIKE EVERYONE ELSE? SURE, I WAS PRETTY GOOD AT IT, BUT IS THAT MY PURPOSE IN LIFE? I WAS SO BUSY RUNNING AROUND THE WORLD I NEVER GOT TO LOOK AT IT!
DEVILS!
CRABS & CLAMS
SKINKS
VOLES
OCELOTS
RATS
LIONS
GORILLAS
TIGERS
BEARS-OH MY!
WILD HUMANS
LEOPARD PIRATES
WHALES
NUCLEAR PEOPLE
BUT--YOUR EXPLORATIONS...
OH, SURE, THEY WERE FUN. EXCEPT FOR ALL THE CONCUSSIONS AND THIRD DEGREE BURNS AND STUFF. BUT THEY DIDN'T COUNT AS EXPLORATIONS, EXACTLY--
GWWHURRRRRRR
NOW, EXCUSE ME--I HEAR COMPANY COMING--
BUT--BUT KAMANDI--!
KAMANDI! WE HAVE GREAT NEED OF YOU! THE TIGERS HAVE BROKEN THEIR TRUCE AND ATTACK US IN WASHINGTON! ONLY YOU CAN REASON WITH--
GWHU
RRR
SEE? SEE WHAT I MEAN? EVERY DAY THE SAME THING!
SNIFF SNIFF
YESTERDAY THE GREEDY SNAKE MEN OF LAS VEGAS! LAST WEEK THE BLIND MOLE MEN OF THE MIDWEST! LAST MONTH THE BRIGHTLY TIE-DYED FERRETS OF BOULDER! I HAVE PROBLEMS OF MY OWN, Y'KNOW!!

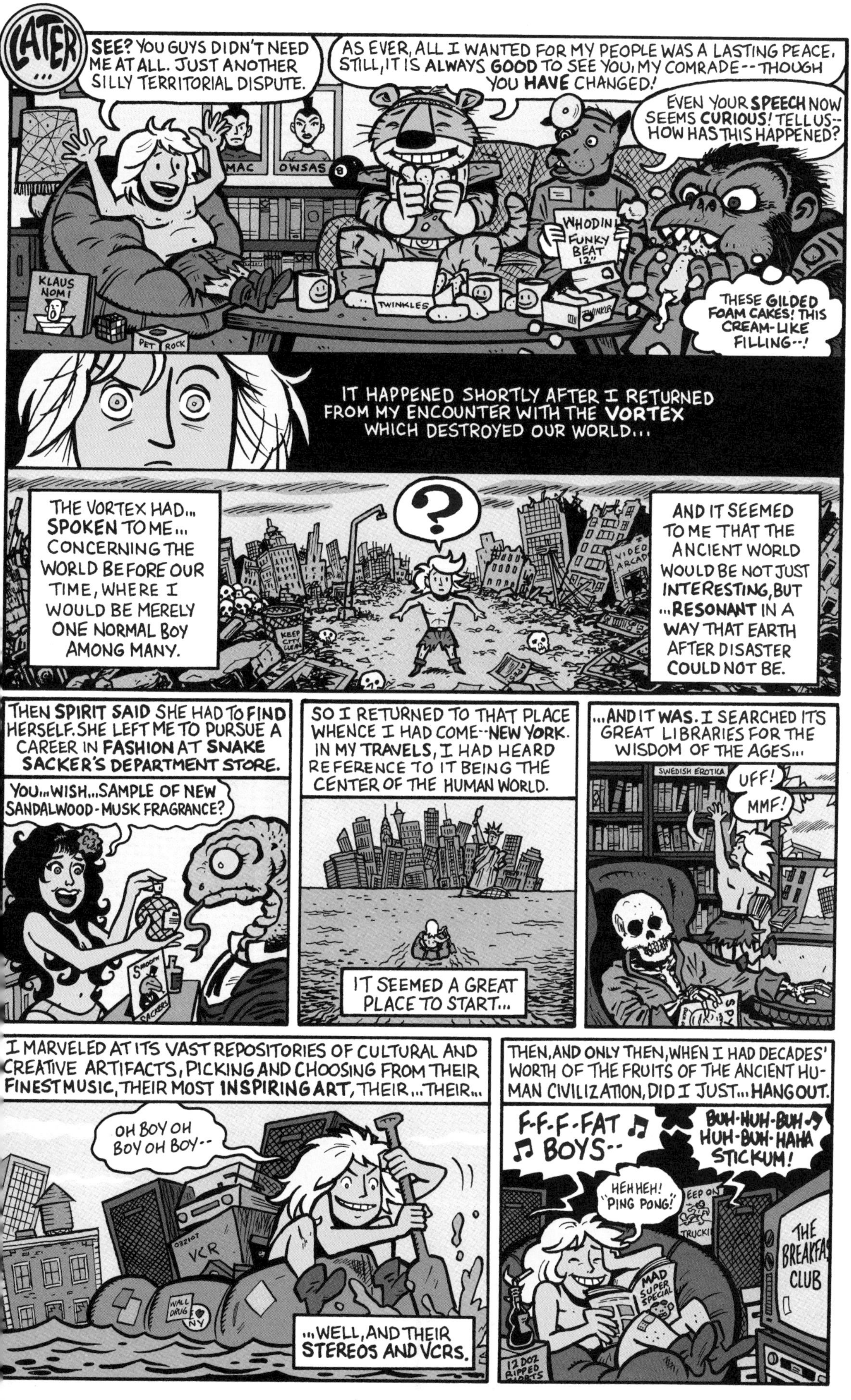
LATER...
SEE? YOU GUYS DIDN'T NEED ME AT ALL. JUST ANOTHER SILLY TERRITORIAL DISPUTE.
AS EVER, ALL I WANTED FOR MY PEOPLE WAS A LASTING PEACE. STILL, IT IS ALWAYS GOOD TO SEE YOU, MY COMRADE--THOUGH YOU HAVE CHANGED!
EVEN YOUR SPEECH NOW SEEMS CURIOUS! TELL US--HOW HAS THIS HAPPENED?
MAC
OWSAS
WHODINI FUNKY BEAT 12"
KLAUS NOMI
TWINKLES
PET ROCK
THESE GILDED FOAM CAKES! THIS CREAM-LIKE FILLING--!
IT HAPPENED SHORTLY AFTER I RETURNED FROM MY ENCOUNTER WITH THE VORTEX WHICH DESTROYED OUR WORLD...
THE VORTEX HAD... SPOKEN TO ME... CONCERNING THE WORLD BEFORE OUR TIME, WHERE I WOULD BE MERELY ONE NORMAL BOY AMONG MANY.
?
VIDEO ARCADE
KEEP CITY CLEAN
AND IT SEEMED TO ME THAT THE ANCIENT WORLD WOULD BE NOT JUST INTERESTING, BUT ...RESONANT IN A WAY THAT EARTH AFTER DISASTER COULD NOT BE.
THEN SPIRIT SAID SHE HAD TO FIND HERSELF. SHE LEFT ME TO PURSUE A CAREER IN FASHION AT SNAKE SACKER'S DEPARTMENT STORE.
YOU...WISH...SAMPLE OF NEW SANDALWOOD-MUSK FRAGRANCE?
SO I RETURNED TO THAT PLACE WHENCE I HAD COME--NEW YORK. IN MY TRAVELS, I HAD HEARD REFERENCE TO IT BEING THE CENTER OF THE HUMAN WORLD.
IT SEEMED A GREAT PLACE TO START...
...AND IT WAS. I SEARCHED ITS GREAT LIBRARIES FOR THE WISDOM OF THE AGES...
SWEDISH EROTICA
UFF!
MMF!
I MARVELED AT ITS VAST REPOSITORIES OF CULTURAL AND CREATIVE ARTIFACTS, PICKING AND CHOOSING FROM THEIR FINEST MUSIC, THEIR MOST INSPIRING ART, THEIR... THEIR...
OH BOY OH BOY OH BOY--
VCR
WALL DRUG
NY
...WELL, AND THEIR STEREOS AND VCRS.
THEN, AND ONLY THEN, WHEN I HAD DECADES' WORTH OF THE FRUITS OF THE ANCIENT HUMAN CIVILIZATION, DID I JUST... HANG OUT.
F-F-F-FAT ♫ ♫ BOYS--
BUH-HUH-BUH ♫ HUH-BUH-HAHA STICKUM!
HEH HEH! "PING PONG!"
KEEP ON TRUCKI
THE BREAKFAS CLUB
MAD SUPER SPECIAL
12 DOZ RIPPED SHORTS

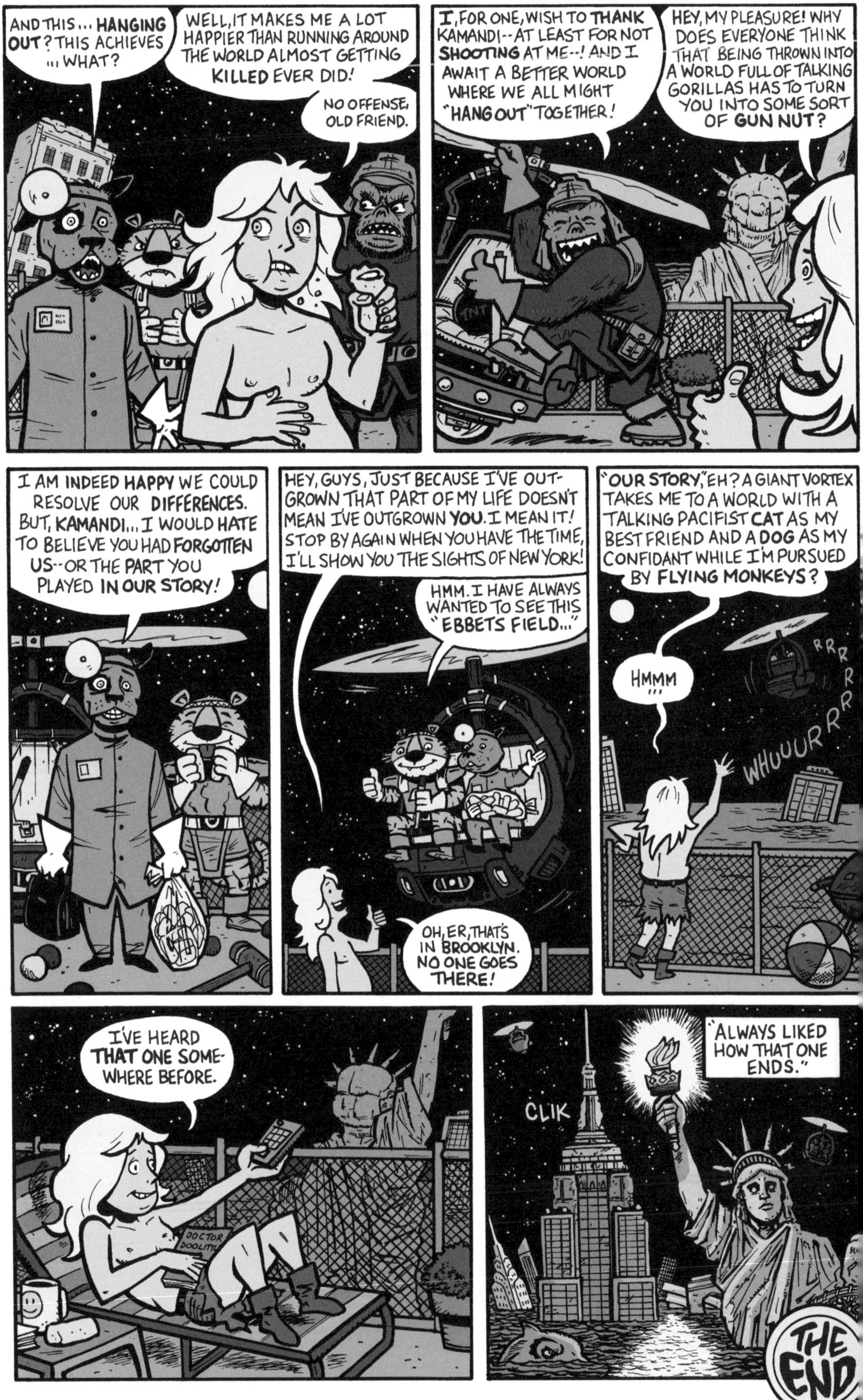
AND THIS... HANGING OUT? THIS ACHIEVES ...WHAT?
WELL, IT MAKES ME A LOT HAPPIER THAN RUNNING AROUND THE WORLD ALMOST GETTING KILLED EVER DID!
NO OFFENSE, OLD FRIEND.
I, FOR ONE, WISH TO THANK KAMANDI--AT LEAST FOR NOT SHOOTING AT ME--! AND I AWAIT A BETTER WORLD WHERE WE ALL MIGHT "HANG OUT" TOGETHER!
HEY, MY PLEASURE! WHY DOES EVERYONE THINK THAT BEING THROWN INTO A WORLD FULL OF TALKING GORILLAS HAS TO TURN YOU INTO SOME SORT OF GUN NUT?
TNT
I AM INDEED HAPPY WE COULD RESOLVE OUR DIFFERENCES. BUT, KAMANDI... I WOULD HATE TO BELIEVE YOU HAD FORGOTTEN US--OR THE PART YOU PLAYED IN OUR STORY!
HEY, GUYS, JUST BECAUSE I'VE OUTGROWN THAT PART OF MY LIFE DOESN'T MEAN I'VE OUTGROWN YOU. I MEAN IT! STOP BY AGAIN WHEN YOU HAVE THE TIME, I'LL SHOW YOU THE SIGHTS OF NEW YORK!
HMM. I HAVE ALWAYS WANTED TO SEE THIS "EBBETS FIELD..."
OH, ER, THAT'S IN BROOKLYN. NO ONE GOES THERE!
"OUR STORY," EH? A GIANT VORTEX TAKES ME TO A WORLD WITH A TALKING PACIFIST CAT AS MY BEST FRIEND AND A DOG AS MY CONFIDANT WHILE I'M PURSUED BY FLYING MONKEYS?
HMMM
RRRRRR
WHUUURRR
I'VE HEARD THAT ONE SOMEWHERE BEFORE.
DOCTOR DOOLITTLE
CLIK
"ALWAYS LIKED HOW THAT ONE ENDS."
THE END

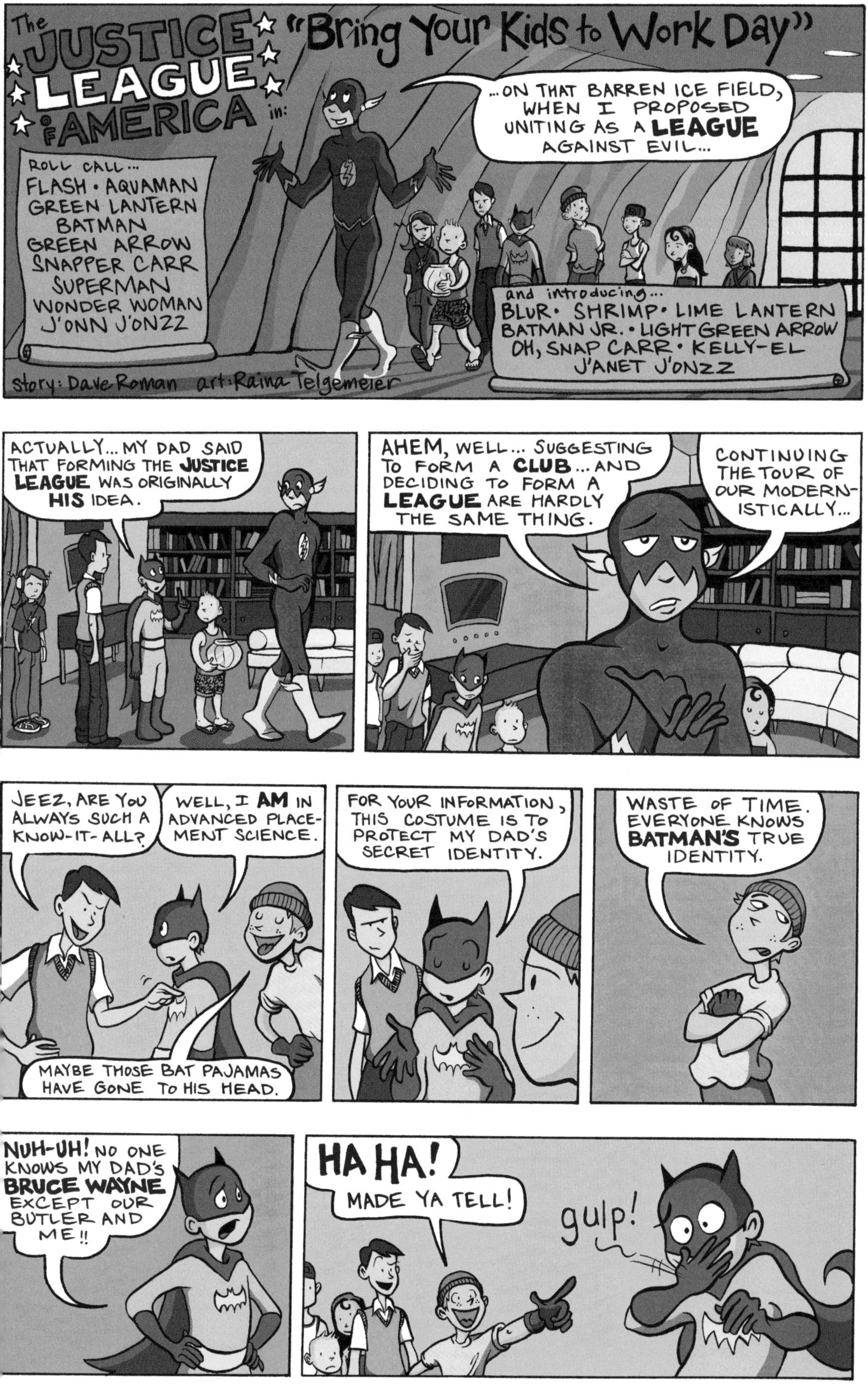
The JUSTICE LEAGUE OF AMERICA in:
"Bring Your Kids to Work Day"
...ON THAT BARREN ICE FIELD, WHEN I PROPOSED UNITING AS A LEAGUE AGAINST EVIL...
ROLL CALL... FLASH • AQUAMAN GREEN LANTERN BATMAN GREEN ARROW SNAPPER CARR SUPERMAN WONDER WOMAN J'ONN J'ONZZ
and introducing... BLUR • SHRIMP • LIME LANTERN BATMAN JR. • LIGHT GREEN ARROW OH, SNAP CARR • KELLY-EL J'ANET J'ONZZ
story: Dave Roman art: Raina Telgemeier
ACTUALLY... MY DAD SAID THAT FORMING THE JUSTICE LEAGUE WAS ORIGINALLY HIS IDEA.
AHEM, WELL... SUGGESTING TO FORM A CLUB... AND DECIDING TO FORM A LEAGUE ARE HARDLY THE SAME THING.
CONTINUING THE TOUR OF OUR MODERNISTICALLY...
JEEZ, ARE YOU ALWAYS SUCH A KNOW-IT-ALL?
WELL, I AM IN ADVANCED PLACEMENT SCIENCE.
MAYBE THOSE BAT PAJAMAS HAVE GONE TO HIS HEAD.
FOR YOUR INFORMATION, THIS COSTUME IS TO PROTECT MY DAD'S SECRET IDENTITY.
WASTE OF TIME. EVERYONE KNOWS BATMAN'S TRUE IDENTITY.
NUH-UH! NO ONE KNOWS MY DAD'S BRUCE WAYNE EXCEPT OUR BUTLER AND ME!!
HA HA! MADE YA TELL!
gulp!

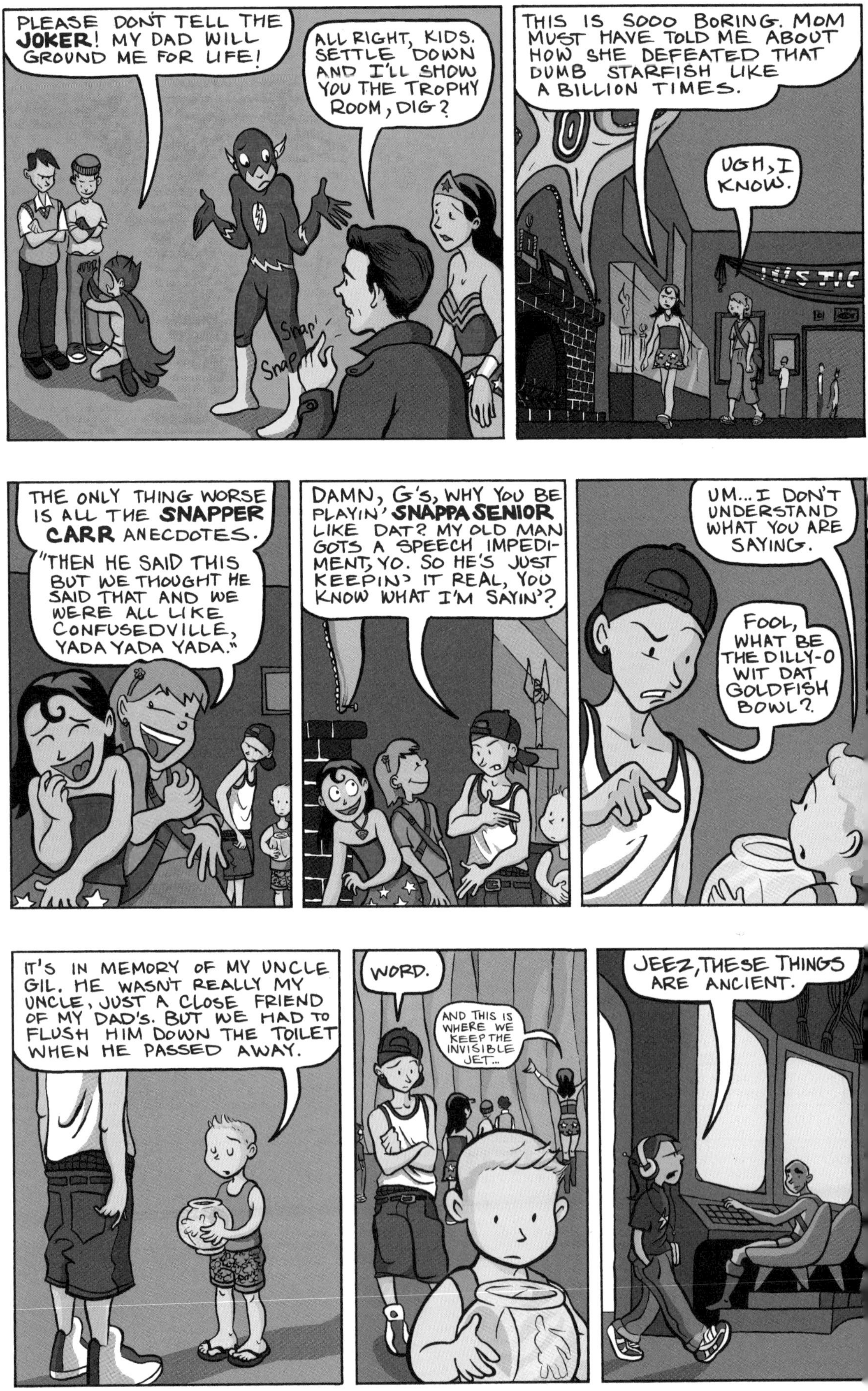
PLEASE DON'T TELL THE JOKER! MY DAD WILL GROUND ME FOR LIFE!
ALL RIGHT, KIDS. SETTLE DOWN AND I'LL SHOW YOU THE TROPHY ROOM, DIG?
Snap! Snap!
THIS IS SOOO BORING. MOM MUST HAVE TOLD ME ABOUT HOW SHE DEFEATED THAT DUMB STARFISH LIKE A BILLION TIMES.
UGH, I KNOW.
THE ONLY THING WORSE IS ALL THE SNAPPER CARR ANECDOTES.
"THEN HE SAID THIS BUT WE THOUGHT HE SAID THAT AND WE WERE ALL LIKE CONFUSEDVILLE, YADA YADA YADA."
DAMN, G'S, WHY YOU BE PLAYIN' SNAPPA SENIOR LIKE DAT? MY OLD MAN GOTS A SPEECH IMPEDIMENT, YO. SO HE'S JUST KEEPIN' IT REAL, YOU KNOW WHAT I'M SAYIN'?
UM... I DON'T UNDERSTAND WHAT YOU ARE SAYING.
FOOL, WHAT BE THE DILLY-O WIT DAT GOLDFISH BOWL?
IT'S IN MEMORY OF MY UNCLE GIL. HE WASN'T REALLY MY UNCLE, JUST A CLOSE FRIEND OF MY DAD'S. BUT WE HAD TO FLUSH HIM DOWN THE TOILET WHEN HE PASSED AWAY.
WORD.
AND THIS IS WHERE WE KEEP THE INVISIBLE JET...
JEEZ, THESE THINGS ARE ANCIENT.

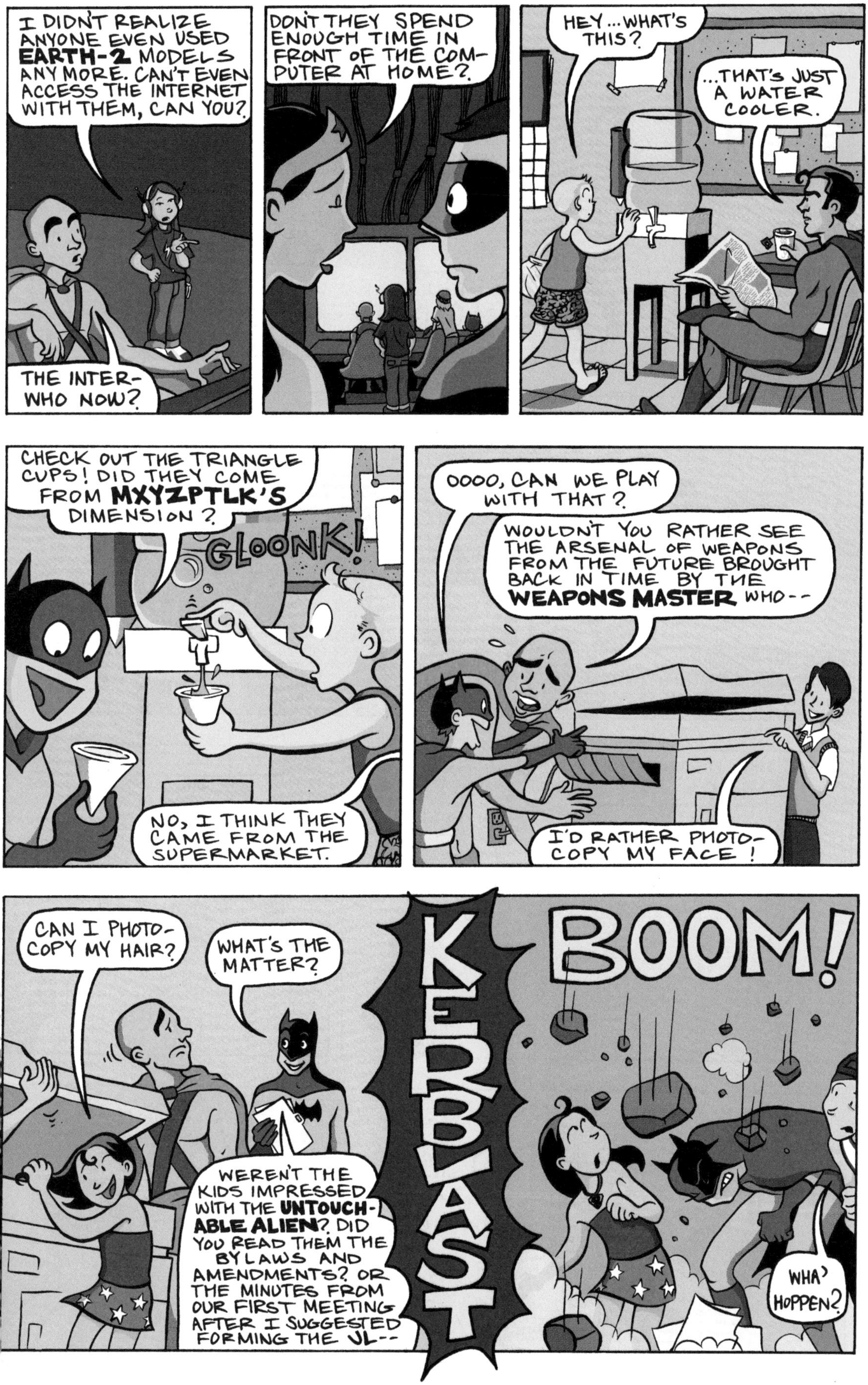

I DIDN'T REALIZE ANYONE EVEN USED EARTH-2 MODELS ANY MORE. CAN'T EVEN ACCESS THE INTERNET WITH THEM, CAN YOU?
THE INTER-WHO NOW?
DON'T THEY SPEND ENOUGH TIME IN FRONT OF THE COMPUTER AT HOME?
HEY... WHAT'S THIS?
...THAT'S JUST A WATER COOLER.
CHECK OUT THE TRIANGLE CUPS! DID THEY COME FROM MXYZPTLK'S DIMENSION?
GLOONK!
NO, I THINK THEY CAME FROM THE SUPERMARKET.
OOOO, CAN WE PLAY WITH THAT?
WOULDN'T YOU RATHER SEE THE ARSENAL OF WEAPONS FROM THE FUTURE BROUGHT BACK IN TIME BY THE WEAPONS MASTER WHO--
I'D RATHER PHOTOCOPY MY FACE!
CAN I PHOTOCOPY MY HAIR?
WHAT'S THE MATTER?
WEREN'T THE KIDS IMPRESSED WITH THE UNTOUCHABLE ALIEN? DID YOU READ THEM THE BYLAWS AND AMENDMENTS? OR THE MINUTES FROM OUR FIRST MEETING AFTER I SUGGESTED FORMING THE JL--
KERBLAST
BOOM!
WHA' HOPPEN?

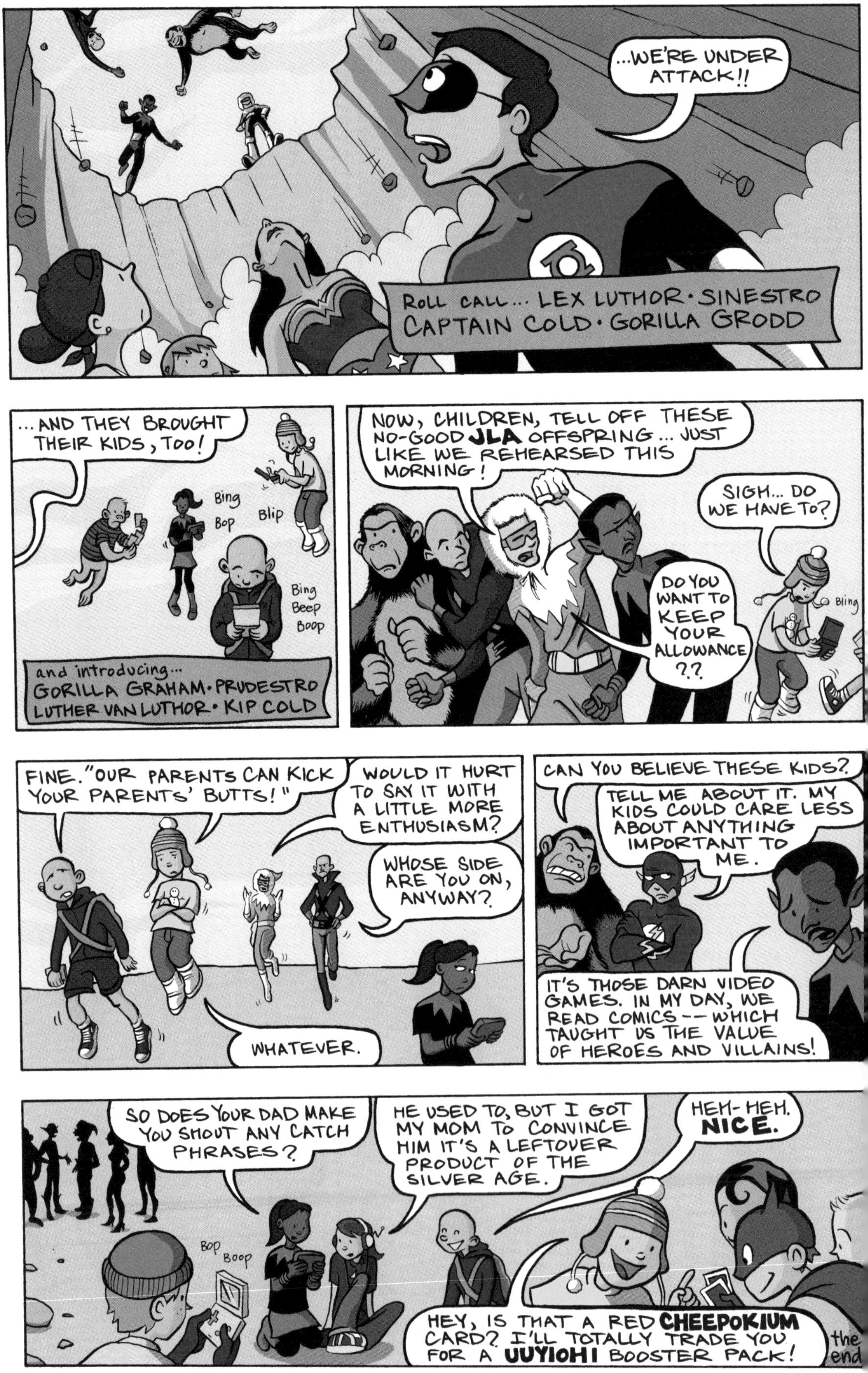
...WE'RE UNDER ATTACK!!
ROLL CALL... LEX LUTHOR • SINESTRO CAPTAIN COLD • GORILLA GRODD
...AND THEY BROUGHT THEIR KIDS, TOO!
Bing
Bop
Blip
Bing
Beep
Boop
and introducing...
GORILLA GRAHAM • PRUDESTRO LUTHER VAN LUTHOR • KIP COLD
NOW, CHILDREN, TELL OFF THESE NO-GOOD JLA OFFSPRING... JUST LIKE WE REHEARSED THIS MORNING!
SIGH... DO WE HAVE TO?
DO YOU WANT TO KEEP YOUR ALLOWANCE ??
Bling
FINE. "OUR PARENTS CAN KICK YOUR PARENTS' BUTTS!"
WOULD IT HURT TO SAY IT WITH A LITTLE MORE ENTHUSIASM?
WHOSE SIDE ARE YOU ON, ANYWAY?
WHATEVER.
CAN YOU BELIEVE THESE KIDS?
TELL ME ABOUT IT. MY KIDS COULD CARE LESS ABOUT ANYTHING IMPORTANT TO ME.
IT'S THOSE DARN VIDEO GAMES. IN MY DAY, WE READ COMICS -- WHICH TAUGHT US THE VALUE OF HEROES AND VILLAINS!
SO DOES YOUR DAD MAKE YOU SHOUT ANY CATCH PHRASES?
HE USED TO, BUT I GOT MY MOM TO CONVINCE HIM IT'S A LEFTOVER PRODUCT OF THE SILVER AGE.
HEH-HEH. NICE.
Bop
Boop
HEY, IS THAT A RED CHEEPOKIUM CARD? I'LL TOTALLY TRADE YOU FOR A UUYIOHI BOOSTER PACK!
the end

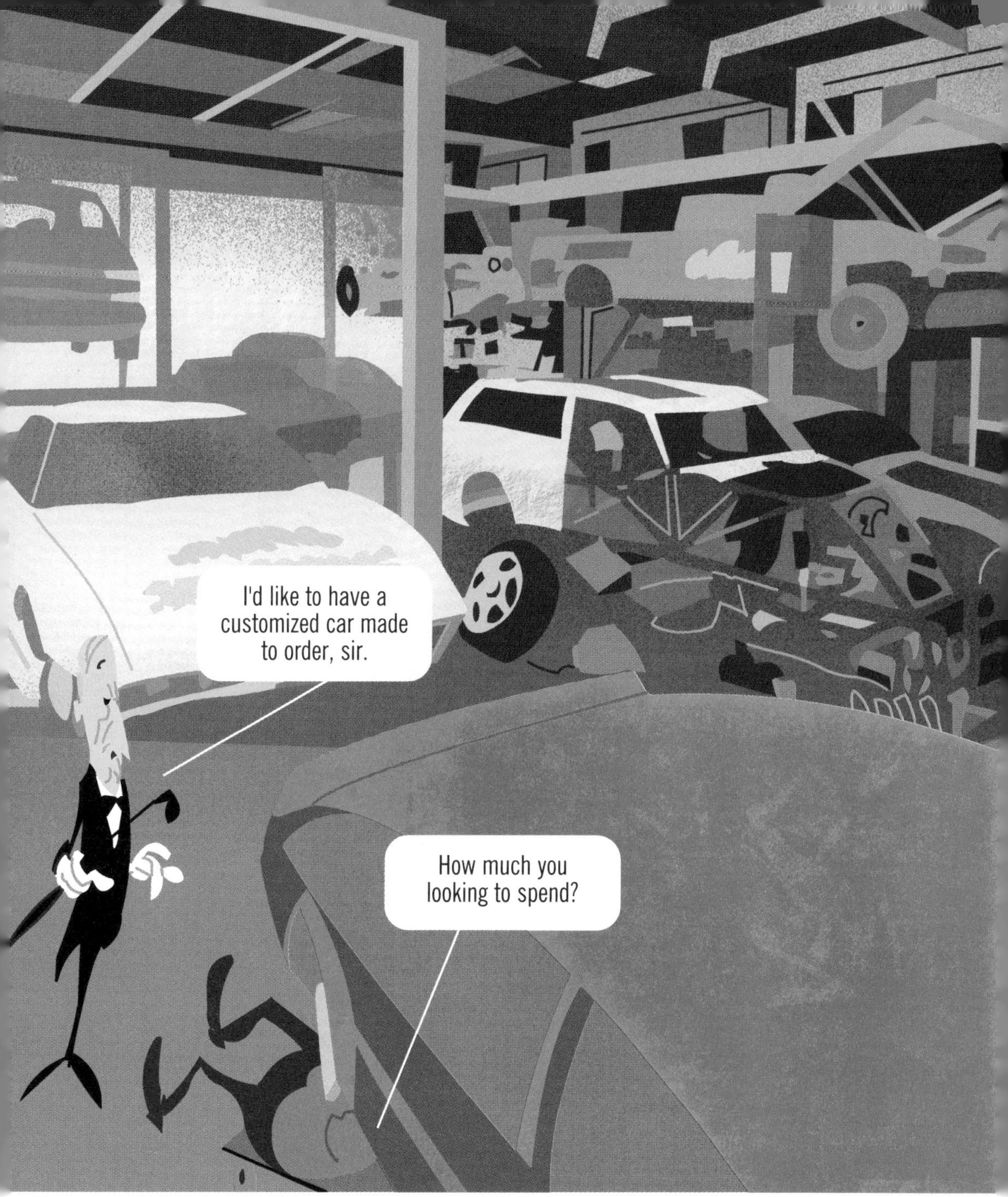
I'd like to have a customized car made to order, sir.
How much you looking to spend?

Personal Shopper

Written by Kyle Baker & Elizabeth Glass

Illustrated by

KYLE BAKER

Batman created by Bob Kane

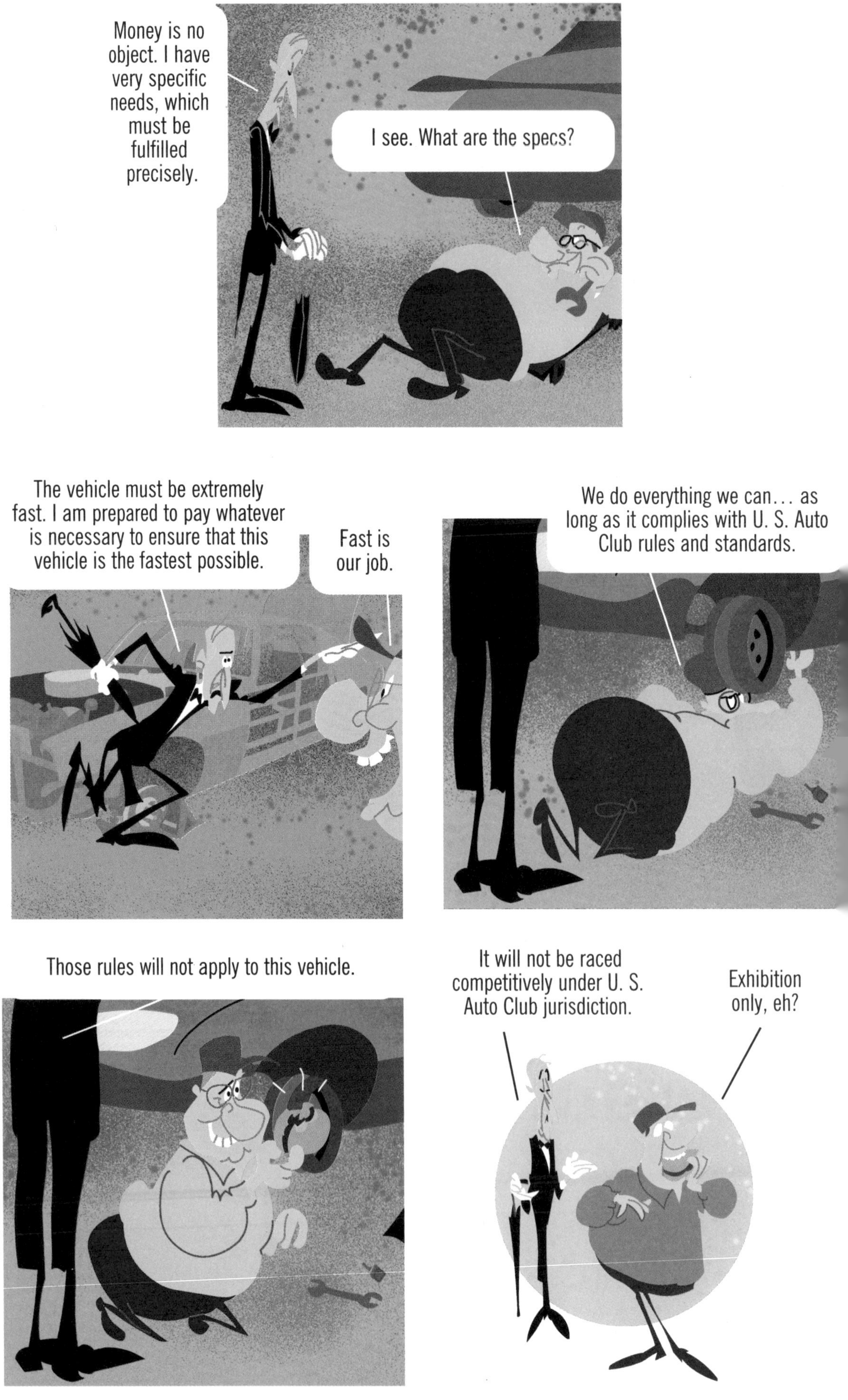
Money is no object. I have very specific needs, which must be fulfilled precisely.
I see. What are the specs?
The vehicle must be extremely fast. I am prepared to pay whatever is necessary to ensure that this vehicle is the fastest possible.
Fast is our job.
We do everything we can… as long as it complies with U. S. Auto Club rules and standards.
Those rules will not apply to this vehicle.
It will not be raced competitively under U. S. Auto Club jurisdiction.
Exhibition only, eh?

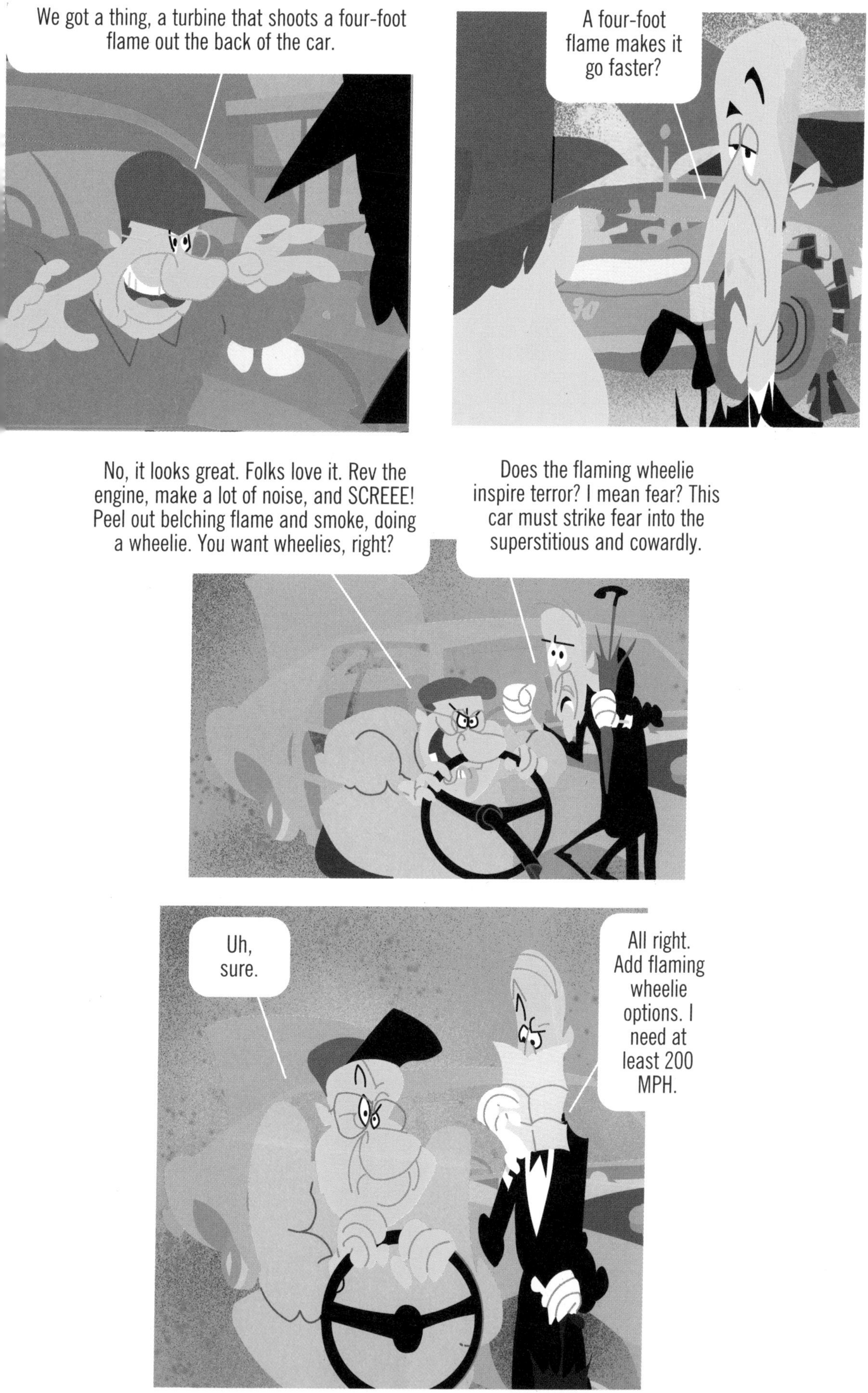
We got a thing, a turbine that shoots a four-foot flame out the back of the car.
A four-foot flame makes it go faster?
No, it looks great. Folks love it. Rev the engine, make a lot of noise, and SCREEE! Peel out belching flame and smoke, doing a wheelie. You want wheelies, right?
Does the flaming wheelie inspire terror? I mean fear? This car must strike fear into the superstitious and cowardly.
Uh, sure.
All right. Add flaming wheelie options. I need at least 200 MPH.

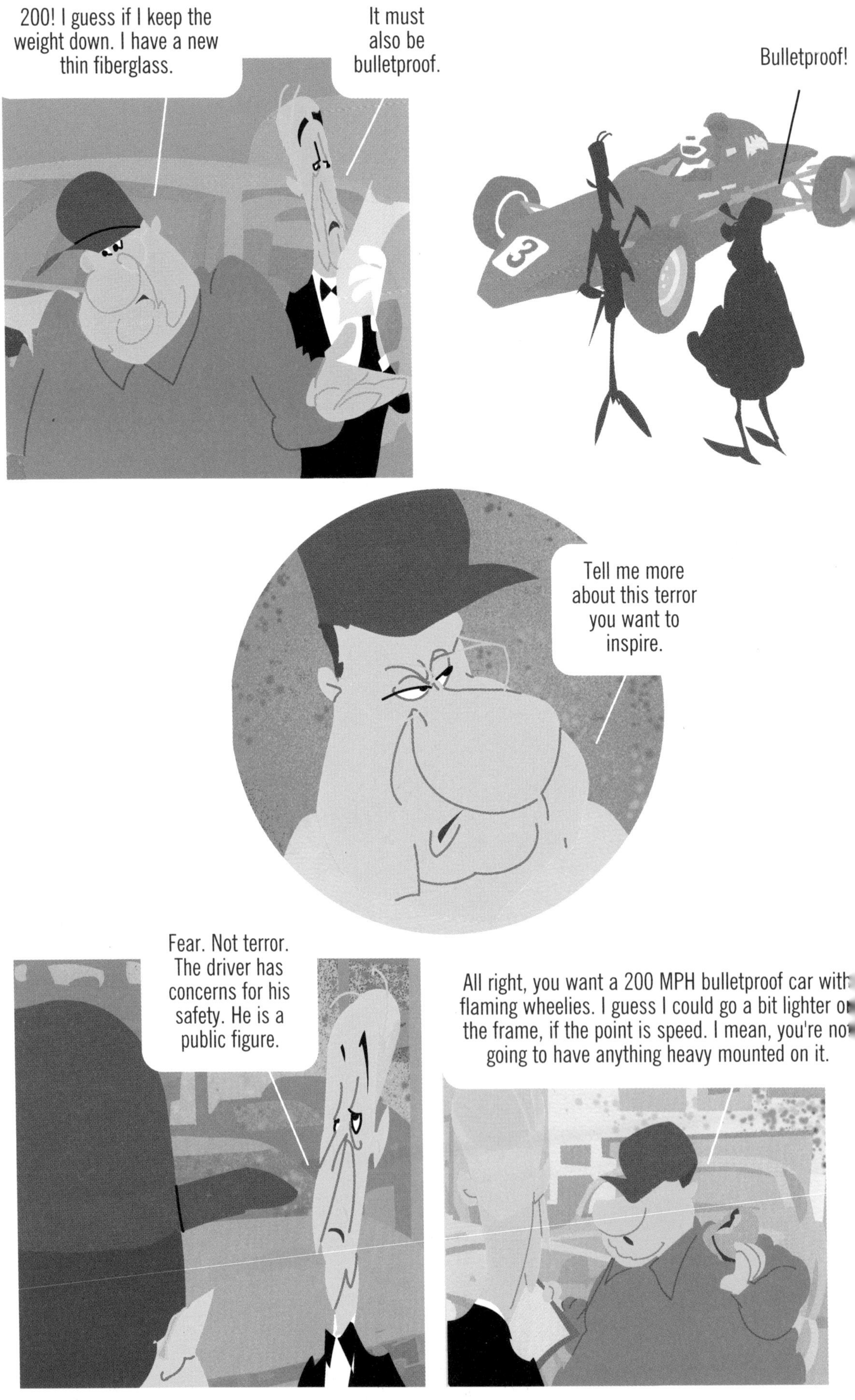
200! I guess if I keep the weight down. I have a new thin fiberglass.
It must also be bulletproof.
Bulletproof!
Tell me more about this terror you want to inspire.
Fear. Not terror. The driver has concerns for his safety. He is a public figure.
All right, you want a 200 MPH bulletproof car wit flaming wheelies. I guess I could go a bit lighter o the frame, if the point is speed. I mean, you're no going to have anything heavy mounted on it.

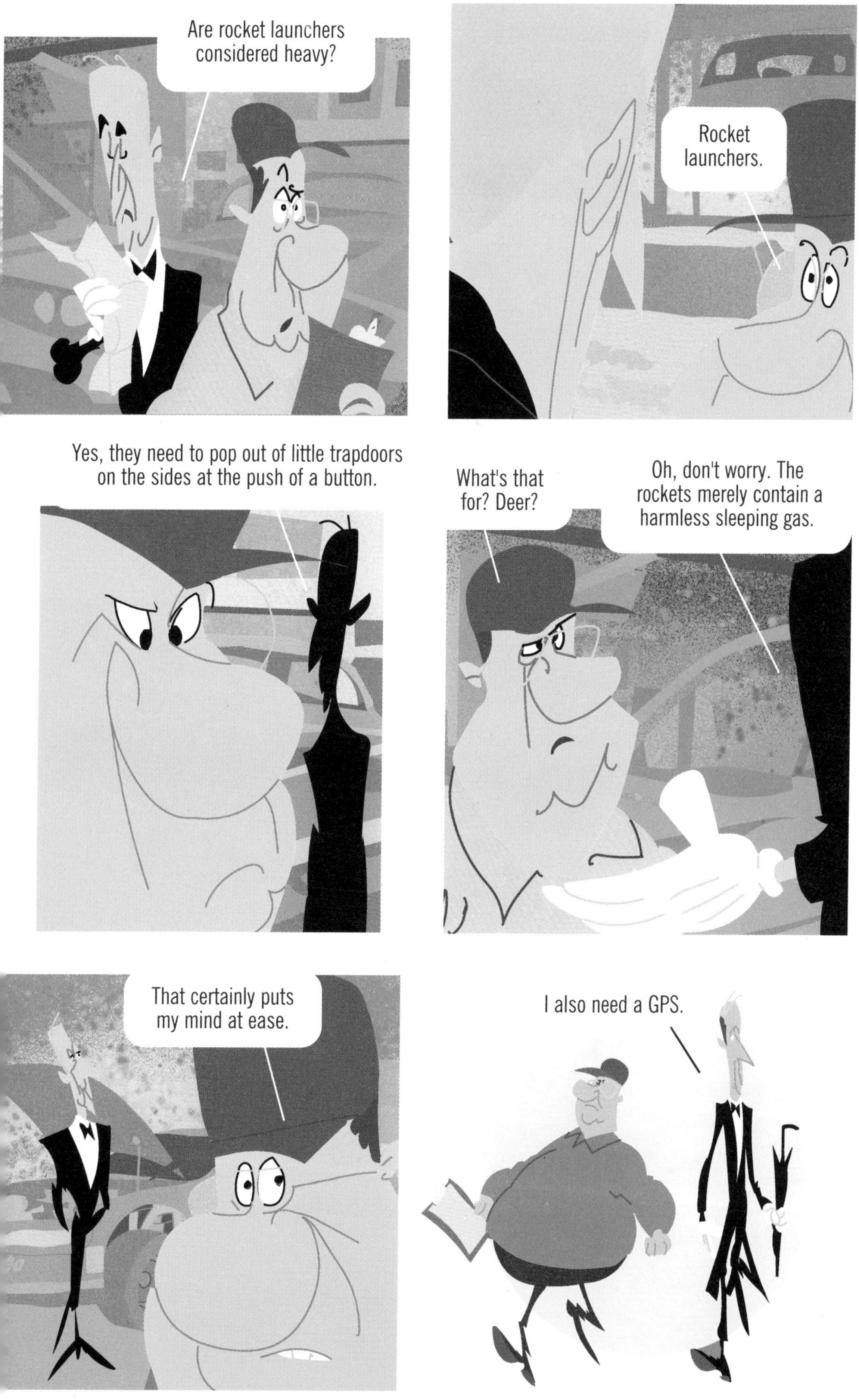
Are rocket launchers considered heavy?
Rocket launchers.
Yes, they need to pop out of little trapdoors on the sides at the push of a button.
What's that for? Deer?
Oh, don't worry. The rockets merely contain a harmless sleeping gas.
That certainly puts my mind at ease.
I also need a GPS.

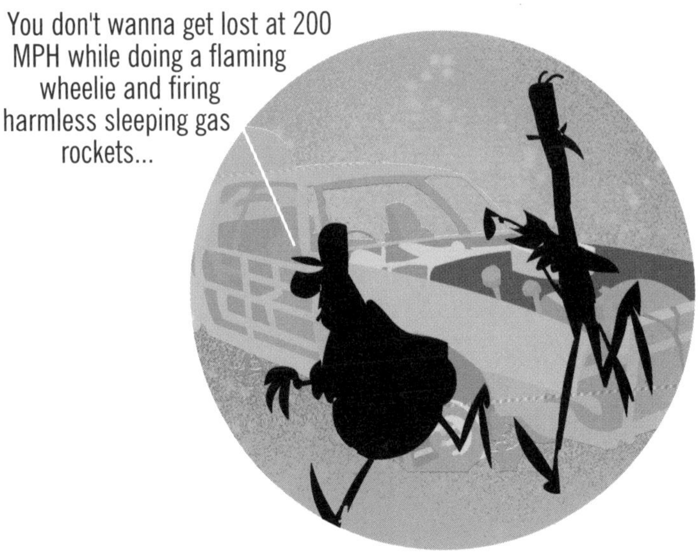
You don't wanna get lost at 200 MPH while doing a flaming wheelie and firing harmless sleeping gas rockets...

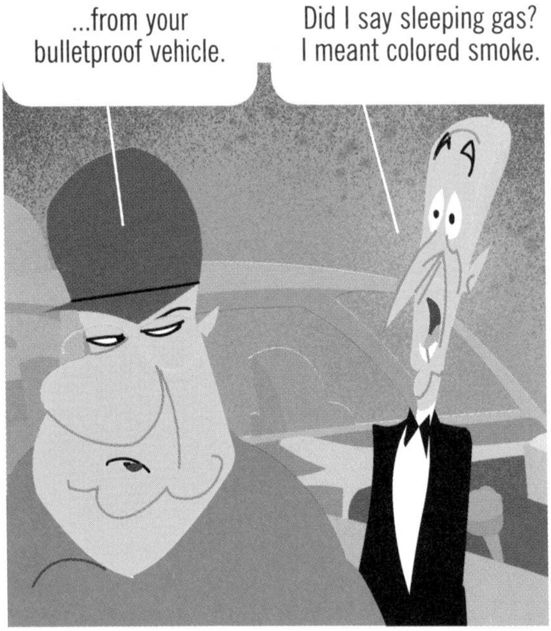
...from your bulletproof vehicle.
Did I say sleeping gas? I meant colored smoke.

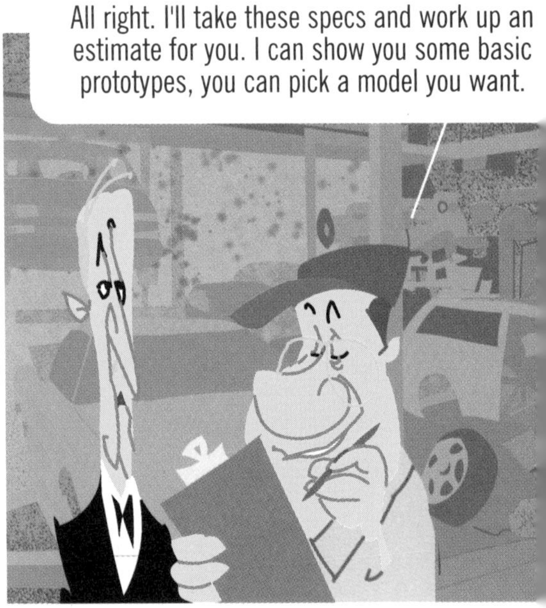
All right. I'll take these specs and work up an estimate for you. I can show you some basic prototypes, you can pick a model you want.

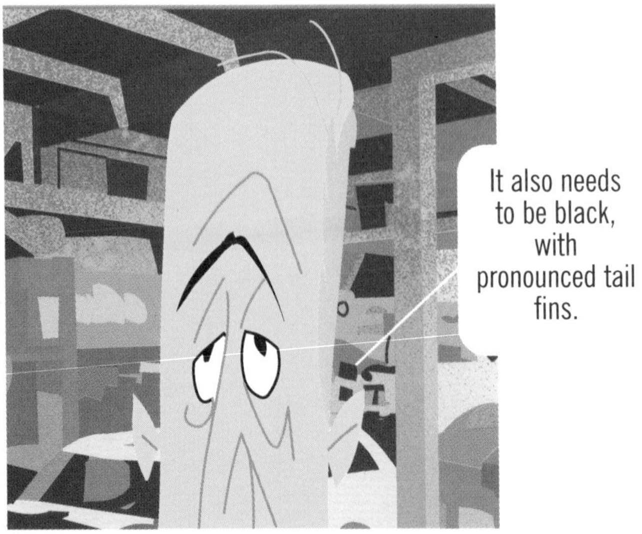
It also needs to be black, with pronounced tail fins.

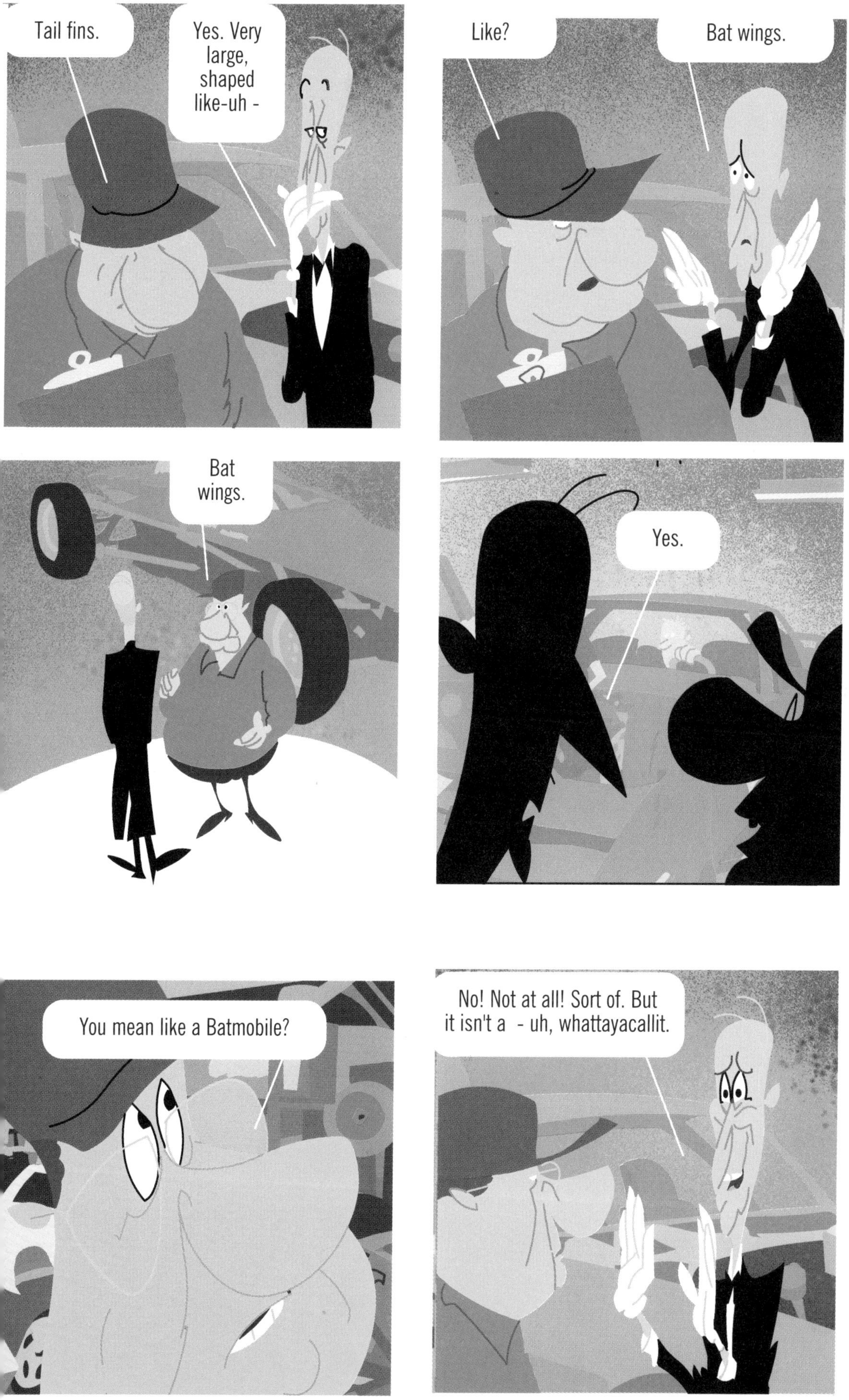
Tail fins.
Yes. Very large, shaped like-uh -
Like?
Bat wings.
Bat wings.
Yes.
You mean like a Batmobile?
No! Not at all! Sort of. But it isn't a - uh, whattayacallit.

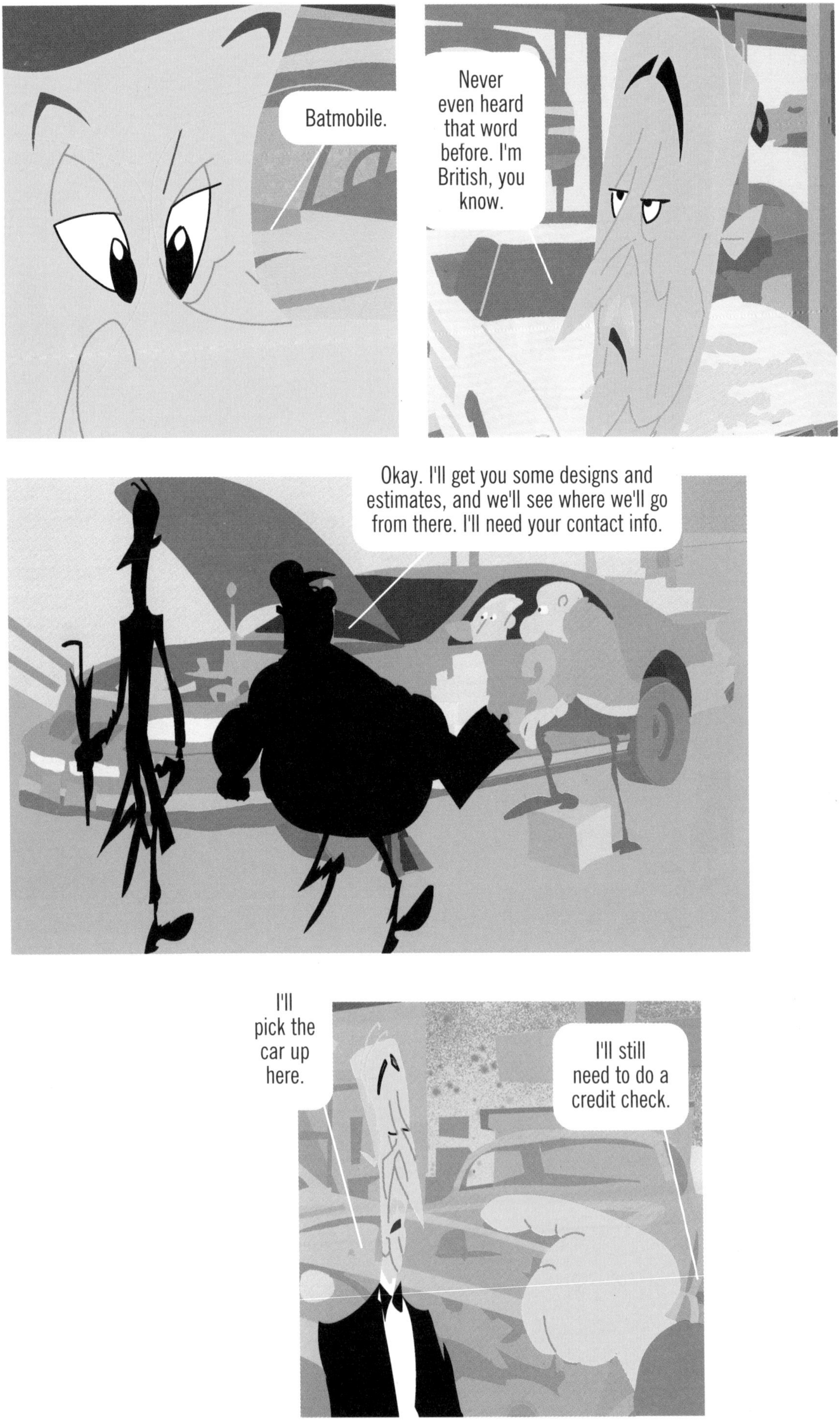
Batmobile.
Never even heard that word before. I'm British, you know.
Okay. I'll get you some designs and estimates, and we'll see where we'll go from there. I'll need your contact info.
I'll pick the car up here.
I'll still need to do a credit check.

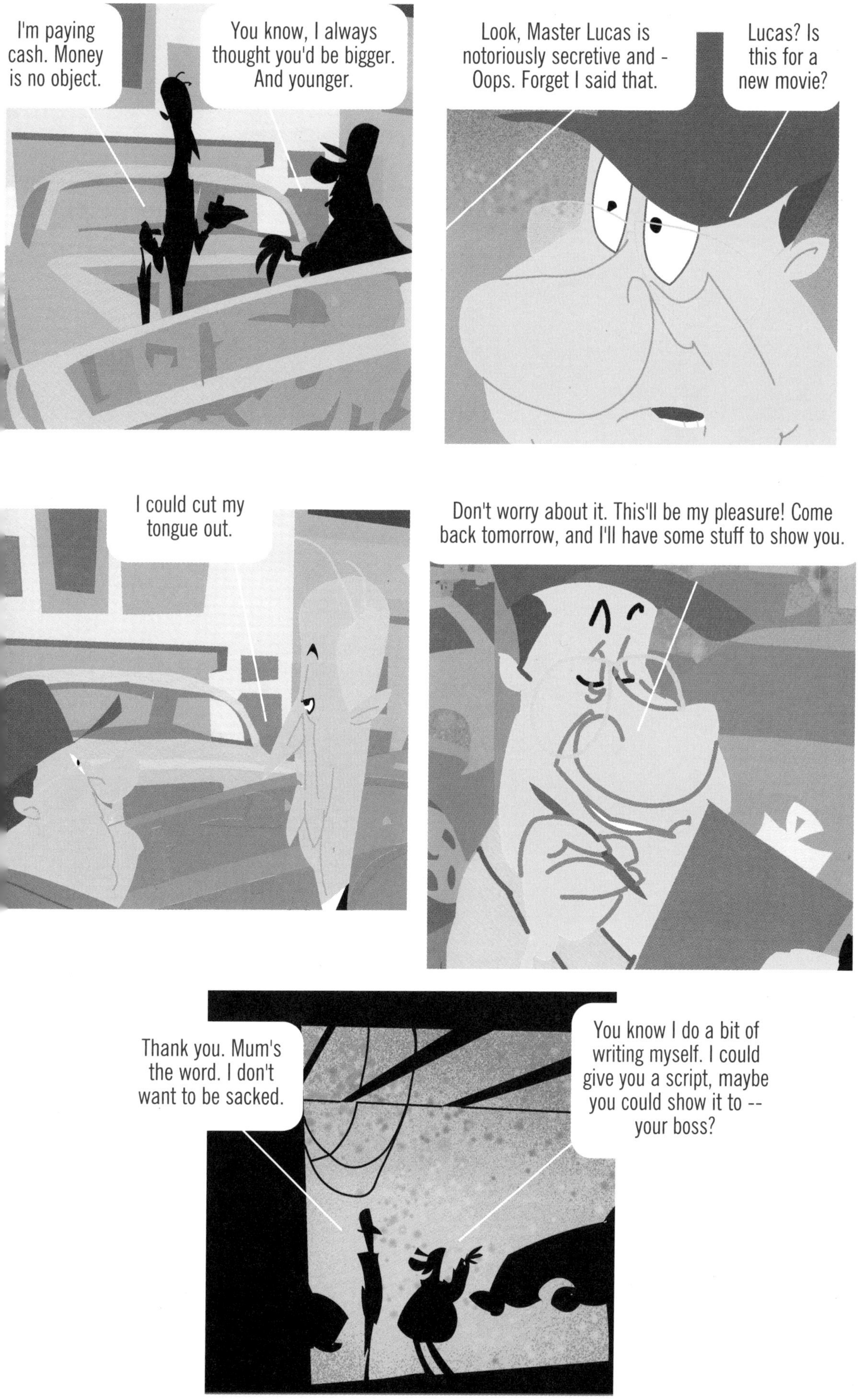

I'm paying cash. Money is no object.
You know, I always thought you'd be bigger. And younger.
Look, Master Lucas is notoriously secretive and - Oops. Forget I said that.
Lucas? Is this for a new movie?
I could cut my tongue out.
Don't worry about it. This'll be my pleasure! Come back tomorrow, and I'll have some stuff to show you.
Thank you. Mum's the word. I don't want to be sacked.
You know I do a bit of writing myself. I could give you a script, maybe you could show it to -- your boss?

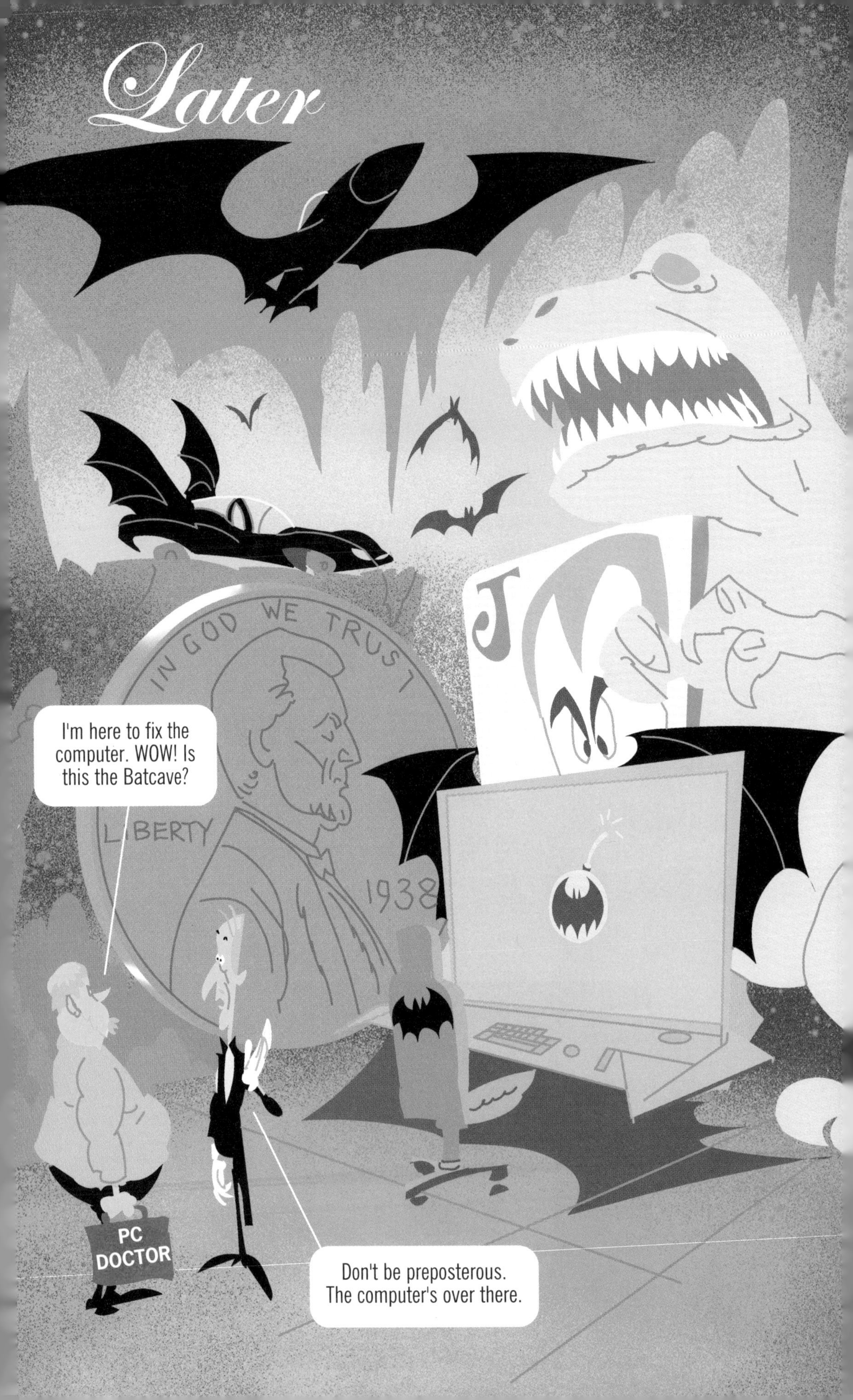
Later
IN GOD WE TRUST
LIBERTY
1938
I'm here to fix the computer. WOW! Is this the Batcave?
PC DOCTOR
Don't be preposterous. The computer's over there.

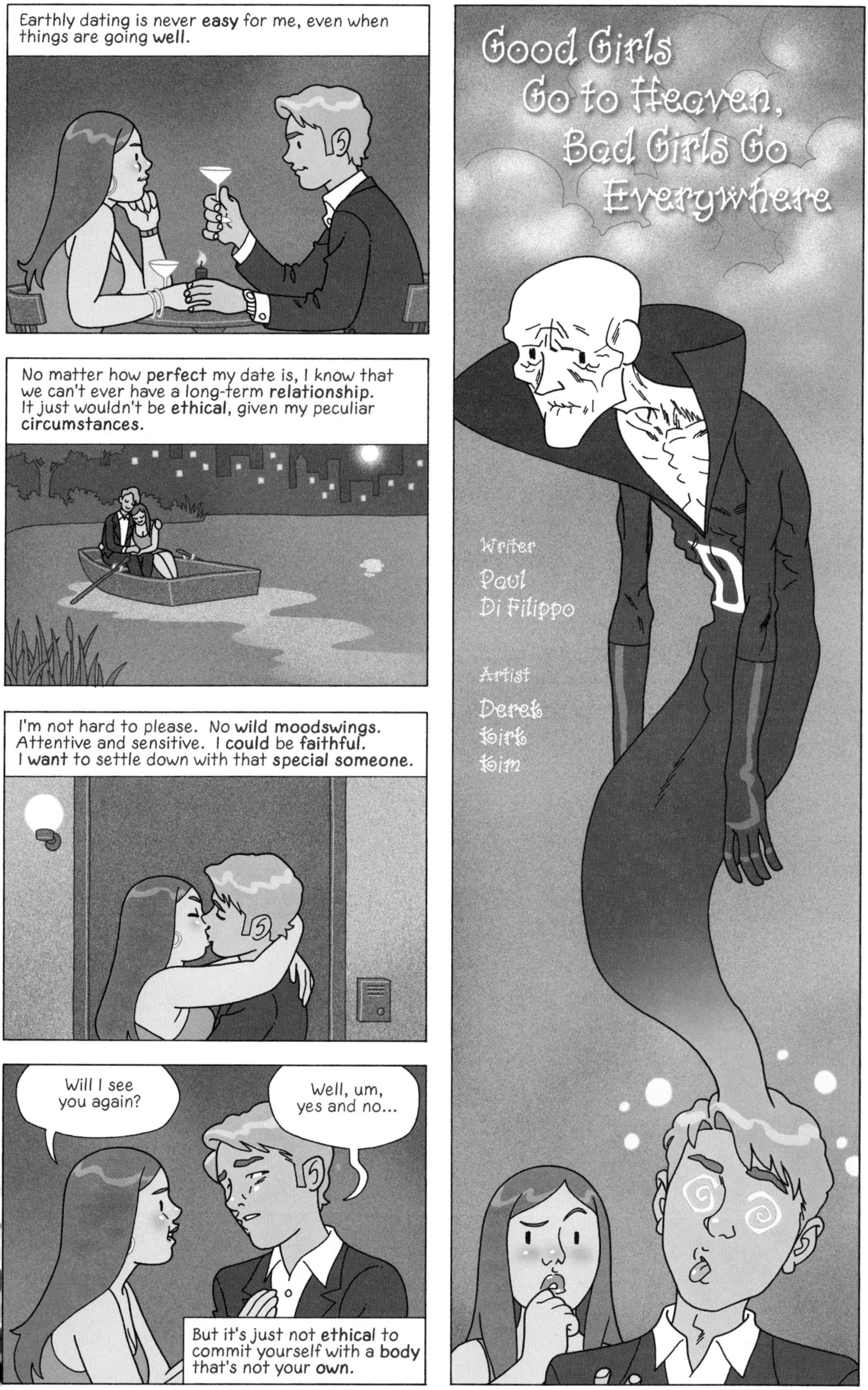

Earthly dating is never easy for me, even when things are going well.
No matter how perfect my date is, I know that we can't ever have a long-term relationship. It just wouldn't be ethical, given my peculiar circumstances.
I'm not hard to please. No wild moodswings. Attentive and sensitive. I could be faithful. I want to settle down with that special someone.
Will I see you again?
Well, um, yes and no...
But it's just not ethical to commit yourself with a body that's not your own.
Good Girls Go to Heaven, Bad Girls Go Everywhere
Writer
Paul Di Filippo
Artist
Derek Kirk Kim

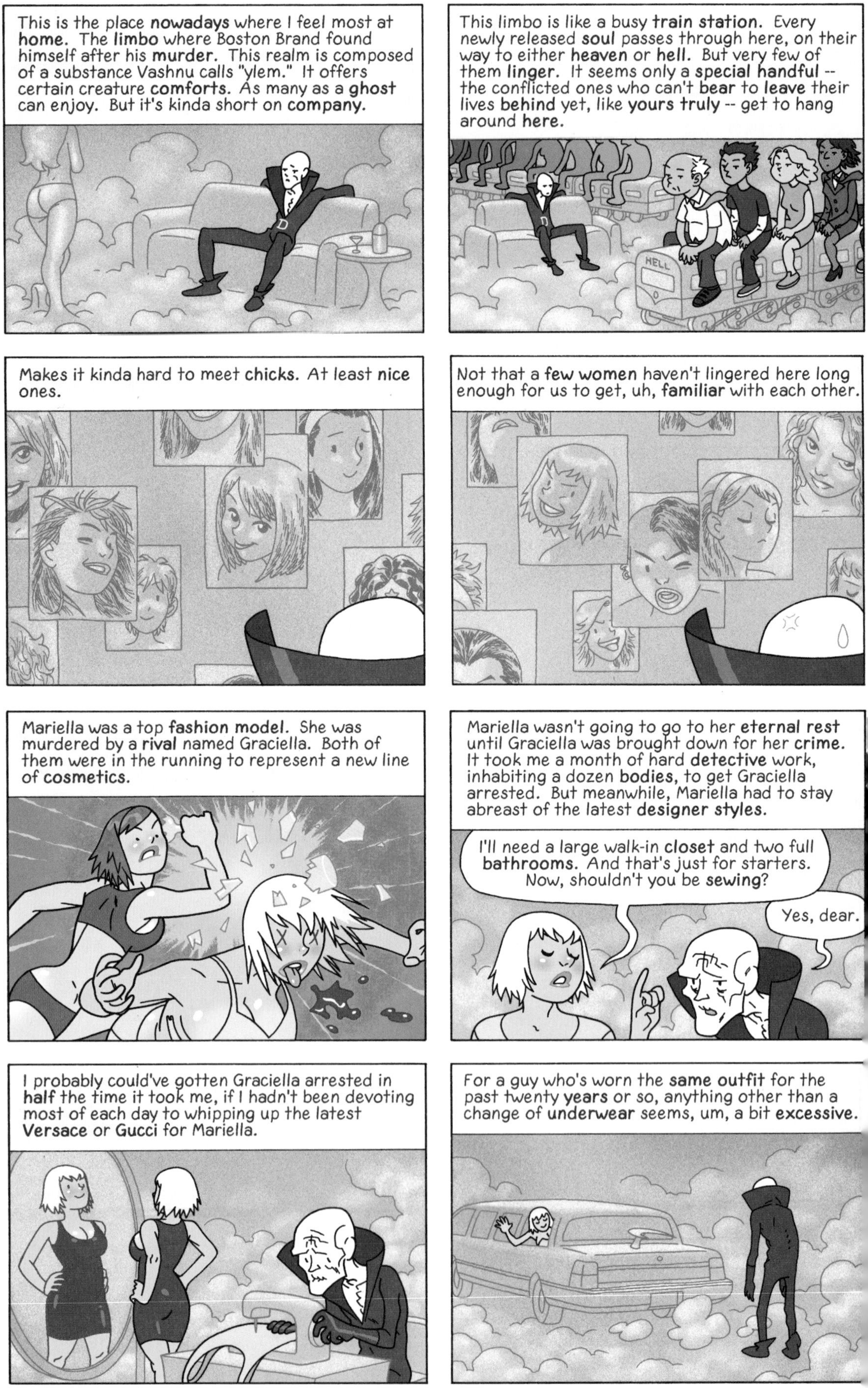
This is the place nowadays where I feel most at home. The limbo where Boston Brand found himself after his murder. This realm is composed of a substance Vashnu calls "ylem." It offers certain creature comforts. As many as a ghost can enjoy. But it's kinda short on company.
This limbo is like a busy train station. Every newly released soul passes through here, on their way to either heaven or hell. But very few of them linger. It seems only a special handful -- the conflicted ones who can't bear to leave their lives behind yet, like yours truly -- get to hang around here.
HELL
Makes it kinda hard to meet chicks. At least nice ones.
Not that a few women haven't lingered here long enough for us to get, uh, familiar with each other.
Mariella was a top fashion model. She was murdered by a rival named Graciella. Both of them were in the running to represent a new line of cosmetics.
Mariella wasn't going to go to her eternal rest until Graciella was brought down for her crime. It took me a month of hard detective work, inhabiting a dozen bodies, to get Graciella arrested. But meanwhile, Mariella had to stay abreast of the latest designer styles.
I'll need a large walk-in closet and two full bathrooms. And that's just for starters. Now, shouldn't you be sewing?
Yes, dear.
I probably could've gotten Graciella arrested in half the time it took me, if I hadn't been devoting most of each day to whipping up the latest Versace or Gucci for Mariella.
For a guy who's worn the same outfit for the past twenty years or so, anything other than a change of underwear seems, um, a bit excessive.

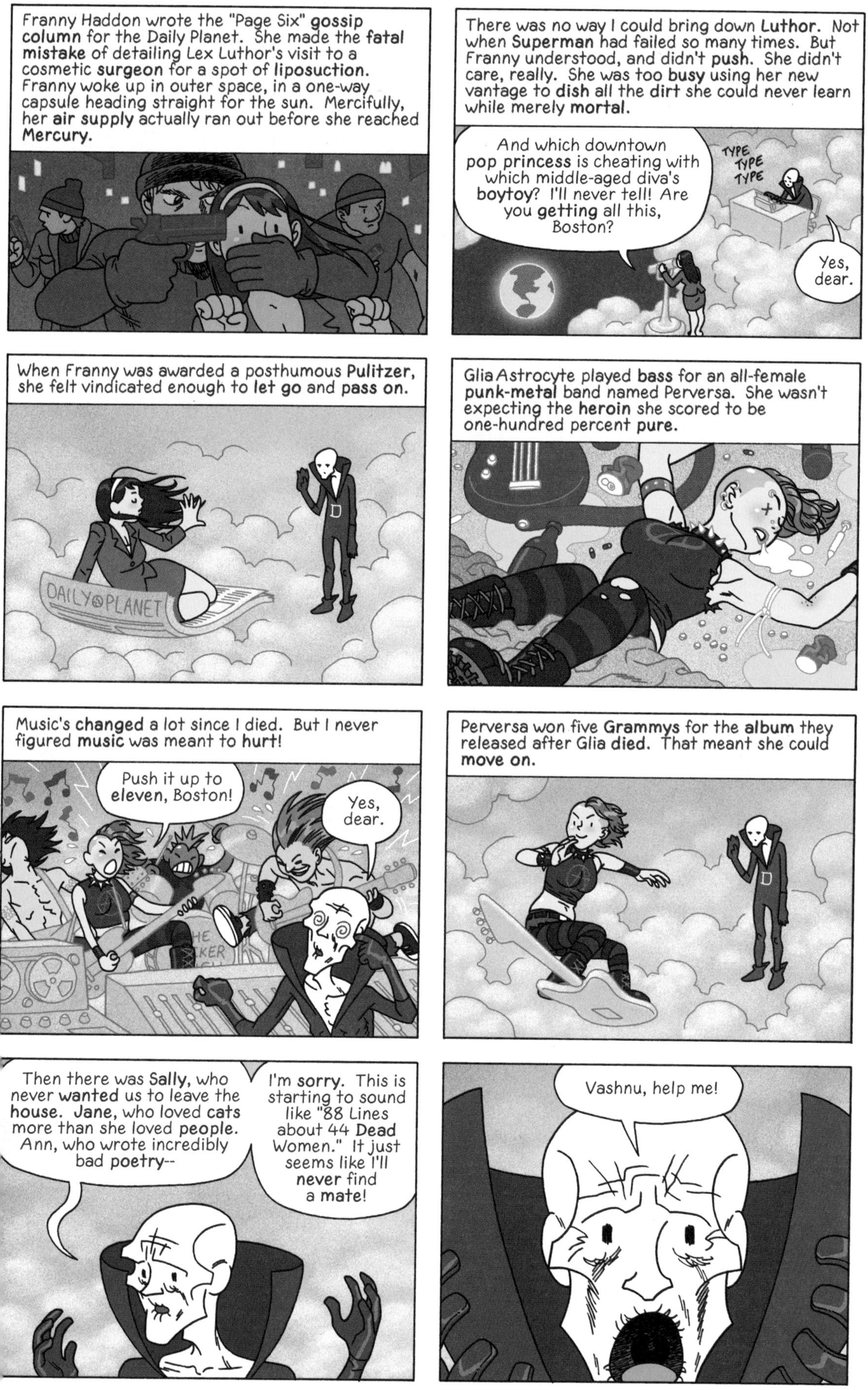
Franny Haddon wrote the "Page Six" gossip column for the Daily Planet. She made the fatal mistake of detailing Lex Luthor's visit to a cosmetic surgeon for a spot of liposuction. Franny woke up in outer space, in a one-way capsule heading straight for the sun. Mercifully, her air supply actually ran out before she reached Mercury.
There was no way I could bring down Luthor. Not when Superman had failed so many times. But Franny understood, and didn't push. She didn't care, really. She was too busy using her new vantage to dish all the dirt she could never learn while merely mortal.
And which downtown pop princess is cheating with which middle-aged diva's boytoy? I'll never tell! Are you getting all this, Boston?
TYPE TYPE TYPE
Yes, dear.
When Franny was awarded a posthumous Pulitzer, she felt vindicated enough to let go and pass on.
DAILY PLANET
Glia Astrocyte played bass for an all-female punk-metal band named Perversa. She wasn't expecting the heroin she scored to be one-hundred percent pure.
Music's changed a lot since I died. But I never figured music was meant to hurt!
Push it up to eleven, Boston!
Yes, dear.
Perversa won five Grammys for the album they released after Glia died. That meant she could move on.
Then there was Sally, who never wanted us to leave the house. Jane, who loved cats more than she loved people. Ann, who wrote incredibly bad poetry--
I'm sorry. This is starting to sound like "88 Lines about 44 Dead Women." It just seems like I'll never find a mate!
Vashnu, help me!

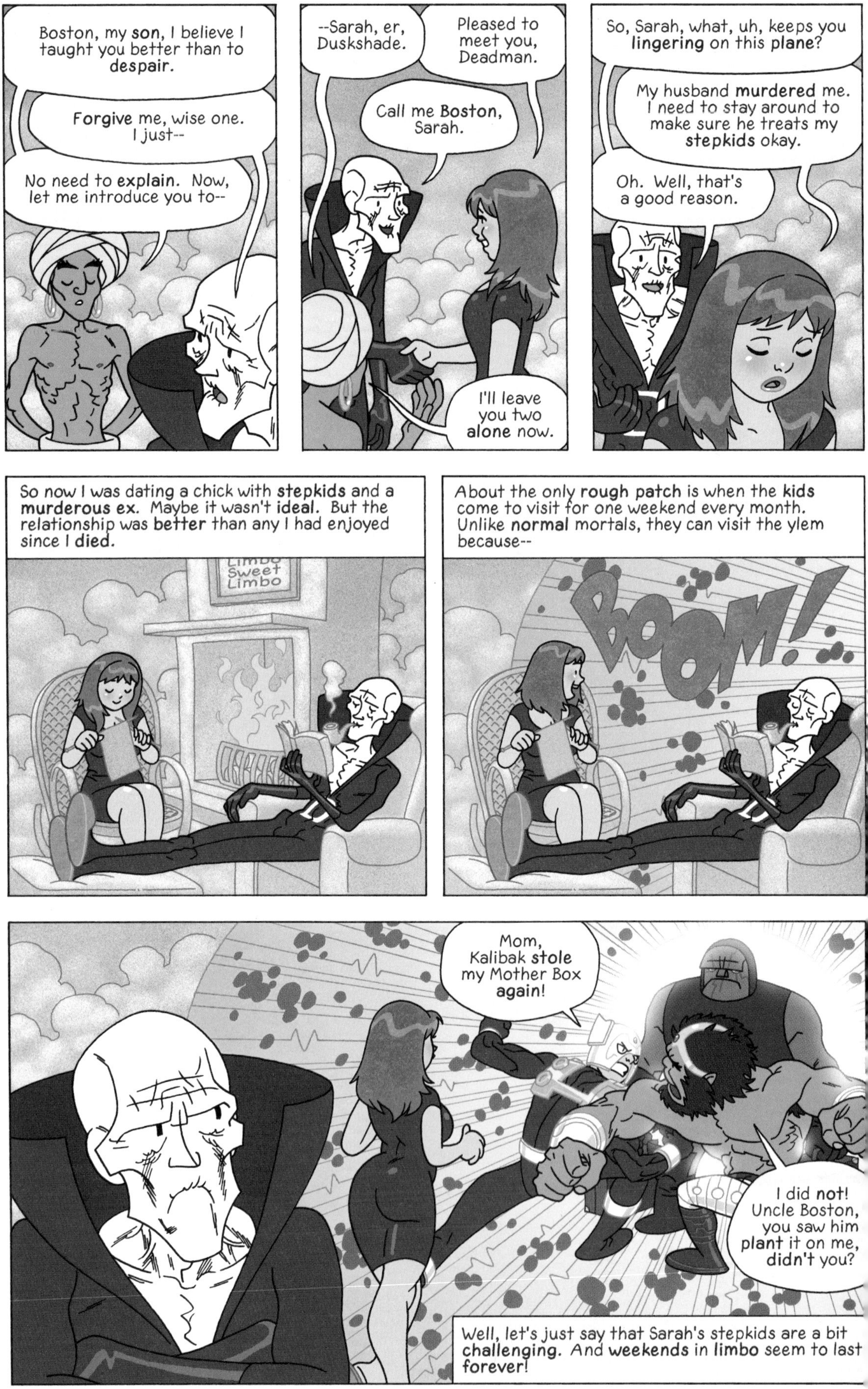

Boston, my son, I believe I taught you better than to despair.
Forgive me, wise one. I just--
No need to explain. Now, let me introduce you to--
--Sarah, er, Duskshade.
Pleased to meet you, Deadman.
Call me Boston, Sarah.
I'll leave you two alone now.
So, Sarah, what, uh, keeps you lingering on this plane?
My husband murdered me. I need to stay around to make sure he treats my stepkids okay.
Oh. Well, that's a good reason.
So now I was dating a chick with stepkids and a murderous ex. Maybe it wasn't ideal. But the relationship was better than any I had enjoyed since I died.
Limbo Sweet Limbo
About the only rough patch is when the kids come to visit for one weekend every month. Unlike normal mortals, they can visit the ylem because--
BOOM!
Mom, Kalibak stole my Mother Box again!
I did not! Uncle Boston, you saw him plant it on me, didn't you?
Well, let's just say that Sarah's stepkids are a bit challenging. And weekends in limbo seem to last forever!

Todd Alcott spent a decade writing experimental plays in downtown New York, then somehow got the gig co-writing the movie *Antz*. The rest is history, or will be, assuming that he ever gets another movie made.

Rick Altergott is the artist behind the comic characters "Doofus" and his pal "Henry Hotchkiss." Both appear in his ongoing series published by Fantagraphics Books, *Raisin Pie*, a comic book he shares with his wife, Ariel Bordeaux. They live in Pawtucket, Rhode Island with their cat, Buster. Rick also does illustration work.

Peter Bagge is best known as the creator of *Hate Comics* (Fantagraphics Books), which has followed the adventures and foibles of the semiautobiographical Buddy Bradley since 1990. He also created the titles YEAH! and SWEATSHOP for DC Comics. Currently, Bagge is a regular contributor to *Reason* magazine and *The Weekly World News*.

Kyle Baker is the author of the graphic novels YOU ARE HERE, THE COWBOY WALLY SHOW, KING DAVID and WHY I HATE SATURN. He has published his own anthologies, *Kyle Baker, Cartoonist, Vols. 1 and 2*. He writes and draws PLASTIC MAN for DC Comics.

Charles Berberian was born in Baghdad, Iraq in 1959. With his partner, Philippe Dupuy, he is responsible for the series *Monsieur Jean*, the fourth album of which won the prize for Best Album at the Festival d'Angoulême.

Aaron Bergeron was nominated for an Emmy Award for his writing at *The Daily Show with Jon Stewart*. He's made dozens of sketch appearances on *Late Night with Conan O'Brien* – most notably in a scene with Jim Carrey featured on *Late Night's 10th Anniversary Special*. His comic, *Aaron Bergeron's You've Got a Crush on Aaron Bergeron*, was recently adapted into a stage show.

Ariel Bordeaux has been writing and drawing comics since 1993. Her past work includes the self-published mini-comic series "Deep Girl" and a novella, "No Love Lost." Her current work can be seen in the comic book series *Raisin Pie* (Fantagraphics), a "split" book in collaboration with husband Rick Altergott. Ariel lives in Pawtucket, Rhode Island, with Rick and the world's greatest cat, Buster.

Rand and David Borden spent their youth together reenacting world wars in 1/10 scale. They've since grown up and co-founded Studio Kaiju, an independent Boston-based performance and media group and created Kaiju Big Battel, the world's only live monster mayhem spectacle. These live tournament-style performances are a character-driven, tongue-in-cheek hybrid of American pro wrestling, Japanese monster movies, and lowbrow pop culture. These multimedia events can be enjoyed from a safe distance thanks to the Kaiju Big Battel DVD series and the Hyperion Books release *Kaiju Big Battel: A Practical Guide to Giant City-Crushing Monsters*. Look for the newest Kaiju Big Battel DVD, *Shocking Truth*, this fall.

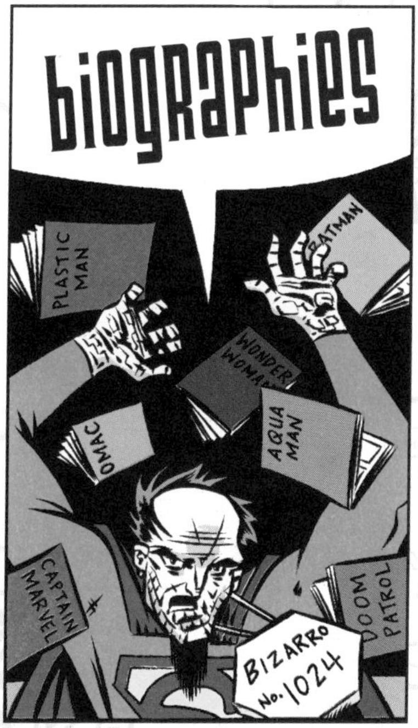
biographies
PLASTIC MAN
BATMAN
WONDER WOMAN
AQUA MAN
OMAC
CAPTAIN MARVEL
DOOM PATROL
BIZARRO No. 1024

Ivan Brunetti was born in a small town in Italy in 1967. At the tender age of 8, he moved from his grandparents' farm there to the industrial South Side of Chicago. He has lived in this fair city for about 5,000 years, rarely venturing outside its bittersweet confines. Fantagraphics Books publishes his autobiographical series *Schizo*, and a collection of morally inexcusable gag cartoons, *HAW!* He's also working on another, smaller gag book, *HEE!*, as well as a memoir of his painful childhood, *Concrete Playground*. He's fat.

Eddie Campbell decided to be an artist shortly after he realized that being a cowboy wasn't a feasible ambition. After twenty-five years, he started to ask if he's sure this one is feasible either. He put his observations into *How To Be an Artist*. In his next big project, he asks what does it all add up to anyway in *The Fate of the Artist*.

Jim Campbell is known as a colorist for Tony Millionaire in works like his recent "Uncle Gabby" hardcover book. He has made comics of his own in anthologies such as *Meathaus* for a few years. His first solo book, *Krachmacher*, has been published in full color with a generous grant from the Xeric Foundation.

Dave Cooper was born in a tiny fishing village in Eastern Canada in 1967. Since then he has produced a number of graphic novels, short animated films, toys, and prints for clients all over the world. For the time being, Dave is concentrating on drawing and oil painting, amassing work for *four* solo gallery shows in 2005 and 2006. He lives in Ottawa, Canada with his wife Julie and his greatest work of art– his two-year-old son, Jake.

Leela Corman is an illustrator, cartoonist, and bellydancer. She also sings in two bands. She likes long walks in the park, library books, and anything with a lot of sequins.

Farel Dalrymple began producing his own comics in 1999 with *Smith's Adventures in the Supermundane*. The first issue of his series, *Pop Gun War*, was published with the help of a Xeric grant. Subsequent issues were published by Absence of Ink, which, in 2003, were collected into a trade paperback by Dark Horse Comics. Farel co-founded the experimental comic anthology *Meathaus*, edited its first five issues, and continues to contribute to it. In 2002, Farel was nominated for a Russ Manning Award and was awarded a gold medal from the Society of Illustrators. In 2003 he was nominated for a Harvey Award.

Paul Di Filippo is the author of well over a hundred short stories and six novels. His publications for 2005 include the story collection *The Emperor of Gondwanaland and Other Stories* and the humor collection *Plumage from Pegasus*. He lives in Providence, Rhode Island, and maintains a flourishing second career as tour guide to H. P. Lovecraft's gravesite.

Paul Dini spent a number of years writing animation for Warner Bros. and comics for DC. He now splits his time between the North Pole and an island someplace in the South Pacific.

Evan Dorkin is the Harvey, Eisner, and Ignatz award-winning creator of *Milk and Cheese* and *Dork*. He's doodled and/or typed for *Esquire, Spin, The Onion, MAD, Disney Adventures, Nickelodeon Magazine*, and the TV shows *Space Ghost Coast to Coast, Superman*, and *Batman Beyond*. He is currently working on his second failed pilot for the Cartoon Network's Adult Swim.

Mike Doughty, once the singer/songwriter in Soul Coughing, is now driving around North America in a rental car, playing shows alone – just himself and a guitar. His fourth solo record, produced by Dan Wilson, is imminent. He lives in New York.

Eric Drysdale is a writer and comedian in New York City. He writes for Comedy Central's *The Daily Show with Jon Stewart* during the day, and performs for drunk people at night. He has some weekend afternoons free.

Chris Duffy wrote a chunk of the first BIZARRO COMICS anthology. He's a Senior Editor at *Nickelodeon Magazine* and also writes the comic strip "Old Wise Basset" for *Family Dog* magazine. Chris thanks his wife, Peggy, and his son, Peter, for their love and support.

Ben Dunn was born in Ping-Tung, Taiwan on April 17, 1964. He immigrated to the U.S. in 1965. Ben started Antarctic Press in 1985 and began to publish manga-inspired stories with *Mangazine* and started "Ameri-manga." He created *Ninja High School* in 1987 which is currently the longest-running Ameri-manga title.

Philippe Dupuy was born in Sainte-Adresse, France in 1960. With his partner, Charles Berberian, he has collaborated on a series of albums based on their character Henriette, as well as several sketchbooks of drawings of life in Lisbon, Barcelona and New York.

Sarah Dyer is the creator and editor of the *Action Girl Comics* anthology. She has written for the TV shows *Space Ghost Coast to Coast, Superman*, and *Batman Beyond*. Her Eisner Award-nominated coloring work has been seen in David Lapham's *Amy Racecar* specials as well as numerous comics and magazines. Currently she's writing the American-version scripts for Tokyopop's *Kodocha, DNAngel* and *Snowdrop* manga titles.

Phil Elliott is currently coloring Paul Grist's *Jack Staff* comic and getting ready to start drawing a new Tupelo miniseries, to follow the recent *Tupelo – The World's Forgotten Boy* book published by Slave Labor. He's also learning to play guitar, to emulate the great Captain Tupelo, of The Famous Monsters, star of said book. The other week he made some pine cupboards for the kitchen.

Hunt Emerson has drawn comics since 1972. His characters include Firkin the Cat, Calculus Cat and PussPuss – do you detect a pattern here? But he has also drawn birds (Charlie Chirp the Tweeting Twerp), rabbits (Alan Rabbit a.k.a. Bill the Bunny), jazz saxophone players (Max Zillion), 18th Century lechers (Casanova) and old sailors (The Rime of the Ancient Mariner). Likes: Laurel and Hardy, sleeping, beer. Dislikes: the international political situation.

Maggie Estep saw her debut "horse noir" novel, *Hex*, named a Notable Book of 2003 by *The New York Times. Gargantuan*, the sequel to *Hex*, will be out in July 2004. Maggie's writing has appeared in many magazines and anthologies, most recently *The Best American Erotica 2004* and *Brooklyn Noir*. She lives in Brooklyn, NY, has a foster horse named Dalton, and likes to hang out at racetracks cheering on longshots.

Bob Fingerman is the creator of the award-winning, critically acclaimed graphic novel *Beg the Question*, as well as many other comics. Bob was delighted to work with the delightful and cuddly Patton Oswalt on his BIZARRO WORLD yarn and looks forward to the opportunity to reduce other DC stalwarts to their most demented incarnations yet. But with love. Always with love.

Abe Foreu began writing at age six, when he won the prestigious Excellence in Unwritten Writing Award, an annual award from the National Congress of Literature. After an eventful tour through school, Abe produced a kidney stone, some unremarkable letters of complaint, and several heartbreaking grocery lists. More than anything, he lives in rural Minnesota with his wife, three cats, and the baby they've been expecting for five years.

Ellen Forney has had work in many publications including *LA Weekly, Bust, Nickelodeon Magazine*, and *The Stranger*. Her book of autobiographical comic strips, *Monkey Food: The Complete "I Was Seven in '75" Collection* (Fantagraphics Books) was nominated for several national comics awards. She has been teaching Comics at Cornish College of the Arts since 2002.

Elizabeth Glass is married to Kyle Baker and they have three children, Lillian, Isaac, and Jacqueline. They live in New York City.

Paul Grist is a British cartoonist who writes and draws the popular comic books *Jack Staff, Kane* and *Burglar Bill*, all published by Image Comics. He currently lives in the year 1985.

Dean Haglund is the writer/actor best known for his portrayal of Langly, one of the Lone Gunmen, on *The X-Files* and, appropriately enough, *The Lone Gunmen*. He has also written extensively, including a sitcom in Canada called *Channel 92* and the hilarious sketch show *Never a Dull Moment*. You might see him live as he tours across the country as a stand-up comic when he is not busy improvising with the likes of Peter Murrieta.

Asaf Hanuka was born in Israel in 1974. He began working for American magazines around 2001. Since, he's had work in *The New York Times, Rolling Stone, Spin, Time, The Source*, and others. He is constantly adapting Etgar Keret's stories into comics form. Two books have appeared in Hebrew: *Street of Rage* and *Pizzeria Kamikaze*. He illustrates French graphic novels such as *Carton Jaune!* with French writer Didier Daeninckx, and *Cassidy* with writer Roger Martin. He also collaborates with Tomer Hanuka, his twin brother, on an experimental comic book, *Bipolar*.

Tomer Hanuka is a cartoonist and an illustrator. His work regularly appears in national magazines, among them *The New Yorker, The New York Times, Time, Rolling Stone* and *Spin*. Tomer also created covers for DC Comics' Vertigo and Focus imprints. With his twin brother Asaf, he co-creates the comic *Bipolar*, published by Alternative Comics.

Tom Hart is the creator of the Hutch Owen graphic novels and weekly strip, featuring his surly antagonistic street bum who hassles – to varied degrees of success – corporations, politicians, and any embodiment of "the man." His non-Hutch material includes *The Sands, Banks/Eubanks, New Hat*, and the short-lived daily "Trunktown," which he created with Shaenon Garrity.

Dean Haspiel was nominated for an Eisner for his semi-autobiographical collection *Opposable Thumbs*, and an Ignatz for *Aim to Dazzle*. His major credits include BIZARRO COMICS, BATMAN ADVENTURES, and JUSTICE LEAGUE ADVENTURES for DC. *Muties, Spider-Man's Tangled Web, X-Men Unlimited, Captain America: Red, White & Blue*, and *The Thing: Night Falls on Yancy Street* for Marvel. Dino is also a regular contributor to Harvey Pekar's *American Splendor*.

Danny Hellman is a commercial artist whose work has appeared in a wide variety of publications, including *Time* and *The Wall Street Journal*. He also edits and publishes the critically acclaimed anthology *Legal Action Comics*. He and his wife live in New York City.

Gilbert Hernandez is currently working on *Love & Rockets, Luba, Luba's Comics and Stories*, and will soon unleash a new DVD project that he wrote and starred in about contacting life on other worlds called *The Naked Cosmos*. He lives with his wife Carol and daughter Natalia in Las Vegas, the hotbed of celestial communication.

Jaime Hernandez is the co-creator of *Love & Rockets*, and has been drawing it for 22 years. Along with the comic, he has just published a 700-page collection of his work, entitled *Locas*.

Dylan Horrocks is the author of *Hicksville* (published by Drawn & Quarterly), a graphic novel about comics, which was nominated for awards in the USA, France, Italy, and Spain. His current series is *Atlas* (also Drawn & Quarterly), but he's also working on a new graphic novel for Top Shelf and various other bits and bobs. He's also written HUNTER: THE AGE OF MAGIC for Vertigo and BATGIRL for DC. He lives by the beach in New Zealand, far from the madding crowd.

Paul Hornschemeier is the Eisner, Harvey, and Ignatz nominated author of *Mother, Come Home*, from Dark Horse Books and founder of the art collective The Holy Consumption of Chicago. The next volume of his ongoing full-color series, *Forlorn Funnies*, will be published by Fantagraphics in June 2005.

Rian Hughes, under the name Device, provides design and illustration for advertising campaigns, record sleeves, book jackets, graphic novels and TV. He has been a comics artist, notably on *Dare* with Grant Morrison, and has worked extensively for the British and American comic industries as designer, typographer and illustrator. Recent work includes poster designs for Tokyo fashion company Yellow Boots, the animated on-board safety film for Virgin Airlines, and a range for Swatch. He has an extensive collection of *Thunderbirds* memorabilia, a fridge full of vodka, and a stack of easy listening albums which he plays very quietly.

John Kerschbaum is, among other things, the cartoonist responsible for *The Wiggly Reader* and *Petey & Pussy*, both published by Fontanelle Press. His work has appeared in *The New York Times*, *The New Yorker*, *Nickelodeon Magazine* and *The Village Voice*. He lives in New York City with his wife and family and is working on an all-new Petey & Pussy graphic novel.

Chip Kidd am greatest writer ever! His novel *The Cheese Monkeys* was big flop!

Except for in Calgary. Yay! And the sequel, *The Learners*, is not written! It is only in his head, which is full of holes. His essay in *McSweeney's #13* was hated by everyone, but he is loved by all on The Comics Journal Message Board! Love love love!!!

Derek Kirk Kim is the Eisner, Harvey, and Ignatz Award-winning writer/artist of *Same Difference and Other Stories*. He is currently working on the debut issue of his ongoing one-man anthology, *Lowbright*.

James Kochalka lives in Burlington, Vermont with his wife, baby, and cat. He draws a daily diary comic strip called "American Elf." You can find it on the Internet. Get a computer. He draws a lot of other comics that aren't on the Internet, like *Peanutbutter & Jeremy's Best Book Ever*. For these, you don't need the computer because they're on paper. So, grab your little hatchet and start chopping down trees!

John Krewson has written for national weekly newspaper *The Onion* since 1991.

Michael Kupperman illustrates and does comics in New York City. His book *Snake'n'Bacon's Cartoon Cavalcade* was published by HarperCollins in 2000. His illustrated version of Robert Coover's *Stepmother* was published by McSweeney's in 2004. He is currently doing comics for *The Believer*.

Tim Lane is the creator and writer of *Happy Hour in America* and *Belligerent Piano*. His illustrations have appeared in the *New York Press*, where he maintained a column entitled "The Intersection."

Roger Langridge has been a professional cartoonist since 1988. He has done work for most major comics publishers in the English-speaking world, including Marvel, DC, Dark Horse, Fleetway/2000AD, Heavy Metal, Deadline, Fantagraphics and others. Most recently, he has been self-publishing his own comic, *Fred the Clown*, which has been nominated for two Eisner Awards (Best Series, Humor and Best Writer-Artist, Humor) and an Ignatz Award (for Outstanding Series).

Carol Lay has drawn comics and illustrations for many publications including *MAD*, *The Wall Street Journal*, and *The New Yorker*. Her weekly comic strip "WayLay" can be found on the Internet. Her work appears in many weekly and daily strips here and abroad.

Rob Leigh is a graduate of the Joe Kubert School of Cartoon and Graphic Art. His lettering first received critical notice in 1972, when he was sent home

with a note for writing a four-letter word on the blackboard of Miss Tuschmann's second-grade class. In addition to lettering, Rob has inked many titles for DC. He lives in northern New Jersey with his wife Vaughan and homicidal cat Barley.

Ken Lopez, master calligrapher, heads the lettering department at DC Comics.

Matt Madden (NYC 1968) lives in Brooklyn, New York. A cartoonist and illustrator who also teaches comics and drawing at the School of Visual Arts, he has worked as a colorist for various comics from DC, Marvel, and Nickelodeon. His most recent graphic novel is *Odds Off* (Highwater Books, 2001). He is currently serializing his new work in a series for Alternative Comics called *A Fine Mess*.

Andy Merrill has been a writer/producer at Cartoon Network for at least 11 years. He co-created *Space Ghost Coast to Coast* in 1994 and went on to write and produce *Cartoon Planet* and *The Brak Show*. He is the voice of Brak and Locar on *Space Ghost Coast to Coast* and the villain Oglethorpe on *Aqua Teen Hunger Force*. Currently, he is working on packaging for *Cartoon Network's Fridays*, a "Laugh-In" for kids. On the show, he is the voice and puppeteer for Long Haul, the Puppet Trucker and the voice of Motor Baby among others. He lives in Atlanta, Georgia with his lovely wife Stacey and his two dogs and a cat.

Tony Millionaire is the creator of the weekly comic strip "Maakies," which has been recently collected by Fantagraphics. He also creates the ongoing adventures of Sock Monkey, published by Dark Horse Comics. He has won four Eisner Awards including Best Writer/Artist-Humor, as well as two Harvey Awards. His illustration work has appeared in *The Village Voice*, *The Wall Street Journal* and *The New Yorker*. He now lives in Pasadena, California with his wife and two daughters.

Scott Morse has been carving simultaneous niches into the comics and animation fields for the past ten years. He is the author of ten graphic novels, including *Soulwind, Magic Pickle, The Barefoot Serpent, Spaghetti Western*, and *Southpaw*. His more recent work can be seen in BATMAN: ROOM FULL OF STRANGERS and periodically in PLASTIC MAN.

Peter Murrieta is the writer/producer who created and wrote the WB's hilarious sitcom *Greetings from Tucson* which was largely based on his experiences growing up. He has since written and produced such shows as *All about the Andersons* and *Hope and Faith*. He also runs an improv theatre in the heart of Hollywood called "Bang" where he regularly performs his show "Peter Murrieta is Always Right" with such guests as Dean Haglund.

Bill Oakley was one of the best letterers in our field, a gentleman, and a craftsman who enjoyed the respect of all of his colleagues. He died in 2002. We miss him.

Patton Oswalt lives in Burbank, California, where he drinks.

Jason Paulos was born in Brisbane in 1969, and since age seven has harbored a (not very) secret desire to draw comics. After a two-year stint at Queensland College of Art, he moved to Sydney and embarked on a career as a graphic designer. In 1989, he self-published the first issue of the now-legendary misadventures of Hairbutt The Hippo, a hippo-humanoid private eye. Since that fateful first issue, he has self-published a dozen Hairbutt comics, collecting accolades and loyal hippophiles along the way. Jason's latest work can be seen in *Soft Boiled Tales*, a funnybook that features his usual blend of high art and lowbrow humor.

Harvey Pekar, a native of Cleveland, Ohio, is best known for his award-winning, autobiographical slice-of-life comic book series cum feature film *American Splendor*. Pekar also collaborated with his wife, Joyce Brabner, on *Our Cancer Year*. Harvey has written THE QUITTER, an original graphic novel being drawn by Dean Haspiel for DC/Vertigo.

Brian Ralph teaches Sequential Art and Character Development at the Maryland Institute College of Art. His comic "Reggie-12" appears in *Giant Robot* magazine and will soon be a series from Highwater Books. Look for his books *Cave-In* and *Climbing Out* wherever graphic novels are sold. Brian lives in Baltimore.

Dave Roman is the co-creator of the Harvey Award-nominated series *Quicken Forbidden*, and the Ignatz Award-winning *Teen Boat* (with artist John Green). He works for *Nickelodeon Magazine*, where he is Associate Comics Editor. Dave's own illustrated work has appeared in *Not My Small Diary*, and *Alternative Comics' 9-11: Emergency Relief*.

Johnny Ryan was born in Boston, Massachusetts. He draws several

comics, including *Angry Youth Comix*, *The Rusty Trombone*, and *Blecky Yuckerella*. His work can also be seen in *Nickelodeon Magazine*, the *Seattle Stranger*, and *National Geographic Kids*. He lives in Los Angeles, California.

Coco Shinomiya is a Los Angeles-based freelance art director and graphic designer. Also known as Monster X, she has received numerous awards including two Grammy nominations for album packaging. She shares her home with a guinea pig named Roscoe and two hot rods – a '32 Ford Tudor Sedan and a '27 T Roadster project. She enjoys going fast.

R. Sikoryak draws comic strip adaptations of classic literature for the anthology *Drawn & Quarterly*. His comics and illustrations have also appeared in *The New Yorker*, *Nickelodeon Magazine*, *Raw*, *Fortune*, and *GQ*, among many other publications, as well as on *The Daily Show with Jon Stewart* and in *America (The Book): A Citizen's Guide to Democracy Inaction*. In his spare time, he curates the cartoon slideshow series *Carousel*.

Don Simpson illustrated "Supply Side Jesus" and "Chickenhawks: Episode One" for Al Franken's #1 mega-bestseller *Lies and the Lying Liars Who Tell Them: A Fair and Balanced Look at the Right*. Don is best known as the creator of *Megaton Man* and *Border Worlds* and is currently at work on new material for both series.

Dave Stewart started as a design intern at Dark Horse Comics. Current projects include CATWOMAN, NEW FRONTIER, and Daredevil. He currently resides in Portland, Oregon with his wife Michelle and his dangerous mutt Spike.

Raina Telgemeier is the creator of *Take-Out*, which was nominated for two Ignatz Awards. She was also the recipient of the Friends of Lulu's Kim Yale Award for Promising New Talent in 2003. Her comics have appeared in *Broad Appeal*, *Not My Small Diary*, *Moo-Cow Fan Club Magazine*, *Reflux*, *Meathaus*, and other publications. She is working on a graphic novel based on the popular *Baby-sitters Club* series for Scholastic.

Craig Thompson is responsible for the universally revered *Good-Bye, Chunky Rice*; and the Eisner and Harvey-nominated epic breakout hit *Blankets*, both from Top Shelf Productions. 2004 saw the release of a "soundtrack" to *Blankets*, a travelogue/sketchbook titled *Carnet de Voyage*, and a joint publication with James Kochalka titled *Conversation*, also from Top Shelf.

M. Wartella is an award-winning NYC underground cartoonist. His detailed artwork and comics have appeared on candy wrappers, in dozens of alt-weekly papers across the country, and in magazines including *Interview* and *Nickelodeon*. He is also the creator behind the country music spoof *Mazey Gardens & The Brick Hit House Band*.

Andi Watson is the Eisner and Harvey-nominated creator of: *Samurai Jam*, *Skeleton Key* and *Slow News Day* published by Slave Labor Graphics, and *Geisha*, *Breakfast After Noon*, *Dumped* and *Love Fights* published by Oni Press. His work has also appeared in innumerable anthologies and in illustration and animation. He lives in Staffordshire, England, with his wife, daughter and cat.

Mo Willems is a six-time Emmy Award-winning writer and animator who currently serves as head writer for Cartoon Network's *Codename: Kids Next Door*. The creator of CN's *Sheep in the Big City*, Mo's other comix work includes DC's 9-11 anthology (vol. 2), the Monkeysuit Press anthologies, and DC's Cartoon Cartoons monthly. Mo's drawings have been exhibited in The Museum of Television and Radio and the U.S. Library of Congress and his first children's book, *Don't Let the Pigeon Drive the Bus!*, was awarded a Caldecott Honor. Upcoming work includes a comic for Jon Scieszka's *Guys Read* anthology and a book about an invisible invention machine.

Kurt Wolfgang lives and draws comics in Collinsville, where he is working on a 5600-page, wordless adaptation of Pinocchio, as well as a number of stories for the exciting new *Mome* anthology project. He once won a Major Award.

Jason Yungbluth rose from the dead to avenge his lover's murder, but found comics to be a more productive use of his eldritch power. He is the creator of *Deep Fried*, his comic book and newspaper strip.

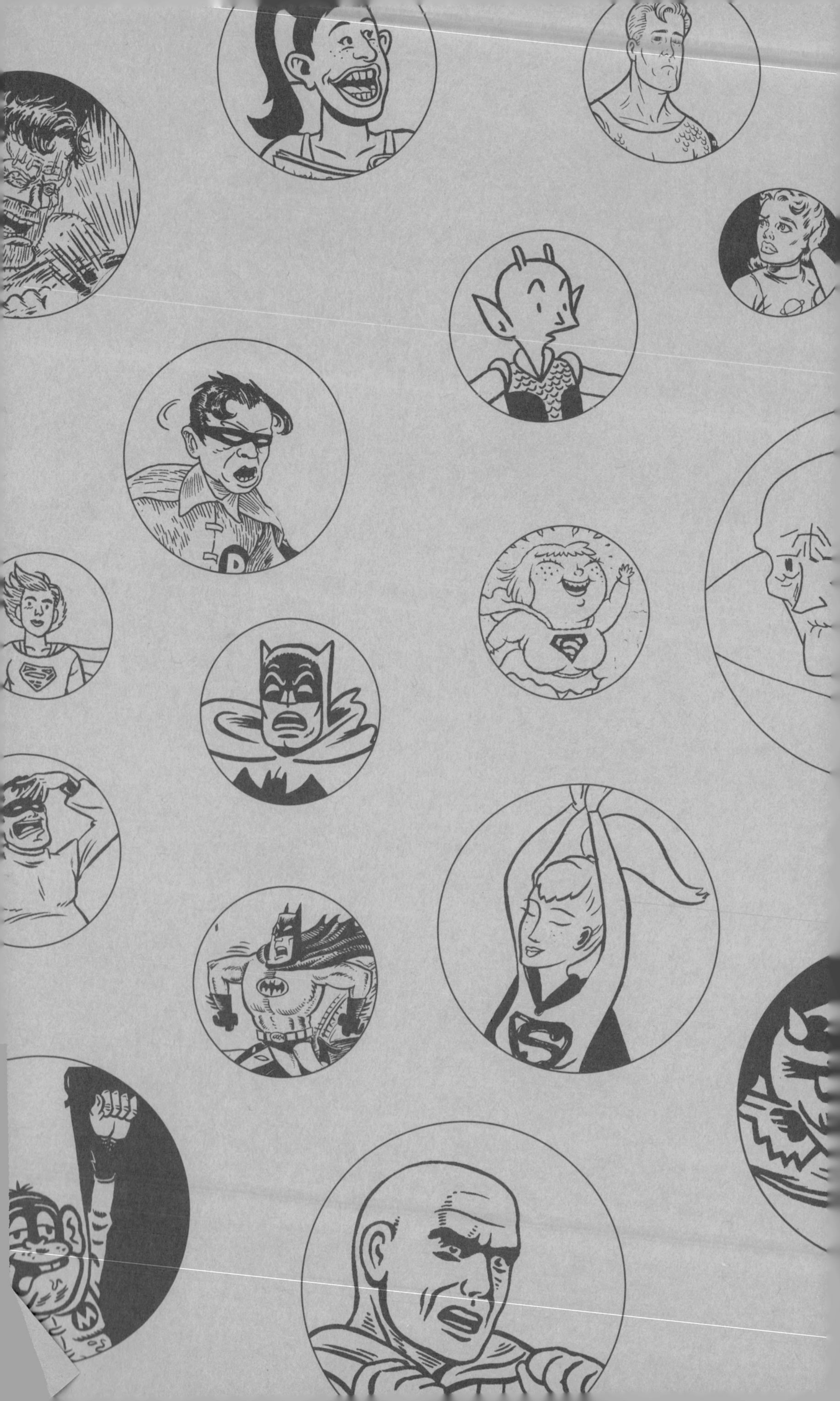